BLACK AMERICAN WOMEN NOVELISTS

THE
MAGILL
BIBLIOGRAPHIES

Other Magill Bibliographies:

The American Presidents—Norman S. Cohen

Classical Greek and Roman Drama—Robert J. Forman

Contemporary Latin American Fiction—Keith H. Brower

Masters of Mystery and Detective Fiction—J. Randolph Cox

Nineteenth Century American Poetry—Philip K. Jason

Restoration Drama—Thomas J. Taylor

Twentieth Century European Short Story—Charles E. May

The Victorian Novel—Laurence W. Mazzeno

Women's Issues—Laura Stempel Mumford

BLACK AMERICAN WOMEN NOVELISTS

An Annotated Bibliography

Craig Werner

Professor of Afro-American Studies
University of Wisconsin

SALEM PRESS

Pasadena, California   Englewood Cliffs, New Jersey

∞The paper used in these volumes conforms to the
American National Standard for Permanence of Paper
for Printed Library Materials, Z39.48-1984.

Library of Congress Cataloging-in-Publication Data

Werner, Craig Hansen, 1952–
    Black American women novelists / Craig Werner.
        p.   cm. — (Magill bibliographies)
    ISBN 0-89356-651-1
    1. American fiction—Afro-American authors—
History and criticism—Bibliography.   2. American
fiction—Women authors—History and criticism-
Bibliography.   3. Afro-American women novelists—
Biography—Bibliography.   4. Women and literature—
United States—Bibliography.   5. Afro-Americans in
literature—Bibliography. I. Title.   II. Series.
Z1229.N39W47   1989
[PS153.N5]
016.813009 ' 9287—dc20   89-10826
                                                                        CIP

CONTENTS

CONTENTS

CONTENTS

EDITORIAL STAFF

BLACK AMERICAN
WOMEN
NOVELISTS

INTRODUCTION

Black women novelists, individually and collectively, differ. Situated in literary and social contexts in which differences are perceived primarily as emblems of superiority or inferiority, black women novelists have quietly and forcefully asserted the value of difference, their own and others. Resisting hierarchical attitudes and institutions that fragment human community and individual psyches, novelists from Harriet Wilson through Zora Neale Hurston to Toni Cade Bambara have celebrated *relationship* as the crucial resource for human survival and fulfillment. Negotiating their experience of triple jeopardy—the multiplicative combination of race, class, and gender oppression—black women have struggled, not always successfully, to conceive and realize processes capable of freeing the energies that throughout American history have been frozen into stereotypes that discourage or preclude real dialogue between black women and those who could benefit from their insights and help alter the circumstances that make their survival a minor miracle. Until their recent rediscovery by spiritual daughters, literary mothers from Pauline Hopkins and Nella Larsen to Ann Petry and Gwendolyn Brooks have been rendered invisible in the literary world. Excluded from the canons of American and, with a few exceptions, Afro-American literature, their novels, when discussed at all, have been dismissed as trivial, condemned for their unwillingness to take risks, their inability to break free from conventional literary forms.

The pioneering efforts of June Jordan, Barbara Smith, Alice Walker, Mary Helen Washington, and Barbara Christian have generated a wholesale revision of this image. As a second generation of black women critics including Deborah McDowell, Hazel Carby, and Hortense Spillers have demonstrated, black women's writing draws on Afro-American cultural traditions in a way that anticipates many of the more radical insights of mainstream critical theory: the paradoxical centrality of the "marginal"; the ideological function of "aesthetic" conventions; the oppressive political impact of binary thought structures; the metaphysical ambiguities of speech and writing. A growing multicultural community of readers and scholars centered on the circle of black daughter/critics including McDowell, Carby, Spillers, Karla Holloway, Trudier Harris, Claudia Tate, Gloria Hull, Thadious Davis, and Nellie McKay have established variety and risk as fundamental characteristics of black women's novels. Because they have valued communication with actual and acting people in an unrelentingly, if not simplistically, real world, black women have frequently written in the forms most likely to attract an audience. Not incidentally, these superficially safe forms are also those which offered the only hope, however slim, for a black woman seeking to earn a living through what was and is, in the most fundamental sense, her real work. Like the writers of the slave narratives and numerous Afro-American musicians before them, these novelists have tested a variety of subversive rhetorical strategies derived from African, Afro-American, and, in a slightly different manner, women's folk practices. Like Jane Austen,

George Eliot, Charles Chesnutt, and Ralph Ellison, the most powerful black women novelists are able to transform apparently conventional forms into a literature of relationship and possibility. Although the determination of the grandmothers suggests that novelists such as Gloria Naylor, Octavia Butler, Virginia Hamilton, and Sherley Anne Williams would have continued writing under any circumstances, the call and response that has developed between black women novelists and their critics has played a not inconsiderable role in broadening the audience for and deepening the comprehension of their work.

Contemporary approaches to black women's novels must be understood in relationship to the long struggle against stereotypes of black women as mammies, primitive exotics, and tragic mulattos. As most black women critics have noted, the form and content of the earliest novels by black women must be understood as direct responses to these images, which served to justify racist institutions. Despite the profound psychological and economic impact of these stereotypes, most early commentary on figures such as Frances E. W. Harper, Pauline Hopkins, Jessie Fauset, Nella Larsen, and Zora Neale Hurston failed to acknowledge the cultural circumstances in which they wrote. White reviewers, working on the assumption that these novelists were attempting to write the same type of novels as their white contemporaries, concluded that black women had simply failed to live up to the aesthetic standards of their time. In contrast, pioneering Afro-American scholars such as W. E. B. DuBois and Alain Locke recognized and responded to the general problem of stereotyping, which affected black men as well as black women. Sterling Brown's *The Negro in American Fiction* (1937) avoided most of the shortcomings that would characterize criticism of black women's novels for another half century. Black academic journals such as *Phylon* and *CLA Journal* provided vitally important forums for early work in the field which came to be known as Black Studies. The contributions of critical grandfathers such as Brown, J. Saunders Redding, Charles and Arthur Davis, George Kent, Richard Barksdale, and Blyden Jackson are all the more remarkable given the extreme demands made upon them as teachers and administrators at predominantly black, and badly underfunded, colleges and universities in the South.

While these critics did not always treat the work of black women novelists with the same respect given Jean Toomer's *Cane* or Richard Wright's *Native Son*, their paternalism contrasts sharply with the contemptuous dismissals in the earliest mainstream studies of Afro-American literature. Vernon Loggins' *The Negro Author: His Development in American to 1900* (1931) and Hugh Gloster's *Negro Voices in American Fiction* (1948), which asserts that Afro-American novels are "lacking in enduring beauty and universal appeal," established a perspective typical of white academic criticism through the 1960's. Although it is frequently singled out for criticism, Robert Bone's *The Negro Novel in America* (1958, rev. 1965) is in fact much more sensitive than Roger Rosenblatt's *Black Fiction* (1974) or David Littlejohn's *Black on White: A Critical Survey of Writing by American Negroes* (1966), which presents a stark image of the intellectual and cultural obstacles confronted by black women at the height of the civil rights movement. Littlejohn argues that the technical and intellectual shortcomings of writers such as Larsen, Hurston, and Paule Marshall typify a "depressing enterprise" in which "the responding spirit is dulled, finally, bored by the iteration of hopelessness, the sordid limitation of the soul in the tight closet of the black imagination."

What distinguishes Littlejohn's statement is its explicitness. Most standard studies of American literature have tacitly supported Littlejohn's blanket condemnation by omitting all mention of black women's novels. Richard Chase's *The American Novel and Its Tradition* and Leslie Fiedler's *Love and Death in the American Novel*, which focuses on the nexus of race and sex in the American imagination, are only two of many examples. The same could be said, it should be noted, of most novels by black men; only in the far-from-unambiguous case of Richard Wright was the pattern substantially altered prior to the academic recognition of Ralph Ellison's *Invisible Man* during the 1960's. Practically no critic prior to the 1980's seems to have sensed even dimly that Hopkins and Larsen were not trying to write *Little Women*, *The House of Mirth*, or *The Rise of Silas Lapham*; that Hurston was not trying to write *The Grapes of Wrath*, *Ulysses*, or *Native Son*. The "loss" of Harriet Wilson's *Our Nig* (1859), which was not recognized as the first novel published by a black woman until 1982, is only an extreme version of what happened to many other novels.

It is profoundly ironic that even the black men most responsible for increasing general awareness of the problem of invisibility seem to have been unable to recognize the difference in black women's writing. Richard Wright and Ralph Ellison, normally extremely sensitive readers, issued vicious attacks on Hurston: Wright condemned *Their Eyes Were Watching God* for perpetuating minstrel stereotypes, while Ellison dismissed *Moses, Man of the Mountain* as "calculated burlesque." As Mary Helen Washington has demonstrated, early reviewers who gave detailed attention to Ellison's *Invisible Man* granted only perfunctory attention to Gwendolyn Brooks's *Maud Martha*. Reflecting the total absence of countervailing voices in the mainstream literary world—and the observation raises questions concerning the relationship between literary journalism, academic criticism, and the publishing industry that have not been adequately addressed—many important novels were simply not available in any accessible editions. When I first began teaching courses in Afro-American literature at the University of Mississippi in 1979, no edition of *Their Eyes Were Watching God* was in print. A decade later, when the activities of Beacon Press, the Feminist Press, Indiana University Press, and the University of Illinois Press have brought many important novels back into print, several significant lacunae remain, among them *Maud Martha*, most of Fauset's fiction, and Hurston's *Seraph on the Suwanee*.

Various currents of literary criticism during the 1960's and 1970's both extended and mitigated the problems of silence and condemnation. Bone's *The Negro Novel in America* established the framework within which white academic discussion of Afro-American fiction developed during the 1960's. Congruent with the perspectives of influential critics such as Irving Howe, Bone's study established the trinity of Wright, Ellison, and James Baldwin—and to a lesser degree Jean Toomer—at the center of the Afro-American tradition. Still, in relation to his predecessors and contemporaries, Bone is not blatantly sexist in his judgments. Although his list of four "major" novels is limited to those of Wright, Ellison, Baldwin, and Toomer, two of the four novels he identifies as "superior" are by women (*Their Eyes Were Watching God* and Petry's *Country Place*) as are two of the seven he labels "good" (Larsen's *Quicksand* and Dorothy West's *The Living Is Easy*). Despite his careful scholarship and "objective" stance, however, Bone's commitment to formalist aesthetic criteria interferes with his appreciation of black women's fiction. He has been frequently, and justifiably, criticized for his condescending tone, found at its most extreme in his dismissal of Fauset's novels as "uniformly sophomoric, trivial, and dull." More common than blatant condemnation (though still less prevalent than silence), liberal condescension grew increasingly common during the 1960's. Although his premises limited his insight, Bone's work, as noted above, was clearly superior to later overviews such as Littlejohn's *Black On White* or Rosenblatt's *Black Fiction*, both of which attained undeserved recognition because they were published by mainstream publishers with substantial advertising budgets.

Recognizing the implicit biases of ostensibly objective academic studies, literary criticism generated by the Black Power and Women's Liberation movements helped established premises that have been extended by contemporary black women critics. "Black Aestheticians" such as Ed Bullins, Addison Gayle, Amiri Baraka, and Ron Karenga confronted the racism of white academic approaches to black culture. Part of an outpouring of cultural activity directed specifically to the black community, Gayle's anthology *The Black Aesthetic* (1971) helped define the cultural practices and political needs that distinguish the Afro-American experience. In "Black Cultural Nationalism," Karenga sounds several themes of lasting importance when he approaches Afro-American art as an extension of communal and functional African aesthetics. Reflecting his specific political agenda, Karenga argues that black art should "expose the enemy," "praise the people," and "support the revolution." The assertion of a specifically black cultural tradition, the focus on identifying the institutional and psychological mechanisms of oppression, and the desire to celebrate the unrecognized beauty and strength of ordinary black people have all been maintained as guiding principles, though in crucially different phrasing, in the best work of and about black women novelists.

The equally fundamental, but equally problematic, contribution of the Women's Liberation movement can be related directly to the limitations of the Black Aesthetic movement, which all too frequently ignored the concerns of black women on the grounds of a historically necessary, but extremely limited, commitment to the recovery of "black manhood." The sexism and homophobia of some elements of the Black Arts movement reaches its peak in Eldridge Cleaver's *Soul On Ice* (1968), which both justifies rape and viciously attacks Baldwin as an affront to black manhood. However unintentionally, such attacks served to fragment the Black

Power movement. Equally important, they perpetuated the binary structures—the hierarchical division of the world into black/white, male/female, mind/body, good/ evil—which provided the intellectual justification for a wide range of politically oppressive institutions. As Baraka acknowledges in his autobiography, the sexual chauvinism of the Black Arts movement, combined with a tendency to confuse rhetoric with political action, subverted the valuable core of its agenda. Recognizing the sexism of progressive movements of all racial compositions, many feminists responded with a wide-ranging critique, including a substantial amount of literary criticism, focused on resisting patriarchal attitudes. Exploring the undervalued novels of white American women such as Kate Chopin, Willa Cather, and Gertrude Stein, studies such as Nina Baym's *Women's Fiction: A Guide to Novels by and About Women in America, 1820-1870* (1978), Annette Kolodny's *The Lay of the Land* (1975), and Annis Pratt's *Archetypal Patterns in Women's Fiction* (1981) radically increased academic awareness of the difference between men's and women's expression. Very few of the white feminist critics—Pratt and historian Gerda Lerner would be the notable exceptions—gave more than token consideration to black women. As a result, theoretical formulations generated within the field of Women's Studies frequently pertained exclusively to the experience of white middle-class women.

The recent recognition of black women's literature, originating in the work of June Jordan, Barbara Smith, Robert Hemenway, Alice Walker, Mary Helen Washington, and Barbara Christian, has developed the insights of the Black Aesthetic and feminist criticism while acknowledging the limitations of these approaches. Published in the leading black nationalist magazine *Black World*, Jordan's 1974 essay "Notes Toward a Black Balancing of Love and Hatred" argued that Hurston's affirmative vision of black life was as central to the Afro-American tradition as Wright's angry protest. At about the same time, Alice Walker embarked on the well-publicized spiritual quest which culminated in her placement of a headstone on Hurston's previously unmarked grave. Originally published in *Ms.*, probably the most influential white feminist magazine, Walker's essay "Looking for Zora" marked a crucial step toward establishing Hurston as a major figure in the feminist literary tradition. In retrospect, Jordan's essay seems particularly crucial both because it contributed to the rediscovery of Hurston and because, in an accessible vocabulary, it identifies binary thought structures—originating outside but maintained within the black community—as the fundamental source of the distortions that plague black women novelists. Establishing a fundamental position for criticism of black women's fiction, Jordan carefully avoids elevating Hurston above Wright; rather, she insists that the division between the two visions is an artificial fragmentation of a more basic cultural unity. Recent critical work by Hortense Spillers, Deborah McDowell, Henry Louis Gates, Jr., and Houston Baker can be seen as an elaboration of Jordan's critical position.

More immediately influential, in part because of its more assertive tone, Smith's *Toward a Black Feminist Criticism* (1977) issued a clear call for a critical perspective

answering specifically to the needs of black women. Although later critics such as McDowell and Michael Awkward have drawn attention to problems regarding Smith's definition of terms, her monograph occupies a position of importance in Afro-American cultural history equivalent to Langston Hughes's "The Negro Artist and the Racial Mountain" (1926) and Richard Wright's "Blueprint for Negro Writing" (1937), each of which served as a rallying point for a generation of black writers. Extending the energy released by Jordan, Walker, and Smith, scholars such as Robert Hemenway and Barbara Christian helped introduce black women writers in an intelligent and rigorous manner to a broad academic audience. Hemenway's *Zora Neale Hurston: A Literary Biography* (1977)—universally praised as the single best biography of a black woman writer—provides clear evidence that a white male scholar aware of his own critical position and the specific contexts of black women's experience can make a significant contribution to the study of black women's novels. Christian's *Black Women Novelists: The Development of a Tradition, 1892-1976* (1980) both provided an invaluable historical overview of its subject and helped shape critical discussion of the 1980's. Similarly, Washington's editorial work on the anthologies *Midnight Birds* (1980), *Black-Eyed Susans* (1975), and *Invented Lives* (1987) helped diminish resistance to black women's writing within the publishing industry. Repeatedly, anthologies have played an extremely important role in the reassertion of the black women's tradition. In addition to Washington's anthologies, Toni Cade's *The Black Woman* (1970); Barbara Smith's *Home Girls: A Black Feminist Anthology* (1983), which reprints most of the material published in a special issue of the lesbian journal *Conditions*; Roseann Bell, Bettye Parker, and Beverly Guy-Sheftall's *Sturdy Black Bridges* (1979); Gloria Hull, Patricia Bell Scott, and Barbara Smith's *But Some of Us Are Brave* (1982); Mari Evan's *The Black Woman Writer* (1984); and Hortense Spillers and Marjorie Pryse's *Conjuring* (1985) have all played significant roles in the development of Black Women's Studies.

Although they have encountered conscious and unconscious resistance, black women have gradually succeeded in asserting a critical perspective potentially capable—as Toni Morrison observes in her brilliant essay "Unspeakable Things Unspoken: The Afro-American Presence in American Literature"—of enriching the understanding not only of black women's novels but also of American literature as a whole. The resistance extends the previously discussed patterns of condemnation, condescension, and silence. Nathan Scott's chapter "Black Literature" in *The Harvard Guide to Contemporary American Writing* (1979) focuses almost exclusively on black male writers. The vast majority of books on contemporary American fiction continue to ignore black women completely. Only Hurston, Alice Walker, and Morrison—a new, equally misunderstood, mainstream trinity replacing Wright, Ellison, and Baldwin—have received more than token attention in journals not devoted specifically to Afro-American writing. It is particularly disturbing to find that feminist journals such as *Signs* and *Tulsa Studies in Women's Literature* are as guilty of tokenism and the star mentality as are more traditional journals such as *American Literature* or *Novel*.

Yet more problematic is a growing backlash against what has been perceived as an overcompensatory celebration of black women's novels. Although it is extremely difficult to find evidence that black women's novels have been reviewed more leniently than those by other writers, several reviewers have presented unfavorable reviews as principled resistance to reverse discrimination. As the entries in this bibliography demonstrate, however, the uncritical acceptance of black women's novels is almost entirely a figment of the hostile critics' imaginations. Usually identified along with Alice Walker as the primary beneficiary of black women's allegedly favored status, Toni Morrison has in fact seen her novels unfavorably reviewed in *The Village Voice*, which repeatedly criticizes her failure to adhere to a feminist perspective; *The New York Times Book Review*, in which Mel Watkins repeatedly rails against the unmerited elevation of black women novelists; *The New York Review of Books*, where Darryl Pinckney has issued several blanket condemnations of black women as incompetent writers; and *The New Republic*, where *The Village Voice* staff writer Stanley Crouch recently concluded that Morrison's success is proof that "poorly digested folk materials, feminist rhetoric," and "maudlin ideological commercials" can pay off. Not surprisingly, an equivalent academic backlash has emerged in mainstream journals which have published very little favorable comment on black women novelists. Cynthia Edelberg's essay in *American Literature*, for example, condemns Morrison as a romantic whose vision amounts to nothing more than wishful thinking; Dianne Sadoff's essay in *Signs* claims that Walker's celebration of Hurston is largely wishful thinking; and Jennifer Jordan's essay in *Tulsa Studies in Women's Literature*—the first article on a black woman novelist published in the journal—dismisses Hurston as a useful model for black women writers.

This backlash is supported by the widely held belief that black women novelists, like the "castrating bitch" of the patriarchal imagination, are engaged in a constant battle for dominance over black men. This image derives in large part from the controversy over the film version of *The Color Purple* and from the intemperate statements of a few black men with access to influential, white-operated literary forums. Among this group are Watkins, Pinckney, Crouch, and David Bradley, whose lengthy critique of Walker was published in *The New York Times Magazine*. As the entries in this bibliography demonstrate, a larger number of black male critics, including Gates, Awkward, and Richard Wesley, agree with the position of Clyde Taylor, who argues that "instead of creating a separate chamber in African-American literature, black women's writing has flowered in the heart of it." After a somewhat difficult transitional period culminating in Christian's skeptical essay "The Race for Theory," most black critics interested in the theoretical dimensions of Afro-American expression have begun to engage in a constructive dialogue with primary and critical texts by black women writers. Robert Stepto's *From Behind the Veil* (1979), Gates's *The Signifying Monkey* (1988), Baker's *Blues, Ideology, and Afro-American Literature* (1984), and Awkward's *Inspiriting Influences: Tradition, Revision, and Afro-American Women's Novels* (1989) speak to and with the black women's tradition. Similarly, some recent work by white critics suggests that black

women writers are exerting a growing impact on segments of academia that have traditionally ignored their insights. John Callahan's *In the African-American Grain* (1988) and Keith Byerman's *Fingering the Jagged Grain* (1985) are among the most insightful overviews of recent Afro-American fiction. Another white scholar, Joe Weixlmann, has made significant contributions to the criticism of black women's novels as editor of *Black American Literature Forum* and *Studies in Black American Literature*, which established the standard for a striking improvement in the quality and breadth of Afro-American journals, including *Callaloo* and *MELUS*. While some criticism by white feminists, such as Susan Willis' *Specifying: Black Women Writing the American Experience* (1987), is weakened by an inadequate understanding of Afro-American cultural traditions, other works such as Barbara Johnson's *A World of Difference* (1987), Mary Dearborn's *Pocahontas's Daughters: Gender and Ethnicity in American Culture* (1986), and Missy Dehn Kubitschek's forthcoming *Claiming the Heritage* intimate a valuable symbiosis of Afro-American and feminist perspectives.

There is no doubt, however, that black women themselves have played the central role in (re)discovering and defining the field of Black Women's Studies. Extending the work of Jordan, Walker, Smith, Washington, and Christian, critics including Hortense Spillers, Deborah McDowell, Nellie McKay, Trudier Harris, Karla Holloway, Claudia Tate, Gloria Hull, and Hazel Carby have provided the fundamental insights and resources for subsequent work. In addition, many of these critics have contributed an enormous amount of energy in crucial but relatively unrecognized forms such as editing and writing introductions for reprint editions. Perhaps the most impressive contribution of this type has been Harris' editing (with the assistance of another black woman critic, Thadious Davis) of the *Dictionary of Literary Biography* volumes on Afro-American literature. Giving thorough attention to both black women and black men writing in all genres, these volumes are frequently the only source of reliable biographical information or serious commentary on black women novelists less prominent than Hurston, Walker, Morrison, or Petry. McDowell's supervision of the Beacon Press series of black women's fiction; Washington's previously noted anthologies; and McKay's editorial work on several anthologies all have enriched the contemporary critical dialogue.

A certain irony adheres to the fact that these efforts have contributed to a situation in which the real importance of the black women critics, like that of the generation of black scholars including Charles Davis and George Kent, is somewhat obscured by the absence of "major" critical books equivalent to those of Gates, Byerman, Baker, Stepto, or Willis. Many of the personally dynamic younger black women are continually asked to contribute time and energy to the education of their colleagues in white universities, to national conferences, and to the many white women's groups which have recently become aware of the need to establish contact with the black community. The absence of the "big book" reinforces the potential for invisibility inherent in the "star mentality" of American academia and the mass media's continuing search for an "official media spokesman for black literature" —

a role bestowed on a sequence of often reluctant recipients from Wright and Baldwin through Morrison and Gates. As a result, some of the most important black women critics have not yet published their most valuable insights in book form. Only Christian and Carby, whose *Reconstructing Womanhood: The Emergence of the Afro-American Woman Novelist* (1987) joins *Black Women Novelists* as the first of what will surely prove to be many classic academic studies by black women critics, have published books commensurate with the quality of their essays and introductions. Students wishing to benefit fully from the insights of McDowell, Spillers, McKay, or the other black women critics who have inspired the expanding call and response, are encouraged to consult the dispersed sources listed in this bibliography.

This bibliography is the response of a white grandson to calls that my community has, historically and currently, been reluctant or unable to hear. It is intended to serve three primary purposes: (1) to provide a historical overview of commentary on black women novelists and their most important works; (2) to help identify current issues and future directions in the criticism of those works; and (3) to suggest sources of contextual information that will help students and critics avoid serious misunderstanding of those works. Although the amount of published commentary—particularly newspaper reviews—precludes comprehensive coverage, I have attempted to provide a relatively full overview of the historical development of critical commentary on black women's novels. For this reason I have not excluded reviews, articles, or books, such as those by Rosenblatt and Littlejohn, that are badly flawed or those with which I disagree on fundamental points.

The first section of the bibliography, "General Studies," provides an extensive annotated list of books and articles pertaining to the study of black American women novelists. This general section is followed by individual annotated listings for thirty-two writers, treated in alphabetical order. Each individual section includes entries under the headings "Biography" and "Commentary," followed by entries keyed to specific novels, listed in alphabetical order rather than sequence of publication. (In a handful of cases, where all of the significant criticism on a writer is devoted to a single book, the "Commentary" section has been omitted.)

The principles used for selection of materials are as follows:

(1) Books. I have listed every book of which I am aware that focuses specifically on black women novelists or includes substantial discussion of black women novelists in relation to Afro-American, American, or women's fiction. When such books contain substantial discussion of more than one novelist, I have included a separate citation in the section devoted to that novelist. In defining "substantial discussion," I have employed slightly different criteria for different novels and historical eras. When considering the studies that established the framework for later academic discussions of the Afro-American novel—works such as those by Hugh Gloster, Robert Bone, and Addison Gayle—I have annotated discussions as brief as a single paragraph. In processing more recent books, I have generally limited separate annotation to longer sections. I have been more likely to annotate brief discussions

of writers or works that have not received more detailed attention elsewhere. In any case, entries in the "General Studies" section list all of the writers who receive more than passing mention in a given source.

(2) Scholarly journals. The bibliography annotates all essays on black women novelists published in the following journals, chosen on the basis of their visibility and influence in academic discussions of Afro-American literature, Women's Studies, or the American novel: *Black American Literature Forum, CLA Journal, American Literature, Modern Fiction Studies, Novel, Frontiers, Feminist Studies, Signs, Minority Voices, MELUS, Callaloo, Obsidian, Obsidian II, The Journal of Black Studies, The Southern Review*, the *Mississippi Quarterly, Studies in Black American Literature, Sage, Tulsa Studies in Women's Literature, Studies in Black Literature, Studies in American Fiction*, the *Arizona Quarterly*, the *Centennial Review, Critique*, and *Contemporary Literature*. Essays from other academic journals—such as the proceedings of regional conferences—are included only when they have been cited in at least two other essays. Except in a few cases where an essay has played an important role in subsequent discussion of more than one writer, I have provided only a single annotation. Essays concerning literary influence can be found in the section on the younger writer. Again, the "General Studies" entry lists all novelists discussed in each essay. The best sources for updating information in this bibliography, which is current through early 1989, are the chapter on black literature in *American Literary Scholarship*, the annotated bibliographies published in *Callaloo*, and my annual review of Afro-American literary scholarship to be published in the *Mississippi Quarterly* beginning in 1989.

(3) Reviews and articles in the mass media. This is the most selective area of coverage of materials directly related to black women's novels. I have limited coverage to substantive reviews—usually defined as those of more than five hundred words—published in prominent nationally circulated sources including *The New York Times Book Review, The New York Review of Books, The New Yorker, The New Republic, The Nation, Saturday Review, Time, Newsweek*, the *Atlantic*, and more recently *The Washington Post Book World* and *The Village Voice Literary Supplement*. In addition, I have annotated reviews from a number of sources concerned primarily with Afro-American or women's concerns, among them *Ms., Essence, The Women's Review of Books, Black World/Negro Digest*, and *First World*. In a few cases, I have annotated reviews written by notable critics, especially other novelists, published in other sources. Those seeking a more comprehensive sense of the original reception of particular novels should consult the listings in *Book Review Digest* and the *Book Review Index*. Reviews published in *The Black Scholar, Freedomways, The Crisis, Opportunity, Sinister Wisdom*, and *Belles Lettres* in addition to major regional newspapers such as *The Atlanta Constitution, The Denver Post*, the *Los Angeles Times*, and *The Chicago Tribune* are crucial to understanding the overall reception of black women's work. I have annotated personality profiles only when they include information not readily available in the biographical sketches printed on book jackets.

(4) Reference sources. I have listed entries in various reference books for those without access to extensive research libraries. Clearly the most important of these are the compilations of excerpts from reviews and criticism in *Contemporary Literary Criticism*, *Twentieth-Century Literary Criticism*, and the *Children's Literature Review*; and the invaluable entries in the volumes of the *Dictionary of Literary Biography* edited by Trudier Harris and Thadious Davis. Those seeking a more comprehensive list of sources of basic biographical information should consult the most recent volumes of *Contemporary Authors*.

(5) Contextual materials. In contrast to the principles of selection outlined above, my choice of contextual materials has been frankly personal and highly selective. Because I believe a great deal of commentary on black women's novels has been seriously damaged by ignorance of important backgrounds, I have attempted to identify some of the most accessible and useful sources of information in the fields of African, Afro-American, and Women's Studies. I strongly urge students not already grounded in these areas to establish at least some familiarity with the following basic sources of contextual information before reaching conclusions on particular writers or texts: Robert Farris Thompson's *Flash of the Spirit*; Bell Hooks' *Ain't I a Woman*; Rachel Blau DuPlessis' *Writing Beyond the Ending*; Lawrence Levine's *Black Culture and Black Consciousness*; Angela Davis' *Women, Race, and Class*; Annis Pratt's *Archetypal Patterns in Women's Fiction*; Sara Evans' *Personal Politics*; John Hope Franklin's *From Slavery to Freedom*; Ralph Ellison's *Shadow and Act*; and Deborah White's *Ar'n't I a Woman?* W. E. B. DuBois' *The Souls of Black Folk* and Barbara Christian's *Black Women Novelists* should be considered required reading for all students of Afro-American women's writing. Anthologies such as *But Some of Us Are Brave*, *This Bridge Called My Back*, *Home Girls*, and *Black Women in White America* can serve both to introduce students to the general currents of discussion of black women's novels and to direct them toward more detailed information in their fields.

(6) Choice of novelists, novels, primary sources. The most difficult aspect of selection I have encountered concerns the choice of novels and novelists. As recent textual scholarship, culminating in the publication of the Schomburg Library of Nineteenth-Century Black Women Writers under the supervision of Henry Louis Gates, demonstrates, the amount of fiction written by black women is far more extensive than has been realized. A comprehensive treatment would require a volume of a larger order of magnitude than the present work. In establishing guidelines, I have attempted to include all black women novelists recognized as major figures in any published book in the field of Afro-American Studies. In addition, I have attempted to recognize at least the most prominent figures in fields that have traditionally been marginalized in literary scholarship. Among these are Octavia Butler in science fiction; Ann Shockley in lesbian fiction; and Joyce Carol Thomas, Virginia Hamilton, and Mildred Taylor in children's and juvenile fiction. In choosing specific novels, I have usually selected those which have received the most extensive commentary. Particularly in the cases of the more prolific writers, I

have often selected one or two books, trusting that the sources listed in the "Biography" and "Commentary" sections—particularly the compilations of material in *Children's Literature Review* and *Contemporary Literary Criticism*—will lead interested readers to sources of information on other books.

Most of the black women novelists who do not appear in this volume belong to one of two groups. A few, including Mary Elizabeth Vroman, Arthenia Bates Millican, and Sharon Bell Mathis, are writers of an older generation who have received very little critical attention. The best source of information on these writers— and I would be surprised if, in another ten years, several do not appear to have been glaring omissions—is Carol McAlpine Watson's *Prologue: The Novels of Black American Women, 1891-1965* (1985). The second, more numerous group, consists of younger novelists who have begun their careers during the 1980's and have received attention only in scattered reviews. I feel confident that over the next decade at least a few novels from a group including Doris Austin's *After the Garden*, Terry McMillan's *Mama*, Andrea Lee's *Sarah Phillips*, Linda Jean Brown's *Rainbow Round My Shoulder*, Xam Carrier Wilson's *Rebop Bebop*, and Marita Golden's *A Woman's Place* will be recognized as significant contributions to the tradition that has recently begun to acknowledge slightly older contemporaries such as Ntozake Shange, Butler, and Barbara Chase-Riboud. Of all my exclusions, I am probably least comfortable with the absence of Afro-Caribbean writers such as Jamaica Kincaid. By way of extenuation, I can only encourage another scholar to focus her or his efforts on the deserving work of black women living elsewhere in the diaspora. In addition, I would stress the artificiality of the generic classification that limits this volume to long works of fiction. Short stories by "novelists" such as Bambara and Walker, as well as others such as Rita Dove, Colleen McElroy, and the wonderfully talented J. California Cooper, clearly contribute to the richness of black women's fiction. Brooks's *Maud Martha*, June Jordan's *His Own Where*, and Sherley Anne Williams' *Dessa Rose* strongly suggest that, in the future as in the past, important novels will be published by black women who are currently known as poets, playwrights, or literary critics.

In conclusion, I would like to thank the many individuals who have contributed directly and indirectly to this bibliography. The Graduate College of the University of Wisconsin-Madison provided valuable support for the research and writing of the manuscript. Julie Chase and Benita Ramsey have provided invaluable assistance in compiling materials. As with all of my academic work, my students have provided much of the energy and encouragement that have kept me working. Amy Bowles, Yasmin Cader, Howard Shack, John Gruesser, Malin Walther, Shawn Peters, Malvina Young, and April Madison are only representative of a much larger group who have taught as much as they have learned. Maggie Brandenberg remains the glue that keeps the Humanities Building and the Department of Afro-American Studies at the University of Wisconsin-Madison from collapsing into chaos. Without easy access to the office libraries of William Van Deburg and Nellie McKay, this project would have taken much longer to complete. Missy Dehn Kubitschek has been

invaluable both in cross-checking elusive bibliographical data and as a source of intellectual community. My wife Leslee Nelson and daughters Riah Wakenda and Kaylee Yasmin Werner have shown infinite patience during my long days at the office. As with all bibliographies, this volume would not have been possible without the previous work of fellow bibliographers, of whom John Reilly and Joe Weixlmann have been the most crucial. Finally, I would like to dedicate this volume to Keneth Kinnamon, who taught me that bibliographical research required equal parts passion and patience; and Nellie McKay, whose presence transforms the Department of Afro-American Studies at the University of Wisconsin from a workplace into a community.

General Studies

Anderson, Jervis. *This Was Harlem: A Cultural Portrait, 1900-1950*. New York: Farrar, Straus & Giroux, 1982.
   Popular history based on articles originally published in *The New Yorker*. Examines the origins of New York's black community, the economic and cultural elements of black-white interaction, and the personalities of leading figures in the Harlem Renaissance, including Hurston and Fauset.

Andrews, William L. *To Tell a Free Story: The First Century of Afro-American Autobiography, 1760-1865*. Urbana: University of Illinois Press, 1986.
   Traces the development of black autobiography through the slavery era with an emphasis on the strategies used to interact with a hostile or indifferent white audience. Black autobiographers were forced to develop rhetorical modes that would shift the battle against racism to grounds not occupied by pro- or antislavery polemics, neither of which admitted the full complexity of black life. An essential work of Afro-American literary studies that identifies strategies adapted by many later black writers. Andrews gives substantial attention to the narratives of black women, providing useful approaches to the study of later novels.

Awkward, Michael. *Inspiriting Influences: Tradition, Revision, and Afro-American Women's Novels*. New York: Columbia University Press, 1989.
   Important study of the relationship between Hurston's *Their Eyes Were Watching God*, Morrison's *The Bluest Eye*, Naylor's *The Women of Brewster Place*, and Alice Walker's *The Color Purple*. Awkward argues that affinities between these texts are best understood not simply as a matter of shared racial and sexual oppression, but as the authors' "conscious acts of refiguration and revision of the earlier canonical texts." Awkward emphasizes that black women novelists approach their predecessors not as antagonists, but as sources of energy and inspiration. Gives detailed attention to strategies of double-voicing which con-

tribute to the protagonists' attempts to put an end to "debilitating psychological disjunction (or double consciousness) and isolation from the larger black community."

_____ . "Race, Gender, and the Politics of Reading." *Black American Literature Forum* 22 (Spring, 1988): 5-27.
Examines the ways in which race and gender effect the concept of "acceptable reading" of literary texts. Addresses the question of how literature relates to the full liberation of black people in America. Analyzes criticism by Barbara Smith and Deborah McDowell in addition to that by white feminist scholars. Concludes that both Afrocentric and feminist criticism can benefit from insights emanating from deconstruction and psychoanalytical theory.

Baker, Houston. *Blues, Ideology, and Afro-American Literature: A Vernacular Theory*. Chicago: University of Chicago Press, 1984.
Advances a theory of Afro-American expression based on the central importance of the "black blues life" as a source of both form and content. The importance of the blues lies both in its encoding of communal perceptions and in its focus on interpreting "the experiencing of experience." Substantial emphasis on the economics of culture. Includes a provocative overview of Afro-American literary criticism and some discussion of Hurston.

_____ . *Modernism and the Harlem Renaissance*. Chicago: University of Chicago Press, 1987.
Studies the development of Afro-American expression from the 1880's through the early 1930's with some attention to Hurston and black women singers such as Ma Rainey. Identifies two basic strategies for black expression: the "mastery of form," in which blacks appropriate dominant economic and expressive forms, and the "deformation of mastery," in which writers assert specifically Afro-American cultural forms.

Baraka, Amiri. "Afro-American Literature and Class Struggle." *Black American Literature Forum* 14 (Spring, 1980): 5-14.
Historical overview of Afro-American literature centering on the dialectic between "capitulationist" literature and the revolutionary tradition. Baraka argues that the "genuinely major" Afro-American writers have been part of the revolutionary tradition. Mentions Margaret Walker, Morrison, and Shange.

_____ . [as LeRoi Jones]. *Blues People*. New York: William Morrow, 1963.
Survey of the development of Afro-American music, emphasizing the ways in which it has responded to changing economic and social experiences of the black community. Traces the development of blues and jazz out of African

traditions and the religious and secular musics of the slave community. An important introduction to the musical tradition drawn on by many black women novelists.

_____ , and Amina Baraka, eds. *Confirmation: An Anthology of African American Women*. New York: Quill, 1983.
Anthology containing selections from the poetry or fiction of most of the writers covered in this bibliography. Amiri Baraka's introduction argues that "the conflict between the masses of black women and the feminist movement is chiefly one of class antagonism" caused by monopoly capitalism. Not feminist per se, *Confirmation* seeks to redress the injustice of black women's absence from mainstream literary recognition. Baraka catalogs a number of concerns linking black women writers, including a willingness to fight for democratic ideals; Pan-African consciousness; critical realism as a fundamental stance; and conscious redefinition of the black woman to herself and others.

_____ . [as LeRoi Jones]. "The Myth of a 'Negro Literature.'" In *Home: Social Essays*. New York: William Morrow, 1966.
Harsh overview of the "mediocrity" of "Negro literature," arguing that the vital center of the Afro-American expressive tradition lies in music. Condemns the middle-class bias of most black writers, who have uncritically accepted white conceptions of culture. Baraka asserts that black writers attempting to create vital art were forced to look outside the mainstream to African, subcultural, or hermetic sources. An influential manifesto that helped inspire the Black Arts movement of the 1960's.

Barksdale, Richard. "Castration Symbolism in Recent Black American Fiction." *CLA Journal* 29 (June, 1986): 400-413.
Discusses the transition from images of physical castration to those of psychological castration of black men in Jones's *Corregidora* and *Eva's Man*, Morrison's *Sula*, Walker's *The Color Purple*, and Marshall's *Praisesong for the Widow*. Detailed examination of Jones's two novels suggests that black men have imitated the behavior of their former masters. Presenting black men who deserve castration or have been symbolically castrated by forces beyond their control, these novelists create depressing role models for younger black male readers.

_____ , and Keneth Kinnamon, eds. *Black Writers of America: A Comprehensive Anthology*. New York: Macmillan, 1972.
Standard anthology including trustworthy overviews of Afro-American history and biographical essays on Harper, Hurston, Margaret Walker, Brooks, Petry, and Marshall.

Barthold, Bonnie J. *Black Time: Fiction of Africa, the Caribbean, and the United States*. New Haven, Conn.: Yale University Press, 1981.

Asserts the existence of an African literary continuum based on notions of time shared by Afro-American, African, and Afro-Caribbean writers. Identifies a polarity between the cyclic (synchronous) configuration of time in traditional agrarian cultures and the linear (diachronous) sense of time in industrialized cultures. Most black writers express a transitional stage in which synchronous and diachronous conceptions of time coexist. Includes discussions of Jones, Hunter, Morrison, Marshall, Alice Walker, and Hurston.

Barton, Rebecca Chalmers. *Race Consciousness and the American Negro*. Copenhagen, Denmark: Arnold Busck, 1934. Reprint. Oakdale, N.Y.: Dowling College Press, 1976.

Early study of black fiction as a source of firsthand insights into Negro life. Emphasizes the refusal of Negro writers to separate life and literature. Includes brief passages on Fauset and Larsen, both of whom are viewed as examples of the "urban-cosmopolitan tendency" in black writing. Both are attracted to the "refinement and sophistication" of middle-class black life.

Baym, Nina. *Women's Fiction: A Guide to Novels By and About Women in America, 1820-1870*. Ithaca, N.Y.: Cornell University Press, 1978.

Ground-breaking work of feminist scholarship arguing that nineteenth century women's novels were addressed primarily to other women and tell an archetypal story. They chronicle the experience of a heroine who overcomes hardships by finding within herself qualities of intelligence, will, resourcefulness, and courage. Baym's typology has been employed and revised by numerous critics of black women's fiction.

Bell, Bernard W. *The Afro-American Novel and Its Tradition*. Amherst: University of Massachusetts Press, 1987.

Comprehensive study of Afro-American fiction, in some ways replacing Bone's *The Negro Novel in America* as an introductory overview. Placing novels in their historical, cultural, and social contexts, Bell defines crucial periods in Afro-American fiction. Contemporary novels can be classified as either "neo-realist" or "modernist/post-modernist." Sections concerning Harriet Wilson, Harper, Fauset, Larsen, Hurston, Petry, Alice Walker, Morrison, and Margaret Walker combine analysis and biographical information.

Bell, Roseann, P., Bettye J. Parker, and Beverly Guy-Sheftall, eds. *Sturdy Black Bridges: Visions of Black Women in Literature*. Garden City, N.Y.: Anchor Press, 1979.

Important anthology of analytical essays, interviews, and creative work by and about black women. Dedicated to bringing literary images of black women

into accord with historical truths. Instrumental in drawing attention to the exclusion of black women from previous histories of Afro-American literature. Emphasizes connections between African, Caribbean, and Afro-American expression. Includes extensive material concerning Hurston, Alice Walker, Petry, Bambara, Morrison, and Jones.

Berry, Mary Frances, and John W. Blassingame. *Long Memory: The Black Experience in America*. New York: Oxford University Press, 1982.
Overview of Afro-American history, including brief discussion of literary images of black women. Organized according to major topics, including economics, education, family and church, criminal justice, political movements, Afro-American culture, sex and racism, and black nationalism. Emphasizes the importance of the memories of Africa and slavery to the shape of contemporary Afro-American society.

Berzon, Judith R. *Neither White Nor Black: The Mulatto Character in American Fiction*. New York: New York University Press, 1978.
Study of the mulatto character in American fiction, including commentary on Harper, Hopkins, West, Larsen, and Hurston. Caught between two cultures, the mixed-blood individual exists in a marginal area between the boundaries of the American caste system. The widespread Afro-American preoccupation with questions of individual and community identity assumes special intensity in the case of the mulatto. Includes detailed discussion of scientific, historical, and sociological backgrounds.

Bigsby, C. W. E. "Judgement Day Is Coming! The Apocalyptic Dream in Recent Afro-American Fiction." In *Black Fiction: New Studies in the Afro-American Novel Since 1945*, edited by A. Robert Lee. New York: Barnes & Noble, 1980.
Examines the apocalyptic dimension of recent black fiction, identifying a contradiction at the heart of much of the revolutionary writing of the 1960's. Beneath the imagery of the apocalyptic racial battle, there is frequently a hope that the possibility of apocalypse will itself be enough to effect a social transformation. Discusses the apocalyptic political theme in Alice Walker's *The Third Life of Grange Copeland* and *Meridian*, and Morrison's *Song of Solomon*.

_____ . *The Second Black Renaissance: Essays in Black Literature*. Westport, Conn.: Greenwood Press, 1980.
Overview of Afro-American literary culture from the 1940's to the 1970's, emphasizing the influence of Richard Wright on the formation of a dominant "liberal" agenda. The struggle to come to terms with an oppressive past generates an ambiguous struggle with language. The central theme of Afro-American writing of the period is "the recreation of self and community." Incorporates little direct analysis of black women's writing.

Bone, Robert. *The Negro Novel in America*. Rev. ed. New Haven, Conn.: Yale University Press, 1965.
First published in 1958, this classic study of Afro-American fiction gives attention to Fauset, Larsen, Hurston, and Petry. Early attempt to separate "social" and "literary" understanding of Afro-American fiction. Uses "assimilationism"—the "attempt to abandon ethnic ties and identify with the dominant majority"—and "Negro nationalism"—"an urge to blackness within the race, which is essentially defensive in character"—as primary categories for discussion of individual novels and the consciousness of historical periods.

——————. "Richard Wright and the Chicago Renaissance." *Callaloo* 28 (Summer, 1986): 446-468.
Important essay proposing the existence of a "Chicago Renaissance" as a major period in Afro-American cultural history spanning the years 1935 to 1950. Bone presents evidence regarding the demographic constitution of the black community in Chicago; the importance of the Sociology Department at the University of Chicago; the patronage provided by the Rosenwald Foundation; and the contents of several literary magazines. Noting the presence of a range of important black writers including Margaret Walker and Gwendolyn Brooks, Bone suggests that the importance of Chicago during the period was equivalent to that of Harlem during the 1920's.

Bontemps, Arna. *The Harlem Renaissance Remembered*. New York: Dodd, Mead, 1972.
Anthology of essays on various aspects of the Harlem Renaissance, including a memoir by Bontemps. Includes essays on Fauset, Larsen, and Hurston.

Brawley, Benjamin. *The Negro in Literature and Art in the United States*. New York: Duffield, 1930.
Early study of Afro-American contributions to American culture, covering work in literary and visual forms. Includes brief comments on Harper, Larsen, and Fauset. Larsen and Fauset are discussed with the "new realists," whose main concern is the situation of attractive women confronting the "ways of the world." *Passing* is praised as a promising performance because of its excellent sense of form.

Brock, Sabine, and Anne Koenen. "Alice Walker in Search of Zora Neale Hurston: Rediscovering a Black Female Literary Tradition." In *History and Tradition in Afro-American Culture*, edited by Gunther H. Lenz. Frankfurt: Campus Verlag, 1984.
Argues for the existence of a distinct Afro-American women's tradition that has been repressed by hostile or misleading critics. Emphasizes the supportive

relationship between black women writers. Includes commentary on Alice Walker, Hurston, Morrison, Marshall, and Bambara.

Broderick, Dorothy M. *The Image of the Black in Children's Fiction*. New York: R. R. Bowker, 1973.
Survey of the treatment of black characters in children's literature published between 1827 and 1967. The vast majority of the images presented by white writers are either condescendingly racist or traditionally liberal in the "do-gooder" mold, advocating tolerance rather than love or understanding. Valuable source of information concerning the problems confronted by black women children's novelists such as Hamilton, Thomas, and Taylor. Includes a brief mention of June Jordan's *His Own Where* as a "landmark title."

Brown, Sterling. *The Negro in American Fiction*. Washington, D.C.: Associates in Negro Folk Education, 1937. Reprint. New York: Atheneum, 1969.
Ground-breaking overview of the treatment of racial issues in fiction by white and black Americans by a black critic widely recognized as the founder of Afro-American literary criticism. Traces the interplay of tendencies derived from the plantation tradition and abolitionist fiction. Includes brief discussions of Harper, Hopkins, Larsen, Fauset, and Hurston.

Bruce, Dickson D., Jr. *Black American Writing from the Nadir: The Evolution of a Literary Tradition, 1877-1915*. Baton Rouge: Louisiana State University Press, 1989.
Overview of Afro-American literary activity from the end of the Reconstruction Era to the beginning of the Harlem Renaissance. Bruce emphasizes the tension between the increasingly racist context confronted by the writers and their commitment to middle-class values. Includes some discussion of Harper and Hopkins.

Bruck, Peter, and Wolfgang Karrer, eds. *The Afro-American Novel Since 1960*. Amsterdam: B. R. Gruner, 1982.
Anthology of critical essays on contemporary Afro-American novelists including Marshall, Alice Walker, and Morrison. Bruck's introduction provides a useful overview of dominant tendencies in the criticism of Afro-American fiction, charting a constitutive tension among "protest," "universality," and "blackness" as basic values. Karrer's introduction grounds recent novels in the social and political contexts of Afro-American life.

Bryan, Beverley, Stella Dadzie, and Suzanne Scafe. *The Heart of the Race: Black Women's Lives in Britain*. London: Virago Press, 1985.
Overview of black women's experience in Britain emphasizing the inspirational impact of black American women's expression. The authors discuss the interaction of race, class, and gender issues, asserting the importance of listen-

ing to their own voices along with those of their mothers, sisters, grandmothers, and aunts. Among the aspects of Afro-Caribbean women's experience discussed are their position in the workplace, their role as cultural preservers, and their contribution to various forms of organization and resistance.
An important part of the international discussion between black women.

Bulkin, Elly, Minnie Bruce Pratt, and Barbara Smith. *Yours in Struggle: Three
Feminist Perspectives on Anti-Semitism and Racism.* Brooklyn: Long Haul
Press, 1984.
Dialogue among three feminist critics—one Jewish, one white Protestant, one
black—concerning the issues of anti-Semitism and racism in the feminist
movement. A valuable document concerning the intellectual and political context of black women's writing in the 1980's.

Bullins, Ed. Introduction to *The New Lafayette Theatre Presents*, edited by Bullins.
Garden City, N.Y.: Anchor Press, 1974.
Important theoretical statement by a black playwright associated with the
Black Arts movement. Bullins identifies two interrelated "dialectics" as the
core of Afro-American expression. The "dialectic of change," which encompasses both traditional "protest" writing and black revolutionary writing, attempts to alter the conditions of black life in a racist society. The "dialectic of
experience" provides the most compelling possible images of the realities of
black life without explicit political commentary. A valuable framework for
approaching black women's writing.

Busia, Abena P. B. "Words Whispered over Voids: A Context for Black Women's
Rebellious Voices in the Novel of the African Diaspora." *Studies in Black
American Literature* 3 (1988): 1-41.
Calls for increased recognition of the ways in which the oral dimension of
black women's literature testifies to a process of self-definition common
throughout the diaspora. Protagonists of black women's fiction—in Africa, the
Caribbean, and the United States—sound a shared set of themes including the
validation of Africa through incorporation of folk culture in the text; the
creation of protagonists capable of telling their own stories; the conquering of
physical space as a metaphor for autonomy; and the reexamination of the role
of women in society. Includes discussion of Morrison's *Sula* and Marshall's
Praisesong for the Widow.

Byerman, Keith. *Fingering the Jagged Grain: Tradition and Form in Recent Black
Fiction.* Athens: University of Georgia Press, 1985.
General discussion of Afro-American fiction since 1950, including discussions
of Morrison, Bambara, Alice Walker, and Gayl Jones. Emphasizes the influence of *Invisible Man* over subsequent approaches to the use of folklore as a

stylistic resource for Afro-American novelists. Grounded in what W. E. B. DuBois called "double consciousness," Afro-American folk traditions suggest a sensibility that resists "closed, oppressive systems . . . whether political, economic, cultural, religious, racial, sexual, aesthetic, or philosophical." This openness resists both the racism of Euro-American institutions and the ideological narrowness of some black nationalist approaches.

Cade [Bambara], Toni. *The Black Woman: An Anthology*. New York: New American Library, 1970.
Anthology of materials concerning the black woman's struggle for liberation from racial, sexual, and economic exploitation. Combines creative and analytical perspectives with emphasis on sociopolitical perspectives. Introduction stresses the need to develop a clear understanding of the meaning of liberation. Because it has been dominated by men, literature provides little guidance. Includes fiction by Marshall and Sherley Anne Williams. This anthology played a crucial role in defining issues involving black women's experience and expression.

Callahan, John. *In the African-American Grain: The Pursuit of Voice in Twentieth-Century Black Fiction*. Urbana: University of Illinois Press, 1988.
Examines the use of oral forms as the foundation of literary voice in Afro-American fiction. Writing explicitly as "agents of change," Afro-American novelists tap call and response forms which enable the individual to preserve a distinct personal voice while simultaneously blending it with those of the community. The emphasis on call and response enables writers to awaken dormant relationships—between different writers, different books, different communities of readers, the writer and her characters—that can be used to create a more democratic vision in the black writer's audience. Includes extended discussion of Hurston and Alice Walker.

Campbell, Jane. *Mythic Black Fiction: The Transformation of History*. Knoxville: University of Tennessee Press, 1986.
Examines the attempts of black writers to fuse history and myth into a new reality that will enable blacks to maintain their humanity despite oppressive forces. Many black novelists invoke myths of the messiah and the garden. The primary literary device for the presentation of myth has been the "romance," which Campbell defines as the mode in which protagonists "depict values that run counter to those of an oppressive culture." Romance transforms white versions of history and reinvents a black reality. Includes discussions of Harper, Hopkins, and Morrison.

Carby, Hazel V. "The Canon: Civil War and Reconstruction." *Michigan Quarterly Review* 28 (Winter, 1989): 35-43.

Response to Toni Morrison's essay in the same issue of the journal. Argues that debates about the literary canon frequently avoid the deeper problem, which concerns "the ways in which our society is structured in dominance." Emphasizes the importance of increasing public awareness that "marginalization is itself central to the formation of the dominant culture." Concludes with the suggestion that rather than "searching for cultural purity, we acknowledge cultural complexity."

───────────── . *Reconstructing Womanhood: The Emergence of the Afro-American Woman Novelist*. New York: Oxford University Press, 1987.
Examines the development of black women's fiction from its nineteenth century origins through the Harlem Renaissance of the 1920's. Literary stereotypes of black women have not been created to reflect reality but to obscure objective social relations, particularly those involving economic power. Black women novelists provide a necessary corrective to dominant myths such as that of the "cult of true womanhood." Early novelists such as Harper and Hopkins engage the relationship between politics and literature by focusing sharply on precisely those issues marginalized in texts by white writers. Concludes with a discussion of how the urban confrontation with issues of race, class, and sexuality has been underemphasized in recent criticism of black women's fiction. Includes extensive discussion of Wilson, Harper, Hopkins, and Larsen.

Chase, Richard. *The American Novel and Its Tradition*. Garden City, N.Y.: Anchor Press, 1957. Reprint. Baltimore: Johns Hopkins University Press, 1980.
Although Chase makes no mention of black novelists, his discussion of the tension between realism and romance in the tradition of American fiction has provided a touchstone for many subsequent discussions, including those on Afro-American fiction. Chase argues that the defining characteristic of the American tradition is its inability to reconcile metaphysical, mythic, and symbolic insights (the romance form) on the one hand, with realistic, social, and historical insights (the novel form) on the other.

Christ, Carol P. *Diving Deep and Surfacing: Women Writers on Spiritual Quest*. Boston: Beacon Press, 1980.
Feminist reading of underlying patterns of women's expression, including a chapter focusing on Shange's drama. Identifies a four-stage progression found in much women's literature. Beginning with the experience of nothingness, female protagonists experience awakenings that lead to increased insight into their circumstances. The process culminates in the protagonist's ability to name her own experience. Influential contribution to the feminist discourse surrounding the rise of black women's fiction in the 1980's.

Christian, Barbara. *Black Women Novelists: The Development of a Tradition, 1892-1976*. Westport, Conn.: Greenwood Press, 1980.

The first full-scale treatment of black women's novels. Explores the ways in which stereotypical images of blacks generally, and black women specifically, contributed to the belief that "the Negro had to be contained by a superior being and was naturally suited to the condition of slavery." The Afro-American oral tradition provides a reservoir of counter-images which have been used by black women to create a literary tradition articulating self-definitions that recognize and celebrate the creative spirit omitted in the stereotypes. Includes discussions of Brooks, Fauset, Harper, Hurston, Margaret Walker, Petry, Larsen, Alice Walker, Marshall, and Morrison.

——————— . *Black Feminist Criticism: Perspectives on Black Women Writers*. Elmsford, N.Y.: Pergamon Press, 1985.
Collection of essays by an important black woman critic. In addition to essays focusing specifically on the work of Alice Walker, Morrison, Marshall, Brooks, and Harper, the collection includes several influential essays on general topics, including the treatment of lesbianism in the work of Audre Lorde, Naylor, Shange, and Alice Walker. "Images of Black Women in Afro-American Literature: From Stereotype to Character" is an early version of themes developed more fully in Christian's *Black Women Novelists*. Christian's discussion of the relationship between the struggle against sexism in the black community and the struggle against racism, in "Trajectories of Self-Definition: Placing Contemporary Afro-American Women's Fiction," has provided a central point of reference for many critics working on related topics.

——————— . "The Race for Theory." *Cultural Critique* 6 (Spring, 1987): 51-63.
Statement by an important black feminist critic concerning the role of literary theory in relation to Afro-American literature. Emphasizes the ways in which theoretical vocabularies have become associated with institutional power structures with little interest in the issues raised in black writing. Focuses on the impact of theoretical discourse on feminist scholarship and raises the central question of audience.

Coleman, Wanda. "On Theloniousism." *Caliban* 4 (1988): 67-79.
Important statement of aesthetics by a black woman poet applicable to the situation of black women novelists. Basing her perspective on the music of jazz pianist and composer Thelonious Monk, Coleman addresses the relationship between "minority" writers and the dominant literary culture. Where white writers can afford to play literary games, black writers face a dangerous situation of potential psychological alienation. The black writer's success will inevitably be devalued by tokenism on one hand and the demand that he or she provide a solution to racial problems on the other. Proposes that black writers employ black music as a resource suggesting possible means of escape from this dilemma.

Conditions 5 (1979).
Special issue of an important journal of lesbian writing. Titled "The Black Woman's Issue," it includes Ann Allen Shockley's essay on the black lesbian in American literature. Most of the contents of the issue were reprinted in *Home Girls: A Black Feminist Anthology*, edited by Barbara Smith.

Cooke, Michael G. *Afro-American Literature in the Twentieth Century: The Achievement of Intimacy*. New Haven, Conn.: Yale University Press, 1984.
Study of the movement toward greater freedom from fixed canons of thought in modern Afro-American literature. Stressing the importance of "signifying" and the "blues" to black literary expression, Cooke outlines a four-stage process advancing from "self-veiling" and "solitude" to "kinship" and "intimacy." The most fully realized texts reflect both a deep involvement with the world and a freedom from "sociopolitical shibboleths." Includes discussions of Larsen, Hurston, Alice Walker, and Gayl Jones.

Crabtree, Claire. "The Confluence of Folklore, Feminism, and Black Self-Determination in Zora Neale Hurston's *Their Eyes Were Watching God*." *Southern Literary Journal* 17, no. 2 (1985): 54-66.
Detailed examination of the ways in which Hurston uses various folk traditions to redefine the position of women in the black community. Crabtree discusses Hurston's use of framing, dialect, and various games.

Cruse, Harold. *The Crisis of the Negro Intellectual: From Its Origins to the Present*. New York: William Morrow, 1967.
Influential discussion of Afro-American intellectual history from the Harlem Renaissance to the mid-1960's. Argues that black intellectuals are socially detached from the black community but not fully integrated into the white intellectual world. Traces the tension between assimilationist and nationalist ideologies, identifying the sometimes unrecognized acceptance of American individualistic values as a source of political and psychological problems. Includes important discussion of black-Jewish relations. Little direct attention to black women novelists but valuable as a widely read interpretation of the intellectual context in which they wrote.

Cunard, Nancy, ed. *Negro: An Anthology*. Private printing, 1934. Reprint edited and abridged by Hugh Ford. New York: Frederick Ungar, 1970.
Massive anthology of material related to Afro-American expression of the Harlem Renaissance era. Includes primary and secondary sources related to black music, history, politics, and literature both in the United States and throughout the diaspora. Includes several essays by Hurston and brief comments on Fauset.

Daly, Mary. *Beyond God the Father: Toward a Philosophy of Women's Liberation*. Boston: Beacon Press, 1973.

Feminist analysis of the sexism of dominant religious systems, incorporating extensive discussion of the psychology of feminist experience. The chapter on "Problem, Purpose, and Method" includes insights directly relevant to criticism of black women's fiction. Daly lists trivialization, particularization, spiritualization, and universalization as strategies that are repeatedly used by hostile, patriarchal writers to dismiss feminist insights.

Dandridge, Rita B. "Male Critics/Black Women's Novels." *CLA Journal* 23 (September, 1979): 1-11.

Argues that exaggerated disparagement by male critics has doomed many black women's novels to unwarranted obscurity. Classifies most male critical approaches to black women's novels into three types: apathetic, chauvinistic, and paternalistic. Apathetic critics such as Robert Bone force novels into prescribed categories or dismiss them as trivial. Chauvinistic critics such as Darwin Turner approach black women's novels with obvious vindictiveness. Paternalistic criticism such as Frank Lamont Phillips' review of Shockley's *Loving Her* disapproves of unconventional content and informs the black woman novelist of how to do better.

——————— . "On the Novels Written by Selected Black American Women: A Bibliographical Essay." In *But Some of Us Are Brave: Black Women's Studies*, edited by Gloria T. Hull, Patricia Bell Scott, and Barbara Smith. Old Westbury, N.Y.: Feminist Press, 1982.

Bibliographical essay containing information on both primary and secondary sources. Includes sections on literary and personal background sources; general criticism; and individual studies of Brooks, Fauset, Hurston, Larsen, Marshall, and Petry, with a brief entry on Morrison and Alice Walker.

Daniel, Walter C. *Images of the Preacher in Afro-American Literature*. Washington, D.C.: University Press of America, 1981.

Surveys the treatment of preachers in black fiction by nineteenth and twentieth century novelists including Hurston and Margaret Walker. Emphasizes the central role of the church in the Afro-American community. Identifies the uneducated emotional preacher who speaks in dialect and the young minister characterized by education and social concern as the poles of presentation.

Davies, Carolyn Boyce. "Mothering and Healing in Recent Black Women's Fiction." *Sage* 2 (Spring, 1985): 41-43.

Discusses Walker's *The Color Purple*, Naylor's *The Women of Brewster Place*, Marshall's *Praisesong for the Widow*, Bambara's *The Salt Eaters*, and Shange's *Sassafrass, Cypress and Indigo* as examples of the connection between mother-

ing and healing in recent black women's fiction. Each novel focuses on a black woman who has become lost in a self-destructive maze of negative behavior created by a combination of racial, sexual, and class oppression. Each is healed through the intervention of a mother-healer who, significantly, is never the biological mother.

Davis, Angela Y. *Women, Culture, and Politics*. New York: Random House, 1989.
Collection of essays and lectures exploring various aspects of the struggle for racial, sexual, and economic equality. Among the topics Davis addresses are the situation of women in the third world; violence against women; women's health issues; the black family; black women in the peace movement; and the significance of cultural activity in effecting political change. The theme of empowerment links most of the essays, which provide a sense of the political context of black women's writing in the 1980's.

_____ . *Women, Race, and Class*. New York: Random House, 1981.
Marxist interpretation of black women's experience in relation to racial, sexual, and class exploitation. Traces the relationship between black and white women from the abolition movement to the women's movement of the 1970's, emphasizing the frequent betrayal of the racial agenda by white feminists. Unexamined myths, such as the myth of the black rapist, uphold economic interests of the dominant class and fragment potential political response. Davis' book was an important part of the debate associated with the emergence of black women's fiction in the 1980's.

Davis, Arthur P. *From the Dark Tower: Afro-American Writers 1900 to 1960*. Washington, D.C.: Howard University Press, 1974.
Overview of the development of Afro-American writing from the time of Chesnutt and Dunbar through the emergence of Baldwin, Ellison, and Brooks. Incorporates biographical sketches with analysis of the major works of writers in various genres, including Fauset, Larsen, Margaret Walker, Brooks (primarily as a poet), and Petry.

_____ . "Novels of the New Black Renaissance, 1960-1977: A Thematic Survey." *CLA Journal* 21 (June, 1978): 457-490.
Proposes that the period since 1960 be called "The New Black Renaissance" because of the characteristics it shares with the "New Negro Renaissance" of the 1920's. Both eras emphasize African cultural roots, racial pride, and militancy. Among the major influences on the new movement were the political context, the Black Arts movement, new black magazines, and an increased awareness of the history of Afro-American fiction. Includes brief discussions of Gayl Jones, Marshall, Hunter, Meriwether, Sarah Wright, Morrison, and Alice Walker.

Davis, Charles T. *Black Is the Color of the Cosmos: Essays on Afro-American Literature and Culture, 1942-1981*. New York: Garland, 1982.

Collected essays of a germinal figure in the development of Afro-American Studies as an academic discipline, including numerous references to black women novelists. Title essay argues that "awareness of being black is the most powerful and the most fertile single inspiration for black writers." Every black text reflects an awareness of a dual heritage: the tradition of American letters, and the tradition of Afro-American folk forms.

Davis, Charles T., and Henry Louis Gates, Jr., eds. *The Slave's Narrative*. New York: Oxford University Press, 1985.

Anthology of primary and secondary sources concerning early Afro-American autobiographical writing. Gates's introduction identifies the crucial problems confronted by black writers attempting to write in any genre during the nineteenth century. Because writing was viewed in European discourse as the visible sign of reason, blacks seeking to enter into public discourse were forced to place a central emphasis on the theme of literacy. A crucial framework for discussion of later black writing in relation to mainstream literary conventions.

Dearborn, Mary V. *Pocahontas's Daughters: Gender and Ethnicity in American Culture*. New York: Oxford University Press, 1986.

Argues for the centrality of the ethnic sensibility to American women's literature. Even women not usually considered "ethnic" reflect characteristics of ethnic writing, including the use of devices such as glossaries and prefaces; generic confusion; dualistic writing styles; and political/aesthetic debates. Writers such as Morrison and Alice Walker contribute to a "radical redemptivism" that transforms what have traditionally been seen as negative characteristics into sources of strength. Includes discussion of Wilson, Fauset, Harper, Larsen, Hurston, Morrison, Jones, and Hopkins. Individual chapters focus on the role of black women writers in the Harlem Renaissance and the theme of the mulatto.

Dixon, Melvin. *Ride Out the Wilderness: Geography and Identity in Afro-American Literature*. Urbana: University of Illinois Press, 1987.

Examination of the "symbolic geography" of Afro-American culture, identifying three principal images—the wilderness, the underground, and the mountaintop—that link literary and oral traditions. The wilderness represents a place of refuge beyond the restrictions of the plantation; the underground is the place where individual strength and determination are tested; the mountaintop represents empowerment and vision. Following an analysis of the origins of these images in slave songs and autobiographical narratives, Dixon explores their relationship to the black attempt to turn the land of bondage into a site of freedom. Includes discussions of Hurston, Morrison, Alice Walker, and Gayl Jones.

DuBois, W. E. B. *The Souls of Black Folk*. Chicago: A. C. McClurg, 1903. Reprint. In *Writings* by W. E. B. DuBois. New York: The Library of America, 1986.

One of the most important books in the development of Afro-American thought. Combining historical, sociological, and cultural perspectives, DuBois introduces a range of fundamental concepts for the study of Afro-American experience. Giving a degree of recognition to black women extremely unusual among writers of the era, DuBois centers his book on the concept of "double consciousness," the feeling of division experienced by blacks attempting to merge their "American" and their "Negro" selves into a "better and truer self."

DuPlessis, Rachel Blau. *Writing Beyond the Ending: Narrative Strategies of Twentieth-Century Women Writers*. Bloomington: Indiana University Press, 1985.

Argues that twentieth century women writers have developed a complex set of strategies to criticize and subvert conventional narrative and mythological structures that circumscribe women's experience. Emphasizes the themes of heterosexual domination, gender polarization, and separate spheres for men and women. Discusses Hurston and Alice Walker in the context of revisions of quest plots.

Edwards, Lee R. *Psyche as Hero: Female Heroism and Fictional Form*. Middletown, Conn. Wesleyan University Press, 1984.

Discusses Morrison's *Sula* and Hurston's *Their Eyes Were Watching God*, along with Harriet Arnow's *The Dollmaker*, as attempts to redefine the role of the woman artist in a society that attempts to deny her forms of expression. All three protagonists reject self-reflective conceptions of the aesthetic masterwork and strive for forms that model people and society. Moving from isolation to radical involvement, their medium is life itself. Sula emphasizes the necessity of negativity to this process, while Janie strives for positive identification of self and society.

Elder, Arlene A. *The "Hindered Hand": Cultural Implications of Early African American Fiction*. Westport, Conn.: Greenwood Press, 1978.

Analyzes Afro-American fiction through Paul Laurence Dunbar and Charles Chesnutt, with some attention to Harper. Nineteenth century black novelists modeled their work on white sentimental and propaganda fiction, and to a lesser degree on black oratory and oral narrative. The conflict between these traditions creates strange effects that diminish the artistic quality of the black novelists' work but provide a clear sense of the destructive context in which they wrote.

Ellison, Ralph. *Shadow and Act*. New York: Random House, 1964.

Important collection of nonfiction prose by a black male novelist. Ellison

develops a complex vision of the relationship between black and white American culture. Among the most important essays are "Change the Joke and Slip the Yoke," "Richard Wright's Blues," and "The World and the Jug," all of which articulate the complexity of the Afro-American sensibility; and "Twentieth-Century Fiction and the Black Mask of Humanity" and "Stephen Crane and the Mainstream of American Fiction," which discuss the moral dimensions of the tradition of the American novel. A central point of reference for discussions of Afro-American culture.

Evans, Mari, ed. *Black Women Writers, 1950-1980: A Critical Evaluation*. Garden City, N.Y.: Anchor Press, 1984.
Anthology of essays, interviews, and bio-bibliographic material on black women writers, including Bambara, Brooks, Childress, Jones, Marshall, Morrison, Alice Walker, and Margaret Walker. Stephen Henderson's introduction emphasizes the ways in which black women have generated a "revolution within the [black] Revolution."

Evans, Sara. *Personal Politics: The Roots of Women's Liberation in the Civil Rights Movement and the New Left*. New York: Alfred A. Knopf, 1979.
Traces the origins of the feminist movement of the 1970's to the involvement of women in earlier progressive movements, with particular emphasis on the Civil Rights movement. An important book for establishing historical and philosophical connections that were frequently unrecognized by many of the first academic studies in the field of Women's Studies.

Exum, Pat Crutchfield, ed. *Keeping the Faith: Writings by Contemporary Black American Women*. New York: Fawcett, 1974.
Anthology of materials by black women focusing on a broad range of topics including politics, the family, and literature. Includes the transcript of a symposium on images of black women in literature, originally published in *Freedomways*, that includes comments by Paule Marshall, Alice Childress, and Sarah Wright.

Fairbanks, Carol, and Eugene A. Engeldinger. *Black American Fiction: A Bibliography*. Metuchen, N.J.: Scarecrow Press, 1978.
Bibliography listing primary and secondary sources relevant to the study of most of the writers included in this bibliography. Valuable for listing of original reviews.

Fisher, Dexter, ed. *The Third Woman: Minority Women Writers of the United States*. Boston: Houghton Mifflin, 1980.
Anthology of writing by Native American, Asian American, Chicana, and

Afro-American women writers, including selections by Alice Walker, Hurston, Morrison, Bambara, Margaret Walker, and Petry. Introduction to Afro-American section identifies the concentration on human relationships within the black community as a fundamental characteristic of black women's writing.

Fisher, Jerilyn. "From Under the Yoke of Race and Sex: Black and Chicano Women's Fiction of the Seventies." *Minority Voices* 2, no. 2 (1978): 1-14.
Discusses Alice Walker, Morrison, and Bambara in the context of recent developments in minority women's fiction. All three novelists portray woman characters who attempt to develop new individual identities grounded in their relationship to larger communities. The first step in this process is separation from and reevaluation of traditional definitions of women's roles in their communities.

Foner, Eric. "The Canon and American History." *Michigan Quarterly Review* 28 (Winter, 1989): 44-49.
Response to Toni Morrison's lecture on the American literary canon published in the same journal. Reiterates the core of Morrison's argument: that the canon is itself is an ideological construction that changes over time in accord with political needs. Discusses Morrison's *Beloved*, which Foner reads as a pessimistic vision comparable in some ways to Stanley Elkins' view of slavery as a dehumanizing institution, as a meditation on history and memory. History for Morrison is "both a burden and a form of self-knowledge."

Fontenot, Chester J., Jr. "Black Fiction: Apollo or Dionysius." *Twentieth Century Literature* 25 (Spring, 1979): 73-84.
Presents a theoretical approach to Afro-American fiction based on the tension between the Apollonian sensibility based on a linear conception of time, and the Dionysian sensibility based on a mythic conception that insists on a continual re-creation of the black historical past. Analyzing several novels including Hurston's *Their Eyes Were Watching God* and Jones's *Corregidora*, Fontenot identifies a movement from tragedy to romance as the constitutive form of black fiction.

Ford, Nick Aaron. *The Contemporary Negro Novel: A Study in Race Relations.* Boston: Meador, 1936. Reprint. College Park, Md.: McGrath, 1968.
Early study of black fiction based on the premise that the "Negro novel is more a creature of environment than that produced by any other group. It fairly screams with condemnation, complaint, abuse, pride, and prejudice." Throughout, Ford asserts the responsibility of the black writer to the political advancement of the race. Includes discussions of Fauset, Larsen, and Hurston.

Concludes that according to "our best American standards" all Negro novels "fall rather low in technique."

Foster, Frances. "'In Respect to Females. . . .': Differences in the Portrayals of Women by Male and Female Narrators." *Black American Literature Forum* 15 (Summer, 1981): 66-70.
Contrasts the portrait of slave women in slave narratives by male and female authors. Grounding her analysis in a discussion of sexual oppression in slavery, Foster observes that male narrators typically portray slave women as victims of illicit intercourse and as childless mothers. Presenting more complex images of their sex, women narrators add an awareness of the malevolence of the white mistresses and present images of successful black women. A valuable source of information concerning the expressive tradition behind the work of black women novelists.

Fox-Genovese, Elizabeth. *Within the Plantation Household: Black and White Women of the Old South*. Chapel Hill: University of North Carolina Press, 1988.
Historical study of the relationship between black and white women during slavery. Argues that class and racial tensions precluded the development of interracial sisterhood. Draws heavily on letters, diaries, and oral histories to examine the realities and limits of intimacy. Extensive reliance on slave women's testimony makes this a valuable point of reference for examination of novels that adapt similar sources.

Franklin, John Hope, and Alfred A. Moss. *From Slavery to Freedom: A History of Negro Americans*. 6th ed. New York: Alfred A. Knopf, 1988.
Standard history of black America, organized chronologically. Includes brief discussions of the development of Afro-American literature. Contemporary black literary expression is dominated by black women, including Naylor, Morrison, Jones, and others. A "gender gap" in black literature has been created by the excessive harshness of some presentations of black men. Important primarily as a basic source of contextual information.

Fredrickson, George M. *The Black Image in the White Mind: The Debate on Afro-American Character and Destiny, 1817-1914*. New York: Harper & Row, 1971.
Intellectual history of the development of race-thinking in the United States during the nineteenth century, focusing on the interaction of racial conceptions with social and political ideologies. White supremacist premises help determine the shape of both "liberal" and "reactionary" political agendas. A valuable study of the intellectual currents influencing the cultural response to black women and their writing.

Gates, Henry Louis, Jr., ed. *Black Literature and Literary Theory*. New York: Methuen, 1984.
Collection of essays by various critics exploring the relationship between Afro-American literature and contemporary literary theory. Gates's introduction argues that the most significant texts in the black tradition are "two-toned" or "double-voiced," combining elements of African and western traditions. He places strong emphasis on the need for careful explorations of the use of figurative language as the key to understanding this relationship. Includes essays on Hurston (Barbara Johnson); Toni Morrison (Susan Willis); and Gwendolyn Brooks (Mary Helen Washington).

_____ , ed. "The Black Person in Art: How Should S/he Be Portrayed." *Black American Literature Forum* 21 (Spring/Summer, Fall, 1987): 3-24, 317-332.
Two-part series intended as a contemporary reconsideration of issues raised in W. E. B. DuBois' 1926 *Crisis* questionnaire. Gates compiled the responses of a range of contemporary critics of Afro-American literature to the original questions, which involve the portrayal of blacks in American literature and the relationship of black artists to the publishing world. Among those responding to the questionnaire are black women critics Barbara Smith and Eugenia Collier.

_____ . *Figures in Black: Words, Signs, and the "Racial" Self*. New York: Oxford University Press, 1987.
Collection of essays by a black critic who occupies a leading position in the movement to consider Afro-American literature in relation to contemporary literary theory. Gates's introduction emphasizes the need for close attention to formal concerns and the text itself as a corrective to the emphasis on politics and content in the Black Arts movement. Includes an important essay on Harriet Wilson, and Gates's much-reprinted essay "The Blackness of Blackness," which places Hurston at the center of the Afro-American literary tradition.

_____ . *"Race," Writing, and Difference*. Chicago: University of Chicago Press, 1986.
Collection of essays, most of which were originally published in the Autumn, 1985 special issue of *Critical Inquiry*. In his introduction, Gates comments that the intent of the volume is to explore from a variety of theoretical and methodological perspectives, the dialectic between "formal language use and the inscription of metaphorical racial difference." Emphasizing the ways in which language creates and enforces power differences, Gates argues that contemporary critical theory can help demystify these ideological relations. Gates asserts that "literacy . . . is the emblem that links racial alienation with economic alienation."

_____ . "Reclaiming Their Tradition." *The New York Times Book Review* 92 (October 4, 1987): 3, 34-35.

Review of Mary Helen Washington's anthology *Invented Lives* arguing that the black women's literary movement has established itself as a distinct period in Afro-American literary history. Claiming that too much has been made of the supposed animosity between black men and black women, Gates asserts that the success of black women writers rests not on any condemnation of black men but on the sheer energy of their "resplendently new black voice." Credits black women writers, supported by a group of critics primarily composed of black women, with effecting a major reshaping of the American literary canon.

_____ . *The Signifying Monkey: A Theory of Afro-American Literary Criticism*. New York: Oxford University Press, 1988.

Important book by a critic interested in exploring the relationship between Euro-American and Continental literary theory and African and Afro-American expressive traditions. Emphasizing the importance of the West African figure of Esu and the black American figure of the signifying monkey, Gates seeks to discover "how the black tradition has theorized about itself." His revision of Afro-American literary history, which Gates recognizes as one of many possible constructions, centers on the relationship between oral and written expression in the works of Hurston and Alice Walker.

Gayle, Addison, Jr., ed. *The Black Aesthetic*. Garden City, N.Y.: Anchor Press, 1971.

Influential anthology of essays on theory, music, fiction, poetry, and drama. Essays by Hoyt Fuller, Larry Neal, Ron Karenga, and Gayle assert the need for and existence of a specifically black sensibility and tradition. Reprints work by W.E.B. DuBois, Langston Hughes, and Alain Locke which influenced the nationalist aesthetic. No essays deal directly with black women's writing. A central point of reference for understanding Afro-American writing of the 1960's and 1970's.

_____ , ed. *Black Expression: Essays By and About Black Americans in the Creative Arts*. New York: Weybright and Talley, 1969.

Anthology collecting a range of the most influential essays concerning Afro-American expression. Gayle's introduction stresses the social role of black art and attributes academic neglect of black critical perspectives to the inability of whites to comprehend black life or expression. Section on fiction includes influential essays by critics such as William Stanley Braithwaite, Benjamin Brawley, LeRoi Jones, Richard Wright, J. Saunders Redding, and Langston Hughes. The absence of direct attention to novels by black women reflects the dominant tendencies in black literary criticism prior to the 1980's.

_____ . *The Way of the New World: The Black Novel in America*. Garden City, N.Y.: Anchor Press, 1975.

Black nationalist approach to the development of the Afro-American novel. Contributing to the development of a "nation within a nation," black novelists undertake "the task of redefining the definitions, creating new myths, symbols, and images, articulating new values, and recording the progression of a great people from social and political awareness to consciousness of their historical importance." This imperative leads to a sense of form and structure as intertwined with an inevitably political content. Includes discussions of Fauset, Hurston, and Petry.

Genovese, Eugene D. *Roll, Jordan, Roll: The World the Slaves Made*. New York: Pantheon, 1974.

Bancroft Prize-winning history of the response of the black community to slavery. Explores the institutional and psychological structures developed to transmit and protect the survival techniques developed in response to an alternately paternalistic and vicious white-dominated context. Includes detailed discussion of the black family, sexual practices, and the significant roles of black women in establishing and maintaining a sense of community.

Giddings, Paula. *Where and When I Enter: The Impact of Black Women on Race and Sex in America*. New York: William Morrow, 1984.

Historical overview of black women's experience in the United States, including a brief section on the contribution of black women novelists to the formation of a more positive self-image. Emphasizes the themes of racism and sexism as interrelated sources of oppression; and the ability of black women to transcend, at a high price, the resulting "double discrimination." Black women have redefined traditional conceptions of womanhood to include work, achievement, and independence.

Gilbert, Sandra M., and Susan Gubar. *No Man's Land: The Place of the Woman Writer in the Twentieth Century*. New Haven, Conn.: Yale University Press, 1988.

The first volume of a planned three-volume feminist study of modern literature. The authors argue that many of the strategies of modernist literature were responses to a masculine resistance to the growing prominence of women in the literary world. Includes brief comments on Hurston and Ann Petry's *The Street*, which represents the battle of the sexes as both a class and racial struggle. Petry makes it clear that urban working-class women have no way out of their dilemma.

Gilligan, Carol. *In a Different Voice: Psychological Theory and Women's Development*. Cambridge, Mass.: Harvard University Press, 1982.

Widely cited study of gender differences as they effect psychological and moral development. Critiques the sexist biases of most psychological theories and argues that girls develop a greater sense of connection with other people and the world than do boys. Draws primarily on the experiences of middle-class white women, but used as a point of reference in numerous studies of black women's novels.

Gloster, Hugh M. *Negro Voices in American Fiction*. Chapel Hill: University of North Carolina Press, 1948. Reprint. New York: Russell & Russell, 1965.
Historical overview of Afro-American fiction from its origins through the Depression. Emphasizing the social backgrounds of the novels, Gloster argues that environmental pressures have forced black writers to become race-conscious and created a preoccupation with political themes. Asserts that black novels are "often lacking in enduring beauty and universal appeal." Includes discussions of Harper, Hopkins, Fauset, Larsen, and Hurston.

Gomez, Jewelle. "A Cultural Legacy Denied and Discovered: Black Lesbians in Fiction by Women." In *Home Girls: A Black Feminist Anthology*, edited by Barbara Smith. New York: Kitchen Table/Women of Color Press, 1983.
Discusses literary images of black lesbians, emphasizing the ways in which most white writing presents black lesbians as marginal and forbidden. Praises Shockley's *Loving Her* as a groundbreaking effort, but criticizes *Say Jesus and Come to Me* for its inability to place the black lesbian in a believable cultural context, a fault shared with most white writing on the subject. Walker's *The Color Purple* marks an advance in the serious treatment of the theme of women loving women. Concludes with a call for the creation of a literature that will keep the experience of black lesbians from being lost.

Grier, William H., and Price M. Cobbs. *Black Rage*. New York: Basic Books, 1968.
Influential study of the emotional conflicts generating anger and rage in black Americans. Chapter on "Achieving Womanhood" emphasizes the impact of racist standards of beauty on black women. Racist pressures crush healthy youthful narcissism and pervert the sexual experience of black girls growing up in the ghetto. Chapter on "Marriage and Love" asserts that racism has under-cut the stability of the black family.

Gutman, Herbert. *The Black Family in Slavery and Freedom, 1750-1925*. New York: Pantheon, 1976.
Important historical work refuting a wide range of myths concerning the absence of strong family structures in Afro-American culture. Gutman traces the ways in which blacks, expressing fundamentally different conceptions of family, developed various patterns of internal support in response to forces that

subverted traditional European family organization. A crucial book for understanding the nature of kinship systems in many black women's novels.

Gwin, Minrose C. *Black and White Women of the Old South: The Peculiar Sisterhood in American Literature*. Knoxville: University of Tennessee Press, 1985.
Explores the image of interracial contact between women in nineteenth and
twentieth century literature. The relationship highlights the tension between
guilt and contact in Southern experience. Despite real bonds of shared suffering and common experience, white women frequently project their own repressed sexual selves onto black women, who serve as symbolic "Others."
Includes Gwin's essay on Margaret Walker's *Jubilee* as an act of symbolic
atonement based on humanistic values.

Harley, Sharon, and Rosalyn Terborg-Penn. *The Afro-American Woman: Struggles
and Images*. Port Washington, N.Y.: Kennikat Press, 1978.
Anthology of essays concerning the tension between public images and historical realities of black women's experience. Individual essays focus on images of
black women in Afro-American poetry, black women in the blues tradition,
black male perspectives on nineteenth century women, and the involvement of
black women in various political struggles. Source of contextual information
for the study of black women's novels.

Harper, Michael, and Robert B. Stepto, eds. *Chant of Saints: A Gathering of
Afro-American Literature, Art, and Scholarship*. Urbana: University of Illinois
Press, 1979.
Important anthology of Afro-American writing based on two special issues of
The Massachusetts Review. Intended to provide an expression of Afro-
American art and culture in the 1970's, the volume marks a departure from the
highly political approach to black aesthetics represented by critics such as
Addison Gayle and Ron Karenga. Includes poetry and an essay by Williams,
and excerpts from fiction and interviews with Morrison and Jones.

Harris, Norman. *Connecting Times: The Sixties in Afro-American Fiction*. Jackson:
University Press of Mississippi, 1988.
Examination of the significance of Vietnam, the civil rights movement, and the
black power movement in Afro-American fiction about the 1960's. Harris
emphasizes the movement from historical illiteracy to historical literacy, which
allows blacks to find precedents in black history that can help them resolve
current problems. Incorporates contextual information in analysis of seven
novels, including Alice Walker's *Meridian*.

Harris, Trudier. "Black Writers in a Changed Landscape, Since 1950." In *The
History of Southern Literature*, edited by Louis D. Rubin, Jr., et al. Baton

Rouge: Louisiana State University Press, 1985.
Discusses Alice Walker and Margaret Walker as two of many black writers who have begun to explore previously taboo subjects in response to changes in the political and social climates. Despite its artistic accomplishments, *Jubilee* failed to inspire a response from younger black writers and was outdated even at the time of its publication. Harris presents a more favorable view of Alice Walker, who depicts the brutal effects of slavery in *The Third Life of Grange Copeland*, and the complex impact of the civil rights movement on the psychology of a committed individual in *Meridian*.

—————— . *Exorcising Blackness: Historical and Literary Lynching and Burning Rituals*. Bloomington: Indiana University Press, 1984.
Historical study of the impact of ritual violence on Afro-American expression, including some discussion of Morrison and Alice Walker. Argues that lynching represents the attempt of white Americans to exorcise the "black beast" from the community. The fear of castration develops into a major theme in the work of black male novelists. Recent novelists, including Morrison, create images of black men who manage to survive despite their participation in events or relationships that have frequently been portrayed as fatal.

—————— . *From Mammies to Militants: Domestics in Black American Literature*. Philadelphia: Temple University Press, 1982.
Focuses on the role of the black woman as domestic worker in Afro-American literature. Basing her approach on the radical aesthetics of the 1960's, Harris contrasts the relatively passive "Southern Mammy" with the "Northern Militant." Primarily concerned with repudiating distorted romantic pictures of black women's working conditions. Includes discussions of works by Morrison, Petry, Childress, and Hunter.

—————— . "Three Black Women Writers and Humanism: A Folk Perspective." In *Black American Literature and Humanism*, edited by R. Baxter Miller. Lexington: University Press of Kentucky, 1981.
Folk culture provides the basic source of the humanistic conceptions on which many black writers base their creations. Literary characters, like their folk counterparts, often reject Christianity in favor of a more exacting humanistic idealism. Includes discussion of novels by Sarah Wright, Paule Marshall, and Alice Walker.

Hedin, Raymond. "The Structuring of Emotion in Black American Fiction." *Novel* 16 (Fall, 1982): 35-54.
Discusses the relationship between two tendencies that define Afro-American fiction: the tendency toward an indirect or muted expression of anger, "the

most 'irrational' of emotions"; and a strategic emphasis on literary structure, "the most rational of literary qualities." Grounding his discussion in slave narratives, Hedin argues that the anger of black experience has generated a very disciplined aesthetic tradition. Includes a brief discussion of Morrison's *The Bluest Eye* as an example of a novel in which the "careful form of the novel intensifies rather than deflects" the reader's sense of Morrison's anger.

Hernton, Calvin C. *The Sexual Mountain and Black Women Writers: Adventures in Sex, Literature and Real Life*. Garden City, N.Y.: Anchor Press, 1987.
Respected black social scientist's impassioned defense of black women writers against attacks from hostile critics, especially black men. Celebrates the literature of contemporary black women writers as a "dialecticial composite of what is known coming out of the unknown." Challenging readers to revise their understandings of form, style, and landscape, black women novelists offer a vision of unfettered human possibility. Includes detailed discussions of Alice Walker and Petry.

Hill, Herbert, ed. *Anger, and Beyond: The Negro Writer in the United States*. New York: Harper & Row, 1966.
Anthology of essays focusing on the political and aesthetic situation of black writers in the mid-1960's. Hill's introduction views black writing as an attempt not only to explain black experience to whites, but to define the racial situation to blacks. Focuses on the relationship between art and ideology. Includes essays by Saunders Redding, LeRoi Jones, Albert Murray, and others. Little direct attention to black women writers, but an important source of information concerning the cultural context of the mid-1960's.

Hogue, W. Lawrence. *Discourse and the Other: The Production of the Afro-American Text*. Durham, N.C.: Duke University Press, 1986.
Study of the impact of ideological pressures on Afro-American literature with some attention to the importance of the relationship between the economics of the publishing industry and editorial decisions. Black novels typically have been received by white reviewers as exotic or sociological. Until recently, only novels that accepted mainstream literary conventions were admitted to the canon. Examines the ways in which specific novels attempt to provide imaginative resolutions to intractable social problems. Includes discussions of Morrison and Alice Walker.

Homans, Margaret. "'Her Very Own Howl': The Ambiguities of Representation in Recent Women's Fiction." *Signs* 9 (Winter, 1983): 186-205.
Discusses Alice Walker and Morrison in the context of the tension between "French" and "American" approaches to feminist literary criticism, especially

as it focuses on the uses of language. Argues that "French" insights concerning the inescapable interrelationship of language and experience are in fact central to the ostensibly pragmatic American emphasis on representing the actuality of female experience. Both Walker and Morrison conclude their representations of language use in ways that call into question the possibility of that representation.

Hooks, Bell. *Ain't I a Woman: Black Women and Feminism*. Boston: South End Press, 1981.
Important theoretical statement on the combined impact of racism and sexism on black women. Traces the roots of contemporary problems to patterns established during slavery. White males frequently employed sexual violence as a form of economic and psychological control over the entire black community. Stereotypical images established to support this system continue to plague black women, creating destructive tensions with black men. Sexism in black political organizations and racism in the white women's movement leave black women in need of a feminist movement answering to their specific needs.

_____ . *Feminist Theory: From Margin to Center*. Boston: South End Press, 1984.
Theoretical analysis of the potential insights generated by the marginal position of black women in American culture. Black women must develop a positive vision of sisterhood and establish constructive relationships with men working against sexism. Hooks cautions that political actions will be doomed to failure if they do not challenge the dualistic thought processes fundamental to institutional oppression.

_____ . *Talking Back: Thinking Feminist, Thinking Black*. Boston: South End Press, 1988.
Collection of essays covering a wide range of topics concerning black women's experience and expression. Several essays—most notably "When I Was a Young Soldier for the Revolution," "Coming to Voice," and "Writing Autobiography"—concentrate on the problems encountered by black women who attempt to speak or write of their specific experiences. A valuable introduction to the context in which contemporary black women novelists write.

Huggins, Nathan Irvin. *Harlem Renaissance*. New York: Oxford University Press, 1971.
Ground-breaking study of the flowering of Afro-American culture centered in Harlem during the 1920's. Emphasizes the common belief of the period that cultural activity provided the true measure of civilization. Responding to this belief, black writers and artists focused their energy on creating works that would command the respect and admiration of a cultural elite. Black intellec-

tuals seeking to define their racial identity grappled with major themes in the general American experience. Includes some discussion of Fauset, Hurston, and Larsen.

_____ , ed. *Voices from the Harlem Renaissance*. New York: Oxford University Press, 1976.

Sourcebook of political and cultural writing from the Harlem Renaissance era including selections from Fauset, Hurston, and West. Organized around themes such as black identity, history and the folk tradition, art and propaganda, Christianity, and the meaning of black anger.

Hughes, Carl Milton. *The Negro Novelist 1940-1950*. New York: The Citadel Press, 1953.

Resisting sociological interpretations of novels by black writers, Hughes develops the thesis that black writers of the 1940's broadened their perspective beyond racial themes, beginning to grapple with problems of humanity in American society. Emphasizes the prevalence of realistic and naturalistic modes. The primary difference between this fiction and earlier black novels lies in their favorable reception by a wider audience. Includes discussions of Petry and Hurston.

Hughes, Langston. "The Negro Artist and the Racial Mountain." *The Nation* 122 (June 23, 1921): 692-694. Reprinted in *The Black Aesthetic*, edited by Addison Gayle, Jr. Garden City, N.Y.: Doubleday, 1971.

One of the most important statements on the position of the Afro-American artist. Hughes discusses the Negro artist's experience of "an undertow of sharp criticism and misunderstanding from his own group and unintentional bribes from the whites." Embraces the expression of the black community, particularly jazz, and concludes with a call for artistic self-determination. Hughes's essay played a major role in shaping aesthetic discussions of the Harlem Renaissance and much subsequent debate on Afro-American literature.

Hull, Gloria T. *Color, Sex, and Poetry: Three Women Writers of the Harlem Renaissance*. Bloomington: Indiana University Press, 1987.

Study of three Harlem Renaissance-era poets, Angelina Weld Grimke, Alice Dunbar-Nelson, and Georgia Douglas Johnson. Hull's discussion of the problems encountered by these poets both at the time and in historical presentations of the era raises issues directly relevant to black women novelists: the sexism of leading male writers and critics; the impact of color (in addition to race) prejudice; and the exclusion of writers who did not live in New York. Comments briefly on Hurston, Larsen, West, and Fauset.

Hull, Gloria T., Patricia Bell Scott, and Barbara Smith. *But Some of Us Are Brave: Black Women's Studies*. Old Westbury, N.Y.: Feminist Press, 1982.

Interdisciplinary anthology advocating the development of a field of study devoted specifically to black women. Only a careful synthesis of black and feminist analyses can provide a foundation for a politically effective academic understanding. Five essays directly address aspects of black women's literature. Includes Barbara Smith's germinal essay "Toward a Black Feminist Criticism" and a valuable bibliographical essay by Rita Dandridge.

Humm, Maggie. "Black and Lesbian Criticism." In her *Feminist Criticism: Women as Contemporary Critics*. Brighton, England: Harvester Press, 1986.
Discussion of the ways in which black and lesbian criticism has transformed the "cultural misogyny of early Black studies." Explicitly refusing the cultural framework of patriarchy, black and lesbian critics insist on their right to speak out on their own experiences. Analyzes critical writing by Audre Lorde, Barbara Smith, Gloria Hull, Toni Cade Bambara, and Alice Walker, noting that their work has inspired a reconsideration of the psychoanalytical and literary historical approaches to feminist criticism generally.

Inge, M. Thomas, Maurice Duke, and Jackson R. Bryer, eds. *Black American Writers: Bibliographical Essays*. 2 vols. New York: St. Martin's Press, 1978.
Bibliographical essays including information on most of the writers covered by this bibliography who began publishing prior to 1970.

Jackson, Blyden. *The Waiting Years: Essays on American Negro Literature*. Baton Rouge: Louisiana State University Press, 1976.
Collection of essays by a distinguished black critic, including his widely reprinted "The Negro's Image of His Universe as Reflected in His Fiction," which originally appeared in *CLA Journal* in 1960. That essay emphasizes the importance of Richard Wright and Ralph Ellison in the shaping of a shared worldview focusing on the experience of the Northern urban environment. Various essays mention Brooks, Fauset, Harper, Petry, Larsen, Marshall, Margaret Walker, and Hurston, whose *Moses, Man of the Mountain* is praised for the "superb rightness" of Hurston's allegorical adaptation of the biblical story to problems of black leadership.

Jahn, Janheinz. *Muntu: The New African Culture*. New York: Grove Press, 1961.
One of the first books to emphasize the deep connection between the various cultures of Africa and the African diaspora. Examines African philosophical principles, religious systems, and a variety of forms of cultural expression, particularly dance and music. Chapter on the "blues" discusses the ways in which African cultural patterns are transformed in the United States. An influential study directly relevant to the exploration of the African elements of black women's novels.

Janeway, Elizabeth. "Women's Literature." In *Harvard Guide to Contemporary American Writing*, edited by Daniel Hoffman. Cambridge, Mass.: Harvard University Press, 1979.

Discusses Brooks's poetry, Morrison's *The Bluest Eye* and Alice Walker's *Meridian* in relationship to the drive toward "metaphoric universality" in women's literature. Notes that black women are less willing to accept the association of sexism and racism than are white women writers. Both Morrison and Walker contribute to the investigation of the "madness-inducing society" in women's literature. Each provides a compelling picture of victimization. Walker's vision of a future society that is not madness-inducing testifies to "another sort of universality of imagination that has grown out of the experience of black women."

Johnson, Abby Arthur, and Ronald Maberry Johnson. *Propaganda and Aesthetics: The Literary Politics of Afro-American Magazines in the Twentieth Century*. Amherst: University of Massachusetts Press, 1979.

Survey of the tension between politics and aesthetics in Afro-American literary magazines. Covers large political and cultural journals such as *Crisis* and *Opportunity* in addition to significant but short-lived magazines such as *Fire!* and *Negro Story*. Includes brief comments on the journalistic activities and/or reception of Brooks, Fauset, Harper, Hopkins, Hurston, Larsen, Petry, Shockley, Margaret Walker, and West.

Johnson, Charles. *Being and Race: Black Writing Since 1970*. Bloomington: Indiana University Press, 1988.

A black novelist's philosophical meditation on contemporary Afro-American fiction. Johnson observes that almost all black writers assume the validity of the traditional correspondence between word and world. He then argues that a deep enough exploration of apparently different perspectives leads to an ultimate transcendence of relativity. Discussion of individual texts divided into chapters on "The Men" and "The Women," with the work of the latter characterized as "politically charged, oppositional fiction." Includes analysis of novels by Jones, Alice Walker, Marshall, Morrison, Bambara, Naylor, Hunter, Southerland, and Butler.

Jones, Jacqueline. *Labor of Love, Labor of Sorrow: Black Women, Work and the Family, from Slavery to the Present*. New York: Basic Books, 1985.

Bancroft Prize-winning examination of the work experiences and family life of black women. Black women working in their own homes and communities sought to nurture their own kin and, increasingly, black people as a whole. As members of the paid work force, black women encountered a variety of forces that reinforced their subordinate status in American society. Includes a few

comments on black women novelists but important primarily as a source of contextual information.

Jordan, Winthrop D. *White Over Black: American Attitudes Toward the Negro, 1550-1812*. Chapel Hill: University of North Carolina Press, 1968.
Standard historical account of the development and relationship of slavery and racism in the United States. Emphasizes the relationship between stereotypical images of blacks and white refusal to acknowledge the bestial aspects of its institutional treatment of blacks. Although the focus is primarily on the experience of black men, includes some discussion of slave women's experiences. Frequently cited as source of historical background in essays on black women novelists.

Joseph, Gloria I., and Jill Lewis. *Common Differences: Conflicts in Black and White Feminist Perspectives*. Garden City, N.Y.: Anchor Press/Doubleday, 1981.
Argues that the tensions between black and white feminists can be reduced only by recognition of differences in experience and perspective. Examines the interaction of racial and sexual factors in the oppression of women. Among the topics addressed are sexuality, marriage, media images, mother-daughter relationships, and the future of the feminist movement. Provides contextual information regarding the political debate surrounding the recognition of black women novelists.

Kellner, Bruce, ed. *The Harlem Renaissance: A Historical Dictionary of the Era*. New York: Methuen, 1987.
Reference book including biographical entries on Hurston, Larsen, Fauset, and West. Appendices list books published by black writers from 1917 to 1940 and a glossary of slang terms that appear in writings of the period.

Kent, George. *Blackness and the Adventure of Western Culture*. Chicago: Third World Press, 1972.
Collected essays of an influential Afro-American literary critic, including an important discussion of Gwendolyn Brooks's poetry and brief comments on several black women novelists. Kent asserts the central importance of the Afro-American folk tradition to the adequate understanding of black literature. The folk tradition engages what Kent calls the "is-ness" of experience in order to obtain an adequate interpretive perspective on the oppressive environment. This sensibility encourages an understanding of "universalism" as full engagement with the specifics of experience rather than reflection of a preexisting conceptual system.

King, Deborah K. "Multiple Jeopardy, Multiple Consciousness: The Context of a Black Feminist Ideology." *Signs* 14 (Autumn, 1988): 42-72.

Presents a vision of black women's cultural and social situation as one of "multiple jeopardy" in which race, gender, and class issues reinforce one another in a synergistic manner. King considers and rejects theories based on the analogy between racial and sexual oppression and on double jeopardy, before considering the relationship of "multiple jeopardy" to race-, gender-, and class-based liberation movements. A clear presentation of one of the central theories informing many black women's novels.

Kolodny, Annette. "The Integrity of Memory: Creating a New Literary History of the United States." *American Literature* 57 (May, 1985): 291-307.
Essay by an important feminist literary critic calling for a rewriting of American literary history, which has repressed the writing and experience of a number of groups including both blacks and women. Among the writers Kolodny argues should receive greater consideration are Hurston, Morrison, Alice Walker, and Harper. An important theoretical perspective on the relationship between Afro-American and mainstream American literature.

Kramer, Victor A., ed. *The Harlem Renaissance Re-examined*. New York: AMS Press, 1987.
Anthology of essays reconsidering the Harlem Renaissance, many of which were originally published in a special 1974 issue of *Studies in the Literary Imagination*. Among the new contributions are several essays focusing specifically on black women playwrights; Hurston; and an interview with Dorothy West.

Kubitschek, Missy Dehn. "Subjugated Knowledge: Toward a Feminist Exploration of Rape in Afro-American Fiction." *Studies in Black American Literature* 3 (1988): 43-56.
Comparative study of the treatment of rape in Euro- and Afro-American texts. White writers present rape in oblique and symbolic terms in contrast to the realistic, complex vision of Afro-American writers. Black writers such as James Baldwin and Alice Walker concentrate on the struggle of women to attain an identity beyond that of rape victim. By reestablishing their connections with their communities, characters such as Celie in *The Color Purple* release their creative potential. Kubitschek calls for a "symbiotic" criticism combining feminist and Afro-American perspectives.

Ladner, Joyce A. *Tomorrow's Tomorrow: The Black Woman*. Garden City, N.Y.: Doubleday, 1971.
Sociological study of black women, concentrating on the period since 1960. Much of the pathological behavior attributed to black women reflects patterns established by the dominant culture. Drawing on specifically black social structures, particularly those involving the extended family, black women have

nonetheless managed to adjust constructively to an oppressive context. Valuable as a source of information concerning the situation of black women novelists prior to the emergence of Morrison and Alice Walker.

Lauter, Paul. "Race and Gender in the Shaping of the American Literary Canon." In *Feminist Criticism and Social Change: Sex, Class, and Race in Literature and Culture*, edited by Judith Newton and Deborah Rosenfelt. New York: Methuen, 1985.
Examination of the process of canon formation, showing how blacks, women, and working-class writers have been excluded. Traces the background of institutional influence over academic and popular conceptions of cultural tradition and calls for a reconsideration of both the concept and content of the canon.

Lee, A. Robert, ed. *Black Fiction: New Studies in the Afro-American Novel Since 1945*. New York: Barnes & Noble Books, 1980.
Anthology of critical essays designed to "offer a fresh estimate of the Afro-American novel since Richard Wright." Includes an essay on Ann Petry (Gross), along with thematically based essays with some attention to black women writers including Hurston, Larsen, Morrison, Alice Walker, Jones, and Polite. Among the topics are the theme of apocalypse (Bigsby), black women's fiction (Pullin), and experimental fiction (Lee).

Lee, Valerie Gray. "The Use of Folktalk in Novels by Black Women Writers." *CLA Journal* 23 (March, 1980): 266-272.
Observes that while the narrative frames of novels by black women are usually written in conventional English, they include numerous scenes written in folk language which capture the more subtle dynamics of black life. Much of the folk talk between mothers and daughters centers on men, reflecting the return to the theme of love in many recent works. Includes discussions of Hurston's *Their Eyes Were Watching God*, Morrison's *Sula*, and Jones's *Corregidora*.

Lenz, Gunther H., ed. *History and Tradition in Afro-American Culture*. Frankfurt: Campus Verlag, 1984.
Anthology of materials on various aspects of Afro-American culture, emphasizing the importance of historical and folk consciousness. Includes interviews with Morrison and Marshall, in addition to essays on several black women novelists.

Lerner, Gerda, ed. *Black Women in White America: A Documentary History*. New York: Random House, 1972.
Indispensable compilation of primary source materials relevant to the experience of black women in the United States. Includes materials by Harper and

Meriwether, but more valuable as a source of contextual information. Individual sections devoted to topics including slavery, institutional racism, and the attempts of black women to accept their blackness and womanhood.

Levine, Lawrence W. *Black Culture and Black Consciousness*. New York: Oxford University Press, 1977.
Study of the Afro-American folk tradition highlighting the sensibility underlying black expression, whether written or oral. Examines the presence of African cultural patterns in Afro-American religion; the relationship between sacred and secular forms; the nature of Afro-American humor; and the significance of various heroic figures. Afro-American expression reflects the intricate adjustment of the black community to an ever-changing array of oppressive forces. A fundamental text in Afro-American Studies.

Lewis, David Levering. *When Harlem Was in Vogue*. New York: Alfred A. Knopf, 1981.
Period history with substantial attention to the importance of the contributions of writers including Fauset, Hurston, and Larsen. Discussion of cultural issues focuses on the influence of white patron Carl Van Vechten, the tension between "genteel" and "folk" sensibilities, and the relationship between art and politics. Emphasizes the position of black intellectuals on the margins of a racist society.

Littlejohn, David. *Black on White: A Critical Survey of Writing by American Negroes*. New York: Grossman, 1966.
A white critic's view of Afro-American literature as a "depressing enterprise" in which "the responding spirit is dulled, finally, bored by the iteration of hopelessness, the sordid limitation of the soul in the tight closet of the black imagination." Includes dismissive references to West, Fauset, Larsen, Marshall, and Hurston. Brooks's *Maud Martha* is praised as a "striking experiment." Gives more detailed attention to Petry.

Locke, Alain, ed. *The New Negro*. New York: Albert and Charles Boni, 1925. Reprint. New York: Atheneum, 1968.
One of the most influential books in Afro-American cultural history, Locke's anthology brings together a wide range of primary and secondary sources related to the Harlem Renaissance. Locke's classic introductory essay identifies Harlem as the key to the advancement of blacks in America and throughout the world. Cultural achievement paves the way for broader social progress. Includes selections by Hurston and Fauset; a survey of black literature by William Stanley Braithwaite; and an essay on the role of black women.

Loewenberg, Bert James, and Ruth Bogin, eds. *Black Women in Nineteenth-Century American Life: Their Words, Their Thoughts, Their Feelings*. University Park:

Pennsylvania State University Press, 1976.
Selection from the writings of black women leaders of the nineteenth century, including some material from Frances Ellen Watkins Harper. Individual sections focus on the family, religion, politics, and education. Introduction stresses the importance of "inner emancipation" to black women in diverse fields. Provides information on intellectual and social context of early black women novelists.

Loggins, Vernon. *The Negro Author: His Development in America to 1900*. New York: Columbia University Press, 1931. Reprint. Port Washington, N.Y.: Kennikat Press, 1964.
Standard historical survey of Afro-American writing prior to the twentieth century, including brief mentions of Harper and Hopkins. In part because of an overly complicated plot, Hopkins fails in her political mission, which is better realized by Walter Stowers' *Appointed*. Hopkins shares Harper's structural weaknesses, but the sensationalism of her novel maintains reader interest.

Lomax, Michael J. "Fantasies of Affirmation: The 1920s Novel of Negro Life." *CLA Journal* 16 (December, 1972): 232-246.
Treats Fauset and Larsen in the context of a discussion of writers who viewed themselves as part of the "advanced element" of urban black society. Like many of their contemporaries, they attempted somewhat hysterically to disassociate themselves from the black masses in order to win mainstream acceptance.

Lorde, Audre. *Sister Outsider: Essays and Speeches*. Trumansburg, N.Y.: Crossing Press, 1984.
Collection of essays by an important black lesbian feminist poet and critic. Among Lorde's themes are the transformative power of black women's expression; the relationship between sexism and racism; racism in the predominantly white women's movement; and the importance of the body and the erotic.

Lupton, Mary Jane. "Clothes and Closure in Three Novels by Black Women." *Black American Literature Forum* 20 (Winter, 1986): 409-421.
Examines the treatment of the Cinderella myth of the escape from drudgery and hand-me-down clothes in the work of Fauset, Alice Walker, and Morrison, all of whom associate clothes imagery with the transformation of self. In *Comedy: American Style*, Fauset subverts the Cinderella story. In *The Color Purple*, Walker uses clothing as a path to women's success. In *Tar Baby*, Morrison's treatment of Jadine shows the story doubling back against itself.

McDowell, Deborah E. "New Directions for Black Feminist Criticism." *Black American Literature Forum* 14 (Winter, 1980): 153-159. Reprinted in *The New*

Feminist Criticism: Essays on Women, Literature, and Theory. New York: Pantheon, 1985.

Calls for the development of a clearer theoretical framework and a greater attention to detail in black feminist criticism, which has to this point been marred by slogans, rhetoric, and idealism. Responding to Barbara Smith's "Toward a Black Feminist Criticism," McDowell emphasizes the need for clear definitions of terms such as "lesbian" and "feminist." Endorses a contextual approach aimed at identifying the thematic, stylistic, and linguistic commonalities among black women writers. Among these commonalities are the theme of the thwarted female artist; the use of "clothing as iconography"; and the motif of the journey.

Major, Clarence. *The Dark and Feeling: Black American Writers and Their Work*. New York: The Third Press, 1974.

Collection of essays by a contemporary black male writer usually associated with the postmodernist stream of American fiction. Major emphasizes the need to resist demands that black writers focus on political or ideological concerns, and condemns the puritanism of many black writers, which makes it difficult for others to deal openly with sexual themes. Includes an open letter to June Jordan concerning their shared problem of censorship.

Margolies, Edward, and David Bakish. *Afro-American Fiction, 1853-1976*. Detroit: Gale Research, 1979.

Bibliography including comprehensive list of novels and short story collections by black writers, excluding children's literature, through 1976. Includes selected annotated bibliography of major writers including Petry, Marshall, and Morrison.

Martin, Tony. *Literary Garveyism: Garvey, Black Arts, and the Harlem Renaissance*. Dover, Mass.: The Majority Press, 1983.

Examines the influence of Garveyism on the artistic expression of the Harlem Renaissance era. Stresses the wide circulation of the *Negro World* newspaper, noting its attempt to encourage artistic expression of black who were not a part of the "talented tenth." Identifies Hurston as a writer who benefited from early exposure in *Negro World* but later repudiated her connection with Garvey in order to strengthen her relationship with white publishing houses. Includes brief mention of Fauset.

Mays, Benjamin E. *The Negro's God as Reflected in His Literature*. Chapman & Grimes, 1938. Reprint. New York: Atheneum, 1968.

Examines the image of God in both "classical" (written) and "mass" (oral) Afro-American expression. Grounding his analysis in the changing social cir-

cumstances of the black community, Mays identifies three basic images: an otherworldly compensatory approach; an image of God as an instrument of social change; and a recent tendency to deny God's relevance or existence. Includes brief discussions of Harper as a proponent of God as social force and Fauset as an agnostic, along with a more extended discussion of Larsen's repudiation of God.

Mbiti, John S. *African Religions and Philosophy*. London: Heinemann, 1969.
Detailed exploration of the internal structure and social realization of African religious and philosophical perspectives. Examines the ways in which African conceptions of time—the collapsing of Western concepts of past, present, and future—inform a range of cultural practices. Includes chapters on "Birth and Childhood," "Initiation and Puberty Rites," and "Marriage and Procreation" that focus specifically on African women. Extremely important as an influence on discussions of the relationship between black women's novels and African culture.

Mickelson, Anne Z. "Winging Upward: Black Women: Sarah E. Wright, Toni Morrison, Alice Walker." In her *Reaching Out: Sensitivity and Order in Recent American Fiction by Women*. Metuchen, N.J.: Scarecrow Press, 1979.
Wright, Morrison, and Walker ground their novels in the collective history of marginalized blacks. Although they recognize the reality of black women's pain, they also emphasize their pride in having survived and grown strong. Mickelson emphasizes that all three novelists make it clear that the conditions which afflict their female protagonists are shared with black men. The dominant theme linking the three writers is that freedom is useless if general social problems such as education and housing are not addressed.

Miles, Rosalind. *The Female Form: Women Writers and the Conquest of the Novel*. New York: Routledge & Kegan Paul, 1987.
Historical overview of women novelists, including mentions of Shange, Morrison, Alice Walker, Guy, Hurston, and Margaret Walker. Notes that while black women have been writing since the eighteenth century, they have only recently emerged as highly visible presences. Identifies the theme of sadness and despair as the central element of black women's writing, but recognizes their spirit of resistance. Incorrectly identifies Rita Mae Brown as a black writer.

Miller, Christopher. *Blank Darkness: Africanist Discourse in French*. Chicago: University of Chicago Press, 1985.
Includes a valuable introduction discussing the premises of European discourse concerning Africa. White writers repeatedly view Africa as "void and

unformed prior to its investment with shape and being" by European masters. Miller's study provides a foundation for understanding the literary dimension of the stereotypes emphasizing the supposed inability of slaves to master written expression. An important source of information concerning the intellectual context of American racism.

Nobel, Jeanne. *Beautiful Also Are the Souls of My Black Sisters: A History of the Black Woman in America*. Englewood Cliffs, N.J.: Prentice-Hall, 1978.
History of black women in various fields of activity, including literature. Focuses on the absence of recognition of black women, the prevalence of stereotypical images, and achievements of women in individual and collective activities.

O'Brien, John, ed. *Interviews with Black Writers*. New York: Liveright, 1973.
Collection of interviews designed to clarify the relationship between individual writers and the black literary tradition. Introduction emphasizes the wide diversity of perspectives, personalities, and literary styles of contemporary black writers. Includes interviews with Petry and Alice Walker.

Ogunyemi, Chikwenye Okonjo. "Womanism: The Dynamics of the Contemporary Black Female Novel in English." *Signs* 11 (Autumn, 1985): 63-80.
Discusses the connections between African and Afro-American women novelists, emphasizing the ways in which both groups distance themselves from positions associated with white feminism. For Ogunyemi, who arrived at the term "womanism" independently of Alice Walker, black women ground their response to sexual oppression in a more holistic sense of racial and class issues. Catalogs shared motifs such as the need for self-healing, the negative portrayal of white women, and the interest in women without men. Includes discussion of Margaret Walker, Alice Walker, Marshall, and Morrison.

Olsen, Tillie. *Silences*. New York: Dell, 1978.
Influential collection of essays exploring the circumstances that obstruct or silence women writers. Examines the interaction of gender, class, and racial factors. Includes brief comments on several black women writers, including Hurston, Petry, Sarah Wright, Alice Walker, and Margaret Walker. Valuable primarily for its insights into the general situation of the woman writer in the United States.

O'Neale, Sondra. "Race, Sex, and Self: Aspects of *Bildung* in Select Novels by Black American Women Novelists." *MELUS* 9 (Winter, 1982): 25-38.
Presents a typology of the *Bildungsroman* as portrayed in black women's novels. O'Neale describes a common pattern in which the main characters begin their passage at a more mature age than in most western growth litera-

ture; relinquish their attempt to find understanding within the black community; and retreat from personal interaction to attain growth. There are no mentors for black women's protagonists and no community to which they can return after their struggle is over. Discussion gives some attention to Harper, Larsen, Fauset, Hurston, Brooks, Marshall, Petry, Jones, Polite, Bambara, and Hunter.

Ordonez, Elizabeth J. "Narrative Texts by Ethnic Women: Rereading the Past, Reshaping the Future." *MELUS* 9 (Winter, 1982): 19-28.
Discusses Morrison's *Sula* as a text exemplifying the emerging currents of an ethnic women's literary tradition which explores particular aspects of ethnic identity while helping to reshape female history, myths, and ultimately personal and collective identity. Discusses *Sula* in relationship to three basic characteristics of ethnic women's literature: the disruption of genre; the displacement of the patriarchal text; and the recovery of a buried or oral matrilineal tradition, usually involving the invention of alternative mythic and historical accounts of women.

Overton, Betty J. "Black Women Preachers: A Literary View." *Southern Quarterly* 23 (Spring, 1985): 157-166.
Discusses the portrayal of black women preachers in the work of a number of black plays and novels, including Shockley's *Say Jesus and Come to Me* and Hunter's *The Soul Brothers and Sister Lou*. Typically, these writers present women preachers as being outside the fold of the traditional church. Basing their ministries on emotionalism rather than a firm grounding in doctrine, these preachers often rely on sensual and sexual appeal to attract a following.

Page, James A. *Selected Black American Authors: An Illustrated Bio-Bibliography*. Boston: G. K. Hall, 1977.
Reference tool including information on family background, education, career development, and publications by a wide range of black American writers, including most of those included in this book. Includes list of biographical entries in other reference sources.

Peplow, Michael W., and Arthur P. Davis, eds. *The New Negro Renaissance: An Anthology*. New York: Holt, Rinehart and Winston, 1975.
Anthology of primary sources from the Harlem Renaissance era including selections from Fauset, Hurston, Larsen, and Margaret Walker. Editors' introduction summarizes the historical forces contributing to the Renaissance and discusses three major characteristics: its unprecedented degree of artistic activity; its great diversity; and its relevance to black writers of the 1960's and 1970's. Selections organized around the themes of protest literature, the genteel tradition, the exotic image of Harlem, the African heritage, race pride, black nationalism, and the image of the folk.

Perry, Margaret. *Silence to the Drums: A Survey of the Literature of the Harle*
Renaissance. Westport, Conn.: Greenwood Press, 1976.
Overview of Harlem Renaissance writing including biographical and critical
comment on Fauset, Larsen, Hurston, and West. Presaging the African Negritude movement, the controlling symbol of the Renaissance was "the primary
idea of blackness." The resulting literature was a combination of "atavistic
racial propaganda and bourgeois romanticism." Includes a valuable appendix
placing events of the Renaissance in relation to historical events and other
cultural movements.

Poirier, Richard. *A World Elsewhere: The Place of Style in American Literature*.
New York: Oxford University Press, 1966.
Although Poirier makes no mention of black writers, his discussion of the
significance of style in American fiction provides a central point of reference
for many later discussions, including several focused explicitly on Afro-
American novels. Poirier argues that the American novel is characterized by a
conflict between environment as a construct of language and environment as a
social-historical force dominating that language. American novelists have
sought to create environments of freedom through the power of words. A
major influence on many discussions of what some critics see as the similar
attempts of black women novelists.

Popkin, Michael, ed. *Modern Black Writers: A Library of Literary Criticism*. New
York: Frederick Ungar, 1978.
Useful compilation of excerpts from critical commentary on black writers from
throughout Africa and the diaspora. Includes entries on Brooks, Hurston,
Morrison, Alice Walker, and Margaret Walker.

Pratt, Annis. *Archetypal Patterns in Women's Fiction*. Bloomington: Indiana University Press, 1981.
Feminist analysis of the ways in which women's writing develops a set of
feminine archetypes that give expression to preliterary folk practices. Emphasizing these patterns as expressions of a repressed tradition in conflict with
patriarchal culture, Pratt discusses four basic types of women's fiction, including novels of development; novels of domestic enclosure; novels of eros; and
novels of rebirth and transformation. Although Pratt gives brief attention to
Hurston, Sarah Wright, Meriwether, Marshall, Morrison, and Margaret Walker,
her book is more important as a framework for later discussions of mythic
patterns in black women's novels.

Pryse, Marjorie, and Hortense J. Spillers, eds. *Conjuring: Black Women, Fiction,*
and Literary Tradition. Bloomington: Indiana University Press, 1985.
Anthology of critical essays on black women writers including Hopkins,

Fauset, Petry, Margaret Walker, Marshall, Morrison, Butler, and Bambara. Also includes thematic essays involving Hurston, Alice Walker, and others. Pryse's introduction observes that black women focus on connection rather than separation; the transformation of silence into speech; and the empowerment of the culturally disenfranchised. Spillers' afterword emphasizes the importance of a community of readers to black women writers, whose novels not only redefine inherited conceptions of literary history but ultimately question the entire idea of tradition.

Pullin, Faith. "Landscapes of Reality: The Fiction of Contemporary Afro-American Women." In *Black Fiction: New Studies in the Afro-American Novel Since 1945*, edited by A. Robert Lee. New York: Barnes & Noble Books, 1980.
Uses Hurston's "revolutionary cultural nationalism and feminism" as a touchstone for an overview of contemporary black women novelists, including analysis of novels by Larsen and Brooks, as well as Morrison, Alice Walker, and Jones, who are identified as major novelists. In addition to refuting stereotypes and asserting the right of black women to define their own experience, recent black women novelists are remarkable for their technical accomplishment and confident experimentation.

Quarles, Benjamin. *The Negro in the Making of America*. 3d ed. New York: Macmillan, 1987.
Widely read history of Afro-Americans in the United States from the first contact between Africa and the New World through the Reagan era. Relates black history to major trends in western history and the African independence movement. Includes a useful bibliography of historical sources.

Raboteau, Albert J. *Slave Religion: The "Invisible Institution" in the Antebellum South*. New York: Oxford University Press, 1978.
Standard study of Afro-American religion during the slavery era. Black religion developed hybrid forms combining African cultural practices with a Christian framework. Emphasizes the tension between religion as a tool for white domination and as a spur for black resistance and rebellion. An essential source of contextual information concerning the historical experience of black women.

Rahming, Melvin B. *The Evolution of the West Indian's Image in the Afro-American Novel*. Millwood, N.Y.: Associated Faculty Press, 1986.
Study of the presentation and implications of West Indian characters in fiction by Afro-American writers. Contrasts the prevalence of stereotypical portraits in early Afro-American fiction to the more complex presentation in recent novels, including those by Morrison and Marshall. In part because they place an inordinate representative weight on Marcus Garvey, black American novel-

ists frequently project their own psychological and cultural ambivalence onto West Indian characters.

Redding, J. Saunders. *To Make a Poet Black*. Chapel Hill: University of North Carolina Press, 1939. Reprint. Ithaca, N.Y.: Cornell University Press, 1988.
Overview of Afro-American literary history by a black critic associated primarily with the "universalist" aesthetic. Redding presents black literature as a "literature of necessity," motivated the need of blacks to adjust to the American environment. Emphasizes the difficulty of simultaneously addressing both black and white audiences. Includes comments on Harper (under the name of Frances Watkins), Fauset, Larsen, and Hurston.

Reilly, John M. "History-Making Literature." *Studies in Black American Literature* 2 (1986): 85-120.
Argues that history must be viewed in part as a branch of literature because our knowledge of history comes primarily through documents that advance an inevitably partial version of events. Failure to acknowledge this complexity has limited the utility of otherwise insightful approaches to Afro-American fiction. Reilly catalogs several different apprehensions of the interaction of literature and history in a manner directly applicable to the attempts of black women to reconstruct the image of their own past.

Rich, Adrienne. *Blood, Bread, and Poetry: Selected Prose, 1979-1985*. New York: W. W. Norton, 1986.
Collection of essays by an influential white lesbian feminist critic who has been deeply involved with the problem of racism within the women's movement. The title essay acknowledges the influence of Afro-American culture on Rich's developing vision of the social significance of literature. Includes an essay on dramatist Lorraine Hansberry where Rich addresses the intersection of racial and gender concerns.

_____ . *On Lies, Secrets, and Silence: Selected Prose 1966-1978*. New York: W. W. Norton, 1979.
Collection of prose that helped shape feminist discourse of the early 1980's. "When We Dead Awaken: Writing as Re-Vision" argues that women writers must both critique existing circumstances and attempt to develop a clear vision of alternative possibilities. "Disloyal to Civilization: Feminism, Racism, Gynephobia" directly engages the relationship between white feminism and racial issues. Rich played a central role in encouraging white feminists to understand the importance of interracial dialogue.

Robinson, Lillian S. *Sex, Class, and Culture*. Bloomington: Indiana University Press, 1978.

Collection of essays by a critic whose work helped shape discussion of black women's fiction during the 1980's. Assuming an activist stance, Robinson emphasizes the ways in which women's work experiences shape their cultural expression. Examines the ways in which mainstream theoretical perspectives repeatedly exclude women's and working-class perspectives. Little direct attention to racial concerns.

Rosenblatt, Roger. *Black Fiction*. Cambridge, Mass.: Harvard University Press, 1974.
Survey of Afro-American fiction in relation to a cyclical conception of history upon which "practically every" piece of black literature has been based. Rosenblatt argues that black novels stand outside the tradition of the American romance because they lack the tendency toward abstraction. Unlike other American heroes, black heroes are not pioneers. While they may believe they control their destinies, they rarely do. Rosenblatt bases his analysis on what he refers to as "the widely agreed-upon, almost institutionalized, absence of a . . . long-reaching black cultural tradition." Badly flawed and occasionally factually inaccurate study, including sections on Hurston and Petry.

Roses, Lorraine, and Ruth E. Randolph. *The Harlem Renaissance and Beyond: 100 Black Women Writers, 1900-1950*. Boston: G. K. Hall, 1989.
Reference guide providing biographical profiles and bibliographical listings for numerous black women writers in various forms, including many of the novelists treated in this bibliography. Profiles include commentary on the influence of earlier black women writers on contemporary novelists such as Alice Walker and Morrison.

Rush, Theressa Gunnels, Carol Fairbanks Myers, and Esther Spring Arata. *Black American Writers Past and Present: A Biographical and Bibliographical Dictionary*. 2 vols. Metuchen, N.J.: Scarecrow Press, 1975.
Reference work containing basic biographical information concerning birth, education, awards, and publications of most of the writers included in this bibliography. Lists primary and secondary sources.

Rushing, Andrea B. "An Annotated Bibliography of Images of Black Women in Black Literature." *CLA Journal* 25 (December, 1981): 234-262.
Annotated listing of articles on the images of women of African descent in the literature of Africa and the New World diaspora. A valuable source of information on a number of issues directly and tangentially related to the subject of this book. Supersedes Rushing's bibliography published in the March, 1978 issue of *CLA Journal*.

Schraufnagel, Noel. *From Apology to Protest: The Black American Novel*. Deland, Fla.: Everett/Edwards, 1973.

Traces the movement of Afro-American fiction since Richard Wright from apology and accommodation to protest. Emphasizes the central role of Wright in establishing the framework within which later writers worked. Accommodationist novels do not avoid racial issues; rather they focus on the development of an individual black character. The dominant form of 1940's protest writing, apologetic protest, gave way to a greater emphasis on militant protest in the 1950's and 1960's. Includes discussions of Brooks, Marshall, Meriwether, Hunter, Hurston, Petry, Sarah Wright, Margaret Walker, Polite, and Dorothy West.

Schultz, Elizabeth. "African and Afro-American Roots in Contemporary Afro-American Literature: The Difficult Search for Family." *Studies in American Fiction* 8 (Autumn, 1980): 127-145.
Uses Morrison's *Song of Solomon* and Alex Haley's *Roots* as touchstones for a discussion of the continuity of traditions within Afro-American families. Although cultural roots have been gnarled and deformed, both writers portray their recovery as more joyous than anguished. *Song of Solomon* insists that identity cannot be assumed but must be constantly struggled for and preserved in ritual. Refers briefly to Meriwether, Margaret Walker, Alice Walker, and Gayl Jones.

_____ . "Free in Fact and at Last: The Image of the Black Woman in Black American Literature." In *What Manner of Woman*, edited by Marlene Springer. New York: New York University Press, 1977.
Valuable overview of literary portraits of black women emphasizing the contrast between white stereotypes of weak black women and black stereotypes of strong black women. Among the issues Schultz discusses are the prevalence of images of working women in black fiction; the significance of color prejudice within the black community; the significance of promiscuous characters; black women's rite-of-passage novels; and the importance of older women in images of liberated black women. Includes comments on Petry, Marshall, Morrison, Margaret Walker, Alice Walker, and Meriwether.

_____ . "Out of the Woods and Into the World: A Study of Interracial Friendships Between Women in American Novels." In *Conjuring: Black Women, Fiction, and Literary Tradition*, edited by Marjorie Pryse and Hortense J. Spillers. Bloomington: Indiana University Press, 1985.
Surveys the presentation of interracial friendships in works by male and female novelists, both white and black. White male novelists perpetuate stereotypical images by reducing women's relationships to power struggles. Among black males, only James Baldwin and Al Young vary this pattern. While white women frequently challenge aspects of racist thought, the friendships rarely survive their novel's conclusions. In novels by black women, interracial friend-

ships are frequently disrupted by power plays on the part of the white women. Comments on work by Marshall, Morrison, Alice Walker, Margaret Walker, and Childress.

Scott, Nathan A., Jr. "Black Literature." In *Harvard Guide to Contemporary American Writing*, edited by Daniel Hoffman. Cambridge, Mass.: Harvard University Press, 1979.
Overview of Afro-American writing since World War II with almost no mention of black women novelists. Emphasizing the importance of Ralph Ellison, James Baldwin, and various writers of the Black Arts movement, Scott mentions Petry briefly in his discussion of naturalism and lists Margaret Walker, Alice Walker, Marshall, Hunter, and Morrison among younger writers who might attain some importance.

Scruggs, Charles. *The Sage in Harlem: H. L. Mencken and the Black Writers of the 1920s*. Baltimore: Johns Hopkins University Press, 1984.
Argues that despite his use of racial slurs and the more visible influence of Carl Van Vechten, Mencken played a central role in shaping the aesthetic premises of the Harlem Renaissance. Among Mencken's influential ideas, which were disseminated through Walter White and George Schuyler, were the view of art as panacea; the novel as foremost literary form; realism as the proper mode for presenting black life; and the novelist as both insider and outsider. Includes comments on Hurston, Fauset, and Larsen, emphasizing the latter two's acceptance of Mencken's principles.

Shinn, Thelma J. *Radiant Daughters: Fictional American Women*. Westport, Conn.: Greenwood Press, 1986.
General historical overview of the ways women writers have used literature to rediscover their own oppression, to reexamine their alternative, and to redefine their lives. Asserts that this process offers the possibility of rediscovering forms of social balance capable of resisting the dualism of American culture. Mentions Bambara, Brooks, and Morrison briefly. Incorporates sections of Shinn's essay on women in the works of Ann Petry.

Shockley, Ann Allen. *Afro-American Women Writers, 1746-1933: An Anthology and Critical Guide*. Boston: G. K. Hall, 1988.
Anthology of writings by black women from the eighteenth to the early twentieth century, including introductions incorporating biographical and critical information. Shockley's introduction traces the historical development of black women's writing with detailed attention to its distorted reception by white and/ or male critics and its serious underrepresentation in Afro-American anthologies. Introductions to each chronological section provide information concerning cultural and literary contexts. Includes selections by and discussions of Harper, Wilson, Hopkins, Fauset, and Larsen.

_____ . "The Black Lesbian in American Literature: An Overview." In *Home Girls: A Black Feminist Anthology*, edited by Barbara Smith. New York: Kitchen Table/Women of Color Press, 1983.

Surveys images of black lesbians in American literature, emphasizing the historical absence of attention and the stereotypical quality of the portrayals that have begun to appear. Shockley attributes the absence of lesbian characters in the work of black women writers to the fear of being labeled lesbian. Comments briefly on her own work and the lesbian themes in the writing of Gayl Jones and in Rosa Guy's *Ruby*. Lists black lesbian writers in various genres. Includes information on publication outlets and black lesbian organizations.

Showalter, Elaine, ed. *The New Feminist Criticism: Essays on Women, Literature, and Theory*. New York: Pantheon, 1985.

Anthology of feminist criticism, including Barbara Smith's "Toward a Black Feminist Criticism" and Deborah McDowell's "New Directions for Black Feminist Criticism." Essays by Alicia Ostriker, Nina Baym, Annette Kolodny, Jane Tompkins, Lillian Robinson, and Showalter address issues of literary politics directly relevant to black women's writing. Provides a useful overview of the political and intellectual backgrounds contributing to the recognition of black women's writing.

Sidran, Ben. *Black Talk*. New York: Da Capo Press, 1971.

Analyzes the ways in which black music transmits the values of African oral culture in a manner reflecting the conditions of blacks in the New World. Extended discussion of the ways in which orality presents a radical critique of Western philosophical, aesthetic, and political systems. Emphasizes the importance of an individual voice grounded in communal experience as a fundamental principle of African-American aesthetics. A valuable introduction to some of the most important recurrent themes in the criticism of black women's novels.

Sims, Janet L. *The Progress of Afro-American Women: A Selected Bibliography and Resource Guide*. Westport, Conn.: Greenwood Press, 1980.

Unannotated bibliography of sources of information concerning various aspects of black women's experience. Includes a section devoted to primary and secondary sources on black women's literature.

Sims, Rudine. *Shadow and Substance: Afro-American Experience in Contemporary Children's Fiction*. Urbana, Ill.: National Council of Teachers of English, 1982.

Overview of recent developments in the treatment of black experience in children's books. Prior to the 1970's, blacks were effectively absent from children's fiction—most of which assumed a white audience—in all but stereo-

typical roles. Examines the sociocultural and historical backgrounds of contemporary realistic fiction alongside three main types of books: social conscience books written to inform whites about black life; melting pot books which assume an assimilationist perspective; and culturally conscious books directed primarily at black readers and intended to recognize the uniqueness of Afro-American culture. Discusses the work of five Afro-American children's writers, including Hamilton.

Singh, Amritjit. *The Novels of the Harlem Renaissance*. University Park: Pennsylvania State University Press, 1976.
Overview of Harlem Renaissance-era fiction, including detailed discussions of Fauset and Larsen. Combining aesthetic and sociocultural analysis, Singh focuses on the intraracial issues of self-definition, class, caste, and color. Argues that while the roots of Afro-American culture lie predominantly in the American context, the implications of the Harlem Renaissance analysis of color continue to have international implications.

Smith, Barbara, ed. *Home Girls: A Black Feminist Anthology*. New York: Kitchen Table/Women of Color Press, 1983.
Influential anthology of black feminist writing including most of the material originally published in "The Black Women's Issue" of *Conditions*. Smith's introductory essay argues that feminism is organic to black experience and explores the practical implications of black feminist thought, raising questions concerning the interaction of black feminists with white feminists and with other women of color. Smith critiques several myths that serve to divert black women from their own freedom. Includes two essays on images of black lesbians in literature (Shockley, Gomez), Hull's essay on Bambara; and Renita Weems's celebration of Morrison.

_____ . *Toward a Black Feminist Criticism*. Trumansburg, N.Y.: Out & Out Books, 1977.
Influential theoretical statement calling for the development of a critical approach grounded in a primary emphasis on the experience of black women, especially black lesbians. Pervasive patterns of racism and sexism render most critical writing on black women novelists either useless or destructive. The failure to recognize the central theme of female bonding generates basic misunderstanding of Morrison's *Sula* and *The Bluest Eye*. A political movement encouraging black lesbians to defend their experience is a precondition for the development of a critical tradition that does not yet exist.

Spillers, Hortense. "A Hateful Passion, a Lost Love." In *Feminist Issues in Literary Scholarship*, edited by Shari Benstock. Bloomington: Indiana University Press, 1987.

Traces the radical innovations of Morrison's *Sula* to their historical antecedents in Margaret Walker's *Jubilee* and Hurston's *Their Eyes Were Watching God*. In bringing to light impulses formerly repressed under the virtuous surface of the characterization of black women, *Sula* provides a literal and figurative break-through to a new dimension of black women's being. If Walker's Vyry is the "woman-for-other," then Sula is the "woman-for-self." Hurston's Janie provides a dialectical point of contact for these antitheses.

_____ . "The Politics of Intimacy: A Discussion." In *Sturdy Black Bridges: Visions of Black Women in Literature*, edited by Roseann P. Bell, Bettye J. Parker, and Beverly Guy-Sheftall. Garden City, N.Y.: Anchor, 1979.
Advances the idea that literary criticism can help provide insight into the "politics of intimacy"—the intricate fabric of feeling presented in fictional situations between men and women—and help black women discover how their freedom, or its negation, are tied to previous ways of saying things. Morrison's *Sula* clearly expresses the need for black women to become their own historical subject, to acquire a language expressing their sense of immediate reality.

Starke, Catherine Juanita. *Black Portraiture in American Fiction: Stock Characters, Archetypes, and Individuals*. New York: Basic Books, 1971.
Historical survey of the presentation of black characters in American fiction from James Fenimore Cooper to the 1960's. Categorizes portraits into three categories: stock characters, usually minor figures used primarily to create atmosphere; archetypes, more complex figures used to embody cultural values; and individuals, characterized by their ability to engage in "transactional re-latedness" with others. Petry's *The Street* reflects the transition from archetype to individual. Hurston's *Their Eyes Were Watching God* and Marshall's *The Chosen Place, The Timeless People* create fully individualized characters.

Steady, Filomina Chioma, ed. *The Black Woman Cross-Culturally*. Cambridge, Mass.: Schenkman, 1981.
Anthology of writings on black women in Africa, the Caribbean, the United States, and Latin America. Individual essays employ a wide range of approaches derived from anthropology, history, and sociology as well as Afro-American and Women's Studies. Unifying themes include the pervasive impact of economic exploitation, the negative influence of stereotypical images of black women in literature, and the ideological necessity of self-reliance.

Stepto, Robert B. *From Behind the Veil: A Study of Afro-American Narrative*. Urbana: University of Illinois Press, 1979.
Theoretically informed study of black narratives from the slave narratives

through *Invisible Man*. Emphasizing the strategies black writers have used to assume control over their own texts, Stepto examines the significance of "authenticating documents" that mediate between black writer and predominantly white audience. Identifies two crucial patterns in Afro-American narrative: "ascent," which involves the movement toward literacy and freedom; and "immersion," a movement back toward racial connection. Includes a brief discussion of *Their Eyes Were Watching God*.

Stepto, Robert B., and Dexter Fisher, eds. *Afro-American Literature: The Reconstruction of Instruction*. New York: Modern Language Association, 1979.
Important anthology of critical essays marking the first major attempt to reorient Afro-American literary criticism away from political and contextual issues toward problems of form, tradition, and theory. Stepto's introduction and several essays by Henry Louis Gates, Jr., are frequently cited as the origins of the theoretical movement in black literary criticism of the 1980's. Also includes important essays by novelist Sherley Anne Williams on the blues roots of Afro-American poetry, and Robert Hemenway on the relationship between folklore and literature.

Sterling, Dorothy, ed. *We Are Your Sisters: Black Women in the Nineteenth Century*. New York: W. W. Norton, 1984.
Compilation of original source materials related to black women's experience in and immediately following slavery. Drawing on letters, interviews, diaries, and organizational documents, the anthology provides insight into common literary themes such as the nature of oppression, the relationship between black and white women, the tension between black and white men, and the role of black women in various political movements. Incorporates some material from the writings of the novelist Frances Ellen Watkins Harper.

Tate, Claudia, ed. *Black Women Writers at Work*. New York: Continuum, 1983.
Collection of interviews with black women writers concerning the influences on their work, their lives, and the increasing recognition of their work. Among the writers interviewed are Bambara, Brooks, Hunter, Jones, Morrison, Shange, Alice Walker, Margaret Walker, and Williams.

Taylor, Clyde. "Black Folk Spirit and the Shape of Black Literature." *Black World* 21 (August, 1972): 31-40.
Argues that the underlying function of Afro-American literature is "to move the process of Black folk art to a further stage of development." Noting that folk art persists as a fragmentary unity capable of bringing moments of human experience to their highest intensity, Taylor presents a typology of Afro-American expression in the form of a complex full-page chart emphasizing the

themes of white brutality; survival; identity crisis; assertion of manhood; and realization of reality. Comments briefly on Brooks and Margaret Walker, but more important as a theoretical framework.

——————— . "Black Writing as Immanent Humanism." *The Southern Review* 21 (July, 1985): 790-800.
Important response of a black male critic to recent developments in black women's writing. Grounding his discussion in the tension between Western and third world conceptions of humanism, Taylor argues that the work of Alice Walker, Morrison, and Marshall stands at the forefront of the understanding of Africa as "spiritual speech" in black American writing. Notes the celebration of Africa as lived experience and the embrace of complexity in black women's novels. Argues that black women writers are fulfilling the call of Richard Wright's "Blueprint for Negro Writing" and concludes that "instead of creating a separate chamber in African-American literature, black women's writing has flowered in the heart of it."

Teish, Luisah. *Jambalaya: The Natural Woman's Book of Personal Charms and Practical Rituals*. San Francisco: Harper & Row, 1985.
Blending autobiography and folk wisdom with analysis of African and African-American philosophical and cultural traditions, *Jambalaya* provides an important entry into the specifically black women's traditions that play a central role in the novels of many contemporary black women. Teish draws connections between aspects of African and Caribbean cosmological thought and the practical problems faced by black women. Central focus on the importance of spiritual awareness to personal identity.

Thomas, H. Nigel. *From Folklore to Fiction: A Study of Folk Heroes and Rituals in the Black American Novel*. Westport, Conn.: Greenwood Press, 1988.
Study of the uses of Afro-American folklore in formal fiction. Thomas catalogs the various types of black expression; examines the treatment of archetypal figures such as the preacher and the "bad nigger"; and the central importance of trickster figures. Includes some discussion of Morrison, Hurston, and Marshall.

Thompson, Robert Farris. *Flash of the Spirit: African and Afro-American Art and Philosophy*. New York: Random House, 1983.
Examination of the presence, adaptation, and transformation of African philosophical attitudes and aesthetic practices in the Western Hemisphere. Emphasizes the psychological and social significance of the African *orisha*, spirits associated with different types of potentially useful energy. While there is little direct reference to literature, Thompson's book recognizes the contributions of black women artists in music and the visual arts. A central point of reference for understanding recent black women's fiction.

Tischler, Nancy M. *Black Masks: Negro Characters in Modern Southern Fiction*. University Park: Pennsylvania State University Press, 1969.
Examines the movement from stereotype to archetype in the presentation of black characters by Southern writers. Observing that stereotypes reflect a refusal to come to terms with human complexity, Tischler praises writers such as Ellison, Wright, Faulkner, and McCullers, who treat blacks not as types but as individuals. Mentions Hurston's *Their Eyes Were Watching God* as an effective attack on black Babbitry, and *Seraph on the Suwanee* as an analysis of the "pet Negro" theme.

Turner, Darwin. *Afro-American Writers*. New York: Appleton, 1970.
Bibliography of secondary sources on Afro-American writers in all genres and related disciplines such as history, music, and folklore. Includes entries on several of the novelists covered in this volume. Valuable for listings of information in popular magazines and encyclopedias.

——————— . "Black Fiction: History and Myth." *Studies in American Fiction* 5 (Spring, 1977): 109-126.
Discusses Hurston's *Moses, Man of the Mountain* and Margaret Walker's *Jubilee* as part of a survey of Afro-American historical novels. Identifying *Moses* as Hurston's best novel, Turner comments on her use of history as satiric commentary on contemporary racial relations. In *Jubilee*, which is surprisingly the first twentieth century black novel to consider the Civil War, Reconstruction and its aftermath, Walker places her hope in the eventual recognition of endurance, good will, and good works.

Van Deburg, William L. *Slavery and Race in American Popular Culture*. Madison: University of Wisconsin Press, 1984.
Focuses on the perception and interpretation of the slave experience in various forms from the seventeenth century to the 1980's. Emphasizes the impact of stereotypes on black expression, which frequently focuses on presenting more realistic images. Characterizations of slavery reveal much concerning both white anxieties and the black drive for self-realization. Frequently cited source of contextual information in criticism of black women's novels. Comments briefly on Margaret Walker.

Wade-Gayles, Gloria. *No Crystal Stair: Visions of Race and Sex in Black Women's Fiction*. New York: Pilgrim Press, 1984.
Thematic readings of twelve novels published by Afro-American women between 1946 and 1976. Asserts the need for understanding the cultural context, emphasizing the failure of both race and gender based organizations to acknowledge black women's specific circumstances. Wade-Gayles' reliance on imagery of darkness and narrowness contributes to a strong impression that

victimization is the core of black women's experience. Among the topics given detailed consideration are the relationship of mothers and daughters; the experience of hopelessness; and the quest for wholeness in the early novels of Alice Walker and Toni Morrison.

Walker, Alice. *In Search of Our Mothers' Gardens*. New York: Harcourt Brace Jovanovich, 1983.
Collection of essays and speeches, including numerous influential pieces concerning black women. Combining political and cultural concerns, Walker advances a "womanist" alternative to mainstream "feminism," which is too often unconscious of its own race- and class-specific attitudes. The lives and cultures of black women, particularly in the South, are the most valuable resources of the younger black woman seeking to find her own voice. The title essay and two essays on Hurston are among the book's highlights.

_____ . *Living by the Word: Selected Writings, 1973-1987*. New York: Harcourt Brace Jovanovich, 1988.
Collection of occasional prose pieces focusing on a range of literary and political concerns. "In the Closet of the Soul" catalogs Walker's responses to the controversy surrounding both the book and movie versions of *The Color Purple*. Walker expresses her disappointment in the refusal of some black men to empathize with black women's suffering under sexism. Walker argues that her critics were not upset by the negative images of black men but by the images of black women with their own agendas for action.

Wallace, Michele. *Black Macho and the Myth of the Superwoman*. New York: Dial Press, 1979.
Attacks stereotypical images of black women which are symptomatic of profound psychological and political problems. Combines autobiographical and analytical sections to explore the ways in which sexual ideologies, held by both black and white men, deny important aspects of black women's experience. Wallace's critiques of Eldridge Cleaver, Richard Wright, James Baldwin, and Norman Mailer were important points of reference in the debate surrounding the emergence of black women novelists in the 1980's.

Washington, Mary Helen, ed. *Black-Eyed Susans: Classic Stories By and About Black Women*. Garden City, N.Y.: Anchor Press, 1975.
The first significant anthology devoted entirely to black women's fiction. Includes influential introduction. The need to correct stereotypical images of black women in writing by whites and often by black men is a primary motivation for black women novelists who attempt to correct distortions and to reclaim control of their own experience. Among the crucial issues discussed are the childhood experiences of black women, the relationship of black

mothers and daughters, the place of the middle-class black woman, and the complex relationship between black women and black men. Includes excerpts from and comments on the work of Morrison, Brooks, Meriwether, Bambara, Alice Walker, Marshall, and Jean Wheeler Smith.

——————— . "I Sign My Mother's Name: Alice Walker, Dorothy West, Paule Marshall." In *Mothering the Mind: Twelve Studies of Writers and Their Silent Partners*, edited by Ruth Perry and Martine Watson Brownley. New York: Holmes & Meier, 1984.
Examines the ways in which Marshall, West, and Alice Walker find in their relationships with their mothers the key to release of their creative powers. Summarizes the writers' comments on their biographical relationship to their mothers and interprets crucial texts as an expression of that relationship. Emphasizes the ways in which the maternal influence helps novelists establish contact with the communal sensibility that informs their literary work. Includes excerpts from an interview with West.

——————— . *Invented Lives: Narratives of Black Women, 1860-1960*. Garden City, N.Y.: Anchor Press, 1987.
Anthology including eight essays by Washington in addition to excerpts from novels, short stories, and nonfiction. Washington's introduction stresses the need to reconstitute a literary tradition that has been repeatedly ignored or distorted. The single distinguishing feature of the tradition is that it focuses on the experience of black women. The success of the quest of the black female protagonist depends largely on her ability to obtain the support of her community. Includes essays and bibliographical notes on Harper, Hopkins, Larsen, Hurston, Petry, West, and Brooks.

——————— . *Midnight Birds: Stories of Contemporary Black Women Writers*. Garden City, N.Y.: Anchor Press, 1980.
Companion anthology to *Black-Eyed Susans*. Introduction titled "In Pursuit of Our Own History" emphasizes the continuing struggle of black women to assume power over the naming of their own experience. Revolting against ideologies that keep black women in literal or figurative bondage, black women writers have presented heroic images of black women struggling to claim an identity wider than that allowed by mainstream society. Emphasizes the need for women to form primary bonds with one another. Brief introductions to selections present biographical and critical commentary on Alice Walker, Shange, Jones, Morrison, Bambara, and Sherley Anne Williams.

——————— . "Teaching *Black-Eyed Susans*: An Approach to the Study of Black Women Writers." *Black American Literature Forum* 11 (Spring, 1977): 20-24. Reprinted in expanded form in *But Some of Us Are Brave: Black Women's*

Studies, edited by Gloria T. Hull, Patricia Bell Scott, and Barbara Smith. Old Westbury, N.Y.: Feminist Press, 1982.

Pedagogical approach to the history of black women writers. Washington describes thematic and historical approaches. She lists several dominant themes in black women's fiction including the black woman as suppressed artist; the impact of color prejudice both outside and within the black community; the cyclic nature of oppression; and the collective and historical violation of black women. The historical approach identifies an evolution from the "suspended woman" through the "assimilated woman" to the "emergent woman." Includes a list of novels according to historical category.

Watkins, Mel. "Hard Times for Black Writers." *The New York Times Book Review* 86 (February 22, 1981): 3, 26-27.

Discusses the problems of black writers attempting to find publishers in the early 1980's. Notes that many young black writers who emerged in the previous decade have been hit hard by the general economic problems of the publishing industry. Among the writers Watkins discusses are Alice Walker, Morrison, Polite, and Bambara. Quotes Morrison on her experience editing *The Salt Eaters* for a white publishing house.

———————— . "Sexism, Racism and Black Women Writers." *The New York Times Book Review* 91 (June 15, 1986): 1, 35-37.

Uses Polite's *The Flagellants* as a touchstone for a discussion of the bitter animosity between black male and black women writers, which derives largely from the unflinchingly candid and negative portraits of black men in black women's novels. Argues that "Although the sexist oppression of women should be explored in literature, some moderation and care should be employed by those who take on the task when it involves or *may even be construed* as involving sweeping condemnations of specific groups."

Watson, Carol McAlpine. *Prologue: The Novels of Black American Women, 1891-1965*. Westport, Conn.: Greenwood Press, 1985.

Study of the development of central themes in black women's novels prior to 1965. The desire of black women to communicate their particular experiences and to play a politically active role leads to an emphasis on content rather than aesthetic concerns. Among the themes Watson emphasizes are religion, prejudice, the issue of color within the black community, and the political purpose of art. Detailed discussion of novels by Harper, Hopkins, Fauset, Hurston, Petry, Marshall, and Hunter. Includes a statistical analysis of themes in novels by black women and an annotated list of novels published prior to 1965.

Weixlmann, Joe. "The Changing Shape(s) of the Contemporary Afro-American Novel." *Studies in Black American Literature* 1 (1984): 111-128.

Examines the development of a self-consciously experimental techniques by recent Afro-American novelists, including Morrison, Jones, and Polite. Two major approaches can be seen: surrealism, and the exploitation of popular cultural forms such as the detective novel. Emphasizes the importance of *Invisible Man* in the development of the experimental tradition. Despite cultural indifference, the search for a new style should be understood as part of the larger struggle for liberation.

Weixlmann, Joe, and Houston Baker, eds. *Studies in Black American Literature* 3 (1988).
This volume is devoted entirely to the topic of "Black Feminist Criticism and Critical Theory." Includes thematically oriented essays by Abena Busia and Missy Dehn Kubitschek in addition to studies of Hurston by Michael Awkward and Larsen by Deborah McDowell.

Werner, Craig. "Minstrel Nightmares: Black Dreams of Faulkner's Dreams of Blacks." In *Faulkner and Race*, edited by Doreen Fowler and Ann J. Abadie. Jackson: University Press of Mississippi, 1987.
Extending the argument presented in his essay "Tell Old Pharaoh," Werner identifies a second phase of the Afro-American response to Faulkner in which black writers move beyond a critique of his limitations to pursue a truly open dialogue on questions of racial and sexual identity. Includes discussion of Naylor's *Linden Hills* and Williams' *Dessa Rose*.

_____ . "New Democratic Vistas: Toward a Pluralistic Genealogy." *Studies in Black American Literature* 2 (1986): 47-83.
Draws on feminist and Afro-American critical approaches to construct a model of a pluralistic approach to Afro-American literature. Emphasizes the ways in which black culture questions white conceptions of "universality." Within Afro-American culture, black women's culture similarly questions theories based primarily on black male experience; and black lesbian experience cautions against theories based primarily on heterosexual experience.

_____ . "Tell Old Pharaoh: The Afro-American Response to Faulkner." *The Southern Review* 19 (October, 1983): 711-735.
Examines the response of contemporary black writers, including Jones, Morrison, and Alice Walker, to Faulkner's treatment of racial issues. Using Robert Stepto's ideas as a critical framework, Werner observes that Faulkner substitutes a static "narrative of endurance" for the kinetic narratives of "ascent" and "immersion." Moving beyond Faulkner's conception of history as torment and trap, Jones, Morrison, and Walker all seek to transform history into a source of individual and communal identity.

West, Cornel. *Prophetic Fragments*. Trenton, N.J.: Africa World Press, 1988.
Collection of essays by a black theologian who occupies a leading position in contemporary African-American intellectual life. West emphasizes the rela tionship between political, cultural, and spiritual aspects of African-American life. Among the topics examined are the relationship between black cultural forms and modernist aesthetics; the role of the black middle class in addressing political problems; and the challenge of liberation theology. A central point of reference in the cultural context of contemporary black women's writing.

White, Deborah Gray. *Ar'n't I a Woman? Female Slaves in the Plantation South*. New York: W. W. Norton, 1985.
Historical study of the experience of black women in slavery provides important contextual information relating to the subject matter of novels by Morrison, Margaret Walker, Williams, and others. Critiques myths of black women as passive-aggressive, nurturing-emasculating, and so on. Black women drew on their African heritage and extended kinship networks to cope with oppression. Unlike the white women with whom they shared certain experiences, black women relied heavily on support from their female peers.

Whiteman, Maxwell. *A Century of Fiction by American Negroes, 1853-1952: A Descriptive Bibliography*. Philadelphia: Albert Saifer, 1955.
Valuable bibliographical source including information about editions and textual variations of fiction by Harper, Hopkins, Larsen, Fauset, West, and Hurston. Includes synopses of novels and information concerning the racial identity of publishers.

Whitlow, Roger. *Black American Literature: A Critical History*. Chicago: Littlefield, Adams, 1974.
Overview of Afro-American literary history including biographical information and brief comments on Harper, Larsen, Hurston, Petry, West, Brooks, Margaret Walker, Marshall, Hunter, and Wright. Untrustworthy synthesis of previously published sources.

Wideman, John. "Defining the Black Voice in Fiction." *Black American Literature Forum* 11 (Fall, 1977): 79-82.
Discussion of the attempt to reclaim the black voice from literary frames which devalue black speech. From the start of the Afro-American tradition, black writers confronted a context in which literary frames denied the sources of moral and aesthetic authority which energized their community's word structures. Wideman builds his analysis around passages from Phillis Wheatley and Gayl Jones's *Corregidora*. In Jones's prose, there is no hierarchical relationship between black speech and a separate literary language.

Williams, Kenny J. *They Also Spoke: An Essay on Negro Literature in America, 1787-1930*. Nashville: Townsend Press, 1970.

Overview of Afro-American literature through the Harlem Renaissance, including comments on Larsen and Fauset. Emphasizes Fauset's stature as a novelist of the middle class who countered stereotypical images of black life and expressed racial pride. Both novelists' characters were caught in the cycle of prejudice.

Williams, Sherley Anne. *Give Birth to Brightness: A Thematic Study in Neo-Black Literature*. New York: Dial Press, 1972.

Critical study of Afro-American literature of the 1960's by a black woman novelist and poet. Williams advances a theory of "Neo-Black" literature as a vision of black life generated within the black community for a specifically black audience. Repudiates the traditional emphasis on protest in favor of a new attention to the possibility of a liberating vision. Detailed attention to forms of rebellion in black literature, with emphasis on the "streetman" and the black musician. Mentions black women writers only in passing.

_____ . "Some Implications of Womanist Theory." *Callaloo* 27 (Spring, 1986): 303-308.

Essay by a black woman novelist, poet, and critic, calling for an expansion in the focus of black women's critical attention to include the ways in which black male writers have presented black men. Charts the shift in attitude toward physical aggression and the black family and community in black male writing, noting the movement from subversion to unconscious acceptance of white value structures since the publication of *Native Son*. Includes a significant discussion of the relationship between (white) feminist and (black) womanist criticism.

Willis, Susan. *Specifying: Black Women Writing the American Experience*. Madison: University of Wisconsin Press, 1987.

Examines the work of Hurston, Marshall, Morrison, Alice Walker, and Bambara as it exemplifies black women's responses to historical forces. The Great Migration of blacks from south to north is presented as a shift from agrarian to industrial modes of economic organization. Discusses the use of forms derived from the oral tradition as they relate to the process of transforming the contradictions of an oppressive history into a fully realized vision of self. A Marxist theoretical approach that makes little attempt to ground its insights in broad discussions of Afro-American culture or folklore theory.

Wintz, Cary D. *Black Culture and the Harlem Renaissance*. Houston: Rice University Press, 1988.

An examination of the literary culture of the Harlem Renaissance era. Views the Renaissance as a shared awareness of a new awakening in black culture. Among the issues discussed are the relationship between art and politics; the interaction between black and white intellectuals; and the role of black women. Recognizes the participation of women "at all levels" in the literary world, despite their difficulty in getting financial support and having their work taken seriously. Includes discussion of Larsen, Fauset, and Hurston.

Wright, Richard. "Blueprint for Negro Writing." *New Challenge* 2 (Fall, 1937): 53-65. Reprinted in *The Richard Wright Reader*, edited by Ellen Wright and Michel Fabre. New York: Harper & Row, 1978.
Influential essay in which Wright focuses on the tension between folk nationalism and sophisticated Marxist analysis as the constituting element of the black literary tradition. Insisting that the Afro-American writer must be free of external constraints on his imagination, Wright concludes with a call for a collective form of cultural work. Wright's highly political perspective was crucial in establishing the framework for most discussion of Afro-American fiction from the 1930's through the 1960's.

Yellin, Jean Fagan. *The Intricate Knot: Black Figures in American Literature, 1776-1863*. New York: New York University Press, 1972.
Useful survey of the presentation of blacks in American literature, emphasizing the ways in which stereotypical images support specific political agendas. Plantation fiction, with its image of helpless blacks, perpetuates the myth that slavery was beneficial and necessary to blacks. Despite its relatively sympathetic political agenda, abolitionist fiction presents blacks primarily as passive victims, testifying to the inability of whites to imagine blacks as effective agents in their own lives. A useful source of information concerning the literary context of black women's novels.

Young, James O. *Black Writers of the Thirties*. Baton Rouge: Louisiana State University Press, 1973.
Overview of Afro-American writing of the Depression era, emphasizing political and economic writing. Comments on fiction stress that black novelists of the period went far beyond the shallowness characteristic of most Harlem Renaissance fiction. Notes that both Hurston and Richard Wright rejected the idea that it was necessary to "escape their blackness in order to dramatize themes of genuinely universal significance." Includes discussion of Hurston and Jessie Fauset, who is presented as an exemplar of the worst Harlem Renaissance tendencies.

TONI CADE BAMBARA

Biography

Bambara, Toni Cade. "Salvation Is the Issue." In *Black Women Writers, 1950-1980: A Critical Evaluation*, edited by Mari Evans. Garden City, N.Y.: Anchor Press, 1984.
Bambara comments on her interest in nonlinear literary conventions; her commitment to a functional art; the problem of individual and communal empowerment; and the significance of Zora Neale Hurston. An important critical foremother, Hurston wrote against the stereotypes of her day and showed how to make use of folk wisdom as the basis of literary art.

―――――――― . "What It Is I Think I'm Doing Anyhow." In *The Writer on Her Work*, edited by Janet Sternburg. New York: W. W. Norton, 1980.
Bambara grounds her work in the global political struggle, presenting her position as a "Pan-Africanist-socialist-feminist" as an advantageous one. Comments on the influence of her mother; the beginning of her writing career; her vision of literature as a collective enterprise; her sense of words as a form of conjuring; and the ways in which she integrates writing into her life.

Deck, Alice. "Toni Cade Bambara." In *Afro-American Writers After 1955: Dramatists and Prose Writers*, edited by Thadious M. Davis and Trudier Harris. Vol. 38 of *Dictionary of Literary Biography*. Detroit: Bruccoli Clark, 1985.
Lengthy biographical essay including analysis of Bambara's short stories and *The Salt Eaters*. Biographical sketch emphasizes the influence of Bambara's mother on her artistic sensibility; her political activism; and her editorial and academic contributions to the awareness of black women's experience. Interprets *The Salt Eaters* as an attempt to build bridges between various parts of the black community, and between that community and other ethnic communities in the United States. The hallmark of Bambara's style is her keen ear for Afro-American dialect.

Guy-Sheftall, Beverly. "Commitment: Toni Cade Bambara Speaks." In *Sturdy Black Bridges: Visions of Black Women in Literature*, edited by Roseann P. Bell, Bettye J. Parker, and Beverly Guy-Sheftall. Garden City, N.Y.: Anchor Press, 1979.
Interview introduced by a headnote stressing Bambara's importance in inspiring new forms of awareness and action among black women. Among the topics discussed are Bambara's early life and the beginning of her writing career; her belief that street life is a more important influence on her work than other

literature; her assessment of black women's literature; and a brief comment on the work-in-progress that developed into *The Salt Eaters*.

Salaam, Kalamu ya. "Searching for the Mother Tongue." *First World* 2, no. 4 (1980): 48-53.
Interview accompanied by Salaam's commentary in which he emphasizes Bambara's concern with finding an African mother tongue, her belief that art can make a real contribution to social transformation, and her recognition of how sexism damages the black liberation movement. In the interview, Bambara comments on black musicians as resources for re-creating black language; her writing process; her interest in film; her analysis of colonialism; and the relationship between art and politics.

Tate, Claudia C. *Black Women Writers at Work*. New York: Continuum, 1983.
Interview including Bambara's comments on the decline in the political energies of the 1960's; the responsibility of the writer to her community; her own writing process; differences in the perspectives of black male and female writers; influences on her writing; and the impact of the women's movement on Afro-American writing.

Commentary

Burks, Ruth Elizabeth. "From Baptism to Resurrection: Toni Cade Bambara and the Incongruity of Language." In *Black Women Writers, 1950-1980: A Critical Evaluation*, edited by Mari Evans. Garden City, N.Y.: Anchor Press, 1984.
Bambara perpetuates the struggles of her people by recording it in their own voices. Her fiction traces the civil rights movement from its inception through its loss of momentum in the 1970's. An innate spirituality is the foundation of a successful struggle. The least successful of Bambara's works, *The Salt Eaters* fails because Bambara has not been able to find a language adequate to the description of the liberating resurrection with which the novel ends.

Byerman, Keith E. "Women's Blues: The Fiction of Toni Cade Bambara and Alice Walker." In *Fingering the Jagged Grain: Tradition and Form in Recent Black Fiction*. Athens: University of Georgia Press, 1985.
Identifies the theme of disintegration as the primary concern of *The Salt Eaters*; Bambara's portraits of the black community and her protagonist, like the book's structure, are decentered. Discussion focuses on the ways in which different systems that attempt to resist oppression take on oppressive characteristics when they seek to compel agreement with their principles. Concludes that the lack of resolution in the novel is necessitated by Bambara's perception that in order to effect real change, her fiction must remain open.

Johnson, Charles. "The Women." In *Being and Race: Black Writing Since 1970*. Bloomington: Indiana University Press, 1988.
Brief comment by a black male novelist praising Bambara as a comic writer with a narrative voice capable of combining diverse forms of specialized diction. In *The Salt Eaters*, Bambara blends satire and grief to batter at social hypocrisy before offering a final measure of hope. Despite its narrative power, *The Salt Eaters* tends to sprawl shapelessly, suggesting that Bambara is still making a transition from short fiction to the novel form.

"Toni Cade Bambara." In *Contemporary Literary Criticism*, vol. 19, edited by Sharon R. Gunton. Detroit: Gale Research, 1981.
Compilation of excerpts from reviews of *The Salt Eaters*, including those by Anne Tyler and John Wideman.

Traylor, Eleanor W. "The Salt Eaters: My Soul Looks Back in Wonder." *First World* 2, no. 4 (1980): 44-47, 64. Reprinted in slightly different form as "Music as Theme: The Jazz Mode in the Works of Toni Cade Bambara." In *Black Women Writers, 1950-1980: A Critical Evaluation*, edited by Mari Evans. Garden City, N.Y.: Anchor Press, 1984.
The Salt Eaters is a rite of transformation told in the jazz mode. Like a jam session, it juxtaposes diverse perspectives to raise questions concerning the various modes of understanding available for use in the community's engagement with its own history. Bambara emphasizes that the individual must draw on the strength of the past in order to move towards the future.

Vertreace, Martha M. "Toni Cade Bambara: The Dance of Character and Community." In *American Women Writing Fiction: Memory, Identity, Family, Space*, edited by Mickey Pearlman. Lexington: University Press of Kentucky, 1989.
Consideration of the problem of personal definition within the context of community, primarily in regard to Bambara's short stories. Bambara's women grow strong not because of an inherent "feminine" quality, but because of the lessons they learn from interacting with others. Identity is achieved, not bestowed. Includes an extensive bibliography of primary and secondary sources, including several reviews of *The Salt Eaters*.

Willis, Susan. "Problematizing the Individual: Toni Cade Bambara's Stories for the Revolution." In, *Specifying: Black Women Writing the American Experience*. Madison: University of Wisconsin Press, 1987.
The Salt Eaters attempts to link the black activism of the 1960's with the changed political situation of the 1980's. Despite Bambara's optimistic vision, however, she fails to offer useful suggestions concerning how change might be produced. Bambara's primary focus is on the lost cohesion between the black

community and its leaders. The novel's primary significance is to be found in its contribution to the project of rewriting history from the woman's perspective.

Selected Title

The Salt Eaters

Hull, Gloria T. " 'What It Is I Think She's Doing Anyhow': A Reading of Toni Cade Bambara's *The Salt Eaters*." In *Conjuring: Black Women, Fiction, and Literary Tradition*, edited by Marjorie Pryse and Hortense J. Spillers. Bloomington: Indiana University Press, 1985.

Like *Invisible Man* in the 1950's and *Song of Solomon* in the 1970's, *The Salt Eaters* defines present conditions and challenges the way to the future. Bambara's treatment of healing involves drawing on ways of knowing—astrology, dreams, witches, voices, visions, and so on—opposed to dominant scientific rational Western modes. A complex view of time, in which past, present, and future coexist, supports Bambara's belief that all knowledge systems are ultimately one meta-system. Bambara focuses her discussion of this multiplicity of perspectives on the well-being of the Afro-American community.

Rumens, Carol. "Heirs to the Dream." *Times Literary Supplement* (June 18, 1982): 676.

An introverted and convoluted performance, *The Salt Eaters* makes few concessions to its audience. Despite the expressive power of Bambara's writing, the novel will communicate only with those already familiar with its material. A hymn to individual courage, it offers a somber message of hope.

Shipley, W. Maurice. Review of *The Salt Eaters*. *CLA Journal* 26 (September, 1982): 125-127.

Favorable review emphasizing the tragic dimension of the novel. *The Salt Eaters* is an unqualified success in its exposure of the flaws in black male-female relationships and the unique pain and despair felt by black women as they search for wholeness. Stylistically, Bambara demonstrates her mastery of the novel form in her interweaving of mythmaking, psychological and sociological drama, literary and factual history, and political and philosophical realities.

Tyler, Anne. "At the Still Center of a Dream." *The Washington Post Book World* (March 30, 1980): 1-2.

Generally favorable review comparing the vitality of Bambara's characters with the Jewish characters of Isaac Bashevis Singer. Not an easy book to read, *The Salt Eaters* resembles a long, rich dream which is brought alive by the power of Bambara's writing.

Wideman, John. "The Healing of Velma Henry." *The New York Times Book Review* 85 (June 1, 1980): 14, 28.

Favorable review praising the boldness of design at the center of black creativity. At its best, the novel recalls Faulknerian montage, the harmonic counterpoints of Jean Toomer, and the rich textures of Toni Morrison and Leslie Silko. Bambara's juxtapositions of the imaginary and the actual are particularly effective. The novel's perspective is multicultural.

GWENDOLYN BROOKS

Biography

Brooks, Gwendolyn. *Report from Part One*. Detroit: Broadside Press, 1972.
Autobiography focusing on the development of Brooks's political and literary perspectives. Brooks describes her early concentration on mastery of Euro-American literary forms which she comes to associate with integrationist politics. Her contact with young black writers and her trip to Africa generate her shift to a black nationalist stance. Includes several interviews detailing her approach to the writer's craft and the implications of her political transformation.

Hull, Gloria T., and Posey Gallagher. "Update on *Part One*: An Interview with Gwendolyn Brooks." *CLA Journal* 21 (September, 1977): 19-40.
Interview focusing on the direction of Brooks's thought and work since *Report From Part One*. Brooks comments on her plans for a sequel to *Maud Martha* and a second volume of her autobiography. Among the other issues discussed are her attempt to find a new poetic voice, her feelings about the importance of love and marriage, and the decreasing emphasis on black women in her recent work.

Israel, Charles. "Gwendolyn Brooks." In *American Poets Since World War II: Part I, A-K*, edited by Donald J. Greiner. Vol. 5 of *Dictionary of Literary Biography*. Detroit: Bruccoli Clark, 1980.
Reference entry including a biographical sketch and analysis of Brooks's poetry. Biographical sections emphasize her grounding in traditional American literature; and her conversion to a black nationalist perspective following her participation in the 1967 Black Writers' Conference at Fisk University and her subsequent trip to Africa.

Kent, George. "Gwendolyn Brooks." In *Afro-American Writers, 1940-1955*, edited by Trudier Harris. Vol. 76 of *Dictionary of Literary Biography*. Detroit: Bruccoli Clark, 1988.
Lengthy reference entry by a distinguished black critic who was completing a full-length biography of Brooks at the time of his death. Includes detailed description of Brooks's childhood, family, and education; her early work experience; the beginning of her poetic career; her commitment to black solidarity and redemption; her public presence in Afro-American culture, especially in Illinois; and her balancing of the roles of mother and writer. Analytical segments focus exclusively on Brooks's poetry.

Tate, Claudia C. *Black Women Writers at Work*. New York: Continuum, 1983.
Includes a relatively brief interview focusing primarily on Brooks's poetry.

Among the topics she discusses are her conversion to a black nationalist perspective; the problems of white critics addressing black literature; and her perspective on literary treatment of black male-female encounters.

Wall, Cheryl A. "Gwendolyn Brooks." In *American Women Writers*, vol. 1, edited by Lina Mainiero. New York: Frederick Ungar, 1979.
Biographical entry including brief commentary on *Maud Martha* and a short bibliography.

Commentary

Davis, Arthur P. "Integrationists and Transitional Writers." In *From the Dark Tower: Afro-American Writers 1900 to 1960*. Washington, D.C.: Howard University Press, 1974.
Biographical sketch accompanied by analysis of Brooks's writing focusing primarily on her poetry. Notes her recent change from integrationist thought to a black nationalist perspective. Brief discussion of *Maud Martha* as a series of vignettes that combine to form a unified picture of a marriage in the urban ghetto. Although the novel has few high points, it is one of Brooks's most sensitive and understanding works.

"Gwendolyn Brooks." In *Contemporary Literary Criticism*, vol. 4, edited by Carolyn Riley (1975); vol. 49, edited by Daniel G. Marowski and Roger Matuz (1988). Detroit: Gale Research.
Compilations of materials relating to Brooks's writing. Vol. 4 includes an excerpt from Annette Shands's *Black World* essay on Brooks as novelist. Vol. 49 includes a biographical headnote and excerpts from critical commentary, mostly on Brooks's poetry. Includes excerpts from Patricia Lattin and Vernon Lattin's essay on *Maud Martha*. Lists entries on Brooks in other reference books.

Loff, Jon N. "Gwendolyn Brooks: A Bibliography." *CLA Journal* 17 (September, 1973): 32-41.
Bibliography listing general sources on Brooks and reviews of *Maud Martha*. Superseded by Miller's *Reference Guide*.

Melhem, D. H. *Gwendolyn Brooks: Poetry and the Heroic Voice*. Lexington: University Press of Kentucky, 1987.
Critical overview of Brooks's career incorporating biographical, historical, and literary approaches. Chapter on *Maud Martha* examines the textual and publication history, identifying the unpublished poetry manuscript *American Fam-*

ily Brown as a primary source. A "masterpiece of classic simplicity and poetic precision," *Maud Martha* weaves together dream and reality, individual and social perspectives. The novel's success derives primarily from Brooks's sensitive presentation of the autobiographical protagonist's unifying consciousness.

Miller, R. Baxter. *Langston Hughes and Gwendolyn Brooks: A Reference Guide*. Boston: G. K. Hall, 1978.
Bibliographical guide including extensive listing of primary and secondary sources concerning Brooks. Includes comprehensive list of original reviews of *Maud Martha*.

Mootry, Maria K., and Gary Smith, eds. *A Life Distilled: Gwendolyn Brooks, Her Poetry and Fiction*. Urbana: University of Illinois Press, 1987.
Collection of critical essays, including essays on *Maud Martha* by Harry Shaw and Barbara Christian. Mootry's introduction emphasizes Brooks's continuing commitment to modernist aesthetics and the ideal of social justice.

Shaw, Harry B. *Gwendolyn Brooks*. Boston: Twayne, 1980.
Overview of Brooks's career including chapters on Brooks's life and *Maud Martha*. Although Brooks employs her "poetic style" effectively in the vignettes which make up the novel, the absence of the political awareness of her later poetry renders the novel somewhat unsatisfying. The war between beauty and people's concepts of beauty provides the thematic center. Shaw's analysis is divided into sections on the themes of death, negative displacement, and the survival of the unheroic.

Selected Title

Maud Martha

Christian, Barbara. "Nuance and the Novella: A Study of Gwendolyn Brooks's *Maud Martha*." In *A Life Distilled: Gwendolyn Brooks, Her Poetry and Fiction*, edited by Maria K. Mootry and Gary Smith. Urbana: University of Illinois Press, 1987.
Explores the question of why *Maud Martha*, which has been identified by Paule Marshall as an important anticipation of *Brown Girl, Brownstones*, received little critical attention when it was first published. Although Brooks's approach to her early poetry reflects the era's belief that poetry should transcend racial boundaries, readers of the 1950's brought a different set of presuppositions to fiction. In its insistence on the "trivial," *Maud Martha* runs directly counter to the tone of the black novel established by books such as *Native Son*. Brooks replaces the expected conventions with a careful rendering of the rituals of ordinary life, where racism is experienced in "sharp nibbles rather than screams."

_____ . "Ordinary Women: The Tone of the Commonplace." In *Black Women Novelists: The Development of a Tradition, 1892-1976*. Westport, Conn.: Greenwood Press, 1980.

Brooks's major theme is the marvelous quality of the commonplace. The lyrical, perhaps autobiographical vignettes in *Maud Martha* emphasize the sensibility of the black girl growing up in an urban community. Although she confronts a range of problems, most notably those connected with distinctions in skin shade, the protagonist is loved by her family and nurtured by communal rituals.

Lattin, Patricia, and Vernon E. Lattin. "Dual Vision in Gwendolyn Brooks; *Maud Martha*." *Critique* 25 (1984): 180-188.

Presents *Maud Martha* as a "comedy of the commonplace" that demonstrates the effects of racism, the absurdity of human behaviour, and the quest of an individual for love, beauty, and meaning. Balancing the individual struggle with an understanding of the limitations of existence, *Maud Martha* remains a fresh novel. Maud's ability to attain human dignity is a significant achievement.

Schraufnagel, Noel. "Accommodationism in the Fifties." In *From Apology to Protest: The Black American Novel*. Deland, Fla.: Everett/Edwards, 1973.

Firmly situated in the accommodationist tradition of Afro-American writing in the 1950's, *Maud Martha* deals with the coming of age of a young black who must make personal adjustments to the effects of racism. Brooks's protagonist is the type of "enduring black woman that has become a stereotype." The elegance and economy of Brooks's language, which makes the novel resemble a series of sonnets, compensates for the relative lack of interesting material.

Shands, Annette Oliver. "Gwendolyn Brooks as Novelist." *Black World* 22 (June, 1973): 22-30.

Emphasizes Brooks's exploration of the "theme of humanness" and ability to give value to things and places through their identification with people and their feelings. Although Brooks believes in the possibility of change, she does not attempt to inspire social advancement. Rather, she urges her readers to accept the challenge of being human and "to assert humanness with urgency."

Shaw, Harry B. "*Maud Martha*: The War with Beauty." In *A Life Distilled: Gwendolyn Brooks, Her Poetry and Fiction*, edited by Maria K. Mootry and Gary Smith. Urbana: University of Illinois Press, 1987.

Analysis of the "black-and-tan motif" in *Maud Martha*. Like Brooks's poetry, the novel makes a sharply ironic commentary on human nature by revealing the ways in which physical appearance generates rejection to a greater extent than deep-rooted differences in culture, religion, or ideology. Employs Grier

and Cobbs's analysis of the impact of color prejudice on black women as a theoretical framework.

Spillers, Hortense J. " 'An Order of Constancy': Notes on Brooks and the Feminine." *Centennial Review* 29 (Spring, 1985): 223-248.
Uses *Maud Martha* as the touchstone of an examination of the meaning and potential power of the "feminine." For Brooks, the feminine is a cause for neither celebration, nor despair, but a particular vantage point capable of providing new insight into the ways in which multiple, and frequently excluded, meanings impinge on a central event. Balancing the perspectives of participant and observer, Maud survives because she weaves diverse acts of form from the details of everyday life. Contrasting Maud's heroic repose with dashing heroic motion, Spillers concludes that for Brooks the feminine constitutes "the particular gift of the hidden and silent faculties."

Wade-Gayles, Gloria. "The Halo and the Hardships." In *No Crystal Stair: Visions of Race and Sex in Black Women's Fiction*. New York: Pilgrim Press, 1984.
Identifies *Maud Martha* as one of the few protagonists in black women's fiction who is neither a hero nor a victim. Compares Maud's response to color prejudice within the black community to that of Morrison's Pauline Breedlove. Neither character considers giving birth to herself without a man in her life. The novel is ultimately a hymn to the beauty of everyday black people.

Washington, Mary Helen. "Plain, Black, and Decently Wild: The Heroic Possibilities of *Maud Martha*." In *The Voyage In: Fictions of Female Development*, edited by Elizabeth Abel, Marianne Hirsch, and Elizabeth Langland. Hanover, N.H.: University Press of New England, 1983.
Interprets Brooks's novel in relation to the silencing of black women in their own historical, cultural, and literary traditions. Another example of women's struggle for language, *Maud Martha* focuses on the protagonist's rich inner understanding of unremarkable external events. Washington analyzes four important racial encounters leading up to Maud's self-affirmation but acknowledges that at the end of the novel she remains alienated from the important women in her life and unable to express the meaning of her growth. Includes a detailed comparison of the critical receptions of *Maud Martha* and *Invisible Man*.

_____ . " 'Taming All That Anger Down': Rage and Silence in the Writing of Gwendolyn Brooks." In *Invented Lives: Narratives of Black Women, 1860-1960*. Garden City, N.Y.: Anchor Press, 1987.
Places *Maud Martha* in the cultural context of the 1950's, emphasizing the prevalence of stereotypical images of black women in Afro-American magazines and newspapers. Dealing with the sexism and racism enshrined in the

novel's condescending reviews, Brooks expresses themes of bitterness, rage, self-hatred, and, most important, the silence that results from suppressed anger. The novel's style—truncated chapters, short sentences, lack of ornamentation, and freeze-frame endings—represents structurally the entrapment Brooks's protagonist feels.

OCTAVIA BUTLER

Biography

Beal, Frances M. "Black Women and the Science Fiction Genre: Interview with Octavia Butler." *Black Scholar* 17 (March/April, 1986): 14-18.
Interview including Butler's comments on the origins of her interest in the science fiction genre; her interest in treating contemporary problems through the projection of ideal alternative societies; the thematic structure of *Kindred*, which is referred to as *Kendra*; the position of blacks and women in the science fiction community; and the general problem of hierarchical behaviour.

Mixon, Veronica. "Futurist Woman: Octavia Butler." *Essence* 9 (April, 1979): 12, 15.
Biographical sketch of Butler including information on her family background, emphasizing the influence of Butler's mother and grandmother. Emphasizes Butler's women characters as survivors who draw on the heritage of their female ancestors. Includes Butler's comments on her interest in the science fiction genre.

O'Connor, Margaret Anne. "Octavia E. Butler." In *Afro-American Fiction After 1955*, edited by Thadious M. Davis and Trudier Harris. Vol. 33 of *Dictionary of Literary Biography*. Detroit: Bruccoli Clark, 1984.
Lengthy critical-biographical entry including discussion of Butler's "Pattern-ist" novels and *Kindred*. Identifies the responsibility of the powerful to the powerless as Butler's central theme. Discusses Butler's position in the science fiction world; her interest in cultural anthropology; the influence of the Clarion Workshop on her career; and her sensitive treatment of themes of race and gender. Bibliography includes a useful list of interviews and reviews published in science fiction magazines.

Weixlmann, Joe. "An Octavia E. Butler Bibliography." *Black American Literature Forum* 18 (Summer, 1984): 88-89.
Bibliography of primary and secondary sources, with a comprehensive list of reviews, including those published in science fiction magazines, of Butler's works through *Clay's Ark*.

Commentary

Carter, Patricia A. "Word Star." *Essence* 18 (September, 1987): 34.
Brief profile including Butler's comment on the beginning of her writing career

and the future of blacks in science fiction. Identifies Butler's characters as ordinary people confronting unusual and terrifying circumstances.

Gomez, Jewelle. "Black Women Heroes: Here's Reality, Where's the Fiction?" *Black Scholar* 17 (March/April, 1986): 8-13.
Discussion of the problem of creating heroic images of black women in a cultural setting that denies or trivializes their accomplishments. Gomez discusses *Kindred* as an example of fiction capable of avoiding idealized concepts of heroism and creating a character who is at once both ordinary and extraordinary. Gomez views science fiction as a potentially useful genre for breaking patterns endemic to the mainstream literary world.

Govan, Sandra Y. "Connections, Links, and Extended Networks: Patterns in Octavia Butler's Science Fiction." *Black American Literature Forum* 18 (Summer, 1984): 82-87.
Discusses the significance of Butler's pairing of female protagonists with strong male characters in the "Patternist" novels and *Kindred*. She uses the juxtaposition to illustrate differences in feminine and masculine values, differences in conceptions of power, and differences in the sense of responsibility on both personal and social levels. Quotes Butler's comment that "I began writing about power because I had so little."

_____ . "Homage to Tradition: Octavia Butler Renovates the Historical Novel." *MELUS* 13 (Spring/Summer, 1986): 79-96.
Butler's *Wild Seed* and *Kindred* define the intersection between the traditions of the slave narrative, the historical novel, and science fiction. The women protagonists of the two novels refuse to yield their integrity or submit to male dominance. Butler creates a speculative past firmly grounded in African and African-American cultural history.

Johnson, Charles. "The Women." In *Being and Race: Black Writing Since 1970*. Bloomington: Indiana University Press, 1988.
Brief comment by a black male novelist praising the fertility of Butler's imagination, but concluding that she has not yet made an important contribution to science fiction. Criticizes the "timid" quality of Butler's prose and the narrative construction of *Wild Seed*.

"Octavia E(stelle) Butler." In *Contemporary Literary Criticism*, vol. 38, edited by Daniel G. Marowski. Detroit: Gale Research, 1986.
Compilation of materials on Butler's fiction including a biographical headnote and excerpts from reviews of her novels through *Clay's Ark*. Includes a lengthy excerpt from Frances Smith Foster's essay on Butler's mythology which was originally published in the science fiction critical journal *Extrapolation*.

Salvaggio, Ruth. "Octavia Butler and the Black Science-Fiction Heroine." *Black American Literature Forum* 18 (Summer, 1984): 78-81.

Identifies the central focus of Butler's work in the response of her black heroines to the barriers to their independence presented by racist and sexist obstacles. Salvaggio focuses on the heroines of *Patternmaster*, *Mind of My Mind*, *Survivor*, and *Wild Seed*. Although Butler's heroines are dangerous and powerful women, they do not seek power. Their heroism derives from their ability to conquer the very idea of tyranny.

Shinn, Thelma J. "The Wise Witches: Black Women Mentors in the Fiction of Octavia E. Butler." In *Conjuring: Black Women, Fiction, and Literary Tradition*, edited by Marjorie Pryse and Hortense J. Spillers. Bloomington: Indiana University Press, 1985.

Identifies the "wise witch"—the black woman who shares her survival skills out of a sense of compassion and responsibility—as a central figure in Butler's fiction. Teaching others is a means of transforming personal power into social power. This conception of power demands the conscious interdependence of leaders and those seeking leadership. Butler uses a range of archetypal frameworks to demonstrate that seemingly insurmountable differences can be seen as artificial polarizations of human qualities.

Williams, Sherley Anne. "Sherley Anne Williams on Octavia E. Butler." *Ms.* 14 (March, 1986): 70-74.

Praises Butler's use of science fiction—which she prefers to call "speculative fiction"—as a way of exploring feminist ideas. Emphasizes the theme of survival and her assumption that black people will play a crucial role in shaping the future. The characters who triumph in her work are those who envision new possibilities and affirm their consciously chosen communities.

Selected Titles

Clay's Ark

Zaki, Hoda M. Review of *Clay's Ark*. *Sage* 2 (Spring, 1985): 67-68.

Review commenting on Butler's relationship to the "soft" science fiction of women novelists who take scientific technology for granted and focus on institutional relationships. As a dystopian novelist in the tradition of George Orwell and Aldous Huxley, Butler paints a grim vision of the future. Her implicit solution is that humanity must learn to tolerate diversity, but her alternative society essentially re-creates patriarchy and authoritarian power structures.

Dawn

Coven, Laurence. Review of *Dawn*. *The Washington Post Book World* 17 (June 28, 1987): 10.

Descriptive review emphasizing the theme of genetic engineering. Although Butler provides all the elements for an adventure story, her creation of Lilith as a resilient, intelligent heroine takes the novel in a different direction. The relationship between Lilith and Nikanj is moving, frightening, funny, and eerily beautiful.

Zaki, Hoda M. "Fantasies of Difference." *The Women's Review of Books* 5 (January, 1988): 13-14.

Favorable review discussing Butler's use of science fiction conventions to explore themes of discrimination, domination, freedom, love, and power. All of Butler's heroines are women of color who use their differences for their survival. Celebrating physical and cultural diversity, Butler asserts the need for tolerance. Concludes with a discussion of the tension between utopian and dystopian elements in Butler's novels.

Kindred

Crossley, Robert. Introduction to *Kindred*. Boston: Beacon Press, 1988.

Places *Kindred* in the context of the Afro-American slave narrative tradition. Like Harriet Jacobs in *Incidents in the Life of a Slave Girl*, Butler's protagonist is forced to make a choice that satisfies neither her internal standards nor the larger feminist principles of sisterhood. Butler emphasizes the unreliability of literary and cinematic images of slavery. Includes a discussion of the involvement of blacks and women in science fiction.

Wild Seed

Lynn, Elizabeth A. "Vampires, Aliens and Dodos." *The Washington Post Book World* 10 (September 28, 1980): 7, 10.

Favorable review grounding Butler's novel in the tradition of literary inquiries into what it means to be human that extend back at least as far as Mary Shelley's *Frankenstein*. Praises Butler's well-controlled prose. Her style is staccato rather than lyrical. The use of a historical backdrop provides a realistic texture that would have been difficult to achieve in a future setting.

BARBARA CHASE-RIBOUD

Biography

McHenry, Susan. "*Sally Hemings*: A Key to Our National Identity." *Ms.* 9 (October, 1980): 35-40.
Profile of Chase-Riboud noting her international reputation as a visual artist. Quotes Chase-Riboud on numerous aspects of *Sally Hemings*, which she sees primarily as a love story despite the attention to the national tragedy of slavery and miscegenation that threatens to overwhelm individual experience. Includes a lengthy biographical section describing Chase-Riboud's family background; her extensive travels; her studies at Temple and Yale; her marriage and children; and her work in a number of visual and literary forms.

Richardson, Marilyn. "Barbara Chase-Riboud." In *Afro-American Fiction Writers After 1955*, edited by Thadious M. Davis and Trudier Harris. Vol. 33 of *Dictionary of Literary Biography*. Detroit: Bruccoli Clark, 1984.
Critical-biographical essay. Biographical section discusses Chase-Riboud's family background; the importance of her extensive travels throughout the world; her work in sculpture; and her poetry. Interprets *Sally Hemings* as a skillful love story that asserts the theme of the need to join apparent opposites: male/female, negative/positive, black/white. Although Chase-Riboud's work raises issues of historical reclamation shared with other black women novelists, the interracial and international aspects of her approach place her in a unique position.

Wilson, Judith. "Barbara Chase-Riboud: Sculpting Our History." *Essence* 10 (December, 1979): 12-13.
Biographical sketch including Chase-Riboud's comments on her motivations in writing on the Thomas Jefferson-Sally Hemings relationship, which she says was not motivated by her own interracial marriage. Summarizes the historical sources of the novel and comments on the difficulty Chase-Riboud experienced in separating herself from the mythology of Jefferson she had previously accepted.

Selected Title

Valide
Gillespie, Marcia. "The Seraglio, the Plantation—Intrigue and Survival." *Ms.* 15 (September, 1986): 20-21.
Favorable review emphasizing the importance of responding to the stereotypi-

cal images of slavery. A powerful historical novel, *Valide* presents a complex tapestry of history as it relates to the intimate life of a woman. Its primary contribution is the willingness to question comfortable assumptions concerning the nature of freedom and slavery.

ALICE CHILDRESS

Biography

Childress, Alice. "A Candle in a Gale Wind." In *Black Women Writers, 1950-1980: A Critical Evaluation*, edited by Mari Evans. Garden City, N.Y.: Anchor Press, 1984.

Childress comments on her grandmother's influence on her upbringing; the emphasis on the "ordinary" in her writing; and the strong influence of theater on her fiction. The role of the black writer is to "explain pain to those who inflict it." Childress emphasizes the importance of multiple points of view in her writing, observing that all of the characters are "telling the truth."

_____ . "The Negro Woman in Literature." *Freedomways* (First Quarter, 1966): 14-19.

Transcript of remarks delivered at a symposium at the New School for Social Research. Childress observes that black women have been omitted from or distorted in American literature; that they have traditionally been portrayed in terms of long-suffering, humility, and patience; and that there is a growing tendency to portray them as domineering and emasculating. Examines American history to refute the "too easy and too misleading conclusion" that there is a core of truth in these images.

Curb, Rosemary. "Alice Childress." In *Twentieth-Century American Dramatists: Part 1, A-J*, edited by John MacNicholas. Vol. 7 of *Dictionary of Literary Biography*. Detroit: Bruccoli Clark, 1981.

Reference entry including a biographical sketch, focusing primarily on Childress' drama. Describes her grandmother's influence on her interest in theater; her self-directed education; her efforts in support of the rights of the impoverished; and the development of her theatrical career. Includes a brief discussion of her children's literature and a bibliography listing commentary on her drama.

Harris, Trudier. "Alice Childress." In *Afro-American Writers After 1955: Dramatists and Prose Writers*, edited by Thadious M. Davis and Trudier Harris. Vol. 38 of *Dictionary of Literary Biography*. Detroit: Bruccoli Clark, 1985.

Extensive discussion of Childress' work in various genres, including a substantial biographical sketch. Biographical section emphasizes Childress' affiliation with the American Negro Theater; her continuing commitment to working within the black community; and the impact of her politics on the reception of her work. Includes lengthy discussions of *A Hero Ain't Nothin' But a Sandwich*, which is realistic without being brutal, and *A Short Walk*, which is at once panoramic and personal.

Commentary

"Alice Childress." In *Children's Literature Review*, vol. 3, edited by Gerard J. Senick. Detroit: Gale Research, 1988.
Compilation of materials relating to Childress' children's books, including excerpts from reviews of *A Hero Ain't Nothin' But a Sandwich* and *Rainbow Jordan*. Also reprints Childress' essay "A Candle in a Gale Wind." Valuable for its inclusion of materials originally published in sources relating specifically to children's literature.

"Alice Childress." In *Contemporary Literary Criticism*, vol. 12, edited by Dedria Bryfonski (1980); vol. 15, edited by Sharon R. Gunton and Laurie Lanzen Harris (1980). Detroit: Gale Research.
Compilations of material relating to Childress' writing. Vol. 12 includes reviews of several of her plays and *A Hero Ain't Nothin' But a Sandwich*. Vol. 15 excerpts three reviews of *A Short Walk*, including those by James Park Sloan and Alice Walker.

Killens, John O. "The Literary Genius of Alice Childress." In *Black Women Writers, 1950-1980: A Critical Evaluation*, edited by Mari Evans. Garden City, N.Y.: Anchor Press, 1984.
Emphasizes Childress' use of satire and humor as weapons against prejudice and hypocrisy. Universal in its implications, *Like One of the Family* belongs in the Afro-American tradition of signifying. *A Short Walk*, Childress' most rewarding novel, brings the Harlem Renaissance era vividly to life.

Selected Titles

A Hero Ain't Nothin' But a Sandwich
Bullins, Ed. Review of *A Hero Ain't Nothin' But a Sandwich*. *The New York Times Book Review* 78 (November 4, 1973): 36-38.
Favorable review of Childress' "real story of the victims of today's worst urban plague, heroin addiction." Bullins, who is a prominent black male playwright, presents the novel as a reaffirmation of the belief that excellent writing can thrive in black America. Childress demystifies the figure of the pusher by centering on the unwilling victim. There is both a suggestion of hope and an unconcealed truth in the novel.

The Washington Post Book World. Review of *A Hero Ain't Nothin' But a Sandwich*. (November 11, 1973): 7C.
Favorable review. Although Childress offers no happy ending, her strong novel is charged with a vitality, personality, and tension that is "anything but defeatist." Praises Childress' "tough, trenchant Harlem idiom" and the brilliant portraits of characters surrounding her protagonist.

Like One of the Family

Harris, Trudier. " 'I Wish I Was a Poet': The Character as Artist in Alice Childress's *Like One of the Family*." *Black American Literature Forum* 14 (Spring, 1980): 24-30.

Drawing on both the oral and written traditions, Childress creates a brilliant character in Mildred, who presents a fully developed theory of artistic expression in the course of the volume. In several situations, Mildred is able to play the role of the trickster from the Afro-American folk tradition. Ultimately, Mildred transcends even the initial intention of her creator.

Rainbow Jordan

Tyler, Anne. "Looking for Mom." *The New York Times Book Review* 86 (April 26, 1981): 52-53, 69.

Favorable review in the context of treatments of mothers in children's literature. Emphasizes the appealing quality of Childress' protagonist, her mother, and her "substitute mother" Miss Josie. *Rainbow Jordan* is a beautiful book with a "heartbreakingly sturdy" central character.

A Short Walk

Sloan, James Park. "Three Novels: *A Short Walk*." *The New York Times Book Review* 84 (November 11, 1979): 14.

Mildly favorable review noting that while Childress' material is not original, the novel as a "stately achievement" including fine set-pieces. Bringing her story to life through rich proverbs and the rich dialect of the Carolina lowlands, Childress enhances the understanding of the black struggle with a meditation on time and change. Childress owes as much to Faulkner and Mann as to Wright and Ellison.

Walker, Alice. "A Walk Through 20th-Century Black America: Alice Childress's *A Short Walk*." *Ms.* 8 (December, 1979): 46, 48.

Mixed review of *A Short Walk*, which Walker identifies as the first fictional treatment of the Garvey movement. Walker states her respect for Childress' historical knowledge but comments that her writing has a "forced folksiness" that renders much of the dialogue unbelievable. Despite the maturity of Childress' mind, her writing lacks passion.

MICHELLE CLIFF

Biography

Cliff, Michelle. *The Land of Look Behind: Prose and Poetry*. Ithaca, N.Y.: Fire-brand, 1985.

Collection including several autobiographical essays. Among the topics Cliff considers are the influence of her family on her writing and her sense of identity; her response to black women writers throughout the African diaspora; the global political situation; and her personal journey from silence to voice.

Selected Titles

Abeng

Levy, Francis. Review of *Abeng*. *The New York Times Book Review* 89 (March 25, 1984): 20.

Brief review concluding that the novel's narrative inconsistencies are compensated for by Cliff's gift for "pithy anecdotal descriptions that bring Jamaica's present and past to life." While the novel centers on Clare's rite of passage and growing awareness of the gulf created by color and caste, Cliff's real subject is "forgotten history." Her style, which frequently digresses from linear form, is an "almost polemical exhuming of Jamaican mythology."

No Telephone to Heaven

Smilowitz, Erika J. "Tales of the Caribbean." *Women's Review of Books* 5 (November, 1987): 13-14.

Generally favorable review emphasizing Cliff's concern with the central issue of Caribbean literature: the question of a Caribbean identity. The novel presents numerous images of the divided self, which is both a personal and a communal dilemma. While Cliff's evocative language and erudition are impressive, her dialogue is at times stilted. Providing no answers, Cliff offers a provocative story rich in both story and substance.

JESSIE FAUSET

Biography

Shockley, Ann Allen. "Jessie Redmon Fauset Harris." In *Afro-American Women Writers, 1746-1933*. Boston: G. K. Hall, 1988.
Biographical headnote including discussion of Fauset's novels. Discusses her family background, education, travels, and literary career. Notes that Fauset's treatment of sexual relationships emphasizes the way people play games for personal benefit. Despite her limitations, Fauset was the "prototype of the new breed of Afro-American women writers."

Sims, Janet L. "Jessie Redmon Fauset, 1885-1961: A Selected Annotated Bibliography." *Black American Literature Forum* 14 (Winter, 1980): 147-152.
Valuable annotated bibliography of primary and secondary sources. List of secondary sources includes biographical and bibliographical notices, critical essays, and contemporary reviews.

Starkey, Marion L. "Jessie Fauset." *Southern Workman* 61 (1932): 217-220.
Valuable early biographical sketch including information on the influence of T. S. Stribling on Fauset's career; her difficulties in balancing her teaching and her literary career; the influence of real experiences on her fiction; and the absence of revision in her writing process.

Sylvander, Carolyn Wedin. "Jessie Redmon Fauset." In *Afro-American Writers from the Harlem Renaissance to 1940*, edited by Trudier Harris. Vol. 51 of *Dictionary of Literary Biography*. Detroit: Bruccoli Clark, 1987.
Lengthy biographical essay including commentary on each of Fauset's novels. Identifies Fauset as a "minor, though pivotal" figure in the Harlem Renaissance. Although her plots are romantic portraits of the black middle class, Fauset can be effective in confronting racial and sexual stereotypes. Sylvander's analysis of the novels is cast in response to what she sees as simplifications by previous critics. Fauset's strongest novel, *Plum Bun*, for example, is a carefully constructed *Bildungsroman* which presents an intricate picture of the psychology of racial difference.

―――――――― . "Jessie Redmon Fauset." In *American Women Writers*, vol. 2, edited by Lina Mainiero. New York: Frederick Ungar, 1980.
Biographical entry including brief commentary on each of Fauset's novels and a short bibliography including listing of entries in other reference works.

―――――――― . *Jessie Redmon Fauset, Black American Writer*. Troy, N.Y.: Whitston, 1981.

Critical biography emphasizing Fauset's awareness of the global implications of the struggle of American blacks, and her understanding of the situation of black women in the United States. Argues that interpretations of Fauset's novels primarily as an expression of her Philadelphia bourgeois background simplify both her life and her writing. Gives substantial attention to Fauset's journalistic work, as well as extended readings of each of her four novels.

Commentary

Bell, Bernard W. "The Harlem Renaissance and the Search for New Modes of Narrative." In *The Afro-American Novel and Its Tradition*. Amherst: University of Massachusetts Press, 1987.
Focuses on Fauset's treatment of the black bourgeoisie. The preciosity and narrowness of her sensibility frequently present problems for contemporary readers. Her treatment of the middle class is more sentimental than satirical. Discusses *Plum Bun* and *Comedy: American Style* as "antiromantic exposures of the tradition of passing."

Bone, Robert. "The Rear Guard." In *The Negro Novel in America*. New Haven, Conn.: Yale University Press, 1965.
Reflecting Fauset's proper "old Philadelphian" background, her novels maintain an irreproachable decorum that renders them "uniformly sophomoric, trivial, and dull." Her dedication to presenting a flattering image of respectable Negro society limits her range. Although her characters are bred to rise above racial discrimination, her novels contain an element of racial protest.

Braithwaite, William Stanley. "The Novels of Jessie Fauset." *Opportunity* 12 (January, 1934): 24-28. Reprint in *The Black Novelist*, edited by Robert Hemenway. Columbus, Ohio: Charles E. Merrill, 1970.
Locates Fauset in the "first rank of American women novelists in general" and identifies her as "the potential Jane Austen of Negro literature." Like Hawthorne, Fauset's philosophical center lies in her "rebuke to an inhuman principle, elevated to an institution." Discusses each of Fauset's novels, concluding that *Plum Bun* is her most perfect artistic achievement.

Brown, Sterling. "The Urban Scene." In *The Negro in American Fiction*. Washington, D.C.: Associates in Negro Folk Education, 1937. Reprint. New York: Atheneum, 1969.
Discusses Fauset's novels as examples of "bourgeois realism." Contrasts Fauset unfavorably with Jane Austen, noting Fauset's sentimentality and her role as apologist. She records the behavior of her class in order to praise her

race. At her best, Fauset succeeds with a realism reminiscent of William Dean Howells. Her novels are flawed by an overreliance on fate and chance.

Carby, Hazel. "The Quicksands of Representation: Rethinking Black Cultural Politics." In *Reconstructing Womanhood: The Emergence of the Afro-American Woman Novelist*. New York: Oxford University Press, 1987.
Fauset advances a middle-class code of morality intended to differentiate her class from the influx of rural blacks. Carby disagrees with Deborah McDowell's defense of Fauset, arguing that the conservatism of her ideology ultimately dominates her texts. Fauset adopts, but does not transcend, the form of the romance.

Christian, Barbara. "The Rise and Fall of the Proper Mulatta." In *Black Women Novelists: The Development of a Tradition, 1892-1976*. Westport, Conn.: Greenwood Press, 1980.
Fauset's novels exemplify the dominant position of Harlem intellectuals of the 1920's. Because Fauset accepts uncritically the values of the American middle class, her novels become "bad fairytales in which she sacrifices the natural flow of life" to the thesis "that blacks are as conventional as whites." Her choice of proper light-skinned women as heroines reflects her acceptance of the conventions of the nineteenth century black novel. Discusses the impact of T.S. Stribling's novel *Birthright* on Fauset's fiction.

Davis, Arthur P. "First Fruits, 1925-1940." In *From the Dark Tower: Afro-American Writers 1900 to 1960*. Washington, D.C.: Howard University Press, 1974.
Emphasizes Fauset's single-minded commitment to the theme that except for superficial differences, middle-class blacks are essentially like better-class whites. The most prolific and representative figure in black middle-class writing, Fauset asserts that her characters are just as interesting as the black "primitives" common in Harlem Renaissance literature. Identifies *There Is Confusion* as Fauset's most representative and fullest novel.

Dearborn, Mary V. "Black Women Authors and the Harlem Renaissance." In *Pocahontas's Daughters: Gender and Ethnicity in American Culture*. New York: Oxford University Press, 1986.
Fauset presents the most extreme and instructive example of ethnic female authorship during the Harlem Renaissance because she gave the issue of black cultural expression the most careful thought and nonetheless "missed the mark most widely." Examines *The Chinaberry Tree*, which reflects Fauset's tendency to confuse "civilization with civility." Despite their genteel texture, Fauset's novels are valuable because they present their subject matter with loving accuracy.

Feeney, Joseph J. "A Sardonic, Unconventional Jessie Fauset: The Double Structure and Double Vision of Her Novels." *CLA Journal* 22 (June, 1979): 365-382.

Rejecting the image of Fauset as a conventional novelist, Feeney emphasizes the deep pain and anger that influence both her form and content. Each of her novels has a double plot. Beneath the surface level of the conventional middle-class love story with a happy ending, each presents a counterstructure which expresses the souring of childhood hopes in either a near-tragic or sardonically comic mode. Includes detailed analysis of the double structure of each of Fauset's novels.

Ford, Nick Aaron. *The Contemporary Negro Novel: A Study in Race Relations.* Boston: Meador, 1936. Reprint: College Park, Md.: McGrath, 1968.

Emphasizes Fauset's treatment of dominant social and political themes of Negro literature of the era. Ford comments on Fauset's images of prejudice between whites and blacks, and between blacks; her disapproval of intermarriage; and her view of whites as untrustworthy. Identifies Fauset as the "greatest exponent" of race pride, who nonetheless is strongly supportive of Americanism. She views the economic independence of the black community as the best solution to racial problems.

Gayle, Addison, Jr. "The Confusion of Identity." In *The Way of the New World: The Black Novel in America.* Garden City, N.Y.: Anchor Press, 1976.

Because she articulates the ability of affluent blacks to serve as mentors to whites and missionaries to poor blacks, Fauset assumed the role of spokesperson for the black middle class during the Harlem Renaissance. Discusses *There Is Confusion* and *Plum Bun* as parables of class relations. Fauset's delineation of the middle-class value structure focuses on marriage, security, family, respectability, and race pride.

Gloster, Hugh. "Fiction of the Negro Renascence." In *Negro Voices in American Fiction.* Chapel Hill: University of North Carolina Press, 1948. Reprint. New York: Russell & Russell, 1965.

Argues that Fauset's main contribution is her demonstration that there are respectable, middle-class blacks whose lives are twisted and distorted by racial prejudice. Identifies *There Is Confusion* as "one of the important novels of American Negro literature." Fauset portrays "Negroes so relentlessly perplexed by racial considerations that they are unable to make a normal approach to living."

Huggins, Nathan. *Harlem Renaissance.* New York: Oxford University Press, 1971.

Emphasizes the conventional quality of Fauset's life and art. *There Is Confusion* exemplifies her use of the clichés of genteel realism to construct stories of the respectable Negro middle class. Her class bias permeates her novels, all of which focus on the themes of uplift, self-perfection, and honor.

"Jessie Fauset." In *Contemporary Literary Criticism*, vol. 19, edited by Sharon R. Gunton. Detroit: Gale Research, 1981.
Compilation of materials on Fauset's novels including excerpts from critical writing by Robert Bone, James Young, Hugh Gloster, and Joseph Feeney. Also includes contemporary reviews of each of her novels.

Johnson, Abby. "Literary Midwife: Jessie Redmond Fauset and the Harlem Renaissance." *Phylon* 39 (1978): 143-153.
Surveys critical reception of Fauset's novels by contemporary reviewers, including W. E. B. DuBois, Alain Locke, and George Schuyler, and later commentators, who are much less favorable in their views. Argues that Fauset's primary contribution to the Harlem Renaissance was as literary editor of *The Crisis*. Fauset sought both to evaluate books by objective literary standards and supported attempts to come to terms with black culture.

Lewis, David Levering. *When Harlem Was in Vogue*. New York: Alfred A. Knopf, 1981.
In terms of "honesty and precocity," Fauset's influence upon the Harlem Renaissance was probably unequaled. Describes Fauset's work with *The Crisis*, her relationship with DuBois, and the significance of her "prim upbringing" and genteel values. Literature, for Fauset, was important as a way of advancing the race. Summarizes the reception of her four novels.

McDowell, Deborah E. "The Neglected Dimension of Jessie Fauset." In *Conjuring: Black Women, Fiction, and Literary Tradition*, edited by Marjorie Pryse and Hortense J. Spillers. Bloomington: Indiana University Press, 1985.
Argues that Fauset employed the conventions of the novel of manners as "protective mimicry, a kind of deflecting mask for her more challenging concerns." Alternately radical and conservative on feminist issues, Fauset nonetheless presents a careful examination of the myriad shadings of sexism and how they impinge on women's development. Fauset's revision of fairy-tale motifs emphasizes that a successful resolution is not marriage but an acceptance of the virtues of black culture and a rejection of conventional attitudes that limit growth.

Perry, Margaret. "The Minor Novels." In *Silence to the Drums: A Survey of the Literature of the Harlem Renaissance*. Westport, Conn.: Greenwood Press, 1976.
Although Fauset's greatest contribution to the Harlem Renaissance was her support of younger writers, her novels presented an image of an aspect of the black world few readers knew existed. *There Is Confusion* introduces Fauset's

basic themes: educated blacks in a hostile world; the schizophrenia of the mulatto; the color caste system among Negroes; and the complex ancestral past of black society. The novel also contains her characteristic stylistic failures: stiff narration; overuse of coincidence; faulty characterization; and unreal dialogue.

Redding, J. Saunders. "The New Negro." In *To Make a Poet Black*. Chapel Hill: University of North Carolina Press, 1939. Reprint. Ithaca, N.Y.: Cornell University Press, 1988.
Unlike Jean Toomer's emphasis on the relationship of the Negro to the soil, Fauset's race pride centers on ancient lineage and cultural heritage. Because her characters seem "actual transcriptions from unimaginative life," her novels resemble dull novels of white middle-class society. Still, her work effectively offsets the artificial glamor of some Harlem Renaissance novels. Because her black characters are no more concerned with race than her white characters, she avoids the "heavier going of propaganda."

Sato, Hiroko. "Under the Harlem Shadows: A Study of Jessie Fauset and Nella Larsen." In *The Harlem Renaissance Remembered*, edited by Arna Bontemps. New York: Dodd, Mead, 1972.
Analyzes each of Fauset's novels with an emphasis on her portrayal of the tragic situation facing black intellectuals who make so much of the white world that they can never escape its influence. The movement in her novels is generated not by what is intrinsic to the middle class but by the forces imposed upon it from without. While Fauset is not a good writer, her social sanity is of value to the advancement of her race.

Singh, Amritjit. "Race and Sex: Approaches to Self-Definition." In *The Novels of the Harlem Renaissance*. University Park: Pennsylvania State University Press, 1976.
Presents Fauset as an exponent of George Schuyler's view that the salvation of America was to become "mulatto-minded." The most prolific Renaissance novelist, Fauset developed this theme in each of her essentially propagandistic novels. All of her fiction centers on the search of a mulatto heroine for happiness. Fauset is of more than simply historical interest because her subject alternates between genteel formulas and the exploration of challenging themes such as incest and self-hatred.

Watson, Carol McAlpine. "Race Consciousness and Self-Criticism, 1921-1945." In *Prologue: The Novels of Black American Women, 1891-1965*. Westport, Conn.: Greenwood Press, 1985.
Fauset's novels espouse the ideal of success, but demonstrate the costs such ambition entails. Her treatment of skin color reveals a similar tension; Fauset

believes both that skin color should not be so important, but that because it is important, it is best to be as white as possible. Contrasts Fauset's middle-class characters with the fiction produced by the black cultural nationalists of the Harlem Renaissance.

Wintz, Cary D. "Literature and Politics." In *Black Culture and the Harlem Renaissance*. Houston: Rice University Press, 1988.
More conservative in style and tone than other Harlem Renaissance writers, Fauset's work resembles that of Edith Wharton. Portraying the experience of the black middle class, she seeks to define "a middle ground" where women can find happiness and fulfillment without renouncing traditional values. In *Plum Bun*, she requires her heroine to make sacrifices for her husband and children while struggling to develop her own artistic talents. Fauset only partially achieved her definition of a fulfilling life.

Young, James O. "Black Reality and Beyond." In *Black Writers of the Thirties*. Baton Rouge: Louisiana State University Press, 1973.
Argues that while the "black middle class was not an invalid subject for fiction," there is little of redeeming value in Fauset's genteel romances. Observing that while the racial identity of Fauset's characters is usually irrelevant, that was precisely Fauset's point. Her "highly idealized" romances are more effective for their unintended satire of black middle-class life than for their dramatic realization.

Selected Titles

The Chinaberry Tree
Feeney, Joseph J. "Greek Tragic Patterns in a Black Novel: Jessie Fauset's *The Chinaberry Tree*." *CLA Journal* 18 (December, 1974): 211-215.
Discusses Fauset's use of elements of Greek tragedy to add a dimension of universality to *The Chinaberry Tree*. Although the tragic elements are alloyed with a great deal of conventional sentiment, Fauset employs aspects of Greek tragedy such as a family curse, a sense that fate rules events, a tragic inevitability, and the use of recognition scenes. She underscores this dimensions with several direct allusions to Greek culture.

Lupton, Mary Jane. "Bad Blood in Jersey: Jessie Fauset's *The Chinaberry Tree*." *CLA Journal* 27 (June, 1984): 383-390.
Compares *The Chinaberry Tree* with the novels of Jane Austen because it demonstrates the constrictions historically placed on women's lives. Examines the theme of "bad blood," which involves racial mixing, moral deficiency, and incest. Concludes with a discussion of the ways in which male critics have failed to comprehend the significance of Fauset's achievement which lies primarily in her ability to create images of "authentic female lives."

Sykes, Gerard. "Amber-Tinted Elegance." *The Nation* 135 (July 21, 1932): 88.
Generally favorable review praising Fauset's psychological insights. A "genuine aristocrat" by temperament, Fauset idealizes the world of educated Negroes in terms of the white standards it has accepted. The primary problem with the novel is that Fauset "is definitely minimizing the colored blood in them." Yet her treatment of the delicate psychological situation of educated blacks makes *The Chinaberry Tree* a valuable book.

Plum Bun
Feeney, Joseph J. "Black Childhood as Ironic: A Nursery Rhyme Transformed in Jessie Fauset's *Plum Bun*." *Minority Voices* 4, no. 2 (1980): 65-69.
Demonstrates Fauset's ironic use of the nursery rhyme "To Market, to Market" in *Plum Bun*. Accompanied by a brief note in which Feeney establishes Fauset's birth date and place as April 26, 1882, in Fredericksville, New Jersey.

K., B. "*Plum Bun*." *The New Republic* 58 (April 10, 1929): 235.
Review describing *Plum Bun* as "a novel of very ordinary sorts about a subject of extraordinary interest." The analysis of Angela's character is admirably handled. The rest of the book, however, is inconsistent, trivial, melodramatic, and unreal. Criticizes Fauset's failure to take advantage of the linguistic resources of the Negro folk idiom.

McDowell, Deborah E. Introduction to *Plum Bun*. Boston: Pandora Press, 1985.
Repudiates the image of Fauset as a "rear guard" writer, emphasizing her treatment of themes which have become central in contemporary feminist criticism: the debate over stereotyping; women's sexualities; and the significance of marriage and motherhood. The controlling theme of *Plum Bun* is the unequal power relationships in American society. She recognizes marriage and passing as the usually futile strategies used by women and blacks who hope to gain access to power. Fauset's treatment of these themes provides a veiled commentary on the literary politics of the Harlem Renaissance era, especially the relationship between black writers and their white patrons and publishers.

There Is Confusion
W., E. D. "*There Is Confusion*." *The New Republic* 39 (July 9, 1924): 192.
Mildly unfavorable review contrasting Fauset's novel unfavorably with works such as *Cane*, which represent the younger generation of Negro writers. Inaccurately identified as the first work of fiction by a Negro woman, *There Is Confusion* is described as a bridge between generations. Not meant for people who know anything about Negro life, the novel is a mediocre work of "puny, painstaking labor."

ROSA GUY

Biography

Guy, Rosa. "Maya Angelou." In *Writing Lives: Conversations Between Women Writers*, edited by Mary Chamberlain. London: Virago, 1988.
Conversation between two black women writers focusing on their responses to the problems each encountered growing up; the difficulties involved with finding their writing voices; their literary influences; their political perspectives; and their feelings concerning the need for love.

Lawrence, Leota S. "Rosa Guy." In *Afro-American Fiction Writers After 1955*, edited by Thadious M. Davis and Trudier Harris. Vol. 33 of *Dictionary of Literary Biography*. Detroit: Bruccoli Clark, 1984.
Substantial critical-biographical essay. Biographical section focuses on Guy's upbringing in a West Indian immigrant family; her involvement with the Harlem Writers Guild; and her political activism. Views *Bird at My Window* as an ambitious first novel examining the impact of racism on family relationships and the psychology of the black man. *A Measure of Time* succeeds as a realistic novel designed to confront blacks who seek to deny harsh realities. Also discusses Guy's juvenile novels.

Wilson, Judith. "Rosa Guy: Writing with Bold Vision." *Essence* 10 (October, 1979): 14, 20.
Biographical sketch emphasizing the importance of the firsthand knowledge of Afro-American-Caribbean life that informs Guy's strong sense of history. Includes brief descriptions of several of her novels, noting that she is best known as a writer of children's books. Guy comments on her interest in Africa and her belief that black women must address the actualities of problems within the black community without undue emphasis on the "positive side" of middle-class life.

Commentary

"Rosa (Cuthbert) Guy." In *Contemporary Literary Criticism*, vol. 26, edited by Jean C. Stine. Detroit: Gale Research, 1983.
Compilation of materials on Guy's adult and juvenile fiction, including a brief headnote and listing of entries in other reference sources. Includes reviews of *Bird at My Window*, *The Friends*, *Ruby*, *Edith Jackson*, *The Disappearance*, and *Mirror of Her Own*.

Selected Titles

Bird at My Window

Johnson, Brooks. Review of *Bird at My Window*. *Negro Digest* 15 (March, 1966):
53, 91.
Generally favorable review placing Guy's novel in the context of previous
writing about Harlem. While she does not provide new insights into Harlem,
Guy presents an effective story of the psychological metamorphosis of a black
man caught in the matriarchy, mores, and manipulations common to black
America. Guy effectively relates social and psychological forces. At times
Guy's dialogue fails to ring true, but the novel is an impressive addition to the
literature of Harlem.

Schraufnagel, Noel. "Apologetic Protest in the Sixties." In *From Apology to Protest: The Black American Novel*. Deland, Fla.: Everett/Edwards, 1973.
Brief discussion of Guy's treatment of the psychological damages of racial
discrimination. Although she has little original to say and is at best a competent artist, Guy's objective analysis of racism rescues the book from oblivion.

A Measure of Time

Isaacs, Susan. "From Montgomery to Harlem." *The New York Times Book Review*
88 (October 9, 1983): 14, 23.
Review praising Guy's treatment of race and racism but criticizing the majority
of characters as one dimensional. Guy stresses the connection between poverty
and powerlessness. Too tough and shrewd to become a victim, Guy's protagonist Dorine takes advantage of the opportunities offered her. Her survival in
Harlem benefits the family she left behind in Alabama.

Neville, Jill. "Making It." *Times Literary Supplement* (August 3, 1984): 864.
Favorable review emphasizing Guy's affirmative vision. Praises both Guy's use
of "jive-talk" and the realism of her street scenes. Criticizes the political
element of the conclusion but calls the novel "the best and liveliest book" the
reviewer has read about being black.

VIRGINIA HAMILTON

Biography

Apseloff, Marilyn F. "Virginia Hamilton." In *American Writers for Children Since 1960: Fiction*, edited by Glenn E. Estes. Vol. 52 of *Dictionary of Literary Biography*. Detroit: Bruccoli Clark, 1986.
Substantial reference entry including biographical sketch and discussion of Hamilton's numerous children's novels. Emphasizes Hamilton's willingness to experiment with new styles from book to book as a way of discovering the different realities of her various characters. Biographical section emphasizes the importance of her Ohio upbringing to the content of her novels. Includes separate discussions of *Zeely*, *The Planet of Junior Brown*, *M. C. Higgins, the Great*, the Justice trilogy, *Junius Over Far*, which is described as her most sophisticated novel, and others.

Ball, Jane. "Virginia Hamilton." In *Afro-American Fiction Writers After 1955*, edited by Thadious M. Davis and Trudier Harris. Vol. 33 of *Dictionary of Literary Biography*. Detroit: Bruccoli Clark, 1984.
Reference entry combining biographical sketch with analysis of Hamilton's novels and nonfiction prose. Biographical section discusses Hamilton's family and educational backgrounds; her experience in Greenwich Village; her travel; and the beginning of her literary career. Discussion of her novels focuses on critical reception and the theme of survival.

Cook, Martha E. "Virginia Hamilton." In *American Women Writers*, vol. 2, edited by Lina Mainiero. New York: Frederick Ungar, 1980.
Biographical entry including brief commentary on *Zeely*, *The House of Dies Drear*, *M. C. Higgins, the Great*, and *The Planet of Junior Brown*. Bibliography includes a list of entries in other reference works.

Commentary

Egoff, Sheila A. "Realistic Fiction" and "Science Fiction." In *Thursday's Child: Trends and Patterns in Contemporary Children's Literature*. Chicago: American Library Association, 1981.
Associates Hamilton's work with the trend of American children's fiction that is more deeply rooted in social realism than most British children's writing. Praises *The Planet of Junior Brown* for its combination of social and historical insight with elements of the fantastic. The first children's writer to view transformation of the human race as a mystical necessity, Hamilton merges allegory

and social dissertation in both *The Planet of Junior Brown* and *Justice and Her Brothers*.

Townsend, John Rowe. "Virginia Hamilton." In *A Sounding of Storytellers: New and Revised Essays on Contemporary Writers for Children*. Philadelphia: J. B. Lippincott, 1979.
Emphasizes the subtlety of Hamilton's writing, identifying her with the symbolist tradition because of her use of dream, myth, and legend to present her awareness of black history. More challenging than most children's literature, Hamilton's work is likely to be appreciated only by a few and perhaps fully understood by none.

Sims, Rudine. "The Image-Makers." In *Shadow and Substance: Afro-American Experience in Contemporary Children's Fiction*. Urbana, Ill.: National Council of Teachers of English, 1982.
Identifies Hamilton as one of the most daring and skilled writers of contemporary children's fiction. Stresses her emphasis on the positive elements of growing up Afro-American. Among her primary themes are Afro-American heritage, black pride, black community, the importance of human relationships within families, a sense of continuity, and the determination to work for survival. Includes brief biographical sketch.

"Virginia (Edith) Hamilton." In *Contemporary Literary Criticism*, vol. 26, edited by Jean C. Stine. Detroit: Gale Research, 1983.
Compilation of material on Hamilton's novels including a biographical headnote and listing of entries in other reference sources. Includes reviews by Alice Walker, Dorothy Sterling, Nikki Giovanni, Kristin Hunter, and a lengthy excerpt from John Rowe Townsend's discussion of Hamilton. Particularly valuable for its inclusion of reviews published in magazines devoted primarily to children's literature.

"Virginia (Esther) Hamilton." In *Children's Literature Review*, vol. 11, edited by Gerard J. Senick. Detroit: Gale Research, 1986.
Extensive compilation of materials concerning Hamilton's children's writing. Reprints excerpts of numerous reviews and critical essays by Townsend, Egoff, and Sims. Valuable for inclusion of reviews and articles originally published in children's magazines. Includes two essays and a lengthy speech and an essay by Hamilton in which she comments on the influence of oral storytelling on her writing; her interest in characters who are survivors; her writing process; and the importance of the audience to her work.

"Virginia Hamilton." In *Children's Literature Review*, vol. 1, edited by Ann Block and Carolyn Riley. Detroit: Gale Research, 1976.

Compilation of excerpts from reviews of Hamilton's children's books, including the novels *The House of Dies Drear*, *Zeely*, and *M.C. Higgins, the Great*. Valuable for its inclusion of materials originally published in periodicals focusing specifically on children's literature.

Selected Title

M. C. Higgins the Great
Gibb, Frances. "Mountain Sickness." *Times Literary Supplement* (May 23, 1975): 577.
Favorable review emphasizing Hamilton's strong sense of her own heritage. Forceful, but never sentimental, Hamilton images the past not in terms of its ghosts but as a source of strength for the present. Her style blends magical images, sensuous descriptions, and a strong sense of landscape. The central tension is that between the rural black community and the miners outside who threaten to destroy its way of life.

Giovanni, Nikki. Review of *M. C. Higgins the Great*. *The New York Times Book Review* (September 22, 1974): 8.
Favorable review emphasizing Hamilton's ability to join the forces of hope with the forces of dreams. Not an easily optimistic book, *M. C. Higgins, the Great* creates a believable world populated by characters with whom it is possible to identify. The novel encourages readers to reconsider the issue of strip mining.

Tucker, Nicholas. *Times Literary Supplement* (July 11, 1975): 766.
Mixed review emphasizing the earnest quality of Hamilton's prose. A sincere, highly original work, the story will hold an adult audience but is likely to lose the interest of younger readers. The excess of feeling described in the book, while authentic as a reflection of adolescence, sometimes causes emotion to slide into overintensity.

FRANCES ELLEN WATKINS HARPER

Biography

Graham, Maryemma. "Frances Ellen Watkins Harper." In *Afro-American Writers Before the Harlem Renaissance*, edited by Trudier Harris. Vol. 50 of *Dictionary of Literary Biography*. Detroit: Bruccoli Clark, 1986.
Lengthy biographical essay including analysis of both *Iola Leroy* and Harper's poetry. An effective antislavery orator and the major black woman poet of the nineteenth century, Harper was an independent woman who directly engaged the major literary and political issues of her era. Written in the tradition of the genteel novel, *Iola Leroy* presents black characters as idealized types but challenges conventions in its presentation of strong women characters. Iola experiences no inner conflict regarding her racial identity.

Shockley, Ann Allen. "Frances Ellen Watkins Harper." In *Afro-American Women Writers, 1746-1933*. Boston: G. K. Hall, 1988.
Biographical headnote to selection of Harper's poetry emphasizing her abolitionist activities and her literary career. Lists other sources of biographical information.

Wall, Cheryl A. "Frances Ellen Watkins Harper." In *American Women Writers*, vol. 2, edited by Lina Mainiero. New York: Frederick Ungar, 1980.
Biographical entry including brief commentary on *Iola Leroy*. Bibliography contains a list of entries in other reference works.

Commentary

Bell, Bernard W. "The Early Afro-American Novel: Historical Romance, Social Realism and Beyond." In *The Afro-American Novel and Its Tradition*. Amherst: University of Massachusetts Press, 1987.
A melodramatic study of the color line, *Iola Leroy* recalls William Dean Howells's *An Imperative Duty* in its emphasis on the moral duty of mulattoes to inspire others through selfless dedication to social reform and to their race. Combining the sentimentality and rhetoric of romance with elements of psychological and social realism, it is the first Afro-American novel to treat the heroism of blacks during and after the Civil War. The major characters reflect Harper's involvement in the abolitionist, temperance, and women's rights movements.

Carby, Hazel. " 'Of Lasting Service for the Race': The Work of Frances Ellen Watkins Harper." In *Reconstructing Womanhood: The Emergence of the Afro-*

American Woman Novelist. New York: Oxford University Press, 1987.
Places Harper's work in her cultural and political contexts, emphasizing the ways in which she attempts to inspire political action in two clearly defined audiences, white and black. This dual address was paralleled by the two major structural influences on the novel: women's fiction and the narratives of Afro-American male writers. Among the many topics discussed are the relation of *Iola Leroy* to Nina Baym's typology of women's fiction; Harper's prefiguration of the concept of the "talented tenth"; her tacit acceptance of the failure of Reconstruction; her treatment of the mulatta figure; and her political activity.

Dearborn, Mary V. *Pocahontas's Daughters: Gender and Ethnicity in American Culture*. New York: Oxford University Press, 1986.
Includes discussions of Harper in relation to the problem of mediation in ethnic women's literature and to the themes of miscegenation and the mulatto. Important as a historical event rather than a text, *Iola Leroy* attempts to mediate black experience for white readers in addition to advancing an assimilationist ideology stressing the similarities between blacks and whites. The protest element of the novel is against the hypocrisies of patriarchal society.

Elder, Arlene A. *The "Hindered Hand": Cultural Implications of Early African-American Fiction*. Westport, Conn.: Greenwood Press, 1978.
Analyzes Harper's treatment of a set of themes present in the work of most nineteenth century black novelists. Elder discusses Harper's use of the mulatto image; her association of the segregation of churches with the white fear of miscegenation; and her skill in recording the ways in which slaves used coded language to deceive their masters.

Foster, Frances Smith. Introduction to *Iola Leroy, or Shadows Uplifted* by Frances E. W. Harper. New York: Oxford University Press, 1988.
Comprehensive overview of Harper's life and writing, with emphasis on the influences shaping *Iola Leroy*, which is viewed as a transition between antebellum fiction and the Harlem Renaissance. An adequate understanding of the novel demands recognition of Harper's knowledge of the preferences of her audience, which was shaped in part by the stereotypical images of blacks in the plantation school writing of Joel Chandler Harris and Thomas Nelson Page. Summarizes both the immediate reception and later critical response to the novel.

"Frances Ellen Watkins Harper." In *Twentieth-Century Literary Criticism*, vol. 14, edited by Dennis Poupard and James E. Person, Jr. Detroit: Gale Research, 1984.
Compilation of materials, including a biographical headnote, relating primarily to Harper's poetry but including some commentary on *Iola Leroy*. Valuable for

excerpts from early materials including statements on Harper by abolitionist William Lloyd Garrison and William Still; and early Afro-American critics
W. E. B. DuBois and Benjamin Brawley. Reprints segments of critical commentary on *Iola Leroy* by Hugh Gloster, Robert Bone, and J. Saunders Redding.
Lists additional sources of information, including other reference books.

Redding, J. Saunders. "Let Freedom Ring." In *To Make a Poet Black*. Chapel Hill:
University of North Carolina Press, 1939. Reprint. Ithaca, N.Y.: Cornell University Press, 1988.
Identifies Harper (who is discussed under her maiden name of Watkins) as the
first black writer to attempt to direct Afro-American literature away from an
exclusive focus on the propagandistic end of abolition. In contrast to this
tendency in her poetry, *Iola Leroy* is frankly propagandistic. Forced, overwrit-
ten, and sensationalistic, it is a failure as a novel.

Selected Title

Iola Leroy
Bone, Robert. "Novels of the Talented Tenth." In *The Negro Novel in America*. New
Haven, Conn.: Yale University Press, 1965.
A transitional work, *Iola Leroy* combines elements of abolitionism with incip-
ient attacks on caste. In part because Harper was sixty-seven years old when
she wrote the novel, it shows little connection with the work of other novelists
of her generation. Her social consciousness, formed by abolitionism, did not
encompass post-Reconstruction repression.

Bruce, Dickson D., Jr. "Foundations of a Literary Tradition." In *Black American
Writing from the Nadir: The Evolution of a Literary Tradition, 1877-1915*. Baton
Rouge: Louisiana State University Press, 1989.
Discusses *Iola LeRoy* as representative of the attempt to "indicate more positive bases" for the black identity of mixed-race protagonists in turn of the
century fiction. Using Iola's life to comment on the central issues of the era,
Harper emphasizes the central theme of "identity and courage" reflected in the
protagonist's choice to remain with her own people. Harper celebrates a black
community within which it is possible both "to maintain genteel ideals and
find a satisfying way of life."

Campbell, Jane. "Female Paradigms in France Harper's *Iola Leroy* and Pauline
Hopkins's *Contending Forces*." In *Mythic Black Fiction: The Transformation
of History*. Knoxville: University of Tennessee Press, 1986.
Discusses Harper's "mythmaking" as a response to the political and cultural
barriers confronting blacks in the post-Reconstruction era. Like Pauline
Hopkins, Harper lauds white American ideals such as the Caucasian standard
of beauty and uncritical admiration of Anglo-Saxon culture. Harper employs

conventions associated with the woman's romance to support her central notion that black women possess the power to effect historical transformation.

Carby, Hazel. Introduction to *Iola Leroy*. Boston: Beacon Press, 1987.
Identifies Harper's novel as a major work of the black woman's renaissance of the 1890's. Carby places the novel in the context of black women's intellectual life at the turn of the century, paralleling Harper's project with those of Ida B. Wells, Anna Julia Cooper, and Victoria Earle Matthews. Intended as a form of political intervention, *Iola Leroy* attempts to create a coherent vision of the relation between mental and manual labor, symbolized in terms of the intellectual and folk communities.

Christian, Barbara. "Shadows Uplifted." In *Black Women Novelists: The Development of a Tradition, 1892-1976*. Westport, Conn.: Greenwood Press, 1980.
Iola LeRoy describes the rise of a black middle class, headed by mulattoes, that aspires to realize the central values of Western Christian civilization. The need to refute stereotypes of black women as mammies or loose women leads Harper to create a heroine who is essentially a missionary to her race.

_____ . "The Uses of History: Frances Harper's *Iola Leroy, Shadows Uplifted*." In *Black Feminist Criticism*. Elmsford, N.Y.: Pergamon Press, 1985.
Approaches *Iola Leroy* as a part of the search for a coherent historical pattern capable of illuminating the work of contemporary black women novelists. Focuses on the question of why Harper's work focuses on exceptional middle-class black women and reveals little of the knowledge of the broader black experience that Harper possessed, as is clear from her journalistic writing. Argues that the conventions of the romance form dictated a particular approach to changing the racial attitudes of the audience, which consisted primarily of white middle-class women.

Gloster, Hugh. "Negro Fiction to World War I." In *Negro Voices in American Fiction*. Chapel Hill: University of North Carolina Press, 1948. Reprint. New York: Russell & Russell, 1965.
Views *Iola Leroy* "almost wholly" as the product of Harper's reading of William Wells Brown's *Clotelle*. The novel helps establish the convention of developing well-mannered, educated black characters to offset the stock figures of the plantation tradition. Despite its sentimentality and idealism, the novel is historically significant as an early attempt to counteract stereotypes.

Kinney, James. "Black Voices, 1891-1914." In *Amalgamation! Race, Sex, and Rhetoric in the Nineteenth-Century American Novel*. Westport, Conn.: Greenwood Press, 1985.
Places *Iola Leroy* in the context of literary treatments of miscegenation. In

addition to countering the common plantation tradition stereotypes of the mulatto, Harper adds another significant dimension to the fictional treatment of the mulatto by treating interracial sex not as an awesome taboo, but as a common fact of life. Harper's primary concern is not with the period of slavery, but with the problem of the freed mulatto after the war.

Lewis, Vashti. "The Near-White Female in Frances Ellen Harper's *Iola Leroy*." *Phylon* 45 (1984): 314-322.
Criticizes Harper for unwittingly perpetuating an image of black women that "suggests that those who have dark skin and whose hair is not straight are not only ugly but also never experience tragedy in their lives." Lewis argues that the harshness of this conclusion should be somewhat mitigated by a recognition that Harper utilized the mulatto stereotype as a way of confronting powerful literary and social forces. Her white audience was willing to sympathize more deeply with racial issues connected with the fate of near-white women with essentially white value structures.

Washington, Mary Helen. "Uplifting the Women and the Race: The Forerunners— Harper and Hopkins." In *Invented Lives: Narratives of Black Women, 1860-1960*. Garden City, N.Y.: Anchor Press, 1987.
The need to defend black women and men against vicious stereotypes exerts a dominating influence on Harper's fiction. Rejecting the concept as marriage as an emotional and economic refuge, Harper gives some attention to women's interaction with other women, their political views, and the possibility of their independence. Although she politicizes marriage as a source of political support as well as romantic attachment, Harper does not fully separate herself from the values associated with the "cult of true womanhood."

Watson, Carol McAlpine. "Uplift and Protest, 1891-1920." In *Prologue: The Novels of Black American Women, 1891-1965*. Westport, Conn.: Greenwood Press, 1985.
The inspirational quality of the protest in *Iola Leroy* reflects Harper's belief that white Americans would not knowingly oppress other decent people. She advances positive images of blacks as models to be emulated. The major conflicts in the novel involve issues of loyalty to race, family, and friends. Discusses Harper's involvement with the temperance movement.

PAULINE HOPKINS

Biography

Campbell, Jane. "Pauline Elizabeth Hopkins." In *Afro-American Writers Before the Harlem Renaissance*, edited by Trudier Harris. Vol. 50 of *Dictionary of Literary Biography*. Detroit: Bruccoli Clark, 1986.
Lengthy biographical sketch recognizing Hopkins' work in theater, the short story, and journalism but stressing the central importance of *Contending Forces* to her reputation. Superficially related to the "women's novels" of the era, *Contending Forces* is a historical romance designed to acquaint Hopkins' predominantly white audience with the historical roles and future potential. Hopkins' work anticipates that of genteel Harlem Renaissance writers such as Jessie Fauset.

Lamping, Marilyn. "Pauline Elizabeth Hopkins." In *American Women Writers*, vol. 2, edited by Lina Mainiero. New York: Frederick Ungar, 1980.
Biographical entry including brief commentary on *Contending Forces*. Bibliography lists entries in other reference works.

Shockley, Ann Allen. "Pauline Elizabeth Hopkins." In *Afro-American Women Writers 1746-1933*. Boston: G. K. Hall, 1988.
Biographical headnote to excerpt from *Contending Forces*, incorporating Shockley's biographical essay originally published in *Phylon* 33 in 1972. Discusses Hopkins' experience as editor, journalist, novelist, playwright, and singer. Emphasizes Hopkins' involvement with the *Colored American Magazine*.

Commentary

Bruce, Dickson D., Jr. "The Color Line and the Meaning of Race." In *Black American Writing from the Nadir: The Evolution of a Literary Tradition, 1877-1915*. Baton Rouge: Louisiana State University Press, 1989.
Discusses Hopkins' short fiction and Iola Leroy as sentimental protest fiction, emphasizing the "depth of Hopkins' assimilationism." Demonstrating the alternative to the sad fate of the tragic mulatto, Hopkins takes the assimilationist argument to its logical conclusion, arguing that "happiness is tied not simply to the absence of exclusion but to the open, ready inclusion of blacks in the larger society." Notes Hopkins' acceptance of a hereditarian position emphasizing individual rather than racial ancestry.

Carby, Hazel. Introduction to *The Magazine Novels of Pauline Hopkins*. New York: Oxford University Press, 1988.

In addition to clarifying Hopkins' formal and political development following the publication of *Contending Forces*, her magazine fiction provides the foundation for an understanding of black popular fiction in the United States. In contrast to the discursive scenes in *Contending Forces*, the magazine fiction expresses social conflict in terms of physical action. Includes detailed analysis of the audience and economics of *The Colored American Magazine*, where the works first appeared; and a short biography of Hopkins emphasizing her awareness of the politics of oppression.

——————— . " 'Of What Use Is Fiction?': Pauline Elizabeth Hopkins" and " 'All the Fire and Romance': The Magazine Fiction of Pauline Hopkins." In *Reconstructing Womanhood: The Emergence of the Afro-American Woman Novelist*. New York: Oxford University Press, 1987.
Wide-ranging discussion of Hopkins' fiction, emphasizing her attempt to encourage her readers to resurrect the spirit of abolitionism. Articulating a complex critique of the pervasive imperialist discourse of the time, *Contending Forces* demonstrates that the political issue behind lynching was not the threat of black sexuality but the potential power of the black vote. Hopkins' treatment of black women emphasizes the ways in which the black female body is colonized by white male power.

Clark, Edward. "Boston Black and White." *Black American Literature Forum* 19 (Summer, 1985): 83-89.
Cites *Contending Forces* and *Of One Blood* in support of the thesis that Afro-American writers portray Boston differently from white novelists. Like other black novelists, Hopkins projects an image of Boston that contrasts sharply with the city's liberal image.

Dearborn, Mary V. "Miscegenation and the Mulatto, Inheritance and Incest: The Pocahontas Marriages, Part II." In *Pocahontas's Daughters: Gender and Ethnicity in American Culture*. New York: Oxford University Press, 1986.
The meaning of interracial romance provides the thematic center of Hopkins' fiction. Especially in her magazine fiction, Hopkins uses melodramatic elements to reveal the remarkable contradictions created by miscegenation. Emphasizes the significance of gothic conventions, particularly the quality of the "uncanny." The mulatto herself is a kind of uncanny text about the coherence and limits of the self. *Of One Blood* is almost a survey of gothic conventions: incest, the return of the repressed in the reanimation of the dead; suicide; and hauntings.

"Pauline Elizabeth Hopkins." In *Twentieth-Century Literary Criticism*, vol. 28, edited by Dennis Poupard. Detroit: Gale Research, 1988.
Compilation of materials including a biographical headnote, a reprint of Hopkins' preface to *Contending Forces*, and a letter and Hopkins' reply pub-

lished in *The Colored American Magazine* in 1903. Also includes excerpts from commentary by Hugh Gloster, Gwendolyn Brooks, Judith Berzon, and Claudia Tate.

Tate, Claudia. "Pauline Hopkins: Our Literary Foremother." In *Conjuring: Black Women, Fiction, and Literary Tradition*, edited by Marjorie Pryse and Hortense J. Spillers. Bloomington: Indiana University Press, 1985.

Hopkins combines the concerns of late nineteenth century black writers who dramatized racial injustice with those of white women writers whose works acclaim Christian virtue. *Contending Forces* presents a program for racial uplift based on black responsibility for advancement. Concepts of duty, virtue, controlled emotion, the institution of marriage, and the vote are key elements of Hopkins' program.

Selected Title

Contending Forces

Brooks, Gwendolyn. Afterword to *Contending Forces*. Carbondale: Southern Illinois University Press, 1978.

Focuses on the tension between Hopkins' assimilationist beliefs and the reality of rage that breaks through her novel intermittently. Hopkins' uncritical acceptance of racist attitudes toward skin color and beauty reveals that she was in some ways "a continuing slave." Nonetheless, her novel is an important piece of testimony, an "essential Black statement of defense and definition." Brooks speculates that the continued presence of the injustices which Hopkins identified in the nineteenth century would have led her to embrace a nationalist perspective if she had lived until the 1970's.

Byrd, James W. "Stereotypes of White Characters in Early Negro Novels." *CLA Journal* 1 (November, 1957): 28-35.

Cites *Contending Forces* several times in the course of an analysis of stereotyping of white characters in Negro novels written before World War I. Notes that Bill Samson conforms to the stereotype of the "poor white villain"; Charles Montford to that of the "kind aristocrat"; Anson Pollock to that of the "mean planter;" and Bill to that of the "brutal overseer."

Campbell, Jane. "Female Paradigms in Frances Harper's *Iola Leroy* and Pauline Hopkins' *Contending Forces*." In *Mythic Black Fiction: The Transformation of History*. Knoxville: University of Tennessee Press, 1986.

Reads *Contending Forces* as a response to stereotypical images of blacks that contributed to an oppressive nineteenth century political context. Hopkins challenges readers to contextualize their myths in order to understand their historical origins. She urges solidarity among women for the purpose of engendering self-esteem and historical transformation. Her primary mythmaking strategy is the romance form of nineteenth century white women's writing.

Gloster, Hugh. "Negro Fiction to World War I." In *Negro Voices in American Fiction*. Chapel Hill: University of North Carolina Press, 1948. Reprint. New York: Russell & Russell, 1965.
Brief discussion emphasizing Hopkins' belief in fiction as an instrument of racial uplift. Badly written and sharing the weaknesses of its genre, *Contending Forces* is most interesting for its interesting sidelights concerning the struggles of the middle-class black family.

Overton, Betty J. "At Best Lukewarm." *Callaloo* 7 (October, 1979): 119-120.
Negative review of reprint edition of *Contending Forces* claiming that the novel fails both in artistic and political terms. The novel reads like a fairytale populated by contrived characters representing black virtue. The characters encounter neither personal nor overt oppressions, rendering the possibility of true self-revelation remote. Though she lacks the artistic power of Fauset or Larsen, Hopkins anticipates aspects of the middle-class domestic novel of the Harlem Renaissance.

Washington, Mary Helen. "Uplifting the Women and the Race: The Forerunners — Harper and Hopkins." In *Invented Lives: Narratives of Black Women, 1860-1960*. Garden City, N.Y.: Anchor Press, 1987.
Although *Contending Forces* rejects the sentimental novel's view of marriage as an economic and emotional refuge for helpless women, Hopkins has not entirely repudiated an ideology that ultimately supports white supremacy. The social hierarchy in her work places dark-skinned blacks in an inferior position to light-skinned blacks. Hopkins' submerged anger creates patterns of avoidance and ambivalence in her treatment of women.

Watson, Carol McAlpine. "Uplift and Protest, 1891-1920." In *Prologue: The Novels of Black American Women, 1891-1965*. Westport, Conn.: Greenwood Press, 1985.
The most forceful protest novel written by a black woman prior to *The Street*, *Contending Forces* criticizes both racial oppression and the self-inflicted compromises of black accommodationists. Discusses the character of Arthur Lewis as a representation of Booker T. Washington. Stresses Hopkins' belief that only a full-scale moral campaign similar to the abolition movement could defeat lynching and racial injustice.

Yarborough, Richard. Introduction to *Contending Forces*. New York: Oxford University Press, 1988.

Biographical sketch including detailed discussion of *Contending Forces*. Emphasizes Hopkins' early interest in theater and black history; her involvement with the *Colored American* magazine; and her position in the Washington-DuBois debate. *Contending Forces* uses conventions of the sentimental novel as part of an overall strategy intended to refute stereotypical images of blacks. Her primary intention is to facilitate racial uplift by presenting black readers with moral guidance through exemplary characters.

KRISTIN HUNTER

Biography

O'Neale, Sondra. "Kristin Hunter." In *Afro-American Fiction Writers After 1955*, edited by Thadious M. Davis and Trudier Harris. Vol. 33 of *Dictionary of Literary Biography*. Detroit: Bruccoli Clark, 1984.
Substantial reference entry incorporating biographical sketch and analysis of Hunter's novels. Biographical section notes the importance of education in her family background and the difficulties she experienced in committing herself to a writing career against her parents' wishes. Her novels are important as part of black women's literature; as children's books that have reached a neglected audience; and as protests against the suffering of black people in urban settings. One of the few sources of information on Hunter that gives detailed attention to works other than *God Bless the Child*.

Reilly, John M. "Hunter, Kristin (Elaine, née Eggleston)." In *Contemporary Novelists*, 4th ed., edited by D. L. Kirkpatrick. New York: St. Martin's Press, 1986.
Reference entry including biographical outline; list of publications, including uncollected short stories; and analysis of *God Bless the Child*, *The Landlord* and *The Lakestown Rebellion*. Quotes Hunter's comment that while all of her work is about black-white relations, she has moved from an "objective" to a more subjective stance. Reilly emphasizes Hunter's portrayal of the contradiction between "reality as it is experienced by the black urban poor and the false optimism of the popular story." *The Lakestown Rebellion*, which is a symbolic enactment of Afro-American cultural history, marks Hunter's fullest achievement.

Tate, Claudia C. *Black Women Writers at Work*. New York: Continuum, 1983.
Includes an interview with Hunter in which she comments on the change in black political energy since the 1960's; the importance of a black female perspective to her writing; her writing process; her sense of responsibility to her audience; the difference in black male and female perspectives in literature; the use of humor in her work; and the role of black women in resolving the debate on sexism.

Commentary

"Kristen Hunter." In *Children's Literature Review*, vol. 3, edited by Gerard J. Senick. Detroit: Gale Research, 1978.
Compilation of materials related to Hunter's children's writing. Includes a

brief interview in which she comments on the absence of black characters in books she read while growing up, and a transcript of a talk she delivered on *The Soul Brothers and Sister Lou*, in which she comments on the negative elements of her portrayal of ghetto life. Reprints excerpts from reviews of *Boss Cat*, *The Survivors*, and *The Soul Brothers and Sister Lou*. Valuable for its inclusion of materials originally published in sources focusing specifically on children's literature.

"Kristin Hunter." In *Contemporary Literary Criticism*, vol. 35, edited by Daniel G. Marowski. Detroit: Gale Research, 1985.
Compilation of materials related to Hunter's adult and juvenile fiction, including a biographical headnote and a listing of entries in other reference sources. Includes excerpts from Gwendolyn Brooks's review of *The Landlord* and Noel Schraufnagel's discussion of Hunter in addition to reviews of *God Bless the Child*, *The Landlord*, *The Soul Brothers and Sister Lou*, *Lou in the Limelight*, *The Survivors*, and *The Lakestown Rebellion*.

Schraufnagel, Noel. "Accommodationism in the Sixties." In *From Apology to Protest: The Black American Novel*. Deland, Fla.: Everett/Edwards, 1973.
Discusses Hunter's three novels in relation to the dominant accommodationist approach in Afro-American fiction of the 1960's. *God Bless the Child* is a great novel that stands alone in terms of categorization and literary quality. The story of Rosie Fleming is a typical American one in that she loses her humanity as a result of her pursuit of material goods. An accommodationist novel inasmuch as the protagonist attempts to adjust by embracing white values, it provides a complex analysis of Rosie's actual psychology. Although it is written in the comic mode, *The Landlord* is another impressive performance. Of lesser magnitude than the first two novels, *The Soul Brothers and Sister Lou* argues for solving racial problems through rehabilitation of the ghettoes.

Selected Titles

God Bless the Child
Bims, Hamilton. Review of *God Bless the Child*. *Negro Digest* 14 (April, 1965): 52, 93.
Unfavorable review criticizing Hunter's acceptance of clichés such as vice, sensuality, brutish materialism, and black inferiority. Her one-dimensional approach badly misrepresents black life. Hunter's psychological descriptions and her high-tension dialogue are redeeming qualities.

Early, Gerald. "Working Girl Blues: Mothers, Daughters, and the Image of Billie Holiday in Kristin Hunter's *God Bless the Child*." *Black American Literature*

Forum 20 (Winter, 1986): 423-442.

Detailed analysis of the significance of Billie Holiday and the song "God Bless the Child" in Hunter's novel. The evocation of Holiday links the life of an ordinary black girl with the prototypical rise and fall of one of the few black women to make a major impact on both popular and highbrow American culture. Indirectly endorsing the feminist plea for reconstruction of the mother-daughter relationship, Hunter employs the specific song to focus on the disruptive effect of money on parent-child bonding.

Saal, Rollene W. "What Made Rosie Run?" *The New York Times Book Review* 69 (September 20, 1964): 36.

Mixed review. Although *God Bless the Child* assumes tragic proportions, Hunter's bitterness is unrelenting. Ultimately, Rosie does not attain a profound understanding or reach a new equilibrium. The real impetus of the novel comes from the opposing values represented by Rosie's amoral, earthy mother and her genteel grandmother.

Turner, Darwin. Introduction to *God Bless the Child*. Washington, D.C.: Howard University Press, 1986.

Places the novel in the context of the "Second Reconstruction," the period of black political gains in the late 1950's and early 1960's. Telling an intensely tragic story, *God Bless the Child* transcends questions of race and criticizes the emptiness of the materialism of the American dream. Includes a biographical sketch and brief discussion of *The Landlord* and Hunter's children's fiction.

Watson, Carol McAlpine. "Racial Issues and Universal Themes, 1946-1965." In *Prologue: The Novels of Black American Women, 1891-1965*. Westport, Conn.: Greenwood Press, 1985.

Contrasts Rosie's development with that of Selina in Marshall's *Brown Girl, Brownstones*. Rosie's life resembles that of a highly active, determined rat caught in a maze. She fails not for lack of effort or courage, but because her values are misplaced. Includes a detailed discussion of Hunter's portrait of Rosie's grandmother, a self-rejecting, malevolent figure whose primary loyalty is to whites. The environmental and personal sources of conflict in Rosie interact synergistically.

Williams, Gladys Margaret. "Blind and Seeing Eyes in the Novel *God Bless the Child*." *Obsidian* 1 (Summer, 1975): 18-26.

Discussion of the techniques used to present the theme of "the futile pursuit of the American dream." Hunter uses tangential characters, parallel subplots, and crucial symbols such as the rainbow bowls to frame her central narrative. She develops her central theme by associating different modes of perception with Rosie, her mother, and grandmother, each of whom has a different relationship to delusion, illusion, and fantasy.

The Landlord

Brooks, Gwendolyn. "Tenant Problems." *The Washington Post Book Week* (May 8, 1966): 14.

Mildly unfavorable review criticizing Hunter's perpetuation of old stereotypes, including the sexual Negro woman and the noisy Black nationalist puppet. Questions the appropriateness of these images for black people who are working hard to confront themselves. The characters in *The Landlord* are not lovable or loathable, but "lookable" as a result of Hunter's "inventiveness and earnestly exercised power."

Chapman, Abraham. "White Invisible Man." *Saturday Review* 49 (May 14, 1966): 45.

Favorable review of *The Landlord* as a "refreshing expression of the diversity of American Negro writing." Emphasizes the satirical elements of the book, which combines absurdity and surrealism with slapstick, the grotesque, and down-to-earth realism. Hunter cuts through stereotypes and myths concerning race to reach the core of "essential human contact and friendship." The most important context for understanding the book is the American quest for identity in an age of alienation.

Sarris, Andrew. "Good Intentions." *The New York Times Book Review* 71 (April 24, 1966): 41.

Favorable review emphasizing the "relative lightness" of *The Landlord*, which represents "an act of emotional restraint, a triumph of form over feeling." Contrasts Hunter's "urbane view of race relations" with the fiery perspectives of James Baldwin and LeRoi Jones. Expresses surprise that a black novelist can generate sympathy for a character with the class condescension of Elgar, who is "an idealist in an insane sort of way."

Whitlow, Roger. "1960 to the Present: Satire, the Past—and Themes of Armageddon." In *Black American Literature: A Critical History*. Chicago: Littlefield, Adams, 1974.

Includes a biographical sketch and analysis of *The Landlord* as a comic account of Elgar's "search for love." Hunter satirizes several recognizable "race types," including the black deluded by his sense of martyrdom, the suffering "super-liberal," and the black who has risen above racial conflict. Hunter has a gift for beautiful writing based on her keen ear for understated tongue-in-cheek humor.

ZORA NEALE HURSTON

Biography

Burke, Virginia M. "Zora Neale Hurston and Fannie Hurst as They Saw Each Other." *CLA Journal* 20 (June, 1977): 435-447.
Examines the relationship between Hurston and Fannie Hurst, comparing the reports included in the autobiographical writing of each. While Hurston was a diverting minor episode in Hurst's life, Hurst played a major role in introducing Hurston to the New York literary scene.

Dance, Daryl C. "Zora Neale Hurston." In *American Women Writers: Bibliographical Essays*, edited by Maurice Duke, Jackson R. Bryer, and M. Thomas Inge. Westport, Conn.: Greenwood Press, 1983.
Fundamental resource for the study of Hurston's novels. Dance's lengthy bibliographical essay includes sections on previous bibliographies; editions of Hurston's works; manuscripts and letters; biographical sources; and criticism, including sections concerning reviews and commentary on each of her novels.

Hemenway, Robert. *Zora Neale Hurston: A Literary Biography*. Urbana: University of Illinois Press, 1977.
Standard biography of Hurston. Details her Florida childhood; her relations with her patron; her role in the Harlem Renaissance; her interaction with other black writers such as Langston Hughes; her use of folk materials; and the relatively obscure final years of her life. Includes interpretations of each of her novels along with summaries of their reception. Along with Alice Walker's introduction, Hemenway's biography played a major role in inspiring the 1980's recognition of Hurston as a major American writer.

Howard, Lillie P. "Zora Neale Hurston." In *Afro-American Writers from the Harlem Renaissance to 1940*, edited by Trudier Harris. Vol. 51 of *Dictionary of Literary Biography*. Detroit: Bruccoli Clark, 1987.
Discussion of Hurston's work in all genres, incorporating biographical information. Presents Hurston's works as manifestos of selfhood that affirm the positive elements of black life. Gives substantial attention to Hurston's work and life following her move away from New York after the publication of *Their Eyes Were Watching God*.

Huggins, Nathan. *Harlem Renaissance*. New York: Oxford University Press, 1971.
Includes sections concerning Hurston's approach to folklore, which is less scholarly than that of Arthur Fauset. Places Hurston in the context of the Harlem Renaissance, emphasizing her relationship with her patron. Summar-

izes the response of other Renaissance writers such as Langston Hughes and Wallace Thurman to Hurston's personality.

Hurston, Zora Neale. *Dust Tracks on a Road*. Philadelphia: J. B. Lippincott, 1942. Reprint, with additional chapters. Urbana: University of Illinois Press, 1984.
Hurston's autobiography, including previously unpublished chapters concerning issues such as race and international politics. Among the topics Hurston discusses are her childhood in an all-black Florida town; the wanderings of her adolescent years; her academic studies and involvement with various figures of the Harlem Renaissance; and her approach to Afro-American folk culture.

Pettis, Joyce. "Zora Neale Hurston." In *American Women Writers*, vol. 2, edited by Lina Mainiero. New York: Frederick Ungar, 1980.
Biographical entry including brief commentary on *Jonah's Gourd Vine*, *Their Eyes Were Watching God*, and *Seraph on the Suwanee*, which includes Hurston's second fully delineated protagonist. *Seraph on the Suwanee* offers a psychologically complete view of the forces that make the life of a Southern rural woman a continuous struggle. Bibliography includes a list of entries in other reference works.

Commentary

Bell, Bernard W. "The Harlem Renaissance and the Search for New Modes of Narrative." In *The Afro-American Novel and Its Tradition*. Amherst: University of Massachusetts Press, 1987.
Hurston's primary legacy is the inspirational love story and compelling modern feminist vision of an autonomous woman in *Their Eyes Were Watching God*. Alienated from both the legitimate and the spurious middle-class values of the black community, Janie is more faithful to her symbolic significance as "bodacious woman" than to the traditional values of black women. Hurston's imaginative use of folklore gives distinction to her pastoral images of rural black life.

Bloom, Harold, ed. *Zora Neale Hurston: Modern Critical Views*. New York: Chelsea House, 1986.
Anthology of commentary on Hurston from her contemporaries to the 1980's. Includes selections from black writers such as Langston Hughes and Alice Walker in addition to many of the essays annotated in this book. Introduction emphasizes the similarity between Hurston's "heroic vitalism" and the worldviews of Theodore Dreiser and D.H. Lawrence. For Hurston, power is identified with the demand for more life. She remains free from the ideological demands that distort reception of her best work.

Bone, Robert. "Aspects of the Racial Past." In *The Negro Novel in America*. New Haven, Conn.: Yale University Press, 1965.

Interprets *Jonah's Gourd Vine* and *Their Eyes Were Watching God* in relation to Harlem Renaissance-era motifs. Although *Jonah's Gourd Vine* has a rich verbal texture, Hurston's treatment of folklore is too anthropological for effective fiction. Even as it reflects the cultural dualism of the Renaissance, *Their Eyes Were Watching God* employs folklore to sound universal themes such as the frustration of individual dreams. Inspired by a failed love affair, the novel ranks with *Native Son* as the best novel of the period.

Brawley, Benjamin. "The New Realists." In *The Negro Genius*. New York: Dodd, Mead, 1937.

Brief comment mentioning *Jonah's Gourd Vine* and *Mules and Men*. Emphasizes Hurston's role as folklorist. The story lines of *Jonah's Gourd Vine* are not well integrated; any interest the novel has derives primarily from the folklore scenes.

Brown, Sterling. "Southern Realism." In *The Negro in American Fiction*. Washington, D.C.: Associates in Negro Folk Education, 1937. Reprint. New York: Atheneum, 1969.

Hurston's command of folklore is unmatched by any previous black novelist. Omitting the bitterness of the rural community, *Mules and Men* presents an image that is somewhat too pastoral. *Their Eyes Were Watching God* is "informed and sympathetic." While there are elements of protest discernible, and while the sketches of the folk community command attention, the love story and the poetic folk speech are the central concerns.

Davis, Thadious M. "Southern Standard-Bearers in the New Negro Renaissance." In *The History of Southern Literature*, edited by Louis D. Rubin et al. Baton Rouge: Louisiana State University Press, 1985.

Discusses Hurston as one of a number of Southern black writers who played significant roles in the Harlem Renaissance. Emphasizes Hurston's interest in folklore and her use of folk elements in her novels. Hurston's primary achievement is her use of the oral tradition to express the vitality of the Southern black heritage. She dismisses the negative impact of racism on her self-contained black worlds.

Dearborn, Mary V. "Black Women Authors and the Harlem Renaissance." In *Pocahontas's Daughters: Gender and Ethnicity in American Culture*. New York: Oxford University Press, 1986.

Views Hurston as the crucial figure linking the Harlem Renaissance and the current renaissance of black women's literature. Despite the fact that her authorship was compromised and threatened, Hurston managed to create an

American classic in *Their Eyes Were Watching God*. Provides a detailed discussion of the financial dependence on others that characterized Hurston's career. Concludes that, even as Hurston played the role of trickster, her implicit "contract" with her patron was remarkably clear to both parties. Relates Hurston's triumph and heroism to those of Janie in *Their Eyes Were Watching God*.

Ford, Nick Aaron. "Postscript." In *The Contemporary Negro Novel: A Study in Race Relations*. Boston: Meador, 1936. Reprint. College Park, Md.: McGrath, 1968.
Report on a visit with Hurston in Florida. Ford quotes Hurston's statement that she no longer thinks in terms of race: "I am interested in the problems of *individuals*, white ones and black ones." Ford comments that attitudes such as Hurston's create problems for other black writers, who, Ford believes, have a primary political duty to their race. Comments briefly on *Jonah's Gourd Vine*, which, despite Hurston's excellent grasp of her material, fails to attain the status of a masterpiece.

Gates, Henry Louis, Jr. "A Negro Way of Saying." *The New York Times Book Review* 90 (April 21, 1985): 1, 43, 45.
Review of reprint editions of *Dust Tracks on a Road* and *Moses, Man of the Mountain* focusing on the question of why Hurston's importance was not recognized for so long. Gates notes that Hurston's mythic realism was regarded as counterrevolutionary by proponents of social realism and that her politics have presented problems for even her most enthusiastic supporters. Nonetheless her achievements have established her as the most important literary source for many contemporary black women writers. Includes a brief comment on *Moses, Man of the Mountain*, suggesting Frances E.W. Harper's "Moses: A Story of the Nile," which also uses multiple voices to present Moses as a conjurer, as the actual source of Hurston's novel.

Gayle, Addison, Jr. "The Outsider." In *The Way of the New World: The Black Novel in America*. Garden City, N.Y.: Anchor Press, 1976.
Hurston's novels image the strength and promise of African-American culture. Hurston went to the proletariat to seek values and to re-create images distorted by white nationalist propaganda. Hurston's treatment of the liberated black woman emphasizes their status as modern women patterned upon historical figures such as Harriet Tubman and Sojourner Truth. Discusses *Jonah's Gourd Vine* and *Their Eyes Were Watching God*.

_____ . "Zora Neale Hurston: The Politics of Freedom." In *A Rainbow Round Her Shoulder: Zora Neale Hurston Symposium Papers*, edited by Ruthe T. Sheffey. Baltimore: Morgan State University Press, 1982.

Hurston anticipates existentialist thought in her insistence that freedom is possible even in the shadows of oppression. To achieve such freedom, Hurston makes it clear that it is necessary to abandon the American value system and become an outsider. Gayle opens with a discussion of the reasons for Hurston's neglect which include the general exclusion of blacks from academic recognition; the impact of sexism; and her refusal to adapt the dominant naturalistic mode of her time.

Gloster, Hugh. "Negro Fiction of the Depression." In *Negro Voices in American Fiction*. Chapel Hill: University of North Carolina Press, 1948. Reprint. New York: Russell & Russell, 1965.

Neglecting the issue of racial tensions, Hurston is more interested in folklore than in social criticism. Compares Hurston's use of folklore favorably with that of Julia Peterkin. Her grasp of characterization shows improvement from *Jonah's Gourd Vine* to *Their Eyes Were Watching God*.

Hemenway, Robert. "Hurston's Buzzards and Elijah's Ravens." In *A Rainbow Round Her Shoulder: Zora Neale Hurston Symposium Papers*, edited by Ruthe T. Sheffey. Baltimore: Morgan State University Press, 1982.

Discusses Hurston's use of the folk tradition, emphasizing the importance of the group of storytellers on the porch of the general store, who are "absolutely central to Hurston's creative imagination." Compares Hurston's practice with that of black male novelists such as Leon Forrest and Ralph Ellison. Analyzes Hurston's presentation of the relationship between cultural frame and folk material in relation to Alice Walker's story "Nineteen Fifty-Five" and the Uncle Remus stories of Joel Chandler Harris.

_____ . "Zora Neale Hurston and the Eatonville Anthropology." In *The Harlem Renaissance Remembered*, edited by Arna Bontemps. New York: Dodd, Mead, 1972.

Emphasizes the importance of Hurston's studies with anthropologist Franz Boas to her participated in the Harlem Renaissance. She was attracted to the scientific study of folklore because it offered a pattern of meaning for material that white racism constantly distorted into stereotypes. Emphasizes the importance of the "Eatonville Anthology" published in *Fire!* to Hurston's developing ability to remove herself from her experience in order to give it form and meaning.

Holloway, Karla F. C. *The Character of the Word: The Texts of Zora Neale Hurston*. Westport, Conn.: Greenwood Press, 1987.

Examines Hurston's adaptation of African conceptions of "the word" to affirm the black self. Contradicting interpretations of black speech as an unsuccessful attempt to mimic white language, Hurston's ability to give spiritual substance to her characters through subtle variations of language—in both direct quotation and narration—gives substance and form to her own "self." Includes summary of Hurston's developing attitude toward language; and detailed discussion of African philosophies of language as they effect each of Hurston's novels.

Howard, Lillie P. "Marriage: Zora Neale Hurston's System of Values." *CLA Journal* 21 (December, 1977): 256-268.
Discusses Hurston's treatment of marriage in several short stories, *Jonah's Gourd Vine*, *Their Eyes Were Watching God*, and *Seraph on the Suwanee*. Rejecting romantic portraits of marriage, Hurston takes a realistic approach acknowledging infidelity, jealousy, violence, and hatred. Her images of successful marriages emphasize the importance of courage, honesty, love, trust, respect, understanding, and a willingness to work together.

———————— . *Zora Neale Hurston*. Boston: Twayne, 1980.
Survey of Hurston's life and career, including analysis of each of her novels. Howard emphasizes Hurston's affirmation of blackness in a black-denying society, identifying her as a "black nationalist when black nationalists were being discredited and deported." Identifies *Their Eyes Were Watching God* as Hurston's primary achievement largely because of its willingness to define marriage in sexual terms.

Johnson, Barbara. "Thresholds of Difference: Structures of Address in Zora Neale Hurston." In *"Race," Writing, and Difference*, edited by Henry Louis Gates, Jr. Chicago: University of Chicago Press, 1986.
Theoretical perspective on Hurston's rhetoric, including some analysis of the frame story of *Mules and Men*. Hurston shows that "questions of difference and identity" are always a function of the specific situation in which they are posed; answers are matters of strategy rather than truth. Hurston undercuts a range of oppositions such as inside/outside. She is both an example of a noncanonical writer and a commentator on the dynamics of attempts to make a statement about difference.

Jordan, June. "Notes Toward a Black Balancing of Love and Hatred." In *Civil Wars*. Boston: Beacon Press, 1981.
Reprints influential essay originally published in *Black World* magazine in 1974. Jordan argues that the widespread emphasis on Richard Wright as the most important black writer seriously distorts the reality of Afro-American experience. Hurston's celebration of the affirmative qualities of black life, based on her own childhood in an all-black town, is as significant as Wright's political confrontation with overwhelming white forces. *Their Eyes Were Watching God* is the prototypical black novel of affirmation.

Kaplan, Deborah. "Zora Neale Hurston." In *Critical Survey of Long Fiction*, vol. 4, edited by Frank N. Magill. Englewood Cliffs, N.J.: Salem Press, 1983.
Lengthy reference entry including biographical sketch and analysis of Hurston's fiction, including some attention to each of her novels. Comments on the political implications of Hurston's use of folk material, particularly in her first two novels. Hurston admires the adaptations to American life expressed in folklore, but worries about its preservation. Hurston does not represent the oppression of blacks in her novels because she refuses to view Afro-American life as impoverished.

Kilson, Marion. "The Transformation of Eatonville's Ethnographer." *Phylon* 33 (Summer, 1972): 112-119.
Discussion of Hurston's academic training in ethnography, which led her to strive for a dispassionate depiction of her rural black characters. Emphasizes that Hurston portrays her characters' frustrations over being unable to attain fundamentally bourgeois ideals. Hurston's "transformation from ethnographic artist to critical ethnographer" occurs in the early 1940's.

Lenz, Gunther H. "Southern Exposures: The Urban Experience and the Re-Construction of Black Folk Culture and Community in the Works of Richard Wright and Zora Neale Hurston." *New York Folklore Quarterly* 7 (1981): 3-39. Reprinted in *History and Tradition in Afro-American Culture*, edited by Lenz. Frankfurt: Campus Verlag, 1984.
Contrasts Hurston's approach to Afro-American folklore with that of Richard Wright. Hurston's attempt to reclaim a folk culture that had been discredited by white stereotypes helped pave the way for more realistic, historically grounded treatments of the 1930's. While Hurston is able to speak in an authentic folk voice, her treatment of the folk community is ahistorical.

Lewis, Vashti Crutcher. "The Declining Significance of the Mulatto Female as a Major Character in the Novels of Zora Neale Hurston." *CLA Journal* 28 (December, 1984): 127-149.
Identifies Hurston as the first black woman novelist to focus on major female characters who were not clearly identifiable mulatto types. In Hurston's work, physical features are secondary to women's intrinsic abilities. The marriage between light-skinned Janie and dark-skinned Tea Cake defies the pattern established by Hopkins, Harper, Larsen, and Fauset, whose mulatto heroines marry men no darker than themselves.

Lowe, John. "Hurston, Humor, and the Harlem Renaissance." In *The Harlem Renaissance Re-examined*, edited by Victor A. Kramer. New York: AMS Press, 1987.
Argues that Hurston's "outrageous sense of humor" played a significant role

both in her artistic success and in the negative response she received from her contemporaries. Summarizes biographical evidence concerning Hurston's humor and analyzes its presence in her fiction. Draws attention to the role of humor in Janie's entertaining narration in *Their Eyes Were Watching God*, and the significance of the Mrs. Turner incident in regard to Hurston's understanding of black laughter.

Newson, Adele S. *Zora Neale Hurston: A Reference Guide*. Boston: G. K. Hall, 1987.
Bibliography of sources concerning Hurston's works in all genres. Particularly valuable for listing of original reviews of her novels.

Rayson, Ann L. "The Novels of Zora Neale Hurston." *Studies in Black Literature* 5 (Winter, 1974): 1-10.
Identifies a common plot formula used in each of Hurston's novels. Her protagonists learn that traditional sexual roles offer the only hope for fulfillment. Thematically, Hurston emphasizes the need to reject bourgeois life, espousing a transcendent philosophy of unity with one's sexuality and the cosmos. Includes analysis of *Jonah's Gourd Vine*, *Their Eyes Were Watching God*, *Moses, Man of the Mountain*, and *Seraph on the Suwanee*.

Sheffey, Ruthe T., ed. *A Rainbow Round Her Shoulder: Zora Neale Hurston Symposium Papers*. Baltimore: Morgan State University Press, 1982.
Collection of papers originally presented at the first scholarly conference devoted wholly to Hurston. Intended to increase community awareness of Hurston's approach to continuing problems in black life, the papers emphasize the ways in which oral traditions influence Hurston's style, the meaning of the blues for her characters, and her vision of the positive connection between the modern black community and African cultural values. Among the contributors are Addison Gayle, Robert Hemenway, James Miller, and Joyce Ann Joyce.

Southerland, Ellease. "The Influence of Voodoo on the Fiction of Zora Neale Hurston." In *Sturdy Black Bridge: Visions of Black Women in Literature*, edited by Roseann P. Bell, Bettye J. Parker, and Beverly Guy-Sheftall. Garden City, N.Y.: Anchor Press, 1979.
After summarizing Hurston's contact with voodoo culture, Southerland catalogs her use of numerological, color, and nature imagery derived from Afro-Caribbean sources. More important, however, is her knowledge and appreciation of the emblems associated with the loa, or gods, of the voodoo pantheon. *Moses, Man of the Mountain* is Hurston's fictional attempt to give full expression to the voodoo religion. The culmination of Hurston's folklore is the form it gave her religious thought.

_____ . "Zora Neale Hurston: The Novelist-Anthropologist's Life and Work." *Black World* (August, 1974): 20-30.

Overview of Hurston's life and works through *Moses, Man of the Mountain*, which Southerland views as a folktale, elaborately related. Refuting claims that Hurston lacked a consciousness of racial issues, Southerland asserts that Hurston and Wright were the major novelists of their era. Hurston shows that African culture survived slavery and Americanization in the form of the oral tradition. Includes comments on *Jonah's Gourd Vine*, *Mules and Men*, and *Their Eyes Were Watching God*.

Turner, Darwin. *In a Minor Chord: Three Afro-American Writers and Their Search for Identity*. Carbondale: Southern Illinois University Press, 1971.

Discusses Hurston alongside Jean Toomer and Countee Cullen as examples of "wanderers," writers who were unable to resolve their search for identity through the patterns offered by the Harlem Renaissance. Highly critical of Hurston's "superficial and shallow" artistic and social judgments. Includes discussions of *Jonah's Gourd Vine*, which is damaged by its exoticism; *Their Eyes Were Watching God*, in which "all Janie wants is to love, to be loved, and to share the life of her man"; *Moses, Man of the Mountain*, which is her most accomplished book; and *Seraph on the Suwanee*, which is Hurston's most ambitious novel but suffers from a prolonged somberness of tone.

Walker, Alice. "Zora Neale Hurston: A Cautionary Tale and Partisan View" and "Looking for Zora." In *In Search of Our Mother's Gardens*. New York: Harcourt Brace Jovanovich, 1983.

Reprints of extremely influential essays which helped inspire the "rediscovery" of Hurston's works and the emergence of black women's fiction in the 1980's. Originally published in *Ms.* magazine in 1975, "Looking for Zora" describes Walker's successful search for Hurston's unmarked grave. Placing Hurston in a "trinity" of black women that includes Billie Holiday and Bessie Smith, "A Cautionary Tale" presents Hurston as an emblem for the collective struggles of black women attempting to find their voices in a hostile context.

Wall, Cheryl A. "Zora Neale Hurston: Changing Her Own Words." In *American Novelists Revisited: Essays in Feminist Criticism*, edited by Fritz Fleischmann. Boston: G. K. Hall, 1982.

Emphasizes the ways in which the black consciousness and feminist movements have generated new understandings of Hurston's works. Recognizing that black culture was in some ways sexist, Hurston nonetheless affirms that black women must attain personal identity by embracing their racial heritage. *Their Eyes Were Watching God*, in which her folk material complements the narrative without overwhelming it, is her most important book. Also includes detailed discussion of *Seraph on the Suwanee*, which restates the major themes of *Their Eyes Were Watching God* in a "misguided attempt to universalize them." Hurston was at her best when she drew her material directly from black folk culture.

Wallace, Michele. "Who Dat Say Who Dat When I Say Who Dat? Zora Neale Hurston Then and Now." *Village Voice Literary Supplement* (April, 1988): 18-21.
Overview of recent critical works on Hurston, arguing that while Hurston can legitimately contribute to the "crucial assault on the logic of binary oppositions of race, class, and sex," she should not be transformed into an unrealistic saint. Includes detailed discussion of the critical positions advanced by black women critics such as Mary Helen Washington and Barbara Christian, whose *Black Women Novelists* remains the "Bible in the field of black feminist criticism"; white women such as Susan Willis and Barbara Johnson; black men such as Henry Louis Gates, Jr., and Houston Baker; and white men such as Harold Bloom.

Washington, Mary Helen. "'I Love the Way Janie Crawford Left Her Husbands': Zora Neale Hurston's Emergent Female Hero." In *Invented Lives: Narratives of Black Women, 1860-1960*. Garden City, N.Y.: Anchor Press, 1987.
Examines the themes of women's relationship to the community and women's relationship to language in *Their Eyes Were Watching God*. While feminist critics have seized upon the text as an expression of female power, a comparison of *Their Eyes* to *Jonah's Gourd Vine* suggests that Hurston's primary concern is women's exclusion from power, particularly from the power of oral speech. Janie's final statement that experience is more important than words implicitly criticizes the tendency in black culture to celebrate orality at the expense of inner growth.

_____ . "Introduction: Zora Neale Hurston, a Woman Half in Shadow." In *I Love Myself When I Am Laughing: A Zora Neale Hurston Reader*, edited by Alice Walker. Old Westbury, N.Y.: Feminist Press, 1979.
Overview of Hurston's life and work emphasizing the ways in which the attention given to Hurston's controversial personality has inhibited objective criticism of her work. Hurston's experience demonstrates that a black woman choosing to work as an artist during the 1940's and 1950's was subjected to the same type of economic violence—generated by publishers and critics—as a black domestic.

Watson, Carol McAlpine. "Race Consciousness and Self-Criticism, 1921-1945." In *Prologue: The Novels of Black American Women, 1891-1965*. Westport, Conn.: Greenwood Press, 1985.
Emphasizes the importance of Hurston's anthropological point of view to her

treatment of moral issues. Includes a relatively lengthy discussion of *Moses, Man of the Mountain*. Written with sustained power, Moses is an allegory in which Jews represent American blacks. The spirit of asceticism and selflessness common in other novels by black women receives its most extreme expression in *Moses, Man of the Mountain*. Hurston believes that the achievement of freedom, which is finally an internal matter, requires unsparing self-sacrifice. Also includes a discussion of *Jonah's Gourd Vine* as an investigation of the tension between African and American cultures.

Willis, Miriam DeCosta. "Folklore and the Creative Artist: Lydia Cabrera and Zora Neale Hurston." *CLA Journal* 27 (September, 1983): 81-90.
Compares the use of black oral expression in the literary works of Hurston and Cuban poet Lydia Cabrera. Both writers returned to their rural homes to collect folklore after formative experiences in urban centers where they had contact with leading intellectuals and artists. Discussion of Hurston, which includes comments on *Mules and Men* and *Their Eyes Were Watching God*, centers on her use of folklore "to dramatize the humanity of Southern blacks."

Willis, Susan. "Zora Neale Hurston's Search for Self and Method." In *Specifying: Black Women Writing the American Experience*. Madison: University of Wisconsin Press, 1987.
The central project of Hurston's work is her attempt to mediate between two deeply polarized worlds. A crucial element of Hurston's incipiently modernist style is her use of images combining elements of specifying—which fixes meaning—and metaphor—which is a multireferential technique. Hurston's most compelling engagement with these issues is *Their Eyes Were Watching God*, which anticipates the dialectical form of much contemporary black women's writing. The dialectic narrative enables Hurston to articulate a vision of a future alternative to the backwards, oppressed, exclusionary community of the rural South.

Wintz, Cary D. "Literature and Politics." In *Black Culture and the Harlem Renaissance*. Houston: Rice University Press, 1988.
Includes a discussion of Hurston and the patronage system of the Harlem Renaissance era and an analysis of *Their Eyes Were Watching God*, which differs from the work of Larsen and Fauset in several ways. In addition to focussing on poor, uneducated blacks living in the rural South, Hurston creates images of strong women who endure and overcome the obstacles placed in their paths. Janie is liberated only when she defies the conventions of her community, asserts herself, and enters into a relationship with a man who loves her for herself.

"Zora Neale Hurston." In *Contemporary Literary Criticism*, vol. 30, edited by Jean C. Stine and Daniel G. Marowski. Detroit: Gale Research, 1984.

Compilation of materials including excerpts from commentary by Darwin Turner, Addison Gayle, Robert Hemenway, Alice Walker, Lillie Howard, and Cheryl Wall. Particularly valuable for its inclusion of numerous reviews of the original editions of Hurston's novels.

Selected Titles

Jonah's Gourd Vine

Daniel, Walter. "Zora Neale Hurston's John Pearson: Saint and Sinner." In *Images of the Preacher in Afro-American Literature*. Washington, D.C.: University Press of America, 1981.

John Pearson is a paradigm for the black community leader who attempts to respond to changes that he has little control over. His decline highlights the change from a personalized oral society to a mechanical nation. Acknowledging both the saint and the sinner in John's character, Hurston provides a complex and authentic image of black Christianity.

Hemenway, Robert. "Are You a Flying Lark or a Setting Dove?" In *Afro-American Literature: The Reconstruction of Instruction*, edited by Robert B. Stepto and Dexter Fisher. New York: Modern Language Association, 1979.

Uses *Jonah's Gourd Vine* to illustrate a methodological approach to the use of folklore in literature. Emphasizing the importance of the actual context to folklore, Hemenway emphasizes that the study of folklore in literature always begins and ends with the text. Examines the use of courtship rituals in *Jonah's Gourd Vine*, particularly the characters' ability to provide "correct" responses, as a key to understanding the relationship between John and Lucy.

Neal, Larry. Introduction to *Jonah's Gourd Vine*. Philadelphia: J. B. Lippincott, 1971.

The central achievement of Hurston's novel is her success in penetrating the romantic surface of rural black life. Although she tends to overwork her dialect and miss some of the real poetry of Southern black speech, she provides a compelling treatment of the theme of the search for spiritual equilibrium. Hurston develops this theme by contrasting two distinct cultural attitudes regarding spirituality. Derived from the slave experience, one conception recognizes no clear distinction between the world of the spirit and the world of the flesh; the other, derived from white Evangelical Christianity, is puritanical.

Wallace, Margaret. "Real Negro People." *The New York Times Book Review* 39 (May 6, 1934): 6-7.

Favorable review identifying *Jonah's Gourd Vine* as "the most vital and original novel about the American Negro that has yet been written by a member of the Negro race." Emphasizes the "brilliantly authentic flavor" of Hurston's dialect, which is rich, expressive and "lacking in self-conscious artifice."

Moses, Man of the Mountain
Ellison, Ralph. "Recent Negro Fiction." *New Masses* 40 (August 5, 1941): 22-26.
Extremely unfavorable review of *Moses, Man of the Mountain* as a novel that reinforces the "blight of calculated burlesque" that has plagued black expression. Hurston does for Moses what *Green Pastures* did for Jehovah. Concludes that the novel contributes nothing to black fiction.

Hutchison, Percy. "Led His People Free." *The New York Times Book Review* 44 (November 19, 1939): 21.
Generally favorable review commenting on Hurston's presentation of the primitive African love of magic which leads to the image of Moses as the greatest magician ever. The narrative possesses great power as a result of its profound eloquence and religious fervor.

Jackson, Blyden. Introduction to *Moses, Man of the Mountain*. Urbana: University of Illinois Press, 1984.
Hurston's most ambitious work, *Moses, Man of the Mountain* presents an allegory relating the biblical story to the experience of contemporary black Americans. She draws freely on Afro-American folklore to develop this allegory and the theme of power. While it lacks the characteristics usually associated with the protest novel, *Moses, Man of the Mountain* invokes the politically charged folk image of Moses to raise questions concerning the struggle for freedom.

Sheffey, Ruthe T. "Zora Neale Hurston's *Moses, Man of the Mountain*: A Fictionalized Manifesto on the Imperatives of Black Leadership." *CLA Journal* 29 (December, 1985): 206-220.
Combining images of Moses from Afro-American folklore and Judeo-Christian tradition—especially Flavius Josephus' *Antiquities of the Jews*—Hurston presents Moses not as a Hebrew, but as an African leader. Unlike the trickster heroes of Afro-American expression, Hurston's Moses emerges as a priest and chief hougan who confronts power and authority directly. Notes that Hurston's identification of Moses as an African was developed contemporaneously with and independently of Freud's similar conclusion in *Moses and Monotheism*.

Mules and Men
Brock, H. I. "The Full, True Flavor of Life in a Negro Community." *The New York Times Book Review* 40 (November 10, 1935): 4.
Favorable review emphasizing the authenticity of Hurston's picture of how blacks speak when whites are not present. Hurston's "native racial quality" is "entirely unspoiled by her Northern college education." Hurston succeeds in

rendering Negro dialect "with rare simplicity and fidelity into symbols so little adequate to convey its true values."

Hemenway, Robert. "That Which the Soul Lives By." In *Mules and Men*. Bloomington: Indiana University Press, 1978.
Introduction to reprint including an overview of Hurston's life and discussing her interest in folklore in relation to the Harlem Renaissance. Presents the book as a collection of folklore, emphasizing the role of vernacular expression in creating a black identity. Discusses criticisms of the "romantic pastoralism" of Hurston's perspective.

Moon, Henry Lee. "Big Old Lies." *The New Republic* 85 (December 11, 1935): 142.
Brief review of *Mules and Men* as a collection of Negro folklore. More than a simple collection of folklore, however, the book also provides a valuable picture of the life of the unsophisticated Negro. The imaginative gift of these Negroes is matched by Hurston's gift for storytelling. She presents the material with little attempt to evaluate it or trace its origins.

Seraph on the Suwanee
Hughes, Carl Milton. "Common Denominator: Man." In *The Negro Novelist, 1940-1950*. New York: The Citadel Press, 1953.
Interprets the novel as an homage to Sigmund Freud. Rather than emphasizing the sexual dimension of Freudian thought, Hurston focuses on the neurotic character. Her treatment of the psychological dilemma of Arvay Henson is a classic study of the neurotic woman. Compares Hurston's sectionalism, reflected in her effective use of Florida dialect, with Petry's treatment of New England. Summarizes the novel's critical reception with excerpts from several reviews.

Schraufnagel, Noel. "The Revolt Against Wright." In *From Apology to Protest: The Black American Novel*. Deland, Fla.: Everett/Edwards, 1973.
Focusing on the psychological problems of a woman unable to face reality, *Seraph on the Suwanee* evinces little interest in broad social concerns. Despite melodramatic contrivances in the plot, Hurston handles the Freudian aspects effectively through most of the novel. Blacks play only a minor role in the novel, which recalls the plantation tradition in its treatment of racial concerns.

Slaughter, Frank G. "Freud in Turpentine." *The New York Times Book Review* 53 (October 31, 1948): 24.
Mixed review emphasizing the importance of Freudian psychology to the characterization of Arvay Henson. Praises Hurston's intimate knowledge of the Florida setting, but criticizes the programmatic Freudianism. The novel is "a curious mixture of excellent background drawing" and mechanical characters.

Their Eyes Were Watching God

Awkward, Michael. " 'The Inaudible Voice of It All': Silence, Voice, and Action in *Their Eyes Were Watching God.*" *Studies in Black American Literature* 3 (1988): 57-109. Reprinted in *Inspiriting Influences: Tradition, Revision, and Afro-American Women's Novels*. New York: Columbia University Press, 1989.

Argues that Hurston's decision not to have Janie narrate her own story is not a failure of Hurston's narrative art but a conscious strategy designed to "blacken" the genre of the novel. The novel explores the tension between saying and doing, between voice and action. Reflecting Janie's insight that the human voice is not in itself empowering, Hurston's narrative structure is an example of the specifically Afro-American pattern of call and response, which conjoins distinct voices by means of emotional and psychological affinity. Includes an insightful discussion of previous interpretations.

Baker, Houston. "Figurations for a New American Literary History: Archaeology, Ideology, and Afro-American Discourse." In *Blues, Ideology, and Afro-American Literature: A Vernacular Theory*. Chicago: University of Chicago Press, 1984.

Uses the concepts of "commercial deportation" and the "economics of slavery" to establish links between *Their Eyes Were Watching God* and the slave narrative tradition. Emphasizes the ways in which Janie's attainment of voice is dependent upon the success of Joe Starks's petit bourgeois enterprises. Nanny is essentially accurate when she claims that only property enables expression. The novel is a commentary on the continuing necessity for blacks to negotiate economically based restrictions if they are to attain expressive wholeness.

Barthold, Bonnie J. "Women: Chaos and Redemption." In *Black Time: Fiction of Africa, the Caribbean, and the United States*. New Haven, Conn.: Yale University Press, 1981.

Although the focus of Janie's story is marriage, Hurston presents marriage as a rebellion first against being a mule, and then against being an inhabitant of no-man's-land. Tea Cake serves as a spiritual guide through whom Janie becomes a celebrant rather than a victim of time. Because neither Tea Cake nor Janie possesses the other, their love locates them in a larger community and celebrates a larger mythic union.

Benesch, Klaus. "Oral Narrative and Literary Text: Afro-American Folklore in *Their Eyes Were Watching God.*" *Callaloo* 36 (Summer, 1988): 627-635.

Asserts that Janie's development is primarily a function of her participation in black folk traditions, and only secondarily dependent on her opposition to gender-based expectations. Her "search for blackness" involves a number of oppositions, including those between people and things, communication and isolation, and, most important, blackness and whiteness. Emphasizes the importance of understanding the relationship between literary and oral style.

Bethel, Lorraine. "'This Infinity of Conscious Pain': Zora Neale Hurston and the Black Female Literary Tradition." In *But Some of Us Are Brave: Black Women's Studies*, edited by Gloria T. Hull, Patricia Bell Scott, and Barbara Smith. Old Westbury, N.Y.: Feminist Press, 1982.
Hurston draws on the oral legacy of black female storytelling and mythmaking to challenge the foundations of the dominant white male culture. Participating fully in the "Black female blues esthetic," Hurston furthers the process of identifying the selves of black women as inherently valuable. Hurston's choice to confront life as an independent, woman-identified black female artist required great courage and strength.

Bloom, Harold, ed. *Zora Neale Hurston's Their Eyes Were Watching God: Modern Critical Interpretations*. New York: Chelsea House, 1987.
Collection of essays including reprints of selections from Stepto, Bethel, Kubitschek, Baker, Johnson, and Meese, and new essays by Gates and Johnson, and Callahan. Introduction emphasizes the "heroic vitalism" of Hurston's and Janie Starks's stances. Hurston's freedom from all ideologies identifies her more closely with Shakespeare's Falstaff and Chaucer's Wife of Bath than with contemporary readers concerned with the advancement of feminist or racial agendas.

Brown, Lloyd W. "Zora Neale Hurston and the Nature of Female Perception." *Obsidian* 4, no. 3 (1978): 39-45.
Explores the contrast between male and female modes of perceiving reality in *Their Eyes Were Watching God*. Her male characters accept the thwarting of dreams with resignation while her women characters embrace a kind of "female transcendentalism," reminiscent of the philosophical analysis of Simone de Beauvoir. Relates the killing of Tea Cake to the "self-defensive" memory which preserves "*selected* images of her dead lover." Janie makes her dream true with a persistence that becomes a "heroic affirmation of her spiritual energy and imaginative power, but which, in the very process emphasizes the limitations of her life and her men."

Brown, Sterling A. "Luck Is a Fortune." *The Nation* (October 16, 1937): 409-410.
Favorable review of the original edition by one of the leading black critics of the era. Hurston's forte is the recording and creation of folk speech. By no means stereotypical primitives, her characters are rich in humor, but are not cartoons. The all-black setting enables Hurston to avoid direct confrontation with the worst pressures of class and caste.

Callahan, John F. "'Mah Tongue Is in Mah Friend's Mouf': The Rhetoric of Intimacy and Immensity in *Their Eyes Were Watching God*." In *In the African-American Grain: The Pursuit of Voice in Twentieth-Century Black Fiction*.

Urbana: University of Illinois Press, 1988.
Study of the ways in which Hurston combines oral and written narrative forms in a challenge to traditional assumptions concerning the distance between narrator and characters, or between author and audience. The resulting "rhetoric of intimacy" draws strongly on African-American call and response forms. Because no single voice seeks to dominate the others, *Their Eyes Were Watching God* advances a democratic, womanist conception of voice and form.

Carr, Glynis. "Storytelling as *Bildung* in Zora Neale Hurston's *Their Eyes Were Watching God*. *CLA Journal* 31 (December, 1987): 189-200.
Argues that an interdisciplinary approach is required to fully appreciate Hurston's *Bildungsroman*, which centers on Janie's increasing mastery of the art of storytelling, both as artistic performance and as affirmation of personal and cultural identity. Hurston structures the novel around a sequence of oppositions involving speech and storytelling.

Christian, Barbara. "The Rise and Fall of the Proper Mulatta." In *Black Women Novelists: The Development of a Tradition, 1892-1976*. Westport, Conn.: Greenwood Press, 1980.
The center of Hurston's sensibility is her love for the rich folk culture and her desire to express the functional beauty of folk language and customs. Unlike her contemporaries in the Harlem Renaissance, she knew this culture intimately. In *Their Eyes Were Watching God*, Hurston draws on the folk culture to revise the mulatta images of her predecessors, pointing the way toward the presentation of more complex women characters. The novel anticipates later works by black women writers who define themselves as persons in a specific black community rather than in relation to whites.

Cooke, Michael G. "Solitude: The Beginnings of Self-Realization in Zora Neale Hurston, Richard Wright, and Ralph Ellison." In *Afro-American Literature in the Twentieth Century: The Achievement of Intimacy*. New Haven, Conn.: Yale University Press, 1984.
Their Eyes Were Watching God is the record of black development from materialism and passivity to self-respect, self-reliance, and qualified self-realization. Janie's inner stability and outer indomitability are new characteristics in black women's fiction. Janie moves from accidental solitude with her grandmother to accepted solitude with Logan and Joe to accomplished solitude when she returns to Eatonville.

Dixon, Melvin. "Keep Me from Sinking Down: Zora Neale Hurston, Alice Walker, and Gayl Jones." In *Ride Out the Wilderness: Geography and Identity in Afro-American Literature*. Urbana: University of Illinois Press, 1987.

Giving compelling expression to the relations between geography and identity, Hurston associates the development of voice with the Florida "muck," from which Janie rises rather than sinks. Contrasts Nanny's desire for land as a means of security with Janie's search for a landscape associated with leadership and autonomy. Hurston's favorable treatment of the South contrasts with the dominant tendency of the Harlem Renaissance.

DuPlessis, Rachel Blau. "Beyond the Hard Visible Horizon." In *Writing Beyond the Ending: Narrative Strategies of Twentieth-Century Women Writers*. Bloomington: Indiana University Press, 1985.
Discusses the image of the horizon in relation to women's narrative strategies centering on the "multiple individual." For Hurston, the horizon and Tea Cake embody the possibility of breaking the frame of individual consciousness. The formation of self in the novel is resolved not in individualistic terms but through Janie's identification with black culture.

Ferguson, Otis. "You Can't Hear Their Voices." *The New Republic* 92 (October 13, 1937): 276.
Unfavorable review criticizing Hurston's "superwordy, flabby" style. The execution is too complex for the unaffected beauty of the Florida Negroes the novel describes. Hurston's dialect is sloppy because she has failed to grasp the first principle of dialect writing: that the key to difference must be indicated by rhythm. The best aspect of *Their Eyes Were Watching God* is its shrewd picture of Negro life in "its naturally creative and unself-conscious grace."

Ferguson, SallyAnn. "Folkloric Men and Female Growth in *Their Eyes Were Watching God*." *Black American Literature Forum* 21 (Spring/Summer, 1987): 185-197.
Discusses Hurston's use of folkloric motifs to characterize the three major male characters in *Their Eyes Were Watching God*. Logan is described in terms of "old man-young woman" marriage tales; Jody comports with the "Jody the Grinder" tale of black folklore; and Tea Cake is a variation on the black folk hero Stackolee. Hurston uses these motifs both to reveal the mens' character flaws and to define the black woman's quest, where her greatest foe is the same one faced by the white woman.

Gates, Henry Louis, Jr. "Zora Neale Hurston and the Speakerly Text." In *The Signifying Monkey: A Theory of Afro-American Literary Criticism*. New York: Oxford University Press, 1988.
Complex discussion of *Their Eyes Were Watching God* as a "speakerly text," in which all other elements are subordinated to the purpose of creating the illusion of oral narration. Contrasting Hurston's emphasis on what is represented—speech—with Richard Wright's emphasis on what it represents—the

experience of black people—Gates credits Hurston with "clearing the rhetorical space" for later writers such as Ralph Ellison and Alice Walker. Emphasizes the importance of "free indirect discourse" to the success of Hurston's strategy.

Gates, Henry Louis, Jr., and Barbara Johnson. "A Black and Idiomatic Free Indirect Discourse." In *Zora Neale Hurston's "Their Eyes Were Watching God,"* edited by Harold Bloom. New York: Chelsea House, 1987.
Stylistic analysis focusing on Janie's verbal attack on Joe Starks. Asserts that Hurston's use of free indirect discourse, which represents not only the individual's speech but also that of her community, is central to her critique of male writing. "Rewriting" Joe's "text of himself," Janie liberates herself. The reversal of authority in the scene is the first truly feminist critique of the fiction of the authority of the male voice in the Afro-American tradition.

Giles, James R. "The Significance of Time in Zora Neale Hurston's *Their Eyes Were Watching God*." *Negro American Literature Forum* 6 (Summer, 1972): 52-53, 60.
Discusses Hurston's use of three competing conceptions of time to sharpen the basic value conflict between the Puritan sense of duty and the primitive sense of hedonism. The first concept of time, presented in the opening metaphor, is time as a deterministic force leading to death. The second, associated with Nannie and Joe Starks, is time as thing to be controlled rationally. The third, associated with Tea Cake, is time as folk hedonism. In the struggle between these conceptions, Tea Cake's fundamentally black version of time triumphs.

Holton, Sylvia Wallace. *Down Home and Uptown: The Representation of Black Speech in American Fiction*. New Brunswick, N.J.: Fairleigh Dickinson University Press, 1984.
Linguistic analysis of the ways in which various writers have represented black speech. Includes brief commentary on Hurston's use of dialect in *Their Eyes Were Watching God*, which is a coherent attempt to merge folklore and fiction. Comments briefly on the relevance of Hurston's novel to contemporary explorations of women's autonomy and identity.

Johnson, Barbara. "Metaphor, Metonymy and Voice in *Their Eyes Were Watching God*." In *Black Literature and Literary Theory*, edited by Henry Louis Gates, Jr. New York: Methuen, 1984. Reprinted in *A World of Difference*. Baltimore: Johns Hopkins University Press, 1987.
Examines Hurston's treatment of the classical rhetorical figure of "metaphor" and "metonymy" as the key to understanding Janie's struggle for voice. Janie's power of voice grows not out of her identity, but out of her "division into

inside and outside." Articulate language requires the simultaneous presence of both poles, not their collapse into oneness. The sign of an authentic voice is not "self-identity" but "self-difference," because unification is a "fantasy of domination." Hurston's project is ultimately one of "de-universalization."

Jordan, Jennifer. "Feminist Fantasies: Zora Neale Hurston's *Their Eyes Were Watching God*." *Tulsa Studies in Women's Literature* 7 (Spring, 1988): 105-117.
Argues that while black and feminist critics of Hurston show an ability judiciously to balance her personal strengths and weaknesses, most recent readings of *Their Eyes Were Watching God* make Hurston a "grand candidate for feminist sainthood." This narrow perspective results in the "unsupportable notion that the novel is an appropriate fictional representation of the concerns and attitudes of modern black feminism." Limited to the experience of the black middle class, Hurston's novel belittles the suffering of working-class black women. Janie ultimately chooses isolation and contemplation over solidarity and action.

Joyce, Joyce Ann. "Change, Chance, and God in Zora Neale Hurston's *Their Eyes Were Watching God*." In *A Rainbow Round Her Shoulder: Zora Neale Hurston Symposium Papers*, edited by Ruthe T. Sheffey. Baltimore: Morgan State University Press, 1982.
Criticizes the thematic emphasis of most previous Hurston criticism and focuses on the use of organic imagery in *Their Eyes Were Watching God*. Discusses Hurston's relationship to the anthropology of Franz Boas and the pragmatic philosophy of William James. Hurston has a philosophical view of life, emphasizing the manner in which chance and change can both restrict and enrich human experience.

Kalb, John D. "The Anthropological Narrator of *Their Eyes Were Watching God*." *Studies in American Fiction* 16 (Autumn, 1988): 169-180.
Detailed stylistic analysis of the narrative voice of *Their Eyes Were Watching God*, which moves freely between the poles of spectator and participant. Argues that this is not simply a split between the first- and third-person sections. Rather, the third-person narrator alters diction and rhythm to assume various positions. Not simply a choice between two extremes, the power of the narrative grows out of the blending of roles that occupies many points on the spectrum of observation and participation.

Kubitschek, Missy Dehn. " 'Tuh de Horizon and Back': The Female Quest in *Their Eyes Were Watching God*." *Black American Literature Forum* 17 (Fall, 1983): 109-115.
Important essay identifying the sexist biases of most previous Hurston criticism and exploring Janie's relationship to the archetypal quest pattern defined by

Joseph Campbell. Previous critics obscure Janie's role as a questing heroine, thereby distorting Hurston's view of the black artist's relationship to the black community. The first half of the novel deals with Janie's resistance to what Campbell labels the "call to adventure"; the second details the trials of her quest. The crucial frame story, ignored by most previous critics, concerns her return to the community. Extending Robert Stepto's idea of ascent and immersion, Kubitschek argues that Janie issues a call for a "group ascent."

Kuyk, Betty M. "From Coon Hide to Mink Skin: Understanding an Afro-American 'Sense of Place' Through *Their Eyes Were Watching God.*" In *A Rainbow Round Her Shoulder: Zora Neale Hurston Symposium Papers*, edited by Ruthe T. Sheffey. Baltimore: Morgan State University Press, 1982.
Focuses on Hurston's conception of "home" as it relates to the resolution of *Their Eyes Were Watching God*. Summarizes African ideas of community and place which parallel Janie's decision to return to her community to teach and mediate, thereby charting her course into the community mythology and affirming her own "everlastingness."

Kuyk, Dirk, Jr. "A Novel from an Oral Tradition: Zora Neale Hurston's *Their Eyes Were Watching God.*" In *A Rainbow Round Her Shoulder: Zora Neale Hurston Symposium Papers*, edited by Ruthe T. Sheffey. Baltimore: Morgan State University Press, 1982.
Focuses on the conflict between "plausibility and situational appropriateness" in Hurston's picture of Janie as storyteller. Resulting from a clash in cultural assumptions, the conflict centers on the problem of inserting oral materials into the novel form. Among the oral elements Hurston employs are proverbs, tales, figures of speech, and rhymes.

McCredie, Wendy J. "Authority and Authorization in *Their Eyes Were Watching God.*" *Black American Literature Forum* 16 (Spring, 1982): 25-28.
Focuses on Janie's "struggle to articulate, to appropriate her own voice, and through her voice, herself." In telling her story, Janie makes her past real as a part of her present. Analysis focuses on the three phases of Janie's process: before, during, and after her relationship with Tea Cake. Near the end of each phase, Janie speaks; each speech represents an advance in her ability to control her own destiny.

Maja-Pearce, Adewale. "Beyond Blackness." *Times Literary Supplement* (May 2, 1986): 479.
Review of reprint edition identifying Hurston as one of the most significant American writers of the century. A black writer who refused to engage in the rhetoric of race, Hurston had the courage to be truthful to her vision. Janie frees herself from the petty concerns of the black community and, like

Hurston, spurns the crippling limitations of other people's expectations, insisting on her right to be free.

Marks, Donald R. "Sex, Violence, and Organic Consciousness in Zora Neale Hurston's *Their Eyes Were Watching God.*" *Black American Literature Forum* 19 (Winter, 1985): 152-157.
Hurston's treatment of Janie's four love relationships demonstrates her acceptance of the organicist ideology of romantic pastoralism and her rejection of the mechanistic ideology of bourgeois capitalism. Her use of metaphors of natural fertility and sexuality in association with Johnny Taylor and Tea Cake contrasts sharply with the metaphors of control associated with Logan and Joe Starks. Hurston's endorsement of the reactionary organicist ideology leads her to portray meaning solely as a matter of Janie's consciousness, distinct from any outside community.

Meese, Elizabeth. "Orality and Textuality in *Their Eyes Were Watching God.*" In *Crossing the Double Cross: The Practice of Feminist Criticism.* Chapel Hill: University of North Carolina Press, 1986.
By transforming Janie's orality into a written text, Hurston creates her story, herself as writer, and an image of Janie creating life through language. Janie moves beyond the use of language as a means of establishing power over others to a wildly radical new way of using language. Janie's participation in the oral tradition of her culture supports her claim to black womanhood and her stature as an artist.

Miller, James A. "Janie's Blues: The Blues Motif in *Their Eyes Were Watching God.*" In *A Rainbow Round Her Shoulder: Zora Neale Hurston Symposium Papers*, edited by Ruthe T. Sheffey. Baltimore: Morgan State University Press, 1982.
One of the first black writers to explore the ideological and aesthetic significance of the blues, Hurston uses the blues on two levels in *Their Eyes Were Watching God*. The first derives from the difficult personal circumstances under which the novel was written; the second from Hurston's exploration of the blues form in the novel itself. Returning to Eatonville to tell the story of her joys and hardships, Janie fulfills the function of a blues singer and emerges as the primary voice in her community.

Pondrom, Cyrena N. "The Role of Myth in Hurston's *Their Eyes Were Watching God.*" *American Literature* 58 (May, 1986): 181-202.
Observes that Hurston's use of myth as a principle of order links her with modernism, and that her insistence on the affirmative potential of myth links her even more strongly with the great female modernists such as H.D. and Virginia Woolf. In *Their Eyes Were Watching God*, Hurston makes extensive

use of the Babylonian myth of Ishtar and Tammuz, the Greek myth of Aphrodite and Adonis, and the Egyptian myth of Isis and Osiris.

Rosenblatt, Roger. "Eccentricities." In *Black Fiction*. Cambridge, Mass.: Harvard University Press, 1974.
Unlike almost every other black character in Afro-American literature, Janie's progress is toward personal freedom. She conceives of breaking the cyclical pattern of black history as a rebellion not to external white forces but to self-manufactured forms of repression. Janie's achievement with Tea Cake is unreal since, although they may escape into a "fantasy of independence," they are aware that the world outside is waiting and able to destroy them.

Schwalbenberg, Peter. "Time as Point of View in Zora Neale Hurston's *Their Eyes Were Watching God*." *Negro American Literature Forum* 10 (Fall, 1976): 104-105, 107-108.
Focuses on the tension between time as a concrete flow of events and more abstract philosophical apprehensions of time in *Their Eyes Were Watching God*. Hurston shifts her focus from one type of time to others as part of her presentation of Janie's changing life experiences. Hurston enables us to view Janie from both intimate and detached perspectives.

Stepto, Robert B. "Literacy and Hibernation: Ralph Ellison's *Invisible Man*." In *From Behind the Veil: A Study of Afro-American Narrative*. Urbana: University of Illinois Press, 1979.
Their Eyes Were Watching God is the only novel published prior to *Invisible Man* to combine coherently the patterns of "ascent"—the movement to literacy and freedom—and "immersion"—the movement back to connection with the black community. A grand effort to demystify the concepts of group- and self-consciousness, the novel calls for a new type of Afro-American fiction in which the narrator achieves control over both her personal history and the way it is told. The one flaw of *Their Eyes Were Watching God* is Hurston's decision to tell the story through an omniscient narrator, which subverts Janie's achievement of voice.

Thornton, Jerome E. " 'Goin' on de Muck': The Paradoxical Journey of the Black American Hero." *CLA Journal* 31 (March, 1988): 261-280.
Uses *Their Eyes Were Watching God* as a touchstone for discussion of the quest pattern in black novels such as Toomer's *Cane* and Amiri Baraka's *The System of Dante's Hell*. "De Muck" becomes a recurring symbolic setting where the black hero can attain self-knowledge. Janie exemplifies the Afro-American pattern in which the hero descends rather than moving "upwards" toward demoralizing white or pretentious black society. Arriving in a cellar, base-

ment, hole, or bottom, the black hero embraces nothingness and begins his or her quest for authentic self.

Walker, S. Jay. "Zora Neale Hurston's *Their Eyes Were Watching God*: Black Novel of Sexism." *Modern Fiction Studies* 20 (Winter, 1974/1975): 519-527.
Views Hurston's emphasis on sexism as "something of a shock" because for politically active black women the "accepted role" is "clearly that of an auxiliary." Hurston is aware both of sexism and the reasons why the feminist movement has not attracted black women. Hurston denies not sexuality, but sex-role stereotypes. Asserting the need for a marriage between acknowledged equals, Hurston shows that the search for the people can be accomplished only through "a person, a man." Like George Eliot and Charlotte Brontë, Hurston embraces the romantic tradition of reciprocal passion.

Williams, Sherley Anne. Foreword to *Their Eyes Were Watching God*. Urbana: University of Illinois Press, 1978.
A black woman novelist's celebration of *Their Eyes Were Watching God* as an expression of aspects of the black "country self" rarely portrayed in literature. Hurston's fidelity to diction, metaphor, and syntax—whether she is writing in rural or urban, Northern or Southern voices—is the key to her literary power. Contains a brief discussion of Janie as a questing hero who is slightly more conventional than her creator.

Wolff, Maria Tai. "Listening and Living: Reading and Experience in *Their Eyes Were Watching God*." *Black American Literature Forum* 16 (Spring, 1982): 29-33.
Argues that *Their Eyes Were Watching God* is concerned not with the truth of Janie's tale, but with its effect on the teller and the impact of its telling. The reader's own experiences determine the significance of the text. Analysis focuses on the ways in which Hurston transforms events into part of an essentially lyrical point of view.

Wright, Richard. "Between Laughter and Tears." *New Masses* 25 (October 5, 1937): 22, 25.
Famous negative review condemning *Their Eyes Were Watching God* for voluntarily perpetuating minstrel tradition stereotypes that were originally forced upon blacks. Wright comments that Hurston has "no desire whatever to move in the direction of serious fiction" and condemns the "facile sensuality" of her prose. While the dialogue accurately reflects the "psychological movement of the Negro folk-mind" in its "pure simplicity," the novel is of no further value.

Young, James O. "Black Reality and Beyond." In *Black Writers of the Thirties*. Baton Rouge: Louisiana State University Press, 1973.

Praises Hurston as a writer who, like Langston Hughes, wrote about Negro folk life because of its own "intrinsic value and interest." Although she was less concerned with conventional racial issues than any other black writer of the period, she discovered much of significance, particularly in *Their Eyes Were Watching God*, which is an example of "feminine and individual protest." Hurston was able to "dramatize elements of universal significance while confining her story entirely within the reality of black experience."

GAYL JONES

Biography

Byerman, Keith. "Gayl Jones." In *Afro-American Fiction After 1955*, edited by Thadious M. Davis and Trudier Harris. Vol. 33 of *Dictionary of Literary Biography*. Detroit: Bruccoli Clark, 1984.
Substantial reference entry including biographical sketch and analysis of both *Corregidora* and *Eva's Man*. Emphasizes the intensity of Jones's writing, which focuses on the madness and violence in the lives of black people, particularly black women. Jones creates "blues narratives" drawing on the Afro-American oral tradition as well as aspects of gothic psychological fiction.

Harper, Michael S. "Gayl Jones: An Interview." In *Chant of Saints: A Gathering of Afro-American Literature, Art, and Scholarship*, edited by Harper and Robert B. Stepto. Urbana: University of Illinois Press, 1979.
Important interview conducted by a leading black poet. Most of Jones's answers are lengthy, amounting to small essays on the topics. Among the issues covered are the autobiographical elements of her writing; her image of herself as storyteller; oral and literary influences on her work; the development of *Corregidora*; the significance of Zora Neale Hurston; Jones's admiration for Chaucer; and her brief comments on the importance of a wide range of Afro-American writers.

Holm, Janis Butler. "Gayl Jones." In *Contemporary Novelists*, 4th ed., edited by D. L. Kirkpatrick. New York: St. Martin's Press, 1986.
Reference entry including biographical outline; list of publications; and brief analysis of *Corregidora* and *Eva's Man*. Emphasizes that what one makes of Jones's writing depends on preconceptions concerning "the function of art—on how, as readers, we enter into the dialogue." Jones's protagonists have been damaged by abuse in ways that deny traditional forms of identification between reader and character.

Jones, Gayl. "About My Work." In *Black Women Writers, 1950-1980: A Critical Evaluation*, edited by Mari Evans. Garden City, N.Y.: Anchor Press, 1984.
Jones identifies her interest in character as the organizing principle of her work. Arguing that political stances can either enhance or damage imaginative literature, she says that she does not have a political stance. Includes Jones's list of influences on her work, commenting on the appeal of the "self-imagined hero" present in Hurston, Morrison, James Joyce, Ralph Ellison, Carlos Fuentes and others.

_____ . "Interview with Lucille Jones." *Obsidian* 3 (Winter, 1977): 26-35.
Interview between Jones and her mother, who has also published several pieces
of short fiction. In her introduction, Jones notes that she sees similarities
between her mother's writing and her own: "the way we go about telling a
story—there are similarities in terms of voice." Interview includes a range of
information concerning Jones's family background and the Kentucky community in which she was reared.

Jones, Judith P. "Gayl Jones." In *American Women Writers*, vol. 2, edited by Lina
Mainiero. New York: Frederick Ungar, 1980.
Biographical entry including brief commentary on *Corregidora* and *Eva's Man*.
Observes that while Jones's writing is neither polemical nor explicitly political,
it reveals a central concern with issues of racism and feminism.

Rowell, Charles H. "An Interview with Gayl Jones." *Callaloo* 16 (October, 1982):
32-53.
Interview covering a wide range of topics, including Jones's use of oral modes
in her writing; her response to Zora Neale Hurston; the nature of black Southern literature; her use of sex as a metaphor; and the influence of history on
personality. Includes extensive discussion of *Corregidora*. Jones emphasizes
that character takes precedence over political themes in all of her writing.

Tate, Claudia C. "An Interview with Gayl Jones." *Black American Literature Forum*
13 (Winter, 1979): 142-148. Reprinted in *Black Women Writers at Work*, edited
by Claudia C. Tate. New York: Continuum, 1983.
Interview including Jones's comments on her revisions of *Corregidora*, partially in response to Toni Morrison's editorial suggestions; the difference between the literary images of black men and black women; the influences on her
work; and her treatment of the lesbian theme in her fiction.

Commentary

Barthold, Bonnie J. "Women: Chaos and Redemption." In *Black Time: Fiction of
Africa, the Caribbean, and the United States*. New Haven, Conn.: Yale University Press, 1981.
Focuses on the characters' apprehension of time in *Corregidora* and *Eva's
Man*. Focusing on the theme of childbirth in *Corregidora*, Barthold emphasizes the tension between the traditional African celebration of childbirth and
the New World "rebellion against history." Relying on black music as an
emblem of the continuity of black experience, Jones generates an act of "rebellious celebration." In *Eva's Man*, the protagonist's rebellion is recurrent and
unredemptive.

Byerman, Keith E. "Beyond Realism: The Fictions of Gayl Jones and Toni Morrison." In *Fingering the Jagged Grain: Tradition and Form in Recent Black Fiction*. Athens: University of Georgia Press, 1985.

Both of Jones's novels create radical worlds which deny readers a "sane" narrative center. *Corregidora* explores the association of racial and sexual domination, concluding that love and history are the creators and preservers of identity. Focusing directly on the theme of madness, *Eva's Man* sees the expression of the self's experiences as the only hope. Both novels consider lesbianism a questionable alternative to the exploitation of heterosexual relationships.

Dixon, Melvin. "Singing a Deep Song: Language as Evidence in the Novels of Gayl Jones." In *Black Women Writers, 1950-1980: A Critical Evaluation*, edited by Mari Evans. Garden City, N.Y.: Anchor Press, 1984. Reprinted in *Ride Out the Wilderness: Geography and Identity in Afro-American Literature*. Urbana: University of Illinois Press, 1987.

Focuses on the regenerative potential of language. Language drawn from musical or sexual idioms of the black American community, when shared with others, can enable predatory characters to recover their lost selves. Comments on Jones's interest in orally based cultures and the writing of novelists (Momaday, Joyce, Tutuola, Fuentes) from strongly oral cultures. While *Corregidora* demonstrates the possibility of "blues reconciliation," *Eva's Man* explores the reality of violence, silence, and disharmony.

"Gayl Jones." In *Contemporary Literary Criticism*, vol. 6, edited by Carolyn Riley and Phyllis Carmel Mendelson (1976); and vol. 9, edited by Dedria Bryfonski (1978). Detroit: Gale Research.

Compilations of reviews of *Corregidora* (vol. 6) and *Eva's Man* (vol. 9). Both volumes include brief excerpts from reviews in *The New Yorker* by John Updike, who focuses on Jones's "sharpened starkness, a power of ellipsis that leaves ever darker gaps between its flashes of rhythmic, sensuously exact dialogue and visible symbol."

Harris, Janice. "Gayl Jones's *Corregidora*." *Frontiers* 5, no. 3 (1981): 1-5.

Emphasizes that the theme of Ursa's growth as an artist is as important as the theme of black female sexuality. Like James Joyce and D. H. Lawrence, Jones uses the tension between her protagonist's calling and the rest of her experiences to provide the structure for her book. Ursa transforms the nets that would limit her artistic flight into sources of support. The real power and originality of the novel lie in Jones's "admission of all that Ursa gives up and becomes in order to sing her old world/new world song." Harris cautions against universalizing Jones's theme, but concludes that what Ursa goes through "includes but also transcends race, class, and sex."

Johnson, Charles. "The Women." In *Being and Race: Black Writing Since 1970*. Bloomington: Indiana University Press, 1988.
Brief comment by a black male novelist praising Jones for her ear for spoken language and her ability to "spin dreamlike erotic narratives that show the darker side of black sexuality." Her prose shares the intimacy of writers grounded in the oral tradition. Her strength is her ability to confront the psychological brutality of black oppression by revealing the depths of another mind.

Wade-Gayles, Gloria. "Journeying from Can't to Can." In *No Crystal Stair: Visions of Race and Sex in Black Women's Fiction*. New York: Pilgrim Press, 1984.
Jones's vision of womanhood is more highly developed in *Eva's Man* than in *Corregidora*. Both novels sound themes of hate, desire, and sexual exploitation. Almost totally devoid of joy, *Eva's Man* adds a preoccupation with raw sexual lust, profanity, and perversion. The novel is an exception to the main currents of black women's fiction because it emphasizes sexual victimization to the exclusion of interest in racial oppression.

Ward, Jerry W., Jr. "Escape from Trublem: The Fiction of Gayl Jones." In *Black Women Writers, 1950-1980: A Critical Evaluation*, edited by Mari Evans. Garden City, N.Y.: Anchor Press, 1984.
Jones focuses on the abuse of women and its psychological results as a way of magnifying the obscenity of racism and sexism in everyday life. Suggesting that disorder is the norm in contemporary life, Jones's narrative strategies raise questions concerning the ways in which individuals derive meaning from texts. *Corregidora* represents the slavery of consciousness; *Eva's Man* centers on the paralysis of consciousness.

Weixlmann, Joe. "A Gayl Jones Bibliography." *Callaloo* 20 (Winter, 1984): 119-131.
Comprehensive bibliography listing Jones's novels, drama, short fiction, poetry, and nonfiction along with reviews, critical essays, and interviews.

Selected Titles

Corregidora

Avant, John Alfred. "*Corregidora.*" *The New Republic* 172 (June 28, 1975): 27-28.
Favorable review emphasizing Jones's emotional power. Despite a rather rigid literary structure, the novel creates the impression of unfiltered experience. The blues power and sexual vernacular reinforce Jones's picture of the "awful complexity" of her protagonist's life. Although Jones avoids ideology, *Corregidora* deals implicitly with racial and feminist issues.

Bell, Roseann P. "Gayl Jones Takes a Look at *Corregidora*: An Interview." In *Sturdy Black Bridges: Visions of Black Women in Literature*, edited by Roseann P. Bell, Bettye J. Parker, and Beverly Guy-Sheftall. Garden City, N.Y.: Anchor Press, 1979.

Brief interview including Jones's comments on the influence of her teacher, black poet Michael Harper; her appreciation for the novels of Carlos Fuentes and Alice Walker; her use of black urban folklore; and her use of the oral tradition as literary resource.

Cooke, Michael G. "After Intimacy: The Search for New Meaning in Recent Black Fiction." In *Afro-American Literature in the Twentieth Century: The Achievement of Intimacy*. New Haven, Conn.: Yale University Press, 1984.

Identifies Jones as a crucial figure in the attempts of younger writers to envision a meaningful "reimmersion" into black experience. In *Corregidora*, the impulse to preserve history gradually degenerates into a rhetorical commitment with little connection to action. The book is characterized by delay, avoidance, and denial. Although it invokes the blues, they are present only in a theoretical sense. The novel takes a spontaneous folk form and fits it into a systematic formal art.

Dearborn, Mary V. "Miscegenation and the Mulatto, Inheritance and Incest: The Pocahontas Marriage, Part II." In *Pocahontas's Daughters: Gender and Ethnicity in American Culture*. New York: Oxford University Press, 1986.

Brief discussion of *Corregidora* as a confrontation with the central paradoxes in ethnic women's fiction. The paradox is twofold: first, Ursa's decision to align herself with her female ancestors aligns her with a tradition of sexual violence and oppression; second, the definition of selfhood based on ownership or descendancy seems contradictory. Jones implies that the women refuse to forget the past, not only because they refuse to forgive, but also because the past, as one's inheritance, defines selfhood.

Sokolov, Raymond. "*Corregidora*." *The New York Times Book Review* 80 (May 25, 1975): 21-22.

Highly positive review praising Jones's ability to negotiate the combination of black blues language and sophisticated modernist literary techniques reminiscent of Molly Bloom's soliloquy in Joyce's *Ulysses*. Praises the complex presentation of a woman trying to make her past and present come to terms with one another. The sexual writing is a model of grace and taste. Not simply a "black women's liberation fable," *Corregidora* testifies to the reality of progress in literature.

Tate, Claudia C. "*Corregidora*: Ursa's Blues Medley." *Black American Literature Forum* 13 (Winter, 1979): 139-141.

Argues that while the emotional intensity of *Corregidora* may suggest that it lacks cohesive structure, the novel possesses an "almost excessive conscious design." Abandoning all authorial intrusion, Jones develops the story entirely in terms of the character's mental processes. The novel's narrative structure is composed of a series of concentric stories of unequal historical range related through monologues that assume the form of an extended blues medley.

Updike, John. "Selda, Lilia, Ursa, Great Gram, and Other Ladies in Distress." *The New Yorker* 51 (August 18, 1975): 79-83.
Favorable review of *Corregidora* as a feminist novel, which Updike defines as a novel about "femaleness that considers itself politically." Jones fuses black history and mythic consciousness with the emotional nuances of contemporary black life. Ursa's primary goal is to transcend a "nightmare black consciousness and waken to her own female, maimed, humanity." Updike locates the novel in a space "between ideology and dream" which he considers appropriate for Jones's material.

Webster, Ivan. "Really the Blues." *Time* 105 (June 16, 1975): 79.
Favorable review emphasizing Jones's ability to illuminate broad questions concerning sexual relationships. Her plot is somewhat melodramatic, hovering between realism and "howling symbolism." No black American novelist since Richard Wright has so effectively traced psychic wounds to their sexual source.

Eva's Man
Byerman, Keith. "Black Vortex: The Gothic Structure of *Eva's Man*." *MELUS* 7 (Winter, 1980): 93-101.
Argues that the obsessive violence and sexuality in *Eva's Man* can be best understood in relation to the "Gothic monomyth" described by G.R. Thompson as a demonic quest-romance in which "a lonely self-divided hero embarks on an insane pursuit of the absolute." Like gothic quest novels, Jones structures her novel around a downward, ever-tightening spiral of the whirlpool. Although the final turn of the vortex involves the reader's willingness to be drawn into Eva's story, Jones clearly distances her own voice from that of her insane protagonist.

Jordan, June. "*Eva's Man*." *The New York Times Book Review* 81 (May 16, 1976): 36-37.
Criticizes Jones's perpetuation of stereotypical images of black women, particularly as they relate to young black girls forced to respond to sexual violation. The "experimental, gruesome narrative," in effect a "blues that lost control," raises disturbing questions concerning the writer's sense of her own identity. The circular, strictly controlled form of the novel reflects an ambivalence reinforced by the constant raising of unresolved questions.

Pinckney, Darryl. *"Eva's Man." The New Republic* 174 (June 19, 1976): 27-28.
    Review stressing Jones's deep exploration of her protagonist's inner life. *Eva's Man* bears no relationship to the polemical tradition of black literature; there is no sense of racial conflict. Relates Jones's concentration on the tyranny of memory and the "paranoia" of Eva's soliloquy to novels concerning homosexuals. Comments briefly on the "lesbian overtones" of the novel.

Updike, John. "Eva and Eleanor and Everywoman." *The New Yorker* 52 (August 9, 1976): 74-77.
    Review of *Eva's Man* and Christina Stead's *Miss Herbert* as novels that "make being a woman sound very depressing." Updike notes that as a male reviewer he feels himself faced "with a sexist mystery, of which these two highly intelligent and earnest authors are as much protectors as celebrants." Praises Jones's powerful sense of "vital inheritance, of history in the blood," particularly in her treatment of the reality of evil. Unlike *Corregidora*, *Eva's Man* sometimes creates the feeling that the characters have been dehumanized by the author's vision as much as by their circumstances.

JUNE JORDAN

Biography

DeVeaux, Alexis. "Creating Soul Food: June Jordan." *Essence* 11 (April, 1981): 82, 138-150.

Lengthy biographical essay including numerous quotations from June Jordan concerning her life and work. The unifying thread of Jordan's career is her attempt to transform anger and silence into an expression of psychological. and political wholeness. Jordan discusses her family both as a problem and a source of sustenance. Other topics include her marriage and experience of motherhood, her ambivalent feelings about the Black Arts movement of the 1960's, and her sense of the beauty of black English.

Erickson, Peter B. "June Jordan." In *Afro-American Writers After 1955: Dramatists and Prose Writers*, edited by Thadious M. Davis and Trudier Harris. Vol. 38 of *Dictionary of Literary Biography*. Detroit: Bruccoli Clark, 1985.

Extended discussion of Jordan's work in all genres, accompanied by a substantial biographical sketch. Identifies power as the central theme uniting her work, which gradually shifts focus from despair to optimism. A part of Jordan's continuing exploration of her relationship with her parents, *His Own Where* combines two aspects of her work which might otherwise seem incongruous: "her experiment with urban planning and her commitment to Black English." The novel attempts to demonstrate that certain ideas of Buckminster Fuller that cannot be realized in real life can be fulfilled in fiction.

Jordan, June. *Civil Wars*. Boston: Beacon Press, 1981.

Collection of essays blending political analysis and personal experience. Introduction provides Jordan's brief overview of the beginnings of her career, but biographical information is interspersed throughout numerous pieces.

_____ . *On Call: Political Essays*. Boston: South End Press, 1985.

Collection of essays on a variety of political and cultural issues. Introduction emphasizes the importance of breaking the silence which has been imposed on black women specifically and black people generally by racist print media. Many of the essays link Jordan's political insights to her personal experiences. Focuses on both international and national issues.

Selected Title

His Own Where

Fabio, Sarah Webster. "His Own Where." *The New York Times Book Review* 76 (November 7, 1971) sec. 2: 6, 34.

Favorable review emphasizing Jordan's sensitive treatment of adolescent feelings of abandonment. Praises her use of black English, which draws readers into the characters' experience rather than distancing them from it. Observes that when language fails the characters, they turn to music for sustenance.

Hentoff, Margot. "Kids, Pull Up Your Socks!" *The New York Review of Books* 18 (April 20, 1972): 13-15.
Discusses *His Own Where* in relation to children's books that present realistic pictures rather than ideal images. Describes the book's "nightmare quality of a world in which adolescents live always at the edge of breakdown and isolation." Accuses Jordan and other similar writers of obsession with the commonplace, cold aspects of life. Doubts that such works help young people attain a sense of their own worth.

NELLA LARSEN

Biography

Davis, Thadious M. "Nella Larsen." In *Afro-American Writers from the Harlem Renaissance to 1940*, edited by Trudier Harris. Vol. 51 of *Dictionary of Literary Biography*. Detroit: Bruccoli Clark, 1987.
Important biographical essay correcting errors and misconceptions in previous presentations of Larsen's biography. Includes detailed analysis of *Quicksand* and *Passing*, which focus on middle-class women who, though cast in traditional roles, assume responsibility for their own lives. Views the novels as valuable for their precise delineation of a social milieu that has passed away and a female perspective that has endured.

Shockley, Ann Allen. "Nella Marian Larsen Imes." In *Afro-American Women Writers, 1746-1933*. Boston: G. K. Hall, 1988.
Biographical headnote exploring Larsen's family background, her marriage, her literary career, and her withdrawal from active participation in Afro-American culture. Includes a detailed discussion of the charges of plagiarism leveled against a Larsen short story. Notes that recent critics have identified sexism, as well as racism and the tragic mulatto, as central themes in Larsen's work.

Wall, Cheryl A. "Nella Larsen." In *American Women Writers*, vol. 2, edited by Lina Mainiero. New York: Frederick Ungar, 1980.
Biographical entry including brief commentary on *Quicksand*, which explores the theme of cultural dualism, and *Passing*, which serves primarily to demonstrate how inconsequential the passing theme was. Bibliography lists entries in other reference works.

Commentary

Bell, Bernard W. "The Harlem Renaissance and the Search for New Modes of Narration." In *The Afro-American Novel and Its Tradition*. Amherst: University of Massachusetts Press, 1987.
Like Fauset, Larsen rejects the romantic extremes of nationalism and assimilation in favor of cultural dualism. Larsen rebels against the assumption that blacks need to deny their color and culture to become first-class American citizens. Praises the convincing quality of Larsen's presentation of her characters' obsession with fashion, decorum, marriage, and housekeeping.

Davis, Arthur P. "First Fruits." In *From the Dark Tower: Afro-American Writers 1900 to 1960*. Washington, D.C.: Howard University Press, 1974.

Presents Larsen as far more intense and bitter than Jessie Fauset in her treatment of themes common to both writers' works. Reflecting her artistic skill, Larsen expresses the agony and frustrations experienced by blacks through realistic and believable characters. Views *Quicksand* as a better novel than *Passing* in part because of Larsen's skillful use of the quicksand motif, which represents Helga's inner self and which is emphasized with images of suffocation, sinking, drowning, and enclosure.

Dearborn, Mary V. *Pocahontas's Daughters: Gender and Ethnicity in American Culture*. New York: Oxford University Press, 1986.

Discusses Larsen, who is presented as a "major novelist of ethnic and female identity," in relationship to the situation of the black woman author in the Harlem Renaissance and to the themes of miscegenation and the mulatto. Examines the reasons behind the underacknowledgement of Larsen's importance, giving careful attention to the accusations of plagiarism that contributed to the silence of her post-Renaissance period. Argues that *Passing* has been misunderstood because critics have assumed Larsen shares Irene's condemnation of Clare. The novel's actual subject is the consequences of repression.

Ford, Nick Aaron. *The Contemporary Negro Novel: A Study in Race Relations*. Boston: Meador, 1936. Reprint. College Park, Md.: McGrath, 1968.

Comments on Larsen's treatment of dominant political and social themes of Negro literature of the era. She is notable for her ironic treatment of the theme of prejudice, and for her portrayal of Negro attempts to reject cultural heritage. She rejects mixed marriage and condemns passing.

Gayle, Addison, Jr. "The Confusion of Identity." In *The Way of the New World: The Black Novel in America*. Garden City, N.Y.: Anchor Press, 1976.

Criticizes Larsen's romantic view of the black poor, which reflects her acceptance of the distorted images of white sociologists. Although Larsen demonstrates that passing entails loss of identity, her novels nonetheless imply the superiority of black middle-class values. *Quicksand* and *Passing* demonstrate that attempts to attain "identity through fantasy" are doomed. Includes brief discussion of the influence of Carl Van Vechten.

Gloster, Hugh. "Fiction of the Negro Renascence." In *Negro Voices in American Fiction*. Chapel Hill: University of North Carolina Press, 1948. Reprint. New York: Russell & Russell, 1965.

In both her novels, Larsen is concerned with the "disintegration and maladjustment wrought by miscegenation." Larsen indicates that "the Negro-white hybrid" rarely attains harmony between personal desires and social status.

Focusing on the psychological problems of Clare Kendry, *Passing* is one of "the significant studies of its kind in American fiction."

Huggins, Nathan. *Harlem Renaissance*. New York: Oxford University Press, 1971.
Responding to the late-1920's attempt to abandon genteel standards, Larsen explores the uncompromising dilemma of the "cultured-primitive Negro." Her characters are pulled between poles of civility and passion. Both *Quicksand* and *Passing* center on the issue of cultural schizophrenia. Although Larsen feels the attraction of black life, she is unable to accept primitivism uncritically. Contradicting the general movement, Larsen exposes the narrowness of black life, its avoidance of experiment. The sharp dichotomy of realism and romance in her novels makes them seem schizophrenic.

McDowell, Deborah E. " 'That nameless . . . shameful impulse': Sexuality in Nella Larsen's *Quicksand* and *Passing*." *Studies in Black American Literature* 3 (1988): 139-167. Reprinted as Introduction to *Quicksand and Passing*. New Brunswick, N.J.: Rutgers University Press, 1986.
Larsen's novels address the dialectic between pleasure and danger. Their reticence about sexuality reflects both the influence of nineteenth century genteel fiction and Larsen's need to refute jazz-age stereotypes of black women as primitive exotics. Their recognition of the reality of female desire— specifically that between Clare and Irene in *Passing*—anticipates more radical feminist insights. Drawing on Afro-American folk traditions of "masking," Larsen creates superficially "safe" plots focused on black middle-class respectability even as she undercuts them with the "dangerous" story of female desire.

"Nella Larsen." In *Contemporary Literary Criticism*, vol. 37, edited by Daniel G. Marowski. Detroit: Gale Research, 1986.
Compilation of materials on Larsen's fiction including a biographical head-note, reprints of contemporary reviews of *Quicksand* and *Passing*, and excerpts from more recent criticism, including selections by Robert Bone, Hiroko Sato, Arthur Davis, Addison Gayle, Claudia Tate, and Mary Helen Washington.

Perry, Margaret. "The Major Novels." In *Silence to the Drums: A Survey of the Literature of the Harlem Renaissance*. Westport, Conn.: Greenwood Press, 1976.
Analysis of *Passing* and *Quicksand* placing strong emphasis on Larsen's awareness of female sexuality. Helga Crane is one of the only Harlem Renaissance era characters who desires sexual fulfillment. Because Larsen uses the black man as an image of gratification, her work reinforces the Renaissance view of the black race as vital, full-bodied, and rich in humaneness.

Sato, Hiroko. "Under the Harlem Shadows: A Study of Jessie Fauset and Nella
Larsen." In *The Harlem Renaissance Remembered*, edited by Arna Bontemps.
New York: Dodd, Meads, 1972.
A much more sophisticated writer than Fauset, Larsen was the first black
writer who demonstrated that a personal problem could be expanded to a
racial problem, then to a universal one. Her "masculine detachment" enables
her to expand on the significance of small, particular situations. Reflecting
Larsen's primary interest in psychological rather than social problems, Helga
Crane anticipates Faulkner's character Joe Christmas in *Light in August*.
Larsen passes no moral judgment on Helga at the end of the book.

Singh, Amritjit. " 'Fooling Our White Folks': Color Caste in American Life." In
The Novels of the Harlem Renaissance. University Park: Pennsylvania State
University Press, 1976.
Relates Larsen's work to the conventional narrative pattern of Harlem Renaissance passing novels. The heroine attempts to pass as mistress or wife of a
bigoted white man and finally returns to black life when she begins to miss its
warmth, color, and vivacity. *Passing* possesses a psychological interest absent
in superficially similar novels by Fauset and Walter White. Not primarily a
study of miscegenation, *Quicksand* focuses on a black woman's acute consciousness and helpless acceptance of white myths concerning miscegenation.

Wall, Cheryl A. "Passing for What? Aspects of Identity in Nella Larsen's Novels."
Black American Literature Forum 20 (Spring/Summer, 1986): 97-111.
Argues that the tragedy for Larsen's mulatto characters is the impossibility of
self-definition. Her protagonists assume false identities in order to ensure
social survial, but the result is psychological suicide. Engaging issues of mar-
ginality and cultural dualism that were central to the Harlem Renaissance,
Larsen demonstrates the psychological costs of racism and sexism. Her treatment of passing expands its significance to encompass the denial of self required of women who conform to restrictive gender roles.

Washington, Mary Helen. "The Mulatta Trap: Nella Larsen's Women of the 1920s."
In *Invented Lives: Narratives of Black Women 1860-1960*. Garden City, N.Y.:
Anchor Press, 1987.
Although Larsen's novels were perceived as "uplift novels" proving that blacks
were as intelligent, moral, and civilized as whites, both *Quicksand* and *Passing*
go far beyond other novels of the "Talented Tenth." Larsen emphasizes "the
chaos in the world of the black elite, the emptiness in the climb to bourgeois
respectability." Larsen's women are stunted by cultural scripts that deny them
the possibility of "awakenings" and punish them for defiance.

Watson, Carol McAlpine. "Race Consciousness and Self-Criticism, 1921-1945." In
Prologue: The Novels of Black American Women, 1891-1965. Westport,

Conn.: Greenwood Press, 1985.
Brief discussion emphasizing Larsen's hostility to the Afro-American church.
Unlike Hurston, who saw black religion as a valuable embodiment of Afro-
American culture, Larsen denounced the church as inimical to political ad-
vancement, offering only a counterfeit freedom that anaesthetized black Amer-
icans to reality.

Wintz, Cary D. "Literature and Politics." In *Black Culture and the Harlem Renaissance*. Houston: Rice University Press, 1988.
Larsen projects very negative images of hopeless and powerless women unable
to establish any control over their destinies. Images of strong women are
lacking in both *Passing* and *Quicksand*. Helga sinks into a psychological quagmire not because she is black, but because she is a woman. Despite a superficial air of success, Larsen's literary career and life were in fact almost as
depressing as those of her characters.

Selected Titles

Passing
"Beyond the Color Line." *The New York Times Book Review* 34 (April 28, 1929): 14.
Generally favorable review praising Larsen's ability to trace the "involved
processes of a mind that is divided against itself, the fights between the dictates
of reason and desire." Larsen's prose is strong and her dialogue convincing,
except when she presents intellectual party talk. The primary difficulty with
the book lies in its unconvincing conclusion.

Cooke, Michael G. "Self-Veiling: James Weldon Johnson, Charles Chesnutt, and
Nella Larsen." In *Afro-American Literature in the Twentieth Century: The
Achievement of Intimacy*. New Haven, Conn.: Yale University Press, 1984.
Reads *Passing* as an example of "self-veiling," the stage of the process toward
intimacy in which the black individual is least aware of her own experience.
The novel reveals that the movement of blacks to the urban North did little to
alter the fundamental problems of the Reconstruction South. Both Irene's
attempt to hide behind the DuBoisean veil and Clare's to break it are doomed
to ironic failure.

Fuller, Hoyt. Introduction to *Passing*. New York: Collier, 1971.
Situates Larsen's novel in regard to the historical significance of passing in
Afro-American life. Her exposure of the emptiness in the lives of upper-class
blacks is the inverse side of the interest in the black community shown by
other Harlem Renaissance writers. An interesting, if flawed, novel, *Passing* is
important for its graphic evocation of upper-class black society.

Seabrook, W. B. "Touch of the Tar-Brush." *The Saturday Review of Literature* 5 (May 18, 1929): 1017-1018.

Generally favorable review praising Larsen for her sense of form, her strongly felt central character, and the generally high quality of her prose, which is marred only when she lapses into literary jargon. Attributes the occasional evidence of self-consciousness to Larsen's awareness that she was writing for a mixed audience.

Tate, Claudia C. "Nella Larsen's *Passing*: A Problem of Interpretation." *Black American Literature Forum* 14 (Winter, 1980): 142-146.

Tate asserts that, while the tragic mulatto theme which has dominated critical attention to *Passing* is an important part of the novel, the novel also centers on jealousy, psychological ambiguity, and intrigue. By focusing on the latter elements, *Passing* is transformed from an anachronistic melodrama into an enduring work of art. The social pretentiousness that most critics have condemned is not a deficiency, but an intentional element of Larsen's art. The conclusion of the novel defies simple analysis, attesting to Larsen's consummate skill at delineating psychological ambiguity.

Youman, Mary Mabel. "Nella Larsen's *Passing*: A Study in Irony." *CLA Journal* 18 (December, 1974): 235-241.

Argues against readings that view Clare as the protagonist of *Passing*, asserting that Irene is the true protagonist who demonstrates that blacks can and do lose the spiritual values of blackness even when they remain in a black world. Quotes Larsen's comments on Walter White and Gertrude Stein to demonstrate her belief that the black heritage is more important than middle-class security. Concludes with the observation that Larsen failed to develop a narrative structure capable of developing the full implications of her theme.

Quicksand

Bone, Robert. "The Rear Guard." In *The Negro Novel in America*. New Haven, Conn.: Yale University Press, 1965.

Part of the "rear guard" which made the last serious attempt to "orient Negro fiction toward bourgeois ideals," Larsen interprets folk culture as a threat, and sees value only in gracious living. Nonetheless, *Quicksand* is an authentic case study that can be profitably approached through psychoanalytic interpretation. The central tension is the conflict between Helga's sexuality and her love of things. Race is functional inasmuch as it helps generate Helga's neurotic withdrawal pattern.

Carby, Hazel. "The Quicksands of Representation: Rethinking Black Cultural Politics." In *Reconstructing Womanhood: The Emergence of the Afro-American Woman Novelist*. New York: Oxford University Press, 1987.

Reflecting Larsen's awareness of the connection between consumerist, capitalist, and sexist ideology, *Quicksand* tears apart the fabric of the romance form. Helga's alienation is not primarily psychological; rather, it is produced by existing social relations and can be altered only by a change in those relations. Rejecting the romantic evocation of folk culture common in the Harlem Renaissance, Larsen is a crucial figure in the neglected tradition of black women's novels concerning the urban confrontation with race, class, and sexuality.

Christian, Barbara. "The Rise and Fall of the Proper Mulatta." In *Black Women Novelists: The Development of a Tradition, 1892-1976*. Westport, Conn.: Greenwood Press, 1980.
Quicksand reveals the hollowness of upper-middle-class Negro society. Larsen employs elements of both the novel of convention and the primitive motif in order to demonstrate their limitations. Her protagonist, a pathetic mulatta, is doomed to become either a self-centered neurotic or a downtrodden peasant. Larsen's life mirrors the tragedy described in her novels.

DuBois, W. E. B. Review of *Quicksand*. *The Crisis* 35 (June, 1928): 202.
Brief favorable notice of *Quicksand* as the best piece of Afro-American fiction since Charles Chesnutt. It ranks with Fauset's *There Is Confusion* for its subtle comprehension of the "curious cross currents that swirl about the black American." DuBois observes that whites will not like the book and encourages his readers to support Larsen's art.

Fleming, Robert E. "The Influence of *Main Street* on Nella Larsen's *Quicksand*." *Modern Fiction Studies* 31 (Autumn, 1985): 547-553.
Although Sinclair Lewis' Carol Kennicott provided a model for Helga Crane's character and life, Larsen's intentions differ greatly from Lewis', as an examination of the resolution of *Quicksand* shows. Like Carol, Helga is a dreamer who marries a small-town professional and ultimately is defeated by her squalid environment. Where Lewis forces his readers to sympathize with other characters, however, Larsen views Helga as the victim of limitations set by both white and black communities.

Hill, Adelaide Cromwell. Introduction to *Quicksand*. New York: Collier, 1971.
Introduction emphasizes the significance of black women as novelists. Following a brief history of black women's fiction, Hill places *Quicksand* in the context of the black nationalist mood of the late 1960's. Black women who minimize their own strengths "in order to build those of the Black man" will resist many of the book's themes, yet Larsen's ability to cover a broad range of issues and succeed as a woman in a hostile context makes the book a significant achievement. Despite its bland style and unreal situations, *Quicksand* broadens the black community's knowledge of the black experience.

Howard, Lillie P. " 'A Lack Somewhere': Nella Larsen's *Quicksand* and the Harlem Renaissance." In *The Harlem Renaissance Re-examined*, edited by Victor A. Kramer. New York: AMS Press, 1987.

Quicksand is important as an examination of the problematic side of the Harlem Renaissance, which contrasts with the superficial image of the era as one of vitality and celebration. Larsen examines a character who is torn asunder by her inability to reconcile the disparate strivings within herself. Helga's tragedy comes in large part from her inability to recognize the alternative paths available to her. Her tragedy is personal rather than social in origin.

Lay, Mary M. "Parallels: Henry James's *The Portrait of a Lady* and Nella Larsen's *Quicksand.*" *CLA Journal* 20 (June, 1977): 475-486.

Examines the parallels between James's and Larsen's novels, including the focus on dissatisfied, sexually confused heroines seeking a happiness they are unable to define; and the similarity of the men with whom they interact. The parallels lead up to strikingly different resolutions, however. Where Isabel Archer is able to make a positive choice at the end, Helga fails, not because of environment, but because of choice and personality.

Lewis, David Levering. *When Harlem Was in Vogue*. New York: Alfred A. Knopf, 1981.

Quicksand is a considerable allegorical achievement with a modern heroine whose destruction is not only racially, but also personally, determined. Larsen, who ultimately may have found the "vagaries of a white identity preferable to the pain of Africa," warns that Afro-Americans who capriciously reject middle-class status risk falling from civilization into atavism. Not to master emotions risks being destroyed by them.

Mays, Benjamin E. "God's Impotence and His Non-Existence." In *The Negro's God as Reflected in His Literature*. Chapman & Grimes, 1938. Reprint. New York: Atheneum, 1968.

Presents *Quicksand* as the most extreme expression of the tendency toward atheism and agnosticism in black writing of the 1920's and 1930's. Revolting against the white man's God and ultimately denying his existence, Helga rejects the idea of a God who loves all people, seeing nothing in black existence to substantiate that belief.

"A Mulatto Girl." Review of *Quicksand. The New York Times Book Review* 33 (April 8, 1928): 16-17.

Favorable review distinguishing *Quicksand* from both the abolitionist stream of American racial fiction and the exotic Harlem novels inspired by Carl Van Vechten. Larsen is aware that the primary purpose of the novel is to deal with individuals rather than with classes. Helga's essential tragedy has little to do with her race. *Quicksand* is an articulate, sympathetic first novel with a wider outlook on life than most novels written by Negroes.

Thornton, Hortense E. "Sexism as Quagmire in Nella Larsen's *Quicksand*." *CLA Journal* 26 (March, 1973): 285-301.
Argues that Helga attains tragic stature and that her fall is created at least as much by sexism as by racism. Reviews previous criticism and analyzes Helga's character, arguing that the hardships of her youth lead her to wear a stoic mask in order to survive. Despite the oppressive forces she confronts, she assumes responsibility for every failure.

PAULE MARSHALL

Biography

Brock, Sabine. "Talk as a Form of Action: An Interview with Paule Marshall." In *History and Tradition in Afro-American Culture*, edited by Gunther H. Lenz. Frankfurt: Campus Verlag, 1985.
Interview in which Marshall discusses various subjects including the influences on her work; the situation of the black woman writer; the civil rights movement; the women's movement; and various aspects of *Brown Girl, Brownstones*, *The Chosen Place, The Timeless People*, and *Praisesong for the Widow*.

Christian, Barbara. "Paule Marshall." In *Afro-American Fiction Writers After 1955*, edited by Thadious M. Davis and Trudier Harris. Vol. 33 of *Dictionary of Literary Biography*. Detroit: Bruccoli Clark, 1984.
Substantial reference entry incorporating biographical sketch and analysis of each of Marshall's novels. Discusses Marshall's failure to attain commercial success despite excellent reviews. Emphasizes the importance of the oral expression Marshall encountered as a child in a Barbadian immigrant family. Marshall's work is characterized by her love of people. Rendering complex women characters in the context of equally complex societies, Marshall maintains a faith in the ability of human beings to transcend their limitations.

Denniston, Dorothy L. "Paule Marshall." In *American Women Writers*, vol. 3, edited by Lina Mainiero. New York: Frederick Ungar, 1981.
Biographical entry including brief commentary on *Brown Girl, Brownstones* and *The Chosen Place, The Timeless People*. Concludes that Marshall's exceptional talent, born of solid scholarship and careful craftsmanship, makes a valuable contribution to understanding of the multidimensional aspects of black experience. Bibliography lists entries in other reference works.

Marshall, Paule. "From the Poets in the Kitchen." *Callaloo* 18 (Spring/Summer, 1983): 23-30. Reprinted in *Reena and Other Stories* by Paule Marshall. Westbury, N.Y.: Feminist Press, 1983.
Important autobiographical essay. Marshall emphasizes the importance of the oral tradition passed down by women to the voice of her fiction. Comments on the political content of black women's talk, which was used to create a refuge from the outside world. Discusses the relationship between the oral tradition and her education in the English and Euro-American literary traditions.

_____ . "The Negro Woman in American Literature." *Freedomways* (First Quarter, 1966): 20-25. Reprinted in *Keeping the Faith: Writings by Contempo-*

rary Black American Women, edited by Pat Crutchfield Exum. New York: Fawcett, 1974.
Transcript of a talk delivered by Marshall at a conference concerning literary images of black women. Marshall criticizes the stereotypical dichotomy between immoral primitives and strong matriarchs in novels by DuBois and West, but praises images created by James Baldwin, John Williams, Alice Childress, and Paule Marshall. Cites Brooks's Maud Martha as the most fully developed image of a black woman in literature.

Reilly, John. "Marshall, Paule (née Burke)." In *Contemporary Novelists*, 4th ed., edited by D. L. Kirkpatrick. New York: St. Martin's Press, 1986.
Reference entry including biographical outline, list of publications, and analysis of Marshall's novels. Emphasizes the ways in which Marshall has transformed the oral tradition she celebrates in her interviews and essays into a more deliberate, "markedly literary" form. Reaching beyond superficial denunciations of modernization, Marshall's complexly realized primary theme is that every woman must gain the power to speak the language of her elder kinswomen.

Washington, Mary Helen. "Paule Marshall Talking with Mary Helen Washington." In *Writing Lives: Conversations Between Women Writers*, edited by Mary Chamberlain. London: Virago, 1988.
Published in slightly different form in *Mothering the Mind*, edited by Ruth Perry and Martine Watson Brownley. New York: Holmes & Meier, 1984. Conversation between Marshall and a prominent black woman critic focusing on Marshall's background in the Barbadian-American community; the impact of women's oral expression on her writing; her transformation of her mother's voice; and the significance of mother-daughter bonds.

Williams, John. "Return of a Native Daughter: An Interview with Paule Marshall and Maryse Conde." *Sage* 3 (Fall, 1986): 52-53.
Conversation between Marshall and an African woman novelist concerning the relationship between Africa and black America. Marshall comments that Africa is both a concrete destination and a spiritual homeland for Afro-Americans. The spiritual return is necessary if blacks are to develop a sense of their collective history. She supports the concept of a universal "African" language and comments on her use of African images and metaphors.

Commentary

Brathwaite, Edward. "Rehabilitations." *Critical Quarterly* 13 (Summer, 1971): 175-184. Published as "West Indian History and Society in the Art of Paule

Marshall's Novel." *Journal of Black Studies* 1 (December, 1970): 225-238.
Essay by an important West Indian writer praising Marshall's important contribution to West Indian Anglophone literature, which has not often addressed
either the communal history or Third World situation of its central theme: the
frustration of the author's persona by a society suffering from a lack of identity. In *The Chosen Place, the Timeless People*, Marshall examines the effects
of the colonial condition and experience on her people. Marshall ultimately
affirms the possibility of rehabilitating the West Indian psyche.

Brock, Sabine. "Transcending the 'Loophole of Retreat': Paule Marshall's Placing
of Female Generations." *Callaloo* 30 (Winter, 1987): 79-102.
Discusses Marshall's image of her heroines' efforts to create a space in which
women will be able to move, thereby challenging the limits of both Anglo-
American discourse and of their closely circumscribed actual lives. This attempt places Marshall near the center of a black feminist tradition which has
struggled against the historical and metaphorical denial of space for black
women. Contrasts *Brown Girl, Brownstones* with *Praisesong for the Widow* to
demonstrate the importance of generational difference in Marshall's treatment
of the theme.

Brown, Lloyd W. "The Rhythms of Power in Paule Marshall's Fiction." *Novel* 7
(Winter, 1974): 159-167.
Emphasizes Marshall's portrayal of the creative willpower, symbolized by the
rhythm of calypso music, that enables her characters to transcend the destructive forces of time and history. Marshall is important as a writer whose
treatment of Pan-African and feminist concerns is grounded in a complex
analysis of power not only as the goal of political movements but as a social
and psychological phenomenon that affects racial and sexual roles, shapes
cultural traditions, and molds the individual psyche.

Christian, Barbara. "Sculpture and Space: The Interdependency of Character and
Culture in the Novels of Paule Marshall." In *Black Women Novelists: The
Development of a Tradition, 1892-1976*. Westport, Conn.: Greenwood Press,
1980.
Emphasizes Marshall's primary devotion to the delineation of character within
the context of a particular culture. As Marshall matures, her emphasis moves
from the way the world affects the individual psyche to how the interaction of
many psyches creates the world. A first-generation descendant of West Indian
immigrants, Marshall experienced the merging and conflict of distinctive black
cultures which provides a central focus of her novels. Includes lengthy discussion of *Brown Girl, Brownstones* and *The Chosen Place, the Timeless People*.

Collier, Eugenia. "The Closing of the Circle: Movement from Division to Wholeness in Paule Marshall's Fiction." In *Black Women Writers, 1950-1980: A*

Critical Evaluation, edited by Mari Evans. Garden City, N.Y.: Anchor Press, 1984.

Identifies the progression from the divided individual self to the self made whole through merging with the community as the dominant pattern in Marshall's fiction. Ritual, particularly dance, is crucial to the realization of unity. *Brown Girl, Brownstones* culminates in a realization of the value of community; *The Chosen Place, the Timeless People* emphasizes the power of the past; and *Praisesong for the Widow* encompasses the lessons of the previous work to assert a vision uniting individual black people with black people worldwide.

Cooke, John. "Whose Child? The Fiction of Paule Marshall." *CLA Journal* 24 (September, 1980): 1-15.

Marshall's work is characterized by her continuing search for a cultural opposition capable of providing an unambiguous political perspective. After exploring the opposition of immigrant versus American in *Brown Girl, Brownstones* and Afro-Caribbean versus white in *Soul Clap Hands and Sing*, she arrives at her resolution in the Western versus Pan-African dichotomy in *The Chosen Place, the Timeless People*. The major problem Marshall encountered in arriving at this perspective was the difficulty of integrating her major subject matter—sexuality—with a political perspective.

DeVeaux, Alexis. "Paule Marshall: In Celebration of Our Triumph." *Essence* 10 (May, 1979): 70-71, 96-98, 123-135.

Lengthy biographical sketch including analysis of *Brown Girl, Brownstones* and *The Chosen Place, the Timeless People*. Emphasizes that while Marshall creates strong women who are centers of power, she is not a "safe" writer and is willing to confront difficult conflicts within the black community. Among the topics discussed are the influence of women's storytelling, which was in part political, on Marshall's consciousness; her work with *Our World* magazine; her commitment to the novel form; and her plans for the novel that eventually became *Praisesong for the Widow*.

Johnson, Charles. "The Women." In *Being and Race: Black Writing Since 1970*. Bloomington: Indiana University Press, 1988.

Brief comment by a black male novelist praising Marshall for her steady production of first-rate fiction and the spiritual balance and emotional maturity of her work. Marshall's strengths are her careful exploration of the theme of the loss of identity and her ability to record the beauty of non-American black voices.

Kapai, Leela. "Dominant Themes and Technique in Paule Marshall's Fiction." *CLA Journal* 26 (September, 1972): 49-59.

Thematic and stylistic overview of Marshall's fiction through *The Chosen Place, the Timeless People*. Kapai discusses the themes of the quest for identity, the race problem, the importance of tradition to black Americans, and the need for sharing in meaningful relationships. Stylistically, she combines a mastery of traditional plot devices to maintain interest while employing a range of experimental techniques such as stream of consciousness and symbolic language to heighten meaning.

Keizs, Marcia. "Themes and Styles in the Works of Paule Marshall." *Negro American Literature Forum* 9 (Fall, 1975): 67, 71-75.
Surveys Marshall's fiction through *The Chosen Place, the Timeless People*, emphasizing the personal and political nature of her vision. Seeking a synthesis of black and third world people, she shapes her fiction around the dichotomies of black/white, man/woman, strong/weak, and life/death. Notes Marshall's concern with refuting myths and stereotypes of black women specifically and black people as a whole.

Kubitschek, Missy Dehn. "Paul Marshall's Women on Quest." *Black American Literature Forum* 21 (Spring/Summer, 1987): 43-60.
Relates Marshall's treatment of questing women to the paradigms of mythologist Joseph Campbell, feminist critic Carol Christ, and Afro-American critic Robert Stepto. Marshall highlights age, continual process and female mentoring as they relate to empowerment and subsequent articulation. Her questers achieve energized and articulate identities, with each quester resolving problems of her particular stage of life. Includes a valuable discussion of Marshall's treatment of lesbian themes.

McCluskey, John, Jr. "And Called Every Generation Blessed: Theme, Setting, and Ritual in the Works of Paule Marshall." In *Black Women Writers, 1950-1980: A Critical Evaluation*, edited by Mari Evans. Garden City, N.Y.: Anchor Press, 1984.
Focuses on Marshall's treatment of two basic themes: the encounter with the past and the need to reverse the present social order. In each of her novels, the major characters experience a terrible loneliness which they attempt to overcome through sharing. One of the basic stylistic features of Marshall's fiction is her reliance on collective rituals used to bind groups of individuals into a cohesive community.

"Paule Marshall." In *Contemporary Literary Criticism*, vol. 27, edited by Jean C. Stine. Detroit: Gale Research, 1984.
Compilation of materials on Marshall's fiction including a brief headnote, excerpts from a range of reviews of her three novels—including Robert Bone's review of *The Chosen Place, the Timeless People* and Darryl Pinckney's review

of *Praisesong for the Widow*—and sections from critical essays by Leela
Kapai and Lloyd W. Brown.

Pannil, Linda. "From the Workshop: The Fiction of Paule Marshall." *MELUS* 12
(Summer, 1985): 63-73.
Emphasizes Marshall's mastery of narrative techniques including comments on
style, plot, and characterization. Contends that critics who view Marshall
primarily in political terms distort her achievement.

Pinckney, Darryl. "Roots." *The New York Review of Books* 30 (April 28, 1983):
26-29.
Unfavorable review of *Praisesong for the Widow* and reprint edition of *Brown
Girl, Brownstones*. Pinckney criticizes the sentimentality of Marshall's titles,
which reflect the romanticized version of Africa which she contrasts with the
evils of the West. Both this simplistic contrast and her portrayal of heroines
who inevitably triumph when they make radical decisions lead to notions that
are "dangerously foolish."

Rahming, Melvin B. "The Rejection of the West Indian Stereotype." In *The Evolution of the West Indian's Image in the Afro-American Novel*. Millwood, N.Y.:
Associated Faculty Press, 1986.
Noting that Marshall's family background gives her a clearer perspective than
that of most American novelists, Rahming praises her treatment of West Indian
culture and psychology. *Brown Girl, Brownstones* embodies two crucial aspects
of West Indian personality: the synthesis of character, place, and community;
and the psychological deracination of those who become racially assertive. *The
Chosen Place, the Timeless People* adds an awareness that the psychological
return from exile is only successful to the extent it reestablishes the synthesis
disrupted by racial awakening.

Waniek, Marilyn Nelson. "Paltry Things: Immigrants and Marginal Men in Paule
Marshall's Short Fiction." *Callaloo* 18 (Spring/Summer, 1983): 46-56.
Discussion of the marginal immigrant men in Marshall's short fiction. Begins
with a brief discussion of *Brown Girl, Brownstones*, which Waniek interprets
as a conflict between Selina's mother and father. While Selina vacillates between extremes, she fails to attain a balance and remains a permanent and
unhappy outsider.

Willis, Susan. "Describing Arcs of Recovery: Paule Marshall's Relationship to
Afro-American Culture." In *Specifying: Black Women Writing the American
Experience*. Madison: University of Wisconsin Press, 1987.
Marshall's primary task is to articulate the difficulties of living in two worlds
simultaneously and the need to unite Afro-American cultures of North Amer-

ica and the Caribbean. Marshall's three novels constitute generationally defined points in a woman's life and confront different aspects of couple relationships as they are defined under capitalism. Each novel suggests a different
politically defined mode. *Brown Girl, Brownstones* concludes with a vision of
open possibility; *The Chosen Place, The Timeless People* focuses on a grim and
contradictory reality; and *Praisesong for the Widow* suggests a visionary sense
of renewal through the recovery of culture.

Selected Titles

Brown Girl, Brownstones
Benston, Kimberly W. "Architectural Imagery and Unity in Paule Marshall's *Brown
    Girl, Brownstones*." *Negro American Literature Forum* 9 (Fall, 1975): 67-70.
    Identifies seven major image patterns, most importantly that involving archi-
    tecture, as Marshall's solution to the problem of unifying her two major
    stories, that of domestic conflict and that of Selina's evolution. Discusses the
    way architecture establishes unity in relation to plot organization; character
    delineation; definition of environment; the novel's language; and inclusive
    metaphorical structure. Other important image clusters involve light and dark;
    water; blindness; silence; color; and machinery.

Butcher, Philip. "The Younger Novelists and the Urban Negro." *CLA Journal* 4
    (March, 1961): 196-203.
    Praises Marshall's "epic of acculturation" as one of the finest works by a
    young black novelist. Marshall delineates in depth a rich assortment of charac-
    ters functioning within a transplanted culture gradually modified to conform to
    the patterns of American life. Marshall expresses the "universal significance"
    of her materials. The only other black woman novelist discussed in Butcher's
    essay is Evelyn West.

Collier, Eugenia. "Selina's Journey Home: From Alienation to Unity in Paule
    Marshall's *Brown Girl, Brownstones*." *Obsidian* 8, nos. 2/3 (1982): 6-19.
    Examines Selina's growth as a journey from alienation to unity, with important
    implications for the black community generally. As Selina grows toward indi-
    vidual wholeness, she also comes to terms with her black heritage. Emphasizes
    the importance of rituals grounded in Caribbean tradition and symbols such as
    the bangles to Marshall's analysis of the difficulties of immersing one's self in
    one's people.

Govan, Sandra Y. "Women Within the Circle: Selina and Silla Boyce." *Callaloo* 18
    (Spring/Summer, 1983): 148-152.
    Favorable review of reprint edition identifying Selina and Silla as the center of
    a circle around which the other events and themes in the novel circulate.

Marshall portrays complicated relationships without clichés or stereotypes, creating classic black women protagonists comparable to Hurston's Janie, Morrison's Sula, and Brooks's Maud Martha.

Harris, Trudier. "No Outlet for the Blues: Silla Boyce's Plight in *Brown Girl, Brownstones*." *Callaloo* 18 (Spring/Summer, 1983): 57-67.

Character analysis of Silla Boyce, stressing the similarity of her plight as an immigrant lost between two cultures to that of the tragic mulatto figure in earlier Afro-American literature. Strong, disappointed, vindictive, and loving, Silla is one of the most complex characters in recent American literature. The powerful unresolved emotions she feels keep her in a state of rage. Although Silla would reject the form, her day-to-day existence exemplifies the blues feeling. Unable to release her pain outward, she can only turn it inward at the cost of her humanity. Silla's philosophy is that of the capitalist, not the humanitarian.

Leseur, Geta J. "*Brown Girl, Brownstones* as a Novel of Development." *Obsidian II* 1 (Winter, 1986): 119-129.

Emphasizes the importance of the Barbadian community to Selina's development from a fragmented self toward a realigned whole. The Barbardians, especially the women, exude a strength based on their wholeness. The confusion that Selina must overcome is based on the "doom" embedded in their double consciousness.

McHenry, Susan. "*Brown Girl, Brownstones*." *Ms.* 10 (November, 1981): 47.

Favorable review of reprint edition identifying the novel as a classic comparable in its treatment of growing up black and female to *Their Eyes Were Watching God* and *Maud Martha*. In its treatment of immigrant experience, it resembles the novels of Agnes Smedley and Anzia Yezierska. Marshall's willingness to allow her protagonist to explore her own sexuality differentiates the novel from other work of the 1950's.

Miller, Jane. "Women's Men." In *Women Writing About Men*. New York: Pantheon Books, 1986.

Focuses on the tension between Barbadian men and women as an influence on Selina's development. Selina experiences a set of irreconcilable oppositions between America and the West Indies, dreams and realities, men and women. She grows up knowing that women find men sexually attractive but that frequently they must submerge their longing in the cause of survival.

Schneider, Deborah. "A Search for Selfhood: Paule Marshall's *Brown Girl, Brownstones*." In *The Afro-American Novel Since 1960*, edited by Peter Bruck and Wolfgang Karrer. Amsterdam: B. R. Gruner, 1982.

Marshall unifies the diverse materials of her novel not through the use of particular image patterns, but through her concentration on Selina's psychological development. Marshall's theme of seeking identity through art and individualism rather than community action links the novel clearly to dominant intellectual trends of the 1950's. Selina shows no awareness that the conflict between her mother and father is related to their sex. The antithetical values associated with each are Selina's projections, not aspects of objective reality.

Troester, Rosalie Riegle. "Turbulence and Tenderness: Mothers, Daughters, and 'Othermothers' in Paule Marshall's *Brown Girl, Brownstones*." *Sage* 1 (Fall, 1984): 13-16.
Focuses on Marshall's use of "othermothers"—women who help guide and form young girls outside the immediate family context—to exemplify values divergent from those of Selina's biological mother. As a result of her turbulent relationship with Silla, Selina turns to Suggie Skeets, Miss Thompson, and Miss Mary for unconditional love. Predictably, Silla harbors animosity toward these women who represent conditions she represses in her own life.

Wade-Gayles, Gloria. "The Halo and the Hardships." In *No Crystal Stair: Visions of Race and Sex in Black Women's Fiction*. New York: Pilgrim Press, 1984.
In *Brown Girl, Brownstones*, the tragic dimensions of black men's realities obscure the harsh realities of black women's lives. Selina begins to understand her parents' relationship on her journey of self-discovery that teaches her to reject capital and material things—the forces that have crushed her father—as the ordering principles of her life. *Brown Girl, Brownstones* is the definitive novel of the West Indian search for a culture combining the old and the new in a Bajan-American synthesis.

Washington, Mary Helen. Afterword to *Brown Girl, Brownstones*. Old Westbury, N.Y.: Feminist Press, 1981.
Recognizing Selina as Marshall's "figure of redemption," Washington identifies Silla Boyce as the monumental tragic figure at the center of the novel. The power, literacy, and community strength of the Barbadians are essential to Marshall's tragic vision, which portrays the characters as inevitably wedded to a "conjugal ritual from which they cannot be released." Miss Thompson is a crucial figure in the novel because she links Selina to the larger black American community which the Barbadians despise.

Watson, Carol McAlpine. "Racial Issues and Universal Themes, 1946-1965." In *Prologue: The Novels of Black American Women, 1891-1965*. Westport, Conn.: Greenwood Press, 1985.
Marshall's novel is unique among postwar tales of ghetto life since it portrays the ghetto as a harsh, but not invincible, environment. Selina's developing

womanhood is the novel's central metaphor. Before she can enter the broader world, Selina must resolve the conflict between her parents' values. Describes Silla's values as "narrow and sometimes ruthless, but sustaining."

The Chosen Place, the Timeless People

Bone, Robert. Review of *The Chosen Place, the Timeless People*. *The New York Times Book Review* 74 (November 30, 1969): 4, 54.

Extremely favorable review identifying *The Chosen Place, the Timeless People* as the best novel ever written by a black woman and, along with William Demby's *The Catacombs*, one of the two important black novels of the 1960's. A parable of Western civilization and its relations with the undeveloped world, Marshall's novel transforms history and politics into ritual and myth. Characterized by a "trim and sprightly prose," Marshall's novel is a compendium of "old-fashioned novelistic virtues." A creation worthy of Camus, the magnificent portrait of Merle Kinbona stands at the center of the novel, an agent for destruction or a catalyst for growth.

Chevigny, Bell Gale. Review of *The Chosen Place, the Timeless People*. *The Village Voice* (October 8, 1970): 6, 30-31.

Favorable review, approaching the novel as evidence that "revolutionary ideas are coming of age." Praises Marshall's intelligent politics and penetrating humanism. Notes that no other contemporary novelist has attempted the balancing of Jewish and black characters. By refusing to compromise her politics or her human understanding, Marshall makes better sense of both.

Harris, Trudier. "Three Black Women Writers and Humanism: A Folk Perspective." In *Black American Literature and Humanism*, edited by R. Baxter Miller. Lexington: University Press of Kentucky, 1981.

Emphasizes the importance of the legend of Cuffee Ned, who led a slave revolt on Bourne Island, as a key to Merle Kinbona's development. Merle's escape from psychological stasis is generated by her acceptance of the guidance of values present in folk culture. Marshall presents the church as an emblem of continued subjugation which must be overcome in order to attain the self-determination which leads to pride and a sense of community.

Rhodes, Richard. "A Serious Matter." *The Washington Post Book World* (December 28, 1969): 10.

Generally favorable review. Although it is not an unqualified success, Marshall has created a monumental book distinguished by its depth of commitment, its complexity, and the evocation of a people. The novel focuses on characters, both black and white, who seek to move beyond the old strictures of race and class.

Schraufnagel, Noel. "Accommodationism in the Sixties." In *From Apology to Protest: Black American Fiction*. Deland, Fla.: Everett/Edwards, 1973.

Marshall's novel bridges the gap between the accommodationist novel and the militant protest novel. Marshall explores the political and racial atmosphere of the island and presents subplots that illuminate the economic exploitation of the native population. Marshall shows how the inhabitants' drive for economic control over their lives frightens the British landowners. Merle embodies the spirit of Cuffee Ned.

Skerrett, Joseph T., Jr. "Paule Marshall and the Crisis of the Middle Years: *The Chosen Place, the Timeless People*." *Callaloo* 18 (Spring/Summer, 1983): 68-73.

Contrasts the focus on public life in *The Chosen Place, the Timeless People* with the focus on private life in Marshall's other novels. Presenting an image of the crisis of the middle years—the crisis of "generativity"—Merle Kinbona is the crucial transitional figure in Marshall's collective history of human psychosocial development. Merle struggles through most of the novel to release herself from an oppressive negative identity. Her triumph is over Harriet, who symbolizes abusive neocolonial power.

Spillers, Hortense J. "Chosen Place, Timeless People: Some Figurations on the New World." In *Conjuring: Black Women, Fiction, and Literary Tradition*, edited by Marjorie Pryse and Hortense J. Spillers. Bloomington: Indiana University Press, 1985.

Argues that the novel requires readers to suspend simplistic expectations and investigates the ways in which Marshall encourages such suspension. Neither a condemnation of oppression nor a celebration of victims, the novel invokes the highest hopes for New World humanity. Discussion based on "four circles of involvement": myth, history, ritual, and ontology. The characters are parts that speak for the whole, just as the whole is constructed out of the combination of their partialness. Thematically, Marshall examines the economics of captivity in both the United States and the Caribbean.

Stoelting, Winifred L. "Time Past and Time Present: The Search for Viable Links in *The Chosen Place, the Timeless People* by Paule Marshall." *CLA Journal* 26 (September, 1972): 60-71.

Focuses on Marshall's attempt to forge viable links between the traditions of the past and the needs of the present. As the epigraph indicates, one of Marshall's main themes is the way in which past mistakes generate suffering both for the oppressed and for those who must bear the burden of guilt. Stoelting analyzes the relationship between Merle and Saul to demonstrate how it is possible to break the chains of psychological dependence, preparing the way for a second coming of Cuffee Ned.

Whalen, Gretchen. "The Long Search for Coherence and Vision." *Callaloo* 25 (Fall, 1985): 667-669.

Review of reprint edition, identifying *The Chosen Place, the Timeless People* as the most political of Marshall's novels. Rather than portraying heroes or villains, Marshall creates characters who combine apparently contradictory qualities. Balancing Marshall's insistence on the need for a reversal of the current order is her recognition of the many times of love possible even in a corrupt world.

Praisesong for the Widow

Christian, Barbara. "Ritualistic Process and the Structure of Paule Marshall's *Praisesong for the Widow.*" *Callaloo* 18 (Spring/Summer, 1983): 74-83.

Praisesong for the Widow explores the cultural continuity of peoples of African descent as a stance from which to critique New World values. Marshall focuses on the consciousness of black people as they develop a sense of spiritual and sensual integrity in response to American materialism. The novel dramatizes the links between Afro-American and Afro-Caribbean cultures, providing the ritualistic basis for Avey Johnson's reconsideration of her life. The ritual in which Avey participates is a collective process of begging pardon, correct naming, celebration, and honoring.

Holloway, Clayton G. Review of *Praisesong for the Widow*. *CLA Journal* 27 (June, 1984): 460-461.

Favorable review emphasizing the technical brilliance of the novel, which is written in a compelling lyric prose. Marshall's central unifying theme is renunciation and affirmation of one's cultural heritage. Through Avey's self-analysis, Marshall presents an image of the moral landscape of human resilience.

Jefferson, Margo. "A Black Woman's Odyssey." *The Nation* 236 (April 2, 1983): 403-404.

Favorable review placing the novel in the context of Marshall's earlier work. Marshall's primary concern is the link between personal and cultural histories. Although Marshall's language is not as rich as in her previous novels, the style is appropriate to her protagonist. Marshall's literary sources included the hymn and case history, as well as African oral tradition.

Sandiford, Keith A. "Paule Marshall's *Praisesong for the Widow*: The Reluctant Heiress, or Whose Life Is It Anyway?" *Black American Literature Forum* 20 (Winter, 1986): 371-392.

Builds on Barbara Christian's analysis of the ritual process to examine the explicit antagonism between the worlds of history and myth which Avey consciously apprehends as the source of her personal dilemma. In expanding Avey's consciousness from the individualism of White Plains to the collectivity of Ibo Landing, Marshall reinstates the preeminence of synchronic mythic awareness.

Tyler, Anne. "A Widow's Tale." *The New York Times Book Review* 88 (February 20, 1983): 7, 34.
Favorable review stressing the maturity of Marshall's later works. An astonishingly moving "universal" story, *Praisesong for the Widow* employs Barbadian speech to create a texture that is at once convincing and "eerily dreamlike." The novel's evocation of early marriage is among the best literary treatments of the subject.

Waxman, Barbara Frey. "The Widow's Journey to Self and Roots: Aging and Society in Paule Marshall's *Praisesong for the Widow*." *Frontiers* 9, no. 3 (1987): 94-99.
Emphasizes the importance of the theme of aging, centering on Avey's attempt to re-create a position for herself in a community which has given little attention to the situation of the older woman. Marshall forces readers to examine their own feelings about aging women by portraying the complex interaction of age, gender, race, and middle-class status. The novel denounces the outmoded separation of youth from old age and old age from place.

Yardley, Jonathan. "Sea Journeys and Soul Searches." *The Washington Post Book World* 13 (January 30, 1983): 3.
Favorable review praising Marshall's "quiet passion" and understanding "that what really counts is the universality of [Avey's] predicament." Marshall's protagonist comes to a sorrowful understanding of the cost of capitulation to the standards of white culture, which sacrifices both personal happiness and racial heritage. *Praisesong for the Widow* is a work of "exceptional wisdom, maturity, and generosity."

LOUISE MERIWETHER

Biography

Dandridge, Rita B. "Louise Meriwether." In *Afro-American Fiction Writers After 1955*, edited by Thadious M. Davis and Trudier Harris. Vol. 33 of *Dictionary of Literary Biography*. Detroit: Bruccoli Clark, 1984.
Substantial reference entry including biographical sketch and discussion of both *Daddy Was a Number Runner* and Meriwether's juvenile biographies. Biographical section focuses on her family background; her early journalistic writing; her experience with the Watts Writers' Workshop; the development of her literary career; and her political activism. Presents Meriwether as a meticulous writer who exposes the insidiousness of racism and the capriciousness of sexism. Describes several works-in-progress.

Selected Title

Daddy Was a Number Runner
Baldwin, James. Foreword to *Daddy Was a Number Runner*. Old Westbury, N.Y.: Feminist Press, 1986.
A brilliantly understated treatment of a major tragedy, Meriwether's novel centers on a child's growing sense of being "one of the victims of a collective rape." The best treatment of a black girl on the edge of womanhood, the novel employs the number game as an effective metaphor for the growing apprehension of life's difficulties.

Dandridge, Rita B. "From Economic Insecurity to Disintegration: A Study of Character in Louise Meriwether's *Daddy Was a Number Runner.*" *Negro American Literature Forum* 9 (Fall, 1975): 82-85.
As the first novelist to examine the impact of the Depression on a poor black urban family, Meriwether has secured a permanent place in the history of American fiction. Emphasizes the importance of recognizing that the Coffins' struggle against economic discrimination is controlled by their idea of maintaining internal peace and an acceptable social image. Three interacting factors—economic insecurity, loss of self-esteem, and self-debasement—contribute to the tragic pattern of family disintegration.

McKay, Nellie. Afterword to *Daddy Was a Number Runner*. Old Westbury, N.Y.: Feminist Press, 1986.
The first fictional account of a girl growing up in Harlem in the midst of the Depression, *Daddy Was a Number Runner* is a book of major historical impor-

tance. Includes detailed examination of Meriwether's women characters, handicapped by an inadequate preparation for dealing with the realities of sexuality, face the triple oppression of class, race, and gender as they wage the struggle between "proud selfhood and starvation." Places the novel in the contexts of black male treatments of growing up in Harlem and of black women's novels of development. Includes a biographical sketch.

Marshall, Paule. Review of *Daddy Was a Number Runner*. *The New York Times Book Review* 75 (June 28, 1970): 31.
Favorable review identifying Meriwether as an exceptional novelist who goes beyond sociological clichés to give a sense of the distinctively black culture of Harlem. Her expression of the tribal or communal quality of black life enables the novel to overcome its structural flaws, primarily relating to the hurried quality of the later chapters. Meriwether celebrates the positive values of the black experience that underlie the often abrasive surface.

Schraufnagel, Noel. "Accommodationism in the Sixties." In *From Apology to Protest: The Black American Novel*. Deland, Fla.: Everett/Edwards, 1973.
Concerned specifically with exposing the hopelessness of ghetto existence, Meriwether's novel emphasizes the facets of Harlem that make life miserable for its inhabitants. She shows how disillusionment becomes the dominant experience of a young girl who discovers that the people she admires are just ordinary human beings. The novel is weak technically, consisting of a series of vignettes revolving around a melodramatic plot.

Sissman, L. E. "Growing Up Black." *The New Yorker* 46 (July 11, 1970): 77-79.
Mildly unfavorable review. While *Daddy Was a Number Runner* is "not a very good novel," its compelling documentation of life in the ghetto during the Depression makes the stylistic weakness almost irrelevant. Meriwether's style is awkward, her characters are unevenly rounded, and the Harlem setting is not brought to life. The central theme of her autobiographical novel is that the hope and innocence of a child are weak weapons against an environment in which the only route to survival is corruption.

The Times Literary Supplement. Review of *Daddy Was a Number Runner*. (January 21, 1972): 57.
Brief review agreeing with James Baldwin's favorable assessment. Meriwether refrains from a justifiably strident response to the problems she describes, presenting a rounded picture of Harlem. Urban documentary fiction of a high order, the novel is depressing without losing its vitality and humor.

Wade-Gayles, Gloria. "The Halo and the Hardships." In *No Crystal Stair: Visions of Race and Sex in Black Women's Fiction*. New York: Pilgrim Press, 1984.

Unlike Brooks's Maud Martha, Meriwether's protagonist is an ordinary woman who rarely feels good about herself. Set in the Depression, the novel focuses on fear, frustration, and unrelenting struggle. There are no bright moments in the Coffins' world. Rejecting the stereotype of the strong black mother, Meriwether develops the image of the distant mother who has no time for her children.

TONI MORRISON

Biography

Bakerman, Jane. "The Seams Can't Show: An Interview with Toni Morrison." *Black American Literature Forum* 12 (Summer, 1978): 56-60.
Interview interspersed with Bakerman's commentary. Among the topics covered are Morrison's decision to become a writer; her attempt to organize and simplify her life; her writing process; her faith in the future of the novel form; her approach to style; her view of the responsibility of the black writer; and her basic themes. Includes Morrison's comment on the early stages of writing *Tar Baby* and her view of Sula and Nel as two sides of one personality.

—————— . "Toni Morrison." In *American Women Writers*, vol. 3, edited by Lina Mainiero. New York: Frederick Ungar, 1981.
Biographical entry including brief commentary on *The Bluest Eye*, *Sula*, and *Song of Solomon*. Morrison's key theme is "the effect of the presence or the absence of love," which can be a liberating and nurturing force.

Blake, Susan. "Toni Morrison." In *Afro-American Fiction Writers After 1955*, edited by Thadious M. Davis and Trudier Harris. Vol. 33 of *Dictionary of Literary Biography*. Detroit: Bruccoli Clark, 1984.
Lengthy reference entry including biographical sketch and analysis of Morrison's novels through *Tar Baby*. Biographical section notes the importance of Morrison's childhood in Depression-era Ohio; the impact of her broad early reading; the importance of her travels in the South; the beginnings of her writing career; and the subsequent success which has made her one of the few successful black women writers and one of the few popular writers to be taken seriously. Analysis of Morrison's novels focuses on her stylistic blending of realism and fantasy, and her thematic emphasis on idiosyncratic individuals in relationship to their communities, which are defined through personal rather than political relationships.

Dowling, Colette. "The Song of Toni Morrison." *The New York Times Magazine* (May 20, 1979): 40-42, 48-58.
Lengthy biographical sketch including information on Morrison's growing public prominence; her family background and education; her experience working with other black writers as an editor at Random House; her appreciation of her women ancestors; and her primary commitment to her writing.

Harris, Jessica. "I Will Always Be a Writer." *Essence* 7 (December, 1976): 54, 56, 90-92.

Biographical sketch including information on Morrison's balancing of her roles as writer, mother, and editor; her sense of the editor's duties; her work with manuscripts by Gayl Jones; her emphasis on rewriting; and the importance of humor.

Heaton, David. "Toni Morrison, (Chloe Anthony Morrison, née Wofford)." In *Contemporary Novelists*, 4th ed., edited by D. L. Kirkpatrick. New York: St. Martin's Press, 1986.
Reference entry including biographical outline and brief analysis of Morrison's novels through *Tar Baby*. Observes that comparisons between Morrison and Faulkner and Joyce are "irresistible." All three writers focus on an "exhaustive, mythical exploration of place" and the "nexus of past and present." Making the legendary new, she focuses on personality and moral character in a manner that is "indisputably universal."

LeClair, Thomas. "The Language Must Not Sweat: A Conversation with Toni Morrison." *The New Republic* 184 (March 21, 1981): 25-29. Reprinted in *Anything Can Happen: Interviews with Contemporary American Novelists*, edited by Tom LeClair and Larry McCaffery. Urbana: University of Illinois Press, 1983.
Interview with Morrison in which she comments on her love of writing; her interest in "village literature"; her understanding of myth; her belief that suggestive and provocative language is the defining element of good writing; her sense of black writing; her interest in eccentric characters; and the visual quality of her prose.

McKay, Nellie. "An Interview with Toni Morrison." *Contemporary Literature* 24 (Winter, 1983): 413-429.
Interview including Morrison's comments on the ability of black women to express themselves creatively outside the public sphere; the characters and treatment of Afro-American life in *Song of Solomon* and *Tar Baby*; the need for a more aware criticism of black literature; and the importance of orality in her work. Includes brief comments on Gayl Jones and Toni Cade Bambara.

Middleton, David L. *Toni Morrison: An Annotated Bibliography*. New York: Garland Publishing, 1987.
Useful bibliography of primary and secondary sources. Includes lengthy annotations of Morrison's essays and reviews; interviews; general critical essays; dissertations; and reviews of Morrison's novels through Tar Baby. Also lists Morrison's awards, honors, memberships, and recordings featuring her work.

Morrison, Toni. "City Limits, Village Values: Concepts of the Neighborhood in Black Fiction." In *Literature and the Urban Experience: Essays on the City and Literature*, edited by Michael C. Jaye and Ann Chalmers Watts. New

Brunswick, N.J.: Rutgers University Press, 1981.
Places Afro-American fiction in the context of the American theme of city versus country. Identifies the white American distrust of the small town, which contrasts with the black American attraction to community, as the source of much cross-cultural misunderstanding since white critics mistrust heroes who prefer the village and its tribal values to loneliness and alienation. Emphasizes that what is missing in city fiction and present in village fiction is the "ancestor." Includes a brief discussion of the village sensibility of Bambara's *The Salt Eaters*.

_____ . "Memory, Creation, and Writing." *Thought* 59 (December, 1984): 385-390.
Emphasizes the importance of memory to the interior growth of the writer. Morrison says that she depends on memory to ignite her creative process because she "cannot trust the literature and the sociology of other people to help me know the truth of my own cultural sources." Observes that she deliberately avoids conscious reference to literary sources when she writes. Comments on the importance of "told stories" to the composition of *The Bluest Eye* and *Tar Baby*.

_____ . "Rediscovering Black History." *The New York Times Magazine* (August 11, 1974): 14-24.
Essay on the intricate interrelationship of black and white history focusing on Morrison's work as an editor on *The Black Book*, a compilation of materials and photographs focusing on Afro-American experience. Morrison emphasizes her desire to go beyond both demeaning white stereotypes and sociology, on the one hand, and accurate, but useless, slogans such as "black is beautiful" on the other. Comments on the ways in which the emphasis on black unity tends to obscure appreciation of differences within the black community.

_____ . "Rootedness: The Ancestor as Foundation." In *Black Women Writers, 1950-1980: A Critical Evaluation*, edited by Mari Evans. Garden City, N.Y.: Anchor Press, 1984.
Morrison comments on the oral quality of African-American writing, and the ways in which black writers respond to their ancestors. Interpreting the novel as the expression of the class or group that writes it, Morrison discusses the ways in which writers can encourage readers to participate in the construction of a book's meaning. Cautions against the limitations inherent in most critical models and observes that political impact and aesthetic beauty are not incompatible.

_____ . "A Slow Walk of Trees (as Grandmother Would Say) Hopeless (as Grandfather Would Say)." *The New York Times Magazine* (July 4, 1976): 104, 150, 152, 156, 160, 162, 164.

Situating her discussion in a social and political context of disappointment over the failure of movements toward change, Morrison analyzes the tension in her own family and the black community generally between distrust of whites and hope for their eventual transformation. Noting that she grew up in "a basically racist household with more than a child's share of contempt for white people," Morrison contrasts her grandfather and father's profound distrust of whites with her mother and grandmother's belief in the possibility of change.

_____ . "Unspeakable Things Unspoken: The Afro-American Presence in American Literature." *Michigan Quarterly Review* 28 (Winter, 1989): 1-34.
Major statement on the American literary tradition, arguing that awareness of racial themes enriches understanding of works by writers of all racial backgrounds. Identifies the cultural biases in most white criticism of Afro-American literature and calls for development of a theory that truly accommodates Afro-American texts. Includes a detailed discussion of *Moby-Dick*, which reveals new richness when approached from this new perspective. Morrison also comments in detail on the ways in which the opening passages of each of her novels can be best understood with an informed awareness of the significance of Afro-American expressive traditions.

Richardson, Robert. "A Bench by the Road." *The World: Journal of the Unitarian Universalist Association* 3 (January/February, 1989): 4-5, 37-41.
Interview preceded by Morrison's statement on her feelings about *Beloved* a year after its publication. Emphasizes the absence of a monument or setting dedicated specifically to remembering the slave community. Interview includes Morrison's comments on the ability of her writing to communicate personally with readers; her sense of the moral question of infanticide; and general comments on her writing career and relationship with other writers.

Stepto, Robert. "'Intimate Things in Place': A Conversation with Toni Morrison." In *Chant of Saints: A Gathering of Afro-American Literature, Art, and Scholarship*, edited by Michael S. Harper and Robert B. Stepto. Urbana: University of Illinois Press, 1979.
Important interview. Among the topics covered are Morrison's sense of place; Sula and Nel as aspects of a fragmented individual; the relationship between grandmothers, mothers, and daughters in *Sula*; the male characters in Morrison's fiction; future directions for black literary criticism; and Morrison's plans for *Song of Solomon*, which had not yet been published.

Tate, Claudia C. *Black Women Writers at Work*. New York: Continuum, 1983.
Includes an interview with Morrison in which she discusses her interest in the pariah figure; her writing process; the differences in approaches between black

male and black female writers; and the impact of her choice of a hero or heroine on the language and stylistic texture of her novels.

Watkins, Mel. "Talk with Toni Morrison." *The New York Times Book Review* 82 (September 11, 1977): 48, 50.
Interview in which Morrison comments on her avoidance of social obligations; the origins of her commitment to writing; her interest in projecting herself into unlikable characters; the prominence of male characters in *Song of Solomon*; the significance of the metaphor of flying; and her admiration for writers including James Dickey, John Gardner, Nadine Gordimer, Eudora Welty, and Lillian Hellman.

Commentary

Adams, Anne. "Straining to Make Out the Words to the 'Lied': The German Reception of Toni Morrison." In *Critical Essays on Toni Morrison*, edited by Nellie Y. McKay. Boston: G. K. Hall, 1988.
Bibliographical essay on the reception of Morrison's work in Germany. Includes a summary of the historical interaction and perception of Afro-American/German relationships. Notes that, despite erratic translations, Morrison is the most widely read Afro-American woman writer in German translation; that she is the most-widely studied in German-speaking universities; and that her novels are frequently read as superficial anthropology.

Bakerman, Jane S. "Failures of Love: Female Initiation in the Novels of Toni Morrison." *American Literature* 52 (January, 1981): 541-563.
Morrison unites her central theme of the search for love with the traditional pattern of the initiation story to make a compelling statement about the failure of human values. The basic pattern is stated most powerfully in *Song of Solomon*, where Milkman's development is framed by the maturation stories of Pilate, Hagar, and Corinthians. Each of these potentially powerful women fails because their families have not prepared them for the transition to maturity.

Begnal, Kate. "Toni Morrison." In *Critical Survey of Long Fiction*, vol. 5, edited by Frank N. Magill. Pasadena, Calif.: Salem Press, 1983.
Lengthy reference entry including biographical sketch and analysis of Morrison's fiction through *Tar Baby*. Analysis emphasizes Morrison's exploration of the conflict between society and the individual. She shows that the individual who defies social pressures can forge a self by drawing on the resources of the natural world, the continuity of the family and the Afro-American tradition, and on various nontraditional sources of psychic power such as dreams.

Bell, Bernard W. "The Contemporary Afro-American Novel, 1: Neorealism." In *The Afro-American Novel and Its Tradition*. Amherst: University of Massachusetts Press, 1987.

Morrison's novels continue the poetic and gothic branches of the Afro-American tradition. Praises the complexity of Morrison's exploration of the impact of sexism and racism on the lives of black women. Analysis of *The Bluest Eye*, *Sula*, and *Song of Solomon* emphasizes gothic techniques and themes; the strength of Morrison's language; and the subtlety of her characterization.

Bischoff, Joan. "The Novels of Toni Morrison: Studies in Thwarted Sensitivity." *Studies in Black Literature* 6 (Fall, 1975): 21-23.

Analyzes *The Bluest Eye* and *Sula* as explorations of the "preternaturally sensitive" but thwarted black girl forced into premature adulthood by the circumstances of her life. For both Pecola and Sula, sensitivity is a curse, not a blessing. Although Morrison finds beauty in sensitive responses, she finds them impractical.

Byerman, Keith E. "Beyond Realism: The Fictions of Gayl Jones and Toni Morrison." In *Fingering the Jagged Grain: Tradition and Form in Recent Black Fiction*. Athens: University of Georgia Press, 1985.

Morrison's novels are characterized by the presentation of disordered, grotesque worlds from the perspective of seemingly stable central characters and narrators, thereby underscoring the violent impact of seemingly ordinary phenomena. Demonstrating the exploitative nature of various symbolic systems, her novels are quest tales in which key characters seek to find sources of strength and identity. Those who realize the original goal of their quest are usually victimized, while those who are diverted toward alternative goals of community, family, or black history are more likely to triumph.

Christian, Barbara. "Community and Nature: The Novels of Toni Morrison." In *Black Feminist Criticism*. Elmsford, N.Y.: Pergamon Press, 1985.

Identifies the relationship between nature and the traditions of particular human communities as the "kernel of the contemporary fable" in Morrison's first three novels. Morrison develops this theme in the manner of an oral storyteller, focusing on the ways in which kinship ties with a specific community are developed through an exploration of the dreams, legends, and subconscious beliefs of its inhabitants.

_____ . "The Concept of Class in the Novels of Toni Morrison." In *Black Feminist Criticism*. Elmsford, N.Y.: Pergamon Press, 1985.

Examines Morrison's treatment of class divisions within the black community in relation to literary images that have created a concept of woman in society that is not only sexist and racist, but also classist. Contrasts Morrison's class-bound characters such as Jadine and Nel with those who challenge boundaries, such as Sula, or exist outside class concerns entirely, such as Pilate. One of the most profound impacts of class distinctions is that they create a need for a feeling of superiority.

_____ . "The Contemporary Fables of Toni Morrison." In *Black Women Novelists: The Development of a Tradition, 1892-1976*. Westport, Conn.: Greenwood Press, 1980.
Compares Morrison's writing to the music of a jazz musician who "finds the hidden melodies within a musical phrase." Christian analyzes *The Bluest Eye* and *Sula*, both of which chronicle the quest of young black girls for womanhood within a community structure. *The Bluest Eye* examines the inversion of truth generated by white imposition of values on black culture. *Sula* concerns a woman's attempt to remake herself in opposition to her own community's norms.

Clark, Norris. "Flying Black: Toni Morrison's *The Bluest Eye*, *Sula*, and *Song of Solomon*." *Minority Voices* 4, no. 2 (1980): 51-63.
Argues that despite Morrison's repudiation of the Black Aesthetic movement, her novels contribute to the movement's fundamental goals. Her careful attention to the realities of black life and her use of Afro-American communal traditions lead to the reclaiming of the black experience.

Davis, Cynthia A. "Self, Society, and Myth in Toni Morrison's Fiction." *Contemporary Literature* 23 (Summer, 1982): 323-342.
Examines the use of myth in Morrison's first three novels in relation to her existentialist approach to heroism. Although the use of myth as an approach to the experience of the oppressed risks accepting the idea of blackness as limitation, Morrison resolves the problem by focusing not on western myths but on myths generated within black culture. Detailed analysis of Morrison's adaptation of the Icarus myth makes it clear that she values myth as a way to design, rather than to confine, reality.

Dearborn, Mary V. "Fathers and Founding Figures: The Making of Little American Women." In *Pocahontas's Daughters: Gender and Ethnicity in American Culture*. New York: Oxford University Press, 1986.
The connection between names and identity is a major theme in *Song of Solomon*, which represents a culmination of an ethnic female tradition that seeks to question the meaning not only of the common language of America, but of language itself. Thematically, Morrison implies that the individual must reanimate language and history. In a larger sense, she argues that the writer must constantly examine the ramifications of American rhetoric.

Denard, Carolyn. "The Convergence of Feminism and Ethnicity in The Fiction of Toni Morrison." In *Critical Essays on Toni Morrison*, edited by Nellie Y. McKay. Boston: G. K. Hall, 1988.

Identifies Morrison as an advocate of "ethnic cultural feminism" but stresses that she does not support as a solution to oppression the type of "existential, political feminism" that alienates black women from their cultural heritage. Discusses Jadine and Sula as Morrison's "objectors" who speak out against women who accept oppressive roles within the community. Her real heroines, however, are Mrs. McTeer, Eva, Pilate, and Ondine, who manage to maintain their sustaining energies despite the absence of social support.

Dixon, Melvin. "Like an Eagle in the Air: Toni Morrison." In *Ride Out the Wilderness: Geography and Identity in Afro-American Literature*. Urbana: University of Illinois Press, 1987.

Reflecting the influence of her Ohio background, Morrison freely explores new physical and metaphorical landscapes in her fiction. Initiating a dialogue with earlier Afro-American texts, most importantly Ralph Ellison's *Invisible Man*, Morrison envisions spaces with fewer historically or politically fixed boundaries. Examines the most significant spatial images in each of Morrison's novels, culminating in a discussion of the use of mountain, farm, and island as stages for dramas of self-creation and racial visibility in *Song of Solomon* and *Tar Baby*. The principal movement in Morrison's fiction is the leap into the sky.

Edelberg, Cynthia Dubin. "Morrison's Voices: Formal Education, the Work Ethic, and the Bible." *American Literature* 58 (May, 1986): 217-237.

Argues that throughout her novels Morrison holds up the value of higher education and the work ethic to ridicule. The unnamed omniscient narrator who tells each of the first four novels asserts that higher education for blacks is "a waste of time at best, truly destructive at worst." Morrison posits a primitivism, but her vision is rhetorical rather than convincing since she shows the defeat of "the funky and the free" in addition to the highly educated. Ultimately, Morrison's values are reduced to wishful thinking.

Harris, Norman. "The Black Univers[e] in Contemporary Afro-American Fiction." *CLA Journal* 30 (September, 1986): 1-13.

Uses Morrison, Charles Johnson, and Ishmael Reed as focal points for a discussion of the changes that have occurred since Blyden Jackson used Wright and Ellison as exemplars of the Afro-American worldview in 1960. Morrison's conception of "village literature" both affirms and extends the principles of the Black Aesthetic movement. A response to the diminution of black values, Morrison's approach focuses not on racism, but on the adaptive and transforming conditions within Afro-American culture.

Holloway, Karla F. C., and Stephanie A. Demetrakopoulos. *New Dimensions of Spirituality: A Biracial and Bicultural Reading of the Novels of Toni Morrison*. Westport, Conn.: Greenwood Press, 1987.
Dialogue between a black woman critic and white woman critic concerning Morrison's development from *The Bluest Eye* through *Tar Baby*. Emphasizes the way in which personal and cultural differences contribute to different understandings of particular works, characters, and techniques. Demetrakopoulos' essays examine the bleak vision of *The Bluest Eye*, the importance of bonding in *Sula* and *Song of Solomon*, and meditate on the white characters in *Tar Baby*. Holloway's essays focus on the modes of survival generated within the world of black women. These modes enable African values to survive in the New World. Includes a valuable chapter summarizing previous criticism of Morrison's work.

House, Elizabeth B. "Artists and the Art of Living: Order and Disorder in Toni Morrison's Fiction." *Modern Fiction Studies* 34 (Spring, 1988): 27-44.
A major theme of Morrison's fiction is that creative pursuits are necessary for the successful balancing of order and disorder in the individual's life. Characters such as Son and Pilate, who find a form of artistic expression, attain an equilibrium and are able to fashion coherent, productive lives. Characters who fail to do so become destructive in various ways. Some such as Shadrack, Soaphead, Mason Dead, and Valerian attempt to impose order on chaos, maiming themselves, other people, and the earth. Others, such as Cholly and Sula, simply lose all control over themselves.

_____ . "The 'Sweet Life' in Toni Morrison's Fiction." *American Literature* 56 (May, 1984): 181-202.
Throughout her novels, Morrison juxtaposes two categories of dreams. One type of dream is idyllic, seeking harmony with people, nature, and racial heritage. The other is materialistic, based on the quest for wealth and power. While Morrison affirms the superiority of the idyllic vision, she acknowledges the difficulty of being altruistic in contemporary America.

Hovet, Grace Ann, and Barbara Lounsberry. "Flying as Symbol and Legend in Toni Morrison's *The Bluest Eye*, *Sula*, and *Song of Solomon*." *CLA Journal* 27 (December, 1983): 119-140.
Morrison employs flight imagery to explore the meaning of a full life. She divides her characters into three types of flyers: nesting birds, who never fly; dangerous flyers whose flights lead to madness and isolation; and soaring flyers, who have a sense of identity and community. Successful flyers, who reflect the Afro-American association of flight with escape from bondage and with equality, appear as mythic images in her first two novels and move toward actualization in *Song of Solomon*.

Johnson, Charles. "The Women." In *Being and Race: Black Writing Since 1970*. Bloomington: Indiana University Press, 1988.

Although Morrison is not formally innovative, she shapes a precise prose that creates musical and mythic elements in her novels. *The Bluest Eye* and *Sula* are stronger, more carefully crafted novels than *Tar Baby* or *Song of Solomon*, which is a mystery novel highly textured with details of black culture. Morrison's fictional universe is lacking in light and balance.

Jones, Bessie W., and Audrey L. Vinson. *The World of Toni Morrison: Explorations in Literary Criticism*. Dubuque, Iowa: Kendall/Hunt, 1985.

Critical study of Morrison's work through *Tar Baby*, emphasizing the use of metaphors of escape which help her characters free themselves from the limitations of their environment. Morrison's mastery of traditional literary techniques and her revision of literary patterns associated with classical tragedy contribute to her treatment of the quest for identity. Includes an interview with Morrison concerning her personal experience and comments on her approach to writing, including her view of folklore as a literary resource.

Joyner, Nancy Carol. "Toni Morrison." In *American Novelists Since World War II*, edited by James E. Kibler, Jr. Vol. 6 of *Dictionary of Literary Biography*. Detroit: Bruccoli Clark, 1980.

Reference entry including biographical sketch and analysis of Morrison's novels through *Song of Solomon*. Emphasizes the grotesque and idiosyncratic elements of her works, each of which deals with class conflicts within the black community rather than with interracial conflict. Notes the importance of allusions to folklore and the Bible. Identifies Morrison as a significant American novelist.

Karl, Frederick R. *American Fictions 1940-1980*. New York: Harper & Row, 1983.

Discusses *Sula* and *Song of Solomon* in the context of a broad survey of contemporary American fiction. Noting that Sula attains a form of personal liberation at the cost of a settled existence, Karl observes that *Sula* focuses on the individual life rather than social or racial issues. Although *Song of Solomon* is Morrison's most ambitious novel, it does not fully cohere, in large part because the ideological struggle between Guitar and Milkman is not well integrated with the other elements.

Lange, Bonnie Shipman. "Toni Morrison's Rainbow Code." *Critique* 24 (1983): 173-181.

Examines use of color symbolism in Morrison's first four novels. Morrison associates blue and white with pleasure; red, pink, and purple with ominous feelings; green with tranquility; brown with domesticity; silver with betrayal; and gold with magic and evil. Morrison's system is clear, consistent, and based on the assumption that people respond to colors in similar ways.

Lee, Dorothy H. "The Quest for Self: Triumph and Failure in the Works of Toni Morrison." In *Black Women Writers, 1950-1980: A Critical Evaluation*, edited by Mari Evans. Garden City, N.Y.: Anchor Press, 1984.

Morrison's novels combine to form a whole. Her preoccupation is with the effect of the community on the individual's ability to form and retain an integrated self. Drawing on myth and legend for narrative patterns, Morrison underscores her quest motif with ironic insights and evocative imagery. The successful quest of *Song of Solomon* contrasts with the failed quests in *Sula* and *The Bluest Eye*. Demonstrating the consistency in Morrison's technique and vision, *Tar Baby* juxtaposes the unresolved quests of Son and Jadine.

McKay, Nellie Y., ed. *Critical Essays on Toni Morrison*. Boston: G. K. Hall, 1988.

Important anthology including two interviews with Morrison; reviews; critical articles (most of them written specifically for the volume) on each of Morrison's novels through *Tar Baby*; and three essays on general topics. McKay's introduction observes that Morrison writes out of both the black and black women's traditions. Her novels are a rejection of white patriarchal modernism, radically revising as well the race- and male-centered Afro-American tradition. She seeks to liberate Afro-American expression from the constraints of social realism. Introduction includes a biographical sketch and detailed examination of the critical reception of Morrison's novels.

Mickelson, Anne Z. "Winging Upward: Black Women: Sarah E. Wright, Toni Morrison, Alice Walker." In *Reaching Out: Sensitivity and Order in Recent American Fiction by Women*. Metuchen, N.J.: Scarecrow Press, 1979.

Overview of Morrison's central themes and characters in *Sula* and *Song of Solomon*. Raising the question of a woman's right to an experimental life, *Sula* focuses on Sula and Nel as symbols of rebellion and conformity. Morrison suggests the radical idea that violence may be endemic to female as well as male psyches. In *Song of Solomon*, Morrison turns her attention to the traditional American theme of the need to free one's self. Mickelson questions the sexual politics of the myth of flying in which Solomon leaves his family behind.

Miller, Jane. "Women's Men." In *Women Writing About Men*. New York: Pantheon, 1986.

Discusses Morrison's treatment of the tension between black men and black women as a result of economic forces and historical oppression. Identifies the scene in which Cholly and Darlene are interrupted by the white men in *The Bluest Eye* as emblematic of Morrison's perspective. The novel's tragedies are all sexual, acts of love truncated by pain. Includes a comparison of Morrison with Jane Austen, who anticipates her awareness that women's psychological problems are not directly attributable to men.

Parker, Bettye J. "Complexity: Toni Morrison's Women—An Interview Essay." In *Sturdy Black Bridges: Visions of Black Women in Literature*, edited by Roseann P. Bell, Bettye J. Parker, and Beverly Guy-Sheftall. Garden City, N.Y.: Anchor Press, 1979.

Report on an interview in which Morrison comments on the presentation of women in *The Bluest Eye* and *Sula*. Morrison comments on her superstitious beliefs; her treatment of the good-evil dichotomy in *Sula*; the significance of Hannah, Eva, and Ajax; and the situation of black women writers.

Smith, Valerie. "Toni Morrison's Narratives of Community." In *Self-Discovery and Authority in Afro-American Narrative*. Cambridge, Mass.: Harvard University Press, 1987.

Morrison suggests that the narrative process leads to self-knowledge because it forces acceptance of the past. Her characters come to an understanding of their lives only when they can tell stories of how they came to be. *Sula* and *The Bluest Eye* employ flashbacks and interpolated stories to show how communal values simultaneously contribute to and subvert the construction of identity. The nonlinear development in *Song of Solomon* portrays a more successful process. The most important formal aspect of the novel concerns the way that every important character tells a story that both helps explain the present and impedes the forward progress of Milkman's central narrative.

Strouse, Jean. "Toni Morrison's Black Magic." *Newsweek* 97 (March 30, 1981): 52-57.

Cover article including biographical sketch, summary of the Afro-American literary tradition, and some analysis of Morrison's novels through *Tar Baby*. Analysis of *Tar Baby* places Son in the tradition of American renegade heroes and argues that the book presents Morrison's "bleakest vision." Examines Morrison's influences in relationship to her "triple consciousness" of herself as American, black, and female. Observes that while Morrison's voice is that of a preacher, she makes no narrowly political points.

"Toni Morrison." In *Contemporary Literary Criticism*, vol. 4, edited by Carolyn Riley (1975); vol. 10, edited by Dedria Bryfonski (1979); vol. 22, edited by Sharon R. Gunton and Jean C. Stine (1982). Detroit: Gale Research.

Compilations of material related to Morrison's novels. Vol. 4 excerpts reviews of *Sula*. Vol. 10 excerpts reviews of *Song of Solomon* and includes a section from Chikwenye Ogunyemi's essay on *The Bluest Eye*. Vol. 22 includes a more extensive range of materials, including a list of entries in other reference sources, excerpts from articles by Phyllis Klotman, Anne Mickelson, and Jane Bakerman, and reviews of *Tar Baby*.

Turner, Darwin T. "Theme, Characterization, and Style in the Works of Toni Morrison." In *Black Women Writers, 1950-1980: A Critical Evaluation*, edited by Mari Evans. Garden City, N.Y.: Anchor Press, 1984.

Morrison's novels focus on individuals isolated by their failures in love and their problems with identity. Her lyrical style enables her to treat grotesque characters and situations without surrendering the beauty of the world. Since her early works, Morrison has expanded her focus from young girls confused by questions of identity to a gallery of men and women in conflict with a wide range of forces.

Wade-Gayles, Gloria. *No Crystal Stair: Visions of Race and Sex in Black Women's Fiction*. New York: Pilgrim Press, 1984.

Examines black women's experiences of oppression and limitation in *The Bluest Eye* and *Sula*, with special attention to the tension between black men and black women; and the interaction of grandmothers, mothers, and daughters. In *The Bluest Eye*, Morrison shows that while Cholly is denied power by racism in the larger society, sexism gives him power in his own home. *Sula* focuses on the problem of the protagonist as an "artist without a form."

Wagner, Linda. "Mastery of Narrative." In *Contemporary American Women Writers: Narrative Strategies*, edited by Catherine Rainwater and William J. Scheick. Lexington: University Press of Kentucky, 1985.

Analyzes the ways in which Morrison's narrative structures create the meaning in her novels through *Tar Baby*. Emphasizes the importance of "context chapters," which resemble the "interchapters" in John Steinbeck's *The Grapes of Wrath*, to enrich the understanding of her central characters' experiences. Among the techniques Wagner discusses are Morrison's use of intentional misdirection; her use of fragmented scenes; and her careful choice of perspective characters. Although all of her novels include at least one climactic scene, these scenes never embody the full meaning of the novel. Establishing meanings on several levels, her endings are never simple resolutions of plot lines. The openness of her form reflects her interest in oral storytelling.

Weems, Renita. " 'Artists Without Art Form': A Look at One Black Woman's World of Unrevered Black Woman." In *Home Girls: A Black Feminist Anthology*, edited by Barbara Smith. New York: Kitchen Table/Women of Color Press, 1983.

Celebration of Morrison as one of the few writers whose work revolves around the lives of black women. The theme of "artists with no art form" provides the focal point of Morrison's first three novels. Recognizing the diversity of black women, Morrison also insists on the importance of their shared peasant heritage. Morrison places special emphasis on the "exquisite idiosyncrasies" that enable black women to survive troubled times.

Weever, Jacqueline de. "The Inverted World of Toni Morrison's *The Bluest Eye* and *Sula*." *CLA Journal* 22 (June, 1979): 402-414.

Emphasizes the bleakness of Morrison's vision, which suggests that the struggle for identity in a hostile environment will sometimes be lost. Like Pauline Breedlove, Sula is an *artiste manquée*; like the protagonist of Jones's *Eva's Man*, she is a "devil figure," a relatively new image in the literary treatment of black women.

Wilkerson, Margaret B. "The Dramatic Voice in Toni Morrison's Novels." In *Critical Essays on Toni Morrison*, edited by Nellie Y. McKay. Boston: G. K. Hall, 1988.
Explores the theatrical and dramatic qualities of Morrison's prose, including her complex, well-developed characters; her sharply defined conflicts; and her crisp, revealing dialogue, which she frequently employs to handle climactic scenes. Includes a brief discussion of Morrison's experience with the theater, consisting primarily of the play *Dreaming Emmett*.

Willis, Susan. "Eruptions of Funk: Historicizing Toni Morrison." In *Specifying: Black Women Writing the American Experience*. Madison: University of Wisconsin Press, 1987.
Morrison disrupts the sensual numbing that accompanies the social and psychological alienation imposed by capitalism through "eruptions of funk," the emergence of repressed historical experience, frequently in the form of metaphors drawn from past moments of sensual fulfillment. Sexuality converges with history and serves as a register of historical change. While *Song of Solomon* treats this material in a liberating manner, *Tar Baby* articulates an essentially pessimistic perspective.

Selected Titles

Beloved
Brown, Rosellen. "The Pleasure of Enchantment." *The Nation* 245 (October 17, 1987): 418-421.
Favorable review emphasizing Morrison's stylistic power and ability to extend our understanding of historical relationships. Identifies two main trends in Morrison's work, "the imagistic and the didactic." *Beloved* is the most "visualizable" of her novels.

Crouch, Stanley. "Aunt Medea." *The New Republic* 197 (October 19, 1987): 38-43.
Extremely unfavorable review condemning Morrison's attempt "to placate sentimental feminist ideology." Morrison's success proves that "poorly digested folk materials, feminist rhetoric, and a labored use of magic realism" can pay off. Morrison explains black behavior entirely in terms of social conditioning and avoids serious confrontation with the complexity of human experience.

Unlike Alice Walker, Morrison has talent, but she perpetually subverts her narrative with "maudlin ideological commercials."

Darling, Marsha Jean. "Ties That Bind." *The Women's Review of Books* 5 (March, 1988): 4-5.
Favorable review accompanied by an interview in which Morrison discusses the writing, plot, and themes of *Beloved*. Darling's review emphasizes the themes of the relationship between living and dead, and the adjustments made by black women responding to the material reality of social oppression. Morrison revoices the African understanding of death as part of her discussion of kinship and family survival.

Gray, Paul. "Something Terrible Happened." *Time* 130 (September 21, 1987): 75.
Generally favorable review praising Morrison's ability to forgo indignation over slavery and let her characters speak for themselves. While Morrison displays slavery in all its cruelty, her unsettling perspective contributes to the creation of a heroine who is both hard to understand and hard to forget. The significance of Beloved in the novel is confusing because she seems to represent both Sethe's guilt and redemption.

Harris, Trudier. "Of Mother Love and Demons." *Callaloo* 35 (Spring, 1988): 387-389.
Generally favorable review focusing on the influence of the past over the present, both psychologically and physically. Stressing Morrison's continuing determination to break down the lines of mortality and immortality, Harris examines her use of the ghost in relation to African conceptions of the return of spirits, concluding that there is a mixture of promise and threat in Beloved's return.

Reed, Dennis. Review of *Beloved*. *CLA Journal* 31 (December, 1987): 256-258.
Favorable review concluding that "Morrison's wordsmithing may be without present day peer." A haunting book with great poetic power, *Beloved* portrays a hidden aspect of a people's historical memory. Exposing the emotional responses to inordinate loss, Morrison creates a work that affirms survival and strength.

Rumens, Carol. "Shades of the Prison-House." *Times Literary Supplement* (October 16, 1987): 1135.
Mixed review praising the power of Morrison's critique of slavery but criticizing the emphasis on the ghost story. Morrison increases the reader's outrage over slavery by describing it not at its worst, but at its most enlightened. While her metaphorical devices work to intensify effects, the sections focusing on the ghost do not resonate as deeply as those concerning actual human beings. As a

family saga, *Beloved* is lopsided and suffers from gaps, suggesting that it may be intended as part of a larger project.

Snitow, Ann. "Death Duties: Toni Morrison Looks Back in Sorrow." *Village Voice Literary Supplement* (September, 1987): 25-26.
Unfavorable review of *Beloved* as an "airless" novel in which Morrison's "undigested insistence on the magical" undercuts the beauty of her prose. Repressing the realities of slavery, Morrison focuses on lonely minds in torment. Morrison's emphasis on the dead child results in a novel where "everything is static and in pieces."

Thurman, Judith. "A House Divided." *The New Yorker* 63 (November 2, 1987): 175-180.
Lengthy, generally favorable review noting that Morrison's power derives in part from the kind of "excesses that Nietzsche objected to in Wagner": melodrama, sentimentality, inflated rhetoric. Observes that Morrison judges her characters according to the risks they take for the autonomy of self and others. Discusses the ghost story in relation to the tradition of the gothic. Includes a detailed contrast of the picture of the black family in *Beloved* and *The Bill Cosby Show.*

The Bluest Eye

Awkward, Michael. "Roadblocks and Relatives: Critical Revision in Toni Morrison's *The Bluest Eye*." In *Critical Essays on Toni Morrison*, edited by Nellie Y. McKay. Boston: G. K. Hall, 1988. Reprinted in expanded form as " 'The Evil of Fulfillment': Scapegoating and Narration in *The Bluest Eye*" in *Inspiriting Influences: Tradition, Revision, and Afro-American Women's Novels*. New York: Columbia University Press, 1989.
Suggests that the works of older Afro-American writers, including James Baldwin and Ralph Ellison, presented "roadblocks" to Morrison's attainment of artistic selfhood. In *The Bluest Eye*, she subjects them to critical revision by grounding their theoretical positions in the concrete experience of black women. Her "revisionary acts," like her complex manipulation of perspective and voice in the prefatory primer, help her give "authentication and voice" to black and feminine experiences whose validity is denied by the earlier texts.

Frankel, Haskel. "*The Bluest Eye.*" *The New York Times Book Review* 75 (November 1, 1970): 46-47.
Mixed review praising Morrison's ability to find beauty in ugliness, but complaining that she "has gotten lost in her construction." She is at her best when handling difficult scenes, yet her style often creates confusion and ambiguity. Approaches Morrison as an "editor who writes novels."

Harris, Trudier. "Reconnecting Fragments: Afro-American Folk Tradition in *The Bluest Eye*." In *Critical Essays on Toni Morrison*, edited by Nellie Y. McKay. Boston: G. K. Hall, 1988.
Reads *The Bluest Eye* as both the story of Pecola's destruction and the story of "Afro-American folk culture in process." Emphasizes the ways in which Morrison's Ohio community shares with historical black folk communities patterns of survival, traditions of comfort, and beliefs that foster enduring creativity. Although Pauline and Cholly have come in contact with sustaining traditions, their move north parallels the dissolution of their ability to use these forms for sustaining purposes.

Klotman, Phyllis R. "Dick-and-Jane and the Shirley Temple Sensibility in *The Bluest Eye*." *Black American Literature Forum* 13 (Winter, 1979): 123-125.
Examines Morrison's use of the three versions of the Dick and Jane reader to juxtapose the fictions of the white educational process with the realities of black children's lives. The three versions symbolize the life-styles portrayed in the novel. The first is that of the alien white world; the second that of the McTeers, who are struggling to succeed despite their poverty; and the third that of the Breedloves, who live in a misshapen world that ultimately destroys Pecola.

Miner, Madonne M. "Lady No Longer Sings the Blues: Rape, Madness, and Silence in *The Bluest Eye*." In *Conjuring: Black Women, Fiction, and Literary Tradition*, edited by Marjorie Pryse and Hortense J. Spillers. Bloomington: Indiana University Press, 1985.
Reads *The Bluest Eye* as a manifestation of the ancient myths of Philomela and Persephone. Although these stories never coalesce with Pecola's to form a unified whole, each contributes to a much larger woman's myth focusing on denial and disintegration. Morrison reveals the concealed connections between male reason, speech, and presence; and female madness, silence, and absence.

Rahming, Melvin B. "West Indian Stereotypes in the Afro-American Novel." In *The Evolution of the West Indian's Image in the Afro-American Novel*. Millwood, N.Y.: Associated Faculty Press, 1986.
Discusses Morrison's characterization of Elihue Whitcombe (Soaphead Church) as a negative, but not stereotypical, portrait of a West Indian afflicted by deep neuroses. Nonetheless, Elihue is "perhaps the most insidious" of West Indian portraits in Afro-American fiction because "through a process of intellection he refines his profound emotional and spiritual illnesses almost beyond recognition."

Rosenberg, Ruth. "Seeds in Hard Ground: Black Girlhood in *The Bluest Eye*." *Black American Literature Forum* 21 (Winter, 1987): 435-445.
Views *The Bluest Eye* as a response to the absence of images of black girls'

experiences in literature for children and adolescents. Working out of her memories of her childhood, Morrison draws attention to problems rarely dealt with in literature: the traumatic aspect of the girl's first menstruation and the reality of color prejudice in the black community. Morrison recognizes the cruel impact of colorist culture on Pecola, but celebrates the children's poignant attempts to assume a maternal role toward the unborn baby.

Royster, Philip M. "The Novels of Toni Morrison: *The Bluest Eye*." *First World* 1 (Winter, 1977): 35-43.
Discusses the novel as a pessimistic narrative focusing on the situation of individuals who have been declared to be scapegoats by the larger society. The novel's weakness lies in the failure of the narrator to present the moments that were crucial to her developing awareness. The novel's strengths, primarily its precise and imaginative style, compensate for this problem. Morrison is particularly acute in showing how history effects present sociological and economic conditions.

Sissman, L. E. "Beginners' Luck." *The New Yorker* 46 (January 23, 1971): 92-94.
Favorable review of *The Bluest Eye* as a beautiful and painful study of black childhood. Dealing with people for whom no glory is possible, Morrison writes in "the freshest, simplest, and most striking prose." Although there are a few stylistic slips—such as the opening primers which are unnecessary and unsubtly ironic—Morrison presents a compelling picture of the relationship between the belief in whiteness that generates first self-hatred and then the overcompensatory counter-statement "Black is beautiful."

Wilder, Charles M. "Novels by Two Friends." *CLA Journal* 24 (December, 1971): 253-255.
Favorable review emphasizing Morrison's mastery of dialogue. Morrison presents a bleak portrait of Pecola as a person who was "doomed from the moment she was conceived." Argues that while Pecola's fate is not representative of poor blacks, her situation is nevertheless real.

Song of Solomon
Bakerman, Jane S. Review of *Song of Solomon*. *CLA Journal* 21 (March, 1978): 446-448.
Favorable review interpreting the novel as a metaphor for the development of Afro-American awareness. Contrasts the stylistic detail and leisurely pacing with the starker quality of Morrison's earlier books. Compares the relationship between Guitar and Milkman with that between Sula and Nel in *Sula*.

Barthold, Bonnie J. "Toni Morrison, *Song of Solomon*." In *Black Time: Fiction of Africa, the Caribbean, and the United States*. New Haven, Conn.: Yale University Press, 1981.

Focuses on Morrison's fusion of past and present into a "temporal resonance" that shapes the novel's thematic focus on heritage. Milkman is caught between two conflicting visions of time. Macon Dead represents the linear sense of time while Pilate embodies the vision of continuity associated with the African sense of cyclic time. In a separate section of the book, Barthold discusses Sula as a conjure woman.

Blake, Susan L. "Folklore and Community in *Song of Solomon*." *MELUS* 7 (Fall, 1980): 77-82.
Song of Solomon develops the tension between individual identity and community through an exploration of folk history as expressed in Morrison's use of the Gullah myth of the flying African. Both Milkman and Morrison return to the past for what is useful and then leave. Morrison adapts the tale to her novel just as Milkman interprets the legend of Solomon in a personal manner.

Brenner, Gerry. "*Song of Solomon*: Morrison's Rejection of Rank's Monomyth and Feminism." *Studies in American Fiction* 15 (Spring, 1987): 13-24.
Discusses Morrison's adaptation and subversion of Otto Rank's concept of the "monomyth." While Morrison's presentation of Milkman follows Rank's pattern, her treatment is satiric. Rejecting the implicit sexism of the monomyth, Morrison surrounds Milkman with women characters who call his heroism into question. Morrison also violates feminist expectations, however, by including a spectrum of women ranging from pathetic to praiseworthy.

Bruck, Peter. "Returning to One's Roots: The Motif of Searching and Flying in Toni Morrison's *Song of Solomon*." In *The Afro-American Novel Since 1960*, edited by Bruck and Wolfgang Karrer. Amsterdam: B. R. Gruner, 1982.
Extending the concerns of her earlier novels, Morrison fuses the theme of initiation with the quest for family roots, which is in turn linked to the search for Afro-American cultural heritage. Reminiscent of a fertility rite, the celebration of mutual love and sensuality in the encounter between Milkman and Sweet celebrates the life-giving force which—in contrast to the alternatives of Ruth, Corinthians, and Hagar—entails the promise of female selfhood.

Butler, Robert J. "Open Movement and Selfhood in Toni Morrison's *Song of Solomon*." *Centennial Review* 28/29 (Fall, 1984/Winter, 1985): 58-75.
Like many of the classic works of American fiction, *Song of Solomon* is deeply preoccupied with the search for human liberation through movement that is not directed toward a particular goal. Morrison's complex treatment of the dialectic between the possibilities of space and the security of place acknowledges that some characters, like Corinthians, may be able to achieve satisfying lives by settling down, while others, like Pilate and Milkman, can attain identity through movement, but only to the extent that they are fully aware of the blues-like paradoxes of modern experience.

Campbell, Jane. "Ancestral Quests in Toni Morrison's *Song of Solomon* and David
Bradley's *The Chaneysville Incident.*" In *Mythic Black Fiction: The Transformation of History.* Knoxville: University of Tennessee Press, 1986.
Thoroughly grounded in the romance mode, *Song of Solomon* argues that the
black American must acknowledge the complexity of black history and reclaim
fundamental aspects of the African heritage: ancestor worship, the super-
natural, and African religion and folklore. Typifying the ideological tendencies
of the romance hero, Milkman Dead provides the focal point for Morrison's
adaptation of the quest motif. Analyzes the novel primarily in relation to
Joseph Campbell's idea of the "monomyth."

Coleman, James W. "Beyond the Reach of Love and Caring: Black Life in Toni
Morrison's *Song of Solomon.*" *Obsidian II* 1 (Winter, 1986): 151-161.
Argues against critics who have seen the conclusion of the novel as positive.
Situated outside the day-to-day affairs of the black community, the example of
Milkman's death, while fulfilling in terms of the novel's mythic pattern, is
primarily a way of getting him outside a situation in which he no longer fits.
The majority of blacks will remain locked in the cycle where survival re-
sponses inevitably merge into strange and destructive patterns of behavior.

De Arman, Charles. "Milkman as the Archetypal Hero: 'Thursday's Child Has Far
to Go.'" *Obsidian* 6, no. 3 (1980): 56-59.
Relates Morrison's characterization of Milkman to the heroic patterns developed by Lord Raglan, Joseph Campbell, and Northrop Frye. Catalogs allusions to mythic heroes, including the association of Pilate with Astarte and
Milkman with Icarus.

Dixon, Melvin. "If You Surrender to the Air. . ." *Callaloo* 4 (October, 1978):
170-173.
Favorable review focusing on the way in which the sustained metaphor of flight
provides a center for Morrison's extremely rich mosaic of narrative and point
of view. *Song of Solomon* captures the pain and beauty of black people's
attempt to discover their names and articulate their meaning. Her language
reveals the connection of classical and biblical myths to the contemporary pain
of the Afro-American community.

Evans, James H. "The Recovery of Sacred Myth: Toni Morrison's *Song of Solomon.*" In *Spiritual Empowerment in Afro-American Literature.* Lewiston,
N.Y.: Edwin Mellen Press, 1987.
Examines the theme of the recovery of sacred myth as Morrison's resolution of
the tension between cultural grounding and cultural uprooting. Analyzes the
interweaving of three mythic strands: the Homeric myth; the myth of the flying

African; and the biblical Song of Solomon. These strands are brought together by Morrison's "strategy of commemoration."

Fabre, Genevieve. "Genealogical Archaeology of the Quest for Legacy in Toni Morrison's *Song of Solomon*." In *Critical Essays on Toni Morrison*, edited by Nellie Y. McKay. Boston: G. K. Hall, 1988.
Views *Song of Solomon* as an incursion into mystery that contributes to the movement away from sociology in recent black women's literature. Morrison treats the experience of legacy with many ironic overtones that highlight the paradoxical qualities of Milkman's quest. Reflecting her grounding in the dynamics of the oral tradition, she offers and withdraws answers, creating a constituting pattern of revelation and deception, of recognition and denial.

Frederick, Earl. "The Song of Milkman Dead." *The Nation* 225 (November 19, 1977): 536.
Favorable review emphasizing the power of Morrison's style, which turns what might be clichés into dazzling sentences carefully balancing language and thought. Her primary theme is that dignity and desperation, along with the abiding need for love, are inseparable aspects of existence. Reminiscent of Faulkner, she is the black writer most capable of achieving to the satisfaction of whites a mix of black form and human content.

Gardner, John. "John Gardner on Fiction." *The New Republic* 177 (December 3, 1977): 33-34.
Includes Gardner's praise of *Song of Solomon* as a "wonderfully vivid, singing book, deeply touching in a way we have learned to expect this writer to be." Gardner observes that he has no way of judging the accuracy of Morrison's portrayals but that the novels are full of convincing characters and wonderful language. Praises "the beauty of the book's construction" in which "meaning rises like a thing of nature, effortlessly flowering."

Gornick, Vivian. "Into the Dark Heart of Childhood." *The Village Voice* (August 29, 1977): 41.
Unfavorable review asserting that *Song of Solomon* fails to attain wholeness because of its "misdirected angle of vision." Gornick argues that Morrison should have chosen one of the women rather than Milkman as her central character. Acknowledges that Morrison is an extraordinary stylist and that the many individual moments of power and beauty help mitigate the implausible nature of Milkman's search.

Harris, A. Leslie. "Myth as Structure in Toni Morrison's *Song of Solomon*." *MELUS* 7 (Fall, 1980): 69-76.
Argues that Morrison uses Afro-American, Judeo-Christian, and Greco-

Roman mythic structure to make Milkman's quest universal. Milkman follows the pattern of the monomyth outlined by Joseph Campbell. Guitar serves as a double who embodies Milkman's negations. Revoicing the myth of Daedalus, Morrison transforms Icarus's doomed flying into Milkman's transcendent leap.

Johnson, Diane. "The Oppressor in the Next Room." *The New York Review of Books* 24 (November 10, 1977): 6-7.
Generally unfavorable review complaining that the praise given Morrison's style has kept readers from considering what she says. Morrison presents an unrelentingly bleak picture of a violent and demoralized black subculture where the women are cleverer, more interesting, and more homicidal than the men. The consideration of Milkman's heritage is the least interesting part of *Song of Solomon*, which sacrifices conventional narrative qualities to achieve the effect of a folktale.

Lardner, Susan. "Word of Mouth." *The New Yorker* 53 (November 7, 1977): 217-221.
Generally favorable review emphasizing Morrison's adaptation of the oral tradition to the form of the novel. The intricate structure, inventiveness, and variety of *Song of Solomon* differentiate it from true oral composition. More worldly-wise than inspired, Morrison recites the facts, no matter how far-fetched, of the Dead clan. Lardner notes the presence of a few patches of "vacant rhetoric" and questions the purpose of Guitar, but concludes that "the current of Morrison's prose is never seriously deflected."

Larson, Charles R. "Hymning the Black Past." *The Washington Post Book World* 7 (September 4, 1977): 1, 4.
Highly favorable review identifying *Song of Solomon* as the best black novel since *Invisible Man* and praising Morrison for her Faulknerian mastery of the mixture of the comic and the grotesque. Milkman's quest for the origins of black consciousness in America inverts the path of Ellison's narrator, moving from North to South. Morrison's marvelous orchestration of her materials enables her to transcend the limited theme of ethnic identity and say something about life and death "for all of us."

Mason, Theodore O., Jr. "The Novelist as Conservator: Stories and Comprehension in Toni Morrison's *Song of Solomon*." *Contemporary Literature* 29 (Winter, 1988): 564-581.
Argues against criticism which views Morrison's primary concern as the revision of modernist or postmodernist literary traditions. Rather, her work relies on linear plotting, the use of rounded characters, and a mimetic conception of the novel. Viewing storytelling as a way of fixing identity, Morrison portrays characters who use stories to create sense out of, and provide significant information about, reality. Both stories that attempt to enhance reality and

those that attempt to control it imply a real connection with the outside world or with other fictions.

O'Shaughnessy, Kathleen. " 'Life life life life': The Community as Chorus in *Song of Solomon*." In *Critical Essays on Toni Morrison*, edited by Nellie Y. McKay. Boston: G. K. Hall, 1988.
Examines the role of the community as a formal chorus in *Song of Solomon*, combining elements of traditional African dance and song with a commentary on the characters' actions. Composed of individuals who act as both observers and participants, Morrison's chorus seeks to involve her community of readers as participants in the experience of her novel.

Pinsker, Sanford. "Magic Realism, Historical Truth, and the Quest for a Liberating Identity: Reflections on Alex Haley's *Roots* and Toni Morrison's *Song of Solomon*." *Studies in Black American Literature* 1 (1984): 183-197.
Morrison's intricate postmodernist attitude and her stylistic use of a "magic realism" comparable to that of Gabriel García Márquez make *Song of Solomon* a much more successful book than *Roots*. Morrison's use of folkloric elements is less strained than Ellison's in *Invisible Man*. Morrison understands that Milkman's struggle is not to recover history but to understand his own relationship to the past.

Price, Reynolds. "Black Family Chronicle." *The New York Times Book Review* 82 (September 11, 1977): 1, 48.
Favorable review of *Song of Solomon*, emphasizing the theme of the possibility of human transcendence within human life. Morrison's negotiations with fantasy, fable, allegory, and song are organically embedded in her narrative. By juxtaposing the individual quest with the larger, freer sphere of human contingency, Morrison reveals the possibility of knowing one's origins and realizing the potential found in the lives of one's ancestors.

Reed, Harry. "Toni Morrison, *Song of Solomon*, and Black Cultural Nationalism." *Centennial Review* 32 (Winter, 1988): 50-64.
Argues that *Song of Solomon* is at once a major contribution to and a serious critique of black cultural nationalism. Even as she recognizes the limitations of nationalist thought of the 1960's—particularly its sexism and its counterproductive elevation of political over cultural perspectives—Morrison asserts fundamental Pan-African motifs expressed through the emphasis on oral tradition and Afro-American musical motifs. Pilate, Circe, and Ruth can all be seen as nationalist archetypes.

Rosenberg, Ruth. "And the Children May Know Their Names: Toni Morrison's *Song of Solomon*." *Literary Onomastics Studies* 8 (1981): 195-219.

Explores Morrison's use of various naming conventions. Morrison uses biblical names to suggest and then subvert allegorical expectations. She examines four generations of naming: the biblical names of slavery; the corrupted names of Reconstruction; the satiric nicknames of the northern migration; and the black militant names of the 1960's. Morrison uses names to underline the theme of the ability of characters to rise above their circumstances.

Royster, Philip M. "Milkman's Flying: The Scapegoat Transcended in Toni Morrison's *Song of Solomon*." *CLA Journal* 24 (June, 1982): 419-440.
Examines *Song of Solomon* as a *Bildungsroman*, contrasting Milkman's changing relationship to the past in the two parts of the novel. In the first section, Milkman functions as a scapegoat who has inherited his family's burden of guilt. In the second part, he becomes the beneficiary of the past. Accepting his past, Milkman transforms himself from scapegoat into "Sugarman."

Samuels, Wilfred D. "Liminality and the Search for Self in Toni Morrison's *Song of Solomon*." *Minority Voices* 5, nos. 1/2 (1981): 59-68.
Discusses Milkman as a heroic figure in relation to the archetypal pattern described by Lord Raglan. Emphasizes the importance of the rites of initiation Milkman undergoes.

Scruggs, Charles. "The Nature of Desire in Toni Morrison's *Song of Solomon*." *Arizona Quarterly* 38 (1982): 311-335.
Concentrates on Morrison's "fascination with the nature of desire." *Song of Solomon* explores two types of desire: one that transcends and one that becomes grotesque. Representing these types, Pilate and Macon Dead represent the fragmented parts of a larger whole; Guitar inherits his father's psychological split; Solomon's flight is liberating and destructive to Ryna; Milkman's integration is accompanied by Hagar's disintegration. The two types of desire are not resolved.

Skerrett, Joseph T., Jr. "Recitation to the Griot: Storytelling and Learning in Toni Morrison's *Song of Solomon*." In *Conjuring: Black Women, Fiction, and Literary Tradition*, edited by Marjorie Pryse and Hortense J. Spillers. Bloomington: Indiana University Press, 1985.
Focuses on the problem of reconciling individual and communal perspectives. If Morrison's protagonists conceive themselves in standard American terms as separate individuals, the community from which they have become isolated is the Afro-American folk community of shared beliefs and practices. Morrison relies heavily on images of folk processes to work out this tension in relation to Milkman Dead. Pilate fulfills the role of the African griot, who teaches Milkman to understand and ultimately participate in these processes.

Spallino, Chiara. "*Song of Solomon*: An Adventure in Structure." *Callaloo* 25 (Fall, 1985): 510-524.
Structuralist analysis of Morrison's use of a fragmented chronology to explore Milkman's maturation as a classic *Bildungsroman* hero. Milkman experiences a series of transformations of consciousness centering on his experience of a "family past" and a "mythic past." The interplay between these time levels is the structural key to the novel. Only by combining the two levels of the past can Milkman free himself to move toward the future.

Tate, Claudia C. Review of *Song of Solomon*. *CLA Journal* 21 (December, 1977): 327-329.
Mildly unfavorable review contrasting the emphasis on intrigue with the rich lyrical quality of Morrison's prose in her previous novels. After the mystery story is resolved, there is little in the book to encourage reexamination.

Wedertz-Furtado, Utelinda. "Historical Dimensions in Toni Morrison's *Song of Solomon*." In *History and Tradition in Afro-American Literature*, edited by Gunther H. Lenz. Frankfurt: Campus Verlag, 1984.
Examines Milkman's quest as an archetypal expression of the experience of black Americans. Emphasizes the significance of the Northern and Southern settings and the family history, which invokes common patterns experienced by the Afro-American community.

Weixlmann, Joe. "Culture Clash, Survival, and Trans-Formation: A Study of Some Innovative Afro-American Novels of Detection." *Mississippi Quarterly* 38 (Winter, 1984/1985): 21-31.
Discusses *Song of Solomon* along with Ishmael Reed's *The Last Days of Louisiana Red* and Clarence Major's *Reflex and Bone Structures* as examples of the ways in which formally innovative Afro-American novels have used popular forms to break the stranglehold of realism and naturalism on black writing. Though not a classic detective story, *Song of Solomon* centers on Milkman's investigation of his ancestry, forcing him to develop unwillingly into "something of a sleuth." Morrison's conclusion is one of the most effective examples of "non-closure" in black literature.

Werner, Craig. "Homer's Joyce: John Updike, Ronald Sukenick, Robert Coover, Toni Morrison." In *Paradoxical Resolutions: American Fiction Since James Joyce*. Urbana: University of Illinois Press, 1982.
Considers Morrison's use of myth in *Song of Solomon* in relation to contemporary American adaptations of Joycean techniques. Relates Morrison's style to the "magic realism" of Gabriel García Márquez and examines the ways in which she resolves the symbolic and realistic meanings of the novel. Discusses the themes of naming and flight as keys to Morrison's resolution of African

and American heritages. Argues that Morrison makes it clear that the theme of flight must be understood from both male and female perspectives.

Sula

Abel, Elizabeth. "(E)Merging Identities: The Dynamics of Female Friendship in Contemporary Fiction by Women." *Signs* 6 (Spring, 1981): 413-435.
  Discusses *Sula* as an illustration of the way in which women writers portray women friends as crucial figures in helping women relax ego boundaries and restore psychic wholeness. Morrison contrasts Sula and Nel's freely chosen friendship to both parental and sexual bonds, asserting the possible conjunction of sameness and autonomy which is attainable only with another version of oneself. Abel revises theoretical formulations of psychologist Nancy Chodorow and literary theorist Harold Bloom.

Banyiwa-Horne, Naana. "The Scary Face of the Self: An Analysis of the Character of Sula in Toni Morrison's *Sula*." *Sage* 2 (Spring, 1985): 28-31.
  Focuses on *Sula* not as a realistic novel but as an exploration of the aspects of the feminine psyche that are often hidden from view because they are too problematic to deal with. Repression of the "scary self" drives the imagination underground, as in the case of Nel. When this self is uncontrolled, however, the result is a decentered personality, as in the case of Sula. Nel and Sula are separate aspects of one being.

Blackburn, Sara. Review of *Sula*. *The New York Times Book Review* 78 (December 30, 1973): 3.
  Mixed review associating the quality of Morrison's characters with those of Gabriel García Márquez, but arguing that she needs to "address a riskier contemporary reality" if she is to "transcend that early and unintentionally limiting classification 'black woman writer' and take her place among the most serious, important, and talented American novelists." Her novels lack immediacy and fail to sustain the intensity of their first reading.

Bryant, Jerry H. "Something Ominous Here." *The Nation* (July 6, 1974): 23-24.
  Review emphasizing the ways in which Morrison, like Ed Bullins and Alice Walker, is challenging the safety of American reality with a chilling detachment expressed through a fascination with evil. Morrison's originality and power can be seen in characters such as Sula who do not fit familiar black images. Concludes that Morrison creates a feeling not of moral complexity, but of a sardonic irony concerning the possibility of ever distinguishing good from evil.

Grant, Robert. "Absence into Presence: The Thematics of Memory and 'Missing' Subjects in Toni Morrison's *Sula*." In *Critical Essays on Toni Morrison*, edited by Nellie Y. McKay. Boston: G. K. Hall, 1988.

Approaches *Sula* as a novel in which "the relative social values of conservancy *and* iconoclasm are exquisitely balanced," emphasizing the difficulty of determining Morrison's moral judgement. Discussing Morrison's "rebel ideas" as the expression of multiple cultural traditions, Grant concludes that the "politico-cultural" relevance of *Sula* lies in its ability simultaneously to shatter boundaries and define new domains.

Hogue, W. Lawrence. "The Song of Morrison's *Sula*: History, Mythical Thought, and the Production of the Afro-American Historical Past." In *Discourse and the Other: The Production of the Afro-American Text*. Durham, N.C.: Duke University Press, 1986.

Lists four basic factors informing the production of *Sula* and its representation of the historical past: the surreal, or elements foreign to rationalism; the need for blacks to reestablish connection with their past; feminism; and Morrison's sense of her audience. Draws on anthropologist Claude Levi-Strauss's concept of the *bricoleur* to describe the naming rituals and conceptual framework of the people of the Bottom. Discusses the community's response to evil, stressing the movement from initial fear through acceptance to an ultimate ability to make evil functional in the way it thinks about the world.

Jefferson, Margo. "Toni Morrison: Passionate and Precise." *Ms.* 3 (December, 1974): 34-39.

Highly favorable review praising the passionate, precise language that combines lyrical and philosophical intensities. Morrison illuminates her tragic materials by grounding them in a rich texture of everyday realities. She convincingly refutes the claims that black writers are incapable of creating great art.

Lounsberry, Barbara, and Grace Ann Hovet. "Principles of Perception in Toni Morrison's *Sula*." *Black American Literature Forum* 13 (Winter, 1979): 126-129.

Sula poses the traditional ordering principles of the Bottom community against the new perspectives of the novel's heroine, showing the constriction and futility created by the dominance of a single ordering principle. Yet the ambivalent portrayal of Sula forces the reader to see the limitation of the concepts of "multiple perspectives" which in themselves do not ensure cultural pluralism.

McDowell, Deborah E. " 'The Self and Other': Reading Toni Morrison's *Sula* and the Black Female Text." In *Critical Essays on Toni Morrison*, edited by Nellie Y. McKay. Boston: G. K. Hall, 1988.

Valuable essay arguing that the next stage of black feminist criticism "must lead us beyond the descriptions that keep us locked in opposition and antagonism." Reads *Sula* as a crucial text in this process because it "transgresses all deterministic structures of opposition." Emphasizes the ways in which Morrison invokes oppositions of good/evil, virgin/whore, and self/other, but moves beyond them, avoiding the false choices they both imply and dictate. Concludes that Morrison intimates a way of conceiving the self which resists stasis and "will glory in difference."

Martin, Odette C. "The Novels of Toni Morrison: *Sula*." *First World* 1 (Winter, 1977): 35-44.
Argues that although *Sula* is usually seen as a celebration of black values, the novel is more important as a prophetic attack on "special Negritude," which she sees as a ethnocentric and romantic response to the complex problems faced by blacks in a technological racist society. Focusing on the suicidal orientation of black values, *Sula* is to Afro-American culture what Chinua Achebe's *Things Fall Apart* is to African culture. Analyzes the novel as a critique of black life, as an allegory of black literary history, and as the narrative of the Peace family.

Matza, Diane. "Zora Neale Hurston's *Their Eyes Were Watching God* and Toni Morrison's *Sula*: A Comparison." *MELUS* 12 (Fall, 1985): 43-54.
Compares the two novels as examinations of the conflict between the individual woman's desire to explore herself and the community's need to stifle her to achieve order and stability. Sharing a belief that writers must be true to their visions, Hurston and Morrison dissect stereotypes, render black speech and folk traditions, and delineate conflicts within the black community.

Middleton, Victoria. "*Sula*: An Experimental Life." *CLA Journal* 28 (June, 1984): 367-381.
Views Sula as fulfilling Simone de Beauvoir's conception of existential heroism because she refuses to accept the submissive female role approved by her community. A "Promethean artist," Sula defies the gods and is superior to other mortals. Contrasts Sula with the conventional Nel and the mad antihero Shadrack.

Munro, C. Lynn. "The Tattooed Heart and the Serpentine Eye: Morrison's Choice of an Epigraph for *Sula*." *Black American Literature Forum* 18 (Winter, 1984): 150-154.
Examines the significance of Morrison's choice of an epigraph from Tennessee Williams' play *The Rose Tattoo*. The choice both identifies the underlying theme and invites a closer examination of parallels between the two works, both of which examine the ravages of time and misbegotten love. Both works identify the tragic quality of even the most mundane lives, which results from individuals' failures to recognize their own self-indulgence.

Ogunyemi, Chikwenye Okonjo. *"Sula*: 'A Nigger Joke.'" *Black American Literature Forum* 13 (Winter, 1979): 130-133.
Sula is a "nigger joke" in which the promiscuous woman turns out to be the hero, while the middle-class prig is the villainess. Its humor presents an accurate image of blacks to the world while providing a modicum of comfort to the reader. Morrison views the lack of fulfillment in life as an inevitable existential reality.

Reddy, Maureen T. "The Tripled Plot and Center of *Sula.*" *Black American Literature Forum* 22 (Spring, 1988): 29-45.
Recognition of the relationship between the theme of death, the split protagonist, and the attention to chronology in *Sula* draws attention to Morrison's antiwar theme. Despite its title, *Sula* has three protagonists: Shadrack, Sula/Nel, and the black community of the Bottom. Each of these three centers develops a different aspect of the antiwar theme. Morrison ultimately asserts the values of communality, of love against death, and of peace against war.

Sokoloff, Janice M. "Intimations of Matriarchal Age: Notes on the Mythical Eve in Toni Morrison's *Sula.*" *Journal of Black Studies* 16 (June, 1986): 429-434.
Analyzes the importance of ancestral ties in *Sula.* The African relationship, presented ironically, is the most striking element of the novel's complex web of familial and communal bonds. Although Morrison portrays her protagonist attempting to kill the ancestor and deny historical connection, she "more fundamentally creates a matriarchal community in which the ancestor becomes the source of vitality and truth" that permits her descendants to prevail.

Stein, Karen F. "Toni Morrison's *Sula*: A Black Woman's Epic." *Black American Literature Forum* 18 (Winter, 1984): 146-150.
Morrison creates a heroic context for her themes and characters by using mythic narrative structures reflecting the patterns identified in Joseph Campbell's *Hero with a Thousand Faces*. Although she grounds *Sula* firmly in the epic tradition, Morrison uses ironic reversals to create a new definition of heroism that will encompass the lives of black women. The fact that most characters in the novel misunderstand Sula and Nel reinforces Morrison's theme of the private nature of heroism.

Wessling, Joseph H. "Narcissism in Toni Morrison's *Sula.*" *CLA Journal* 31 (March, 1988): 281-298.
Uses Christopher Lasch's typology of American narcissism to discuss the generational changes portrayed in *Sula.* The older generation develops a type of narcissism associated with the rugged individualism necessary for survival. Nel's association of the younger generation of blacks with the Deweys suggests that it is developing a more pathological type of narcissism. Includes a discus-

sion of the impact of Sula's and Nel's home environments on the development of their personalities.

Yardley, Jonathan. "The Naughty Lady." *The Washington Post Book World* 4 (February 3, 1974): 3.
Favorable review praising Morrison as a writer who can establish the sense of place in the manner of Flannery O'Connor or Eudora Welty. The quality of Morrison's prose, which has the resonance of poetry without surrendering control, gives *Sula* a genuine distinction. Much more than a portrait of the title character, the novel evokes the way of life of the black communities of the 1920's and 1930's.

Tar Baby

Caplan, Brina. "A Fierce Conflict of Colors." *The Nation* 232 (May 2, 1981): 529-535.
Generally favorable review praising *Tar Baby* as a novel of ideas but observing that, like most novels of the type, it remains "teasingly deficient as a novel of character." Moving beyond the settings of her previous work, Morrison portrays black communities as displaced by the dominant white world in which her "symbolic conflict of colors" takes place. One of Morrison's primary themes is that the contemporary idea that people can be whatever they want to be is "dangerous moral silliness."

Christian, Barbara. "Testing the Strength of the Black Cultural Bond: Review of Toni Morrison's *Tar Baby*." In *Black Feminist Criticism*. Elmsford, N.Y.: Pergamon Press, 1985. Review of *Tar Baby* originally published in *In These Times* (July 14, 1981).
Focuses on Morrison's adaptation of the tar baby folktale to analyze the complexities of class, race, and sex in the Afro-American community. Valerian plays the role of the farmer, Son of the rabbit. The central conflict in the novel, however, is between Jadine, who is individualistic and materialistic, and Son, who is "roots-bound." Raising the question of whether there is a functional black culture in the present-day West, Morrison makes the disturbing suggestion that what were untrue stereotypes—the separation of house and field slaves, for example—have now become true.

Coleman, James. "The Quest for Wholeness in Toni Morrison's *Tar Baby*." *Black American Literature Forum* 20 (Spring/Summer, 1986): 63-73.
Analysis of *Tar Baby* centering on the question of whether the folk values asserted in Morrison's earlier novels can only be achieved in settings removed from those actually experienced by most blacks. Showing Son's inability to adapt to the modern world and leaving him in the wholesome world of the primal where he may be able to avoid dealing with the modern world evades

the issue of whether blacks like Son must abandon traditional values in order to succeed in the modern world. Inasmuch as it fails to address this crucial issue, *Tar Baby* is a failure.

Erickson, Peter B. "Images of Nurturance in Toni Morrison's *Tar Baby*." *CLA Journal* 28 (September, 1984): 11-32.
Focusing on disconnection rather than connection, *Tar Baby* extends the key theme of Morrison's earlier novels—the identity of a black woman—into a larger social and geographical sphere. Analyzes the relationships between Jadine, Ondine, and Therese, with detailed discussion of the suffering associated with Jadine's entry into traditionally male territory. Also discusses Son's nurturant capacity, which is not independent but reached through fusion with the nurturance offered by Therese.

Harris, Trudier. "Beyond the Ritual?" In *Exorcising Blackness: Historical and Literary Lynching and Burning Rituals*. Bloomington: Indiana University Press, 1984.
Discussion of Son in relation to the stereotype of the "nigger rapist," concluding that if Morrison had set her novel in a different location, he would be susceptible to lynching. Emphasizes the importance of distinguishing between the perspectives of the various black women in the novel and comments at length on Valerian's character, which is predicated on his desire to shape other people. Jadine is "potentially as destructive to black men as her historical white counterparts."

Hawthorne, Evelyn. "On Gaining the Double-Vision: *Tar Baby* as Diasporan Novel." *Black American Literature Forum* 22 (Spring, 1988): 97-107.
Examines *Tar Baby* in the context of the historical development of the Diasporean dialogue between black American writers and black writers in the Caribbean and Africa. Morrison transcends cultural insularity to promote an inclusive vision of African peoples and cultures. A contemporary revisioning of racial history, *Tar Baby* makes visible the common identity of blacks in the Diaspora. Includes a valuable summary of the political and cultural dimensions of Diasporean thought.

Howard, Maureen. "A Novel of Exile and Home." *The New Republic* 197 (March 21, 1981): 29-32.
Favorable review identifying *Tar Baby* as an important American novel combining elements of wonder with a comedy of manners. Praises Morrison's ability to create convincing landscapes and her comfortable "pursuit of big themes." Thematically tighter than Morrison's earlier novels, *Tar Baby* presents a vision of a world "which offers the thinness of exile and denies us the comforts of home."

Irving, John. "Morrison's Black Fable." *The New York Times Book Review* 86 (March 29, 1981): 1, 30-31.
Generally favorable review emphasizing Morrison's willingness to "return risk" to contemporary American fiction, but criticizing her decision to base so much of *Tar Baby* on dialogue. Observes that the power of Morrison's picture of racial tension derives from her intense focus on the black characters. Identifies *Tar Baby* as a novel about the black desire "to create a mythology of his own to replace the stereotypes and myths the white man has constructed for him." Also notes the theme of women's anger.

Lardner, Susan. "Unastonished Eye." *The New Yorker* 57 (June 15, 1981): 147-151.
Mixed review discussing the impact of the strange mixture of objective detachment and intense feeling implied in Morrison's style. She employs an omniscient narrator to present opinions, memories, and thoughts for which she is not directly responsible. Her fervent style, however, creates a "disparity between feeling and judgement" in her bleak vision of people divided against one another. Her use of the tar baby image is "an oversimplifying image of manipulation" that makes "nonsense of the complicated racial, sexual, and social battles she is trying to dramatize."

Lepow, Lauren. "Paradise Lost and Found: Dualism and Edenic Myth in Toni Morrison's *Tar Baby*." *Contemporary Literature* 28 (Fall, 1987): 363-377.
Examines Morrison's revision of Milton's *Paradise Lost* as a part of her critique of the self-destructive dualism underlying sexism and racism. Lepow associates the Isles des Chevaliers with Eden; and Valerian, Son, and Jadine with different aspects of Satan. Emphasizes Morrison's refusal to accept any simple allegorical identifications or oppositions between her characters. Urging her readers to transcend dualism and external authority, Morrison portrays Jadine's discovery of her artistic medium as the process of self-creation.

Lydon, Susan. "What's an Intelligent Woman to Do?" *The Village Voice* (July 1, 1981): 40-41.
Generally unfavorable review criticizing Morrison's failure to present Jadine with a viable option. Acknowledges the mythic power of Morrison's style, which creates a strong picture of tensions between master and servant, men and women, blacks and whites. Argues that Morrison is more sympathetic to Son, who is one of the most sexy, interesting male characters in recent literature, than to Jadine, who can only choose whether to fall into the trap of sexism or of racism.

Mobley, Marilyn E. "Narrative Dilemma: Jadine as Cultural Orphan in Toni Morrison's *Tar Baby*." *The Southern Review* 23 (October, 1987): 761-770.
Tar Baby serves both as "a remembrance of a cultural tradition of nurturing

and as a cautionary tale for those like Jadine who define themselves against themselves and their cultural past in the interest of self-fulfillment." A cultural orphan continually in flight from crisis, Jadine risks psychic chaos by denying the sources that could empower her. Emphasizes the tension between Morrison's two central concerns: to affirm the self-reliance and freedom of a black woman who makes her own choices; and to emphasize the importance of cultural grounding.

O'Meally, Robert G. "Tar Baby, She Don Say Nothin'." *Callaloo* 11, 12, 13 (February-October, 1981): 193-198.
Mixed review praising Morrison's ability to create memorable scenes but criticizing her failure to bring her characters fully to life. A classic confrontation between the middle-class black woman and the downhome black man, *Tar Baby*'s greatest achievement is its complex reworking of the "tar baby" folktale, which O'Meally describes in detail. Morrison is most successful when addressing the issue of the relationship of spoken to written language.

Pinckney, Darryl. "Every Which Way." *The New York Review of Books* 28 (April 30, 1981): 24-25.
Unfavorable review asserting that Morrison's "writing is so elaborate that it distracts and obscures." Pinckney identifies "labored metaphors" and "convoluted verbal conjurings" as weaknesses which create a "tone that is overreaching, taxing to the ear." Concludes that it is difficult to decide what the characters represent and that Morrison fails to describe the inner world of black women as effectively as Gayl Jones.

Rumens, Carol. "Conflicts of Complexion." *Times Literary Supplement* (October 30, 1981): 1260.
Favorable review praising Morrison's ability to create an amalgamation of diverse elements that gives her work a unique density reinforced by a superb dramatic sense. *Tar Baby* asserts that complexion is a much more subtle issue than a simple polarization of black and white. Morrison's readers must be constantly alert to where metaphor ends and straight narrative begins.

Schott, Webster. "Toni Morrison: Tearing the Social Fabric." *The Washington Post Book World* 11 (March 22, 1981): 1-2.
Mixed review praising Morrison's poetic language, arresting images, and fierce intelligence but criticizing the absence of credible motives for her characters' actions. Emphasizes Morrison's courage in raising issues that might well be declared the product of male chauvinism if they had been presented by John Updike. Presents Son as kin to mythic wayfarers such as Twain's Huck and Jim, but more basically as Morrison's version of the "official heroic black male."

Sheed, Wilfrid. "Improbable Assignment." *Atlantic* 247 (April, 1981): 119-120.
Generally unfavorable review emphasizing the extreme difficulty of combining the comedy of manners in *Tar Baby* with the expansive vision of black America characteristic of Morrison's previous work. Notes that the first part of the book reads more like a play than a novel and that many scenes seem almost parodies of Broadway. While Jadine's struggle speaks to anyone who has attempted to change cultures, Morrison fails to provide an adequate conclusion. Half of the novel is Morrison at her very best, half is Morrison trying something new with only sporadic success.

Sheppard, R. Z. "Black Diamond." *Time* 117 (March 16, 1981): 90, 92.
Mixed review observing that Morrison's attempt to evoke island life through the magic realism of *Song of Solomon* "does not quite work." Assuming the role of the fox in the folktale who traps the unwary reader, Morrison blends elements of racial identity, assimilation, and Caribbean folklore with "an old-fashioned lady-and-the-truck-driver romance."

Traylor, Eleanor W. "The Fabulous World of Toni Morrison: *Tar Baby*." In *Confirmation: An Anthology of African American Women*, edited by Amiri Baraka and Amina Baraka. New York: Quill, 1983. Reprinted in *Critical Essays on Toni Morrison*, edited by Nellie Y. McKay. Boston: G. K. Hall, 1988.
Analyzes Morrison's adaptation of the tar baby story in relation to the theme of disconnection, which provides a fundamental focus of American literature from Crevecoeur and Emerson to the present. Following the dominant tradition of Afro-American fiction, Morrison's treatment of Jadine reinforces the view of individualism as solipsism. Like the collages of Romare Bearden, *Tar Baby* is a modern fable of society in which humanity is black.

Werner, Craig H. "The Briar Patch as Modernist Myth: Morrison, Barthes, and Tar Baby As-Is." In *Critical Essays on Toni Morrison*, edited by Nellie Y. McKay. Boston: G. K. Hall, 1988.
Argues that Morrison extends Roland Barthes's critique of the dehistoricized modernist understanding of myth. Attuned to both folk and literary traditions of double-voicing, Morrison apprehends myth both as a tool of Euro-American power and a reservoir of historical knowledge capable of resisting that power. Traces the development of the tar baby myth from Afro-American oral tradition through the Uncle Remus stories and Walt Disney's *Song of the South*. Focuses on Morrison's characters as representatives of different orientations toward myth. Builds on George Kent's idea of the "is-ness" of Afro-American folk expression to assert that as a modern Brer Rabbit, Son offers a way of revitalizing repressed historical experience.

GLORIA NAYLOR

Biography

Naylor, Gloria, and Toni Morrison. "A Conversation." *The Southern Review* 21 (July, 1985): 567-593.

Lengthy conversation including an introduction by Naylor and an afterword by Morrison. Among the topics discussed are marriage; the process of breaking stereotypes and revising social conceptions of women's roles; the relationship between Sula and Nel in *Sula*; the composition and publication of *The Bluest Eye*, *Beloved*, and *Linden Hills*; and their feelings concerning their black male characters.

Commentary

"Gloria Naylor." In *Contemporary Literary Criticism*, vol. 28, edited by Jean C. Stine. Detroit: Gale Research, 1984.

Excerpts from five reviews of *The Women of Brewster Place*, including Gottlieb's and those published in the daily *New York Times* and *Washington Post*.

Johnson, Charles. "The Women." In *Being and Race: Black Writing Since 1970*. Bloomington: Indiana University Press, 1988.

Brief comment by a black male novelist identifying Naylor as a "profoundly talented" writer. In *The Women of Brewster Place*, Naylor demonstrates a profound knowledge of her women characters, but presents black men in terms of the "Negro beast stereotype." Naylor melds the concerns of feminism and the Black Arts movement.

Selected Titles

Linden Hills

Brown, Joseph A. "With Eyes Like Flames of Fire." *Callaloo* 24 (Spring/Summer, 1985): 484-488.

Favorable review situating the novel in the prophetic, didactic tradition of Afro-American literature. Cautions against too strong an emphasis on Naylor's use of the *Divine Comedy* as structure; argues that the Book of Revelation is an equally significant source. Naylor's call for repentance is accompanied by an uncompromising vision of the pain, destruction, and chaos of what is.

Gomez, Jewelle. "Naylor's Inferno." *The Women's Review of Books* 2 (August, 1985): 7-8.

Extremely unfavorable review stressing Naylor's acceptance of racist symbolism concerning skin color, and the dominance of mad people in her depiction of the black community. Relying totally on Dante for the structure of her novel, Naylor does nothing to utilize African mythology as a way of increasing her story's significance. The tone of relentless gothic horror and an unclear chronological framework are among the novel's many additional problems.

Kaveney, Roz. "Solutions to Dissolution." *Times Literary Supplement* (May 24, 1985): 572.

Mixed review included in a discussion of the ways in which "traditional fictions might not be ideally suited to the depiction of contemporary urban life." Naylor's central theme is the nullity of black lives that are led in imitation of suburban whites. While the melodramatic plot and machinery are obtrusive, Naylor's rich language keeps the problems from becoming "embarrassing." The verbal energy holds together the unintegrated parts of Naylor's "right-on soap opera."

Ward, Catherine C. "Gloria Naylor's *Linden Hills*: A Modern *Inferno*." *Contemporary Literature* 28 (Spring, 1987): 67-81.

Argues that Naylor uses Dante as a framework for *Linden Hills* in order to give "a universalizing mythic dimension to what otherwise might be considered a narrow subject, the price American blacks are paying for their economic and social 'success.'" Basing her story on the physical and moral topography of the *Inferno*, Naylor associates Willie with Dante, Lester with Virgil, and Willa with Count Ugolino. Contains a detailed description of the parallels between the streets in Linden Hills and the circles of Dante's Hell.

Watkins, Mel. "The Circular Driveways of Hell." *The New York Times Book Review* 90 (March 3, 1985): 11.

Mixed review of *Linden Hills* as a flawed work that "tackles a controversial subject with boldness and originality." In Naylor's version of the *Inferno*, blacks who aspire to the material success of the white world "are pawns of the Devil and will experience the torments of hell." Her rigid allegorical structure, however, creates a didactic tendency and aspects of the Nedeed story remain unclear.

Werner, Craig. "Black Dreams of Faulkner's Dreams of Blacks." In *Faulkner and Race*, edited by Doreen Fowler and Ann J. Abadie. Jackson: University Press of Mississippi, 1987.

Discusses *Linden Hills* in the context of Afro-American revisions of William Faulkner. Naylor insists that women's experiences can be understood only through recognition of repeated historical patterns. Acknowledging the complexity of her black male characters, Naylor makes it clear that light- and dark-skinned blacks, men and women, lower- and middle-class individuals can reduce one another to symbolic "otherness." Failing to recognize this generates a destructive pattern similar to that in *Absalom, Absalom!*

Williams, Sherley Anne. "Roots of Privilege: New Black Fiction." *Ms.* 13 (June, 1985): 69-72.
Reviews *Linden Hills* along with Shange's *Betsey Brown* and Andrea Lee's *Sarah Phillips* as examples of a new engagement with the theme of the black middle-class, which has been generally overlooked since the Harlem Renaissance. Emphasizing Naylor's revoicing of motifs from the works of Morrison and Alice Walker, Williams observes that Willie and Lester represent the best of the oral and literate traditions. Although *Linden Hills* has many compelling moments, the "sins" of Naylor's middle class community seem too trivial to carry the weight of her expert literary attention.

Mama Day
Brown, Rosellen. "Mama Day." *Ms.* 16 (February, 1988): 74.
Generally favorable review emphasizing Naylor's treatment of the theme of the costs and benefits of the move from rural to urban, from intuitive to rational, life. Contrasts the protagonists' "social smarts" with the "street smarts" of most fiction about the urban poor. Brown criticizes Naylor's insistence on making everything in the novel symbolic by relating it to her larger scheme. Identifies George as the most sympathetic portrait of a black man to appear in recent fiction by black women.

Mukherjee, Bharati. "There Are Four Sides to Everything." *The New York Times Book Review* 93 (February 21, 1988): 7.
Mixed review praising Naylor's ambitious ability to make the wondrous familiar, but concluding that she fails to establish convincing ties between the love story and issues of large public concern. Notes Naylor's references to *The Tempest* and to slave narratives. Characterized by an excess of plots and characters, *Mama Day* derives its power primarily from the magnificent portrait of the title character.

Pullin, Faith. "Acts of Reclamation." *Times Literary Supplement* (June 3, 1988): 623.
Brief favorable review relating Naylor's novel to the work of Morrison and Alice Walker. Mixing social satire with folk humor, Naylor juxtaposes African past with American present. Naylor's rich, sensuous imagery supports a narrative that swings from myth to social realism. Naylor "doesn't load her narrative with significance that it can't bear."

Simon, Linda. "Black Roots, White Culture." *The Women's Review of Books* 5 (September, 1988): 11.
Unfavorable review criticizing Naylor's failure to explore the central issue of

how the Afro-American heritage is to be passed on and utilized in the real world. Naylor's primary concern is Cocoa's identity as a rural black woman and her confrontation with urban America. If Cocoa is taken as a representative figure, then black women are fearful, defensive, and vulnerable. Her inability to enact the conjurer role in the New York environment signals that she has abandoned her cultural heritage with nothing to replace it.

Southgate, Maria. "Love's Labors." *The Village Voice* (March 15, 1988): 52.
Favorable review of *Mama Day* as an epic, tragic, funny, and unsentimental book about the difficulty of loving well. Describes the interaction of the three primary voices in the novel, those of Cocoa, George, and of the island itself. Where Naylor's earlier novels occasionally strained for effect and sounded like "warmed-over Toni Morrison," here she has attained a fresh assurance of tone.

The Women of Brewster Place
Awkward, Michael. "Authorial Dreams of Wholeness: (Dis)unity, (Literary) Parentage, and *The Women of Brewster Place*." In *Inspiriting Influences: Tradition, Revision, and Afro-American Women's Novels*. New York: Columbia University Press, 1989.
Argues that although Naylor employs a disjunctive narrative structure that differs from those of Hurston, Morrison, and Alice Walker, her relation to those predecessors is not essentially a parodic one. Stresses the ways in which Naylor revoices a wide range of texts, including *The Bluest Eye*, *Cane*, and Langston Hughes's "Montage of a Dream Deferred" to emphasize the extreme difficulty of overcoming the internal divisions of the black community in the urban north.

Branzburg, Judith V. "Seven Women and a Wall." *Callaloo* 21 (Spring/Summer, 1984): 116-119.
Favorable review emphasizing Naylor's effective balancing of political and aesthetic considerations. Without being overtly critical of racism, Naylor's rich language renders the experience of the women in a way that reveals how the economic and social situations of black life become one with personal experience. She makes it clear that socioeconomic forces create black men's tendency to abandon their families. Patterns of attraction and abandonment by men, too much caring for children, and the solace of relationships between women are repeated throughout the novel. The characterizations of Kiswana and the two lesbians are relatively flat.

Gottlieb, Annie. "Women Together." *The New York Times Book Review* 87 (August 22, 1982): 11, 25.
Favorable review emphasizing the primary importance of bonds between women. Although Naylor presents moving images of realities of black life, *The*

Women of Brewster Place is not realistic fiction. Rather it is mythic in the sense that the characters seem constantly on the verge of breaking out into magical powers. Identifies two climaxes in the book, one of healing (focused on Mattie and Ciel) and one of destruction (focused on Lorraine).

Wickenden, Dorothy. Review of *The Women of Brewster Place*. *The New Republic* 187 (September 6, 1982): 37-38.
Favorable review placing Naylor in the context of contemporary black women's fiction that recognizes the reality of violence and abuse while demonstrating the ability of astoundingly resilient black women to draw on the resources of laughter and companionship. *The Women of Brewster Place* is a novel about motherhood, united by the figure of Mattie Michael, in which each woman is a surrogate child or mother to the next. The accumulation of horrific detail may dull some readers' sensibilities before the novel's devastating climax.

ANN PETRY

Biography

Alexander, Sandra Carlton. "Ann Petry." In *Afro-American Writers, 1940-1955*, edited by Trudier Harris. Vol. 76 of *Dictionary of Literary Biography*. Detroit: Bruccoli Clark, 1988.
Substantial reference entry including biographical sketch and discussion of *The Street*, *The Narrows*, and *Country Place*. Biographical section discusses Petry's New England family background; her journalistic work in New York; her early short fiction; and the reception of her novels. Analysis of her novels focuses on her sensitivity to the fate of less fortunate black Americans and her ability to dramatize aspects of the human condition that transcend geographical and racial boundaries.

Emanuel, James A. "Ann (Lane) Petry." In *Contemporary Novelists*, 4th ed., edited by D. L. Kirkpatrick. New York: St. Martin's Press, 1986.
Reference entry including biographical outline, list of publications, and brief analysis of Petry's novels. Quotes Petry's statement that while her style varies from book to book, her underlying theme is race relations in the United States. Emanuel's analysis emphasizes Petry's thematic focus on the hostility of American materialistic society to moral beauty. Petry's "craftsmanship, social truth, and humanity" deserve wider recognition.

Green, Marjorie. "Ann Petry Planned to Write." *Opportunity* 24 (Spring, 1946): 78-79.
Biographical sketch emphasizing the adjustments Petry made in order to become a writer. Includes information on Petry's experience as a pharmacist; her studies in psychology and psychiatry; and her relationship with her publisher.

Ivy, James W. "Ann Petry Talks About First Novel." In *Sturdy Black Bridges: Visions of Black Women in Literature*, edited by Roseann P. Bell, Bettye J. Parker, and Beverly Guy-Sheftall. Garden City, N.Y.: Anchor Press, 1979.
Reprint of early interview with Petry, including biographical sketch and report on Petry's early interaction with *The Crisis* magazine. Petry comments on several of her short stories and *The Street*, which she intended "to show how simply and easily the environment can change the course of a person's life."

O'Brien, John. "Ann Petry." In *Interviews with Black Writers*, edited by O'Brien. New York: Liveright, 1973.
Interview covering topics such as the presence of racial conflicts in Petry's novels; her writing process; and her response to critical definitions of black

literature. Petry states that it is an imposition to ask a writer to explain her work. O'Brien's headnote identifies *The Narrows* as Petry's best novel.

Petry, Ann. "Ann Petry." In *Contemporary Authors: Autobiography Series*, vol. 6, edited by Adele Sarkissian. Detroit: Gale Research, 1986.
Lengthy autobiographical essay in which Petry observes that when she writes for children, she writes about survival, but that when she writes for adults, she writes about the "walking wounded." Among the aspects of her life she discusses are her New England background; several generations of her family heritage; her early reading; her education; her life in New York City; and the writing of *The Street* and *The Narrows*.

Rayson, Ann. "Ann Lane Petry." In *American Women Writers*, vol. 3, edited by Lina Mainiero. New York: Frederick Ungar, 1981.
Biographical entry including brief commentary on *The Street*, *The Narrows*, and *Country Place*, which belong in the "mainstream of American naturalism and realism." Bibliography lists entries in other reference works.

Commentary

"Ann (Lane) Petry." In *Children's Literature Review*, vol. 12, edited by Gerard J. Senick. Detroit: Gale Research, 1987.
Compilation of materials related to Petry's children's writing, including edited transcript of a talk Petry delivered in 1964 in which she discusses the purposes of children's literature. Emphasizes her attempt to assert a set of values differing from those of the commercial world, to "make history speak across the centuries in the voices of people." Entry reprints excerpts from reviews of Petry's juvenile novels *The Drugstore Cat* and *Tituba of Salem Village*. Valuable for its inclusion of materials originally published in sources relating specifically to children's literature.

"Ann Petry." In *Contemporary Literary Criticism*, vol. 1, edited by Carolyn Riley (1973); vol. 7, edited by Phyllis Carmel Mendelson and Dedria Bryfonski (1977); vol. 18, edited by Sharon R. Gunton (1981). Detroit: Gale Research.
Compilations of material relating to Petry's fiction. Vol. 1 includes excerpts from Carol Milton Hughes and Robert Bone. Vol. 7 includes excerpts from David Littlejohn and Thelma Shinn. Vol. 18 reprints excerpts from commentary by Arthur P. Davis and Arna Bontemps, who observes that *The Narrows* resists classification as a "Negro novel."

Bell, Bernard W. "Ann Petry's Demythologizing of American Culture and Afro-American Character." In *Conjuring: Black Women, Fiction, and Literary Tra-*

dition, edited by Marjorie Pryse and Hortense J. Spillers. Bloomington: Indiana University Press, 1985.

Emphasizes Petry's realistic delineation of cultural myths, especially those of the American dream, the city and the small town, and Afro-American character. Focusing on the black community's relation to American history, Petry debunks myths of urban success, of rural innocence, and of pathological blacks. Bell develops these ideas in relation to both *The Street* and *The Narrows*.

——————— . "Richard Wright and the Triumph of Naturalism." In *The Afro-American Novel and Its Tradition.* Amherst: University of Massachusetts Press, 1987.

Petry moves beyond the naturalism of Richard Wright and Chester Himes to demythologize American culture and Afro-American character. Her vision of black personality is more faithful to the complexities and varieties of black women. Examination of her three novels reveals a movement from a naturalistic vision of the big city to an analysis of black-white relations in small-town America. *Country Place* and *The Narrows* emphasize the influence of time and place on the shaping of character.

Davis, Arthur P. "Integrationists and Transitional Writers: Ann Petry." In *From the Dark Tower: Afro-American Writers 1900 to 1960.* Washington, D.C.: Howard University Press, 1974.

Places Petry in the tradition of "hard-hitting social commentary" derived from the naturalism of Richard Wright. *The Street* asserts the thesis that the black poor have little chance of living decent lives. Though it holds the reader's interest, *The Narrows* has serious weaknesses involving narrative structure and believability. A competent writer, Petry does several things well, but none superlatively.

Gross, Theodore L. "Ann Petry: The Novelist as Social Critic." In *Black Fiction: New Studies in the Afro-American Novel Since 1945*, edited by A. Robert Lee. New York: Barnes & Nobel, 1980.

Emphasizes the naturalistic impact and realistic analysis in Petry's novels. Viewing the novel as an instrument of social criticism, Petry is compelled more by setting than by character. The crippling conditions of ghetto life in *The Street* and *The Narrows* and the perverse provinciality of the small town in *Country Place* are the most memorable aspects of her fiction. While she does not dwell on racial conflict, she makes it clear that white society has created the conditions within which blacks live. Ultimately tragic in impact, her fiction focuses on characters who lose socially but triumph in human terms.

Hernton, Calvin C. "The Significance of Ann Petry." In *The Sexual Mountain and Black Women Writers: Adventures in Sex, Literature, and Real Life*. Garden

City, N.Y.: Anchor Press, 1987.

Discusses *The Street* as a point of transition between conventional nineteenth century "colored lady's writing" and "proletarian black woman's fiction." The first novel in which a black man is killed because he oppresses a black woman, *The Street* is also the first work of social realism and naturalism written from a womanist perspective. Extensive comparison of Petry's protagonist Lutie Johnson with Bigger Thomas from Richard Wright's *Native Son*.

Hughes, Carl Milton. *The Negro Novelist, 1940-1950*. New York: The Citadel Press, 1953.

Discusses *The Street* and *Country Place* in relation to the black fiction of the 1940's. A straightforward naturalistic novel with a deterministic perspective, *The Street* is distinguished by Petry's mastery of her craft. Departing from racial themes, *Country Place* asserts Petry's freedom as a creative artist. Although it advances no political thesis, the novel develops social themes— such as the tension between justice and injustice—in the manner of Sinclair Lewis' *Main Street*.

Lattin, Vernon E. "Ann Petry and the American Dream." *Black American Literature Forum* 12 (Summer, 1978): 69-72.

Rejects attempts to categorize Petry in relation to trends in black fiction. The real center of her work lies in the profound rebellion against the falsifications of life embodied in the American dream and its illusions. Whatever its racial content, her fiction seeks a new order beyond the dominant images of America. Develops the theme of the American dream as nightmare in relation to each of Petry's novels.

Littlejohn, David. "Negro Writers Today: The Novelists II." In *Black on White: A Critical Survey of Writing by American Negroes*. New York: Grossman, 1966.

Identifies Petry as perhaps the most important of contemporary black writers. Although she has a tendency to use sordid and melodramatic plots, the intelligence and stylistic polish of her novels compensates for the deficiency. Out of her "female wisdom" and "chewy style" grow characters of shape and dimension. Ranks Petry at the top of the second rank of black novelists, "a place almost as prominent and promising as that of the bigger three" of Wright, Ellison, and Baldwin.

Schraufnagel, Noel. *From Apology to Protest: The Black American Novel*. Deland, Fla.: Everett/Edwards, 1973.

Includes discussions of Petry's novels as they reflect different approaches to the nature of black fiction. *The Street* is a Wrightian protest novel; *Country Place* is one of the few good assimilationist novels; and *The Narrows* combines elements of both approaches, surpassing Petry's earlier novels in its analysis of racism and the human condition.

Shinn, Thelma J. "Women in the Novels of Ann Petry." *Critique* 16 (1975): 110-120.
Surveys the treatment of women characters in Petry's three novels. Petry demonstrates that individual integrity provides no protection against destruction by a changing array of environmental forces. Petry's rebels, black and white, are frequently deluded to the point that they reinforce the forces they are attempting to resist.

Washington, Mary Helen. "'Infidelity Becomes Her': The Ambivalent Woman in the Fiction of Ann Petry and Dorothy West." In her *Invented Lives: Narratives of Black Women, 1860-1960*. Garden City, N.Y.: Anchor Press, 1987.
Criticizes the tendency to view Petry entirely in relation to social protest writing and/or the influence of Richard Wright. While *The Street* does show the environment as a determining force on people's lives, Petry's later works reveal the ability of individuals supported by community and family to resist environmental pressure. In *The Narrows*, Mamie resists entrapment in narrowly defined domestic roles by tapping the power of speech to resist the confinement of the written word.

Watson, Carol McAlpine. "Racial Issues and Universal Themes, 1946-1965." In her *Prologue: The Novels of Black American Women, 1891-1965*. Westport, Conn.: Greenwood Press, 1985.
Discusses each of Petry's novels as they negotiate the tension between racial politics and universal themes. In *The Narrows*, Petry identifies race hatred as a universal problem. Petry's allusions to the Bible and Shakespeare reinforce this central thesis. The central theme of *The Street* is that a black woman, whatever her positive qualities, cannot succeed in the ghetto.

Selected Titles

Country Place

Bone, Robert. "The Contemporary Negro Novel." In his *The Negro Novel in America*. New Haven, Conn.: Yale University Press, 1965.
A novel far superior to *The Street*, which attempts to make racial discrimination responsible for the slums when a wider framework is needed, *Country Place* embodies both the struggle for emancipation and the desire to re-establish ties with the past through art. The basic tension in the novel is between those who embody village values and those who reject them. Petry's realism, which attains a metaphorical depth unique among Wright's disciples, is appropriate to a novel concerned with deflating romantic attitudes.

Rosenblatt, Roger. "White Outside." In his *Black Fiction*. Cambridge, Mass.: Harvard University Press, 1974.

Analyzes Petry's criticism of white American culture in *Country Place*, focusing on the character of Glory. While the essence of the town's limitation is its lack of imagination, the deeper problem Petry identifies is its lack of a usable past.

Smith, John Caswell, Jr. Review of *Country Place*. *Atlantic* 180 (November, 1947): 178, 182.
Generally favorable review of *Country Place* as a fast-moving, melodramatic story that marks an improvement over *The Street*. While most of the characters are well done, Petry's choice of Johnny Roane as a hero was misguided. Petry preaches no sermons; rather she tells a plausible story of real people in a believable situation.

The Narrows
Bontemps, Arna. Review of *The Narrows*. *Saturday Review* 36 (August 22, 1953): 11.
Favorable review of *The Narrows* as a novel about racial conflict that "resists classification as a Negro novel." Petry is essentially a "neighborhood novelist" who chronicles the way of life of an aspect of New England life that is rarely presented in literature. Praises Petry's achievement as one that is "as rare as it is commendable."

McDowell, Margaret. "*The Narrows*: A Fuller View of Ann Petry." *Black American Literature Forum* 14 (Winter, 1980): 135-141.
Although *The Narrows* shares the theme of racial intolerance with *The Street*, Petry's later treatment moves beyond realism to consider larger issues of social and psychological significance. She employs experimental techniques such as interior monologue and sharp juxtaposition to explore the depths of consciousness. In social terms, Petry emphasizes the need for blacks to attain a historical perspective concerning racial prejudice.

McKay, Nellie Y. Introduction to *The Narrows*. Boston: Beacon Press, 1988.
Representing Petry's fiction at its best, *The Narrows* explores the relationship of race, gender, and class to the lives of all Americans and exposes the roles white economic power and sociocultural conventions play in creating racial and class antagonism. Jamesian in style, the novel creates a dense network of multiple points of view to communicate the experience of the protagonist, whose sense of security within his social milieu precludes neither personal nor community tragedy. Gives detailed attention to the portrayal of older black women in the novel.

Time. 62 Review of *The Narrows*. (August 17, 1953): 94, 96.
Generally favorable review. Except for a "deplorable tendency toward short

flights of bogus impressionistic prose," Petry tells a serious story that differs from the conventional settings of novels concerning black and white, love and violence. Neither the smoldering South nor the raw urban North, Petry's picture of life in broken-down Dumble Street is the best thing in her novel.

Weir, Sybil. *"The Narrows:* A Black New England Novel." *Studies in American Fiction* 15 (Spring, 1987): 81-93.
Argues that *The Narrows* belongs to the tradition of New England literature as well as that of Afro-American literature. The New England tradition of domestic feminism and realism is exemplified in Petry's characterization of the black matron Abbie Crunch, who resembles the spinsters of Alcott, Stowe, and Mary Wilkins Freeman. Abbie embraces New England values at the expense of her black heritage. Like Nathaniel Hawthorne, Petry believes in the chain of "dark necessity."

The Street

Butterfield, Alfred. "The Dark Heartbeat of Harlem." *The New York Times Book Review* 51 (February 10, 1946): 6.
Favorable review of *The Street* as one of the rare novels combining social insight with literary quality. The novel is as spiritually and emotionally effective a treatment of black life as has yet been created. Dealing with black characters without condescension or special pleading, it is a gripping story overflowing with "the classic pity and terror of good imaginative writing."

Christian, Barbara. "Ordinary Women: The Tone of the Commonplace." In *Black Women Novelists: The Development of a Tradition, 1892-1976.* Westport, Conn.: Greenwood Press, 1980.
Petry's major concern is the destructive impact of the environment. Harlem does not emerge as a community but as a place where individuals continually attempt to exploit each other. *The Street* differs from other novels by black women because its characters are alienated from all support. It is important as one of the first novels concerning the struggle of an urban black mother.

Dempsey, David. "Uncle Tom's Ghost and the Literary Abolitionists." *Antioch Review* 6 (September, 1946): 442-448.
Petry is a bellwether of the new trend of literary abolitionism because she presents a heroine who represents a new class of black professionals. Lutie is the one protagonist who fails to achieve success, testifying to the ability of segregation to defeat the best and bring out the worst in people.

Gayle, Addison, Jr. "The Black Rebel." In *The Way of the New World: The Black Novel in America.* Garden City, N.Y.: Anchor Press, 1976.
Despite Petry's evasion of the implied political solution to the problems de-

scribed in *The Street*, the novel presents a realistic analysis of American society. Gayle summarizes the similarities between *The Street* and *Native Son* while emphasizing that, unlike Wright, Petry is more interested in the effects of the environment on her characters than in the characters themselves. Argues that Petry is unwilling to accept the novel's implication that blacks must move to establish control over the institutions that control their lives.

Lenz, Gunther H. "Symbolic Space, Communal Rituals, and the Surreality of the Urban Ghetto: Harlem in Black Literature from the 1920s to the 1960s." *Callaloo* 35 (Spring, 1988): 309-345.
Employs Victor Turner's anthropological methodology to study the development of different literary strategies for the portrayal of Harlem. Presents *The Street* as an exemplification of the "(de)formative power of the ghetto environment." Petry presents a negative image of Harlem, making it clear that the street does not reflect a genuine black urban culture; rather it reflects the abject living conditions that create psychic displacement. Petry poses the question of whether there is any meaning left in the black writer's dream of Harlem as the focal point of black urban culture.

Maja-Pearce, Adewale. "Beyond Blackness." *Times Literary Supplement* (May 2, 1986): 479.
Review of reprint edition placing *The Street* in the tradition of American documentary realism of the 1940's. Trapped by their poverty, her characters' lives are determined by external forces. Like many such novels, it is "tolerably well written and frequently convincing in its description of wasted lives."

Moon, Bucklin. "Both Sides of the Street." *The New Republic* 114 (February 11, 1946): 193-194.
Cautious, but generally favorable review, noting that Petry "has it within her power to be a vital force" in the racial protest movement, but that she could as easily become "a popular writer who, within the taboos of marketability, will find success almost too easily." Praises her ability to transform characters who could become stereotypes into living beings, but observes that at times the melodramatic hopelessness of her plot creates banal and contrived sections, most notably Lutie's interaction with Boots Smith.

Pryse, Marjorie. " 'Pattern Against the Sky': Deism and Motherhood in Ann Petry's *The Street*." In *Conjuring: Black Women, Fiction, and Literary Tradition*, edited by Pryse and Hortense J. Spillers. Bloomington: Indiana University Press, 1985.
Examines Petry's novel in relation to the deism of Ben Franklin, who believed that God's active role in the world ended following the creation. Petry reveals

the destructive implications of this philosophy in her presentation of the Harlem environment, which functions as an expression of the "laws" established by absent "white gods." The betrayal of democracy for blacks becomes the destruction of human feeling in the world. Although Lutie Johnson makes a sequence of wrong choices, Pryse argues that the power she needs to counter the white world already exists on the street.

Purdy, Theodore M. "The Ghetto That Is Harlem." *Saturday Review* 29 (March 1, 1946): 30.
Mildly favorable review, praising Petry's emotional intensity and her technical ability, but complaining of occasional overwriting and a serious imbalance in viewpoint. Petry brings Harlem alive in a way that makes the essential truth of her theme clear. By making her characters so unrelentingly evil, however, Petry undercuts her ability to show how the street has changed or deformed them.

Trilling, Diana. "Class and Color." *The Nation* 162 (March 9, 1946): 290-291.
Mixed review comparing Petry's novel with Fannie Cook's *Mrs. Palmer's Honey*, neither of which compares favorably with Lillian Smith's *Strange Fruit*. Although it is "not particularly rewarding as a work of fiction," *The Street* has some interest because it explains how Petry feels about the situation of blacks. Petry identifies the "economic core of the Negro problem" and makes it clear that class feelings run as deeply in the black community as in American society generally. *The Street* is a "straight-forwardly middle-class document."

Wade-Gayles, Gloria. *No Crystal Stair: Visions of Race and Sex in Black Women's Fiction*. New York: Pilgrim Press, 1984.
Discusses *The Street* as an expression of the limitations imposed on black women by racism and sexism. Wade-Gayles devotes substantial attention to the minor women characters, including Min, Mrs. Pizzini, and Mrs. Hedges. Min provides an emblem of a black woman who has been robbed of a positive self-image. Wade-Gayles also compares Lutie Johnson to Richard Wright's Bigger Thomas, noting the interaction of sexual and racial oppression in her experience.

Williams, Sherley Anne. "The Street." *Ms.* 15 (September, 1986): 23.
Favorable review of reprint edition acknowledging Petry's "abiding place among American naturalist novels." While Petry has been praised for her rendering of external details, the real power of *The Street* rests on her understanding of the role gender and sexuality play in the oppression of black women.

CARLENE HATCHER POLITE

Biography

Worthington-Smith, Hammett. "Carlene Hatcher Polite." In *Afro-American Fiction Writers After 1955*, edited by Thadious M. Davis and Trudier Harris. Vol. 33 of *Dictionary of Literary Biography*. Detroit: Bruccoli Clark, 1984.

Reference entry including biographical sketch and analysis of *The Flagellants* and *Sister X and the Victims of Foul Play*. Emphasizes the experimental quality of Polite's work, which reflects her doubts about the traditional form of the novel. Her style is marked by a mastery of language and a love of the rhetoric of the black cultural revolution. Biographical section describes her education; her experience in Greenwich Village; her involvement with the civil rights movement; and the critical reception of her work.

Selected Title

The Flagellants

Howe, Irving. "New Black Writers." *Harper's* 239 (December, 1969): 130-146.

Extremely unfavorable review. Although Polite treats an important subject, she does little but rant. Her characters are simply puppets. The self-pity and verbal excess of their speeches contribute to the "excruciating badness" of the novel.

Lee, A. Robert. "Making New: Styles of Innovation in the Contemporary Black American Novel." In *Black Fiction: New Studies in the Afro-American Novel Since 1945*, edited by A. Robert Lee. New York: Barnes & Noble Books, 1980.

Discusses *The Flagellants* as part of an experimental movement in recent Afro-American fiction that has moved beyond the influences of Wright, Ellison, and Baldwin. Views Polite's novel in relation to Chester Himes's call for a novel based entirely on subconscious attitudes and reactions. The novel takes the form of a baroque, stylized interplay of two voices, each of which is driven and intense. Polite's style functions as a counterpoint to her lovers' erotic fury. Includes a brief discussion of *Sister X and the Victims of Foul Play*.

Sayre, Nora. "Punishing." *The Nation* 205 (October 9, 1967): 334.

Mixed review emphasizing that Polite's novel does not fit into any of the categories of racial tradition, but criticizing her overblown style, which turns *The Flagellants* into an essay rather than a novel. The "abrasive strength" of the novel springs from the combination of anger at whites and even more intense accusations against blacks. Despite the stylistic failings, the ingredients of Polite's novel are too strong to be negated.

Schraufnagel, Noel. "Accommodationism in the Sixties." In *From Apology to Protest: The Black American Novel*. Deland, Fla.: Everett/Edwards, 1973.

Polite explores the psychological problem of a young black intellectual attempting to maintain racial pride in a context which continually asserts white superiority. Polite concentrates on the special efforts needed to overcome the cultural situation in which males feel emasculated and women emerge as dominant forces. Neither of the main characters can transcend the stereotypical positions assigned to them. The novel gradually dissolves into an endless mental debate that loses its poignancy.

Tate, Claudia. Introduction to *The Flagellants*. Boston: Beacon Press, 1987.

Surveys critical reception of the novel, observing that its difference from historical preconceptions concerning black fiction creates a complex and problematic relationship with its audience. Discusses the tension between religious and sexual implications of flagellation. The protagonist is able to perceive the possibility of wholeness only when she confronts her remembered past. Tate notes parallels with French existentialism, particularly in Polite's theme that it is necessary to assume responsibility for one's actions in order to attain freedom.

NTOZAKE SHANGE

Biography

Blackwell, Henry. "An Interview with Ntozake Shange." *Black American Literature Forum* 13 (Winter, 1979): 134-138.
Interview including Shange's comments on regionalism in Afro-American writing; the influence of geographical space on Western writing; the common concerns linking black women writers; the significance of self-reliance; and her generally positive interaction with black male writers.

Brown, Elizabeth. "Ntozake Shange." In *Afro-American Writers After 1955: Dramatists and Prose Writers*, edited by Thadious M. Davis and Trudier Harris. Vol. 38 of *Dictionary of Literary Biography*. Detroit: Bruccoli Clark, 1985.
Lengthy biographical essay including discussion of Shange's poetry, drama, and brief mention of her first novel. Biographical segment focuses on Shange's family background; the turmoil and confusion of her young womanhood; her process of recovery; and the significance of her decision to change her birth name. Shange's importance derives from her ability to give dimension and clarity to the feminist movement. She repudiates images of black women's dependency on men, creating images of self-sufficiency.

Tate, Claudia C. *Black Women Writers at Work*. New York: Continuum, 1983.
Includes an interview in which Shange comments on her writing process; her response to the success of *For Colored Girls Who Have Considered Suicide When the Rainbow Is Enuf*; her responsibility to her audience; her relationship with her parents; and the differences in the approaches of black male and black female writers.

Commentary

"Ntozake Shange." In *Contemporary Literary Criticism*, vol. 38, edited by Daniel G. Marowski. Detroit: Gale Research, 1986.
Compilation of materials on Shange's writing, including a biographical headnote and excerpts from reviews of *Sassafrass, Cypress & Indigo* and *Betsey Brown*.

Selected Titles

Betsey Brown
Wheatley, Patchy. "Waiting for Change." *Times Literary Supplement* (December 6, 1985): 1406.

Favorable review of *Betsey Brown* as a skillful exploration of the Southern black community at a decisive moment in its history. The simple directness of the novel contrasts sharply with the exoticism of *Sassafrass, Cypress & Indigo*. In this semi-autobiographical book, Shange is interested in Betsey's experience of racism only inasmuch as it affects her own black world. Music is an essential element in the Brown home and in the novel, which was originally written as a rhythm-and-blues opera.

White, Evelyn C. "Growing Up Black." *The Women's Review of Books* 3 (November, 1985): 11.

Favorable review emphasizing autobiographical elements. Employing a humorous and melodic style, Shange portrays a black female experience shaped more by privilege than sacrifices. Although Shange writes candidly of racial and class conflicts, *Betsey Brown* is about the human emotions that unify people as well as the political forces that divide them. Shange's image of an "innocent, frail" protagonist complements the more common image of the strong black woman in black women's fiction.

Willard, Nancy. "Life Abounding in St. Louis." *The New York Times Book Review* 90 (May 12, 1985): 12.

Favorable review of *Betsey Brown*, which is less idiosyncratic than *Sassafrass, Cypress & Indigo*. Shange has no ax to grind. Focusing on an "eccentric and marvelous" black family, she emphasizes what brings her characters together rather than what separates them. The novel rejoices in, but does not sentimentalize, the "places on earth where you are accepted, where you are comfortable with yourself."

Williams, Sherley Anne. "Roots of Privilege: New Black Fiction." *Ms.* 13 (June, 1985): 69-72.

Reviews *Betsey Brown* along with Naylor's *Linden Hills* and Andrea Lee's *Sarah Phillips* as part of a return to the theme of the black middle class that has been generally ignored since the Harlem Renaissance. Unlike the other two novels, which suggest that the "only real black is a poor black," *Betsey Brown* depicts an affluence that does not sever connection with black culture and community. Williams praises the complexity of Shange's vision, but criticizes the novel's numerous stylistic and technical shortcomings, including the disturbing similarity of the characters' language and an "unremarked sentimentality."

Sassafras, Cypress & Indigo

Bovoso, Carole. Review of *Sassafrass, Cypress & Indigo*. *Essence* 13 (October, 1982): 20.

Favorable review. Shange's novel is a "golden spell," a powerful "incantation for and about Black women." Emphasizes the importance of mother-daughter relationships and creative forms ranging from food and cooking to magic, love, and art in the novel. The novel includes some of Shange's finest writing, which reminds readers that there is poetry in the mundane details of life.

Grumbach, Doris. "Ntozake Shange's Trio." *The Washington Post Book World* 12 (August 22, 1982): 1-2.
Favorable review identifying Shange as a "unique lyric singer" who provides deep insights into black life. She is notable for her ability to convey the texture of both simple and sophisticated black life. Her spare and original voice is reminiscent of Jean Toomer's *Cane*.

Isaacs, Susan. "Three Sisters." *The New York Times Book Review* 87 (September 12, 1982): 12-13, 16.
Mixed review arguing that Shange fails to sustain the stylistic vitality of the book's early sections. Her combination of narrative, poetry, dreams, recipes, and magical incantations is an attempt to capture the essence of black culture. Readers with knowledge of African and Afro-American history and art will get more from the novel than those who lack such knowledge. Nonetheless, many passages are earthbound, ideological, predictable, and sometimes simply silly.

ANN ALLEN SHOCKLEY

Biography

Dandridge, Rita B. *Ann Allen Shockley: An Annotated Primary and Secondary Bibliography*. Westport, Conn.: Greenwood Press, 1987.
Valuable bibliography describing Shockley's writings and their critical reception. Includes extensive lists of Shockley's journalistic writing. Particularly valuable for its listing of reviews published in the lesbian and gay press. Includes a biographical headnote with some commentary on *Loving Her* and *Say Jesus and Come to Me*.

———————— . "Gathering Pieces: A Selected Bibliography of Ann Allen Shockley." *Black American Literature Forum* 21 (Spring/Summer, 1987): 133-146.
Briefer version of material assembled in the bibliography described in the previous entry.

Houston, Helen R. "Ann Allen Shockley." In *Afro-American Fiction Writers After 1955*, edited by Thadious M. Davis and Trudier Harris. Vol. 33 of *Dictionary of Literary Biography*. Detroit: Bruccoli Clark, 1984.
Reference entry including biographical sketch and analysis of *Loving Her* and *Say Jesus and Come to Me*. Biographical section describes Shockley's childhood involvement with books; her education and journalistic experience; and her work as a librarian and archivist, which has resulted in numerous publications. Attributes the relative obscurity of Shockley's work to her avant-garde subject matter—*Loving Her* was the first novel to deal with interracial lesbian love—and her failure to attract a mainstream publisher. Although her portrayal of the struggles of lesbian women against racism, sexism, and homophobia places her concerns in the mainstream of contemporary black women's fiction, she has attracted very little notice.

Selected Titles

Loving Her
Phillips, Frank Lamont. Review of *Loving Her*. *Black World* 24 (September, 1975): 89-90.
Extremely unfavorable review criticizing the shabbiness of Shockley's writing and her concentration on an interracial love affair. Rejects Shockley's presentation of black male brutality and positive image of the white woman lover. Concludes that novels such as *Loving Her* should not be published.

Say Jesus and Come to Me

Dandridge, Rita. "Shockley the Iconoclast." *Callaloo* 22 (Fall, 1984): 160-164.

Mixed review praising the novel for its important subject—the relationship between Christianity and lesbianism—but criticizing a number of structural flaws. The novel's significance lies in its attack on the black church as a patriarchal bulwark. Shockley heralds the need for black women's spiritual conversion and heightened sexual consciousness. Quotes Shockley's comments on her intent in writing the novel.

ELLEASE SOUTHERLAND

Biography

Brookhart, Mary Hughes. "Ellease Southerland." In *Afro-American Fiction Writers After 1955*, edited by Thadious M. Davis and Trudier Harris. Vol. 33 of *Dictionary of Literary Biography*. Detroit: Bruccoli Clark, 1984.
Substantial reference entry including biographical sketch and analysis of *Let the Lion Eat Straw*. Biographical section notes the influence of Southerland's large and culturally aware family; her musical interests; her sense of the connection between prose and poetry; her work as a caseworker in New York City; and her balancing of teaching and literary careers. Based primarily on her mother's experience, Southerland's novel infuses the biographical with the figurative and affirms that it is possible to find joy alongside the pain.

Fuller, Hoyt. "Two Views: *Let the Lion Eat Straw*." *First World* 2, no. 3 (1979): 52.
Biographical reminiscence by the editor of *Negro Digest/Black World* magazine concerning his original encounters with Southerland's writing. Notes that Southerland, like other writers of her generation, possessed a "natural affinity for modes of expression which owed no conscious debt to the literary gods" blacks were taught to emulate in the educational system. Identifies *Let the Lion Eat Straw* as the fulfillment of her early promise.

Commentary

Johnson, Charles. "The Women." In *Being and Race: Black Writing since 1970*. Bloomington: Indiana University Press, 1988.
Brief comment by a black male novelist praising *Let the Lion Eat Straw* as a "strangely wonderful novel." Southerland disarms the reader with an apparently simple style that creates exactly the right rhythm for tracing the entire life of her heroine. Southerland's characters exemplify the idea of the "folk" whose ability to love and support one another helps them create lives of strength and self-fulfillment during times of hardship.

Selected Title

Let the Lion Eat Straw
Jackson, Angela. "Two Views: *Let the Lion Eat Straw*." *First World* 2, no. 3 (1979): 51-52.
Extremely favorable review heralding Southerland as the prophet of a "new

age of creation" in Afro-American fiction. She fulfills the original function of the storyteller, giving birth to "an evocative world, framed and filled cultural concepts in a compatible and intelligent style." Although the novel appears to be an "easy read," it is enriched by Southerland's precise diction, which reveals the dynamic interaction of style and suffering. Her treatment of oppression is thoroughly contextualized. *Let the Lion Eat Straw* is a call to literacy and to expressed emotion.

Kilgore, James. "Two Views: *Let the Lion Eat Straw*." *First World* 2, no. 3 (1979): 49-51.
Favorable review emphasizing the lyrical beauty of Southerland's "poet's prose," which distills experience in a manner reminiscent of Toomer's *Cane*. The novel is a "love story that is music: Jazz, spirituals, blues, classical." Notes that the title refers to the eleventh chapter of Isaiah, in which the prophet envisions the coming of a new day. Although some might find the novel sketchy, Southerland has attained a level of excellence she may find it difficult to surpass.

The New Yorker. Review of *Let the Lion Eat Straw*. 55 (May 21, 1979): 145.
Brief review identifying the novel as "an unusual story, composed in lilting dialect." Notes that Southerland's "own dreams and memories, as well as her literary style, are imbued with African folklore." Her story seems "less a novel than a myth."

Swan, Annalyn. "Love Story." *Time* 113 (June 18, 1979): 85.
Favorable review praising Southerland's "graceful hymn of love," which draws its power from her spare, unsentimental imagery. Her prose captures the rhythms of ghetto speech, reflecting the lyricism and unabashed emotionalism of old-time religion. She bears witness to a world centered on family, the community, and the Lord.

MILDRED TAYLOR

Biography

Wright, David A. "Mildred D. Taylor." In *American Writers for Children Since 1960: Fiction*, edited by Glenn E. Estes. Vol. 52 of *Dictionary of Literary Biography*. Detroit: Bruccoli Clark, 1986.
Reference entry including biographical sketch and analysis of *Song of the Trees*, *Roll of Thunder, Hear My Cry*, and *Let the Circle Be Unbroken*. Emphasizes Taylor's ability to provide accurate pictures of southern rural black families of the 1930's. While her work reflects her father's stories about life in rural Mississippi, her themes are "universal and timeless." Biographical section recounts Taylor's family background; the influence of storytelling on her imagination; her experience as one of the few blacks in her classes; her Peace Corps experience; and her growing prominence as a writer of children's books.

Commentary

"Mildred D(elois) Taylor." In *Children's Literature Review*, vol. 9, edited by Gerard J. Senick. Detroit: Gale Research, 1985.
Compilation of materials related to Taylor's children's writing, including a biographical headnote and a speech Taylor delivered when accepting the Newbery Award in 1977. Taylor emphasizes the importance of her father's influence on her work, particularly the wisdom "that taught me that anger in itself was futile, that to fight discrimination I needed a stronger weapon." Notes that her novels focus on the "small and often dangerous triumphs" of blacks. Includes excerpts from reviews of *Song of the Trees*, *Roll of Thunder, Hear My Cry*, and *Let the Circle Be Unbroken*. Valuable for its inclusion of materials originally published in sources devoted specifically to children's literature.

"Mildred D(elois) Taylor." In *Contemporary Literary Criticism*, vol. 21, edited by Sharon R. Gunton. Detroit: Gale Research, 1982.
Compilation of material relating to Taylor's children's fiction, including a biographical headnote and a lengthy excerpt from her Newbery Award acceptance speech. Essentially a briefer version of the material included in the previous entry.

Selected Title

Let the Circle Be Unbroken
Eley, Holly. "Cotton Pickin' Blues." *Times Literary Supplement* (March 26, 1982):
     343.
     Favorable review asserting that Taylor accomplishes in fewer pages what Alex
     Haley attempted in *Roots*. She provides a historical perspective on racial issues
     which she insists can be resolved only by recognizing the fundamental equality
     of human beings. Taylor's writing is impressionistic but also detailed.

Jordan, June. "Mississippi in the Thirties." *The New York Times Book Review* 86
     (November 15, 1981): 56, 58.
     Favorable review comparing Cassie Logan to Huckleberry Finn. Taylor's chil-
     dren are exceptional achievements in large part because the author takes them
     seriously. In part because of Taylor's style, which remains accessible to young
     readers, the novel's examination of the collision between New Deal politics
     and the Mississippi politics of race and property is equally compelling for
     thoughtful adults.

JOYCE CAROL THOMAS

Biography

Toombs, Charles P. "Joyce Carol Thomas." In *Afro-American Fiction Writers After 1955*, edited by Thadious M. Davis and Trudier Harris. Vol. 33 of *Dictionary of Literary Biography*. Detroit: Bruccoli Clark, 1984.
Substantial reference entry including biographical sketch and analysis of Thomas' poetry and her juvenile novels. Biographical section observes that she was well established as a poet and playwright in San Francisco prior to the publication of her first novel in 1982. Emphasizes the biographical aspects of her fiction, much of which is set primarily in the part of Oklahoma where she grew up in a large family that made its living picking cotton. Thomas' fiction refuses generalizations and presents realistic pictures of specific families. She re-creates Afro-American rituals, particularly those based on communion with nature. Notes that she plans several more volumes in the Abyssinia series begun in *Marked by Fire* and *Bright Shadow*.

Commentary

"Joyce Carol Thomas." In *Contemporary Literary Criticism*, vol. 35, edited by Daniel G. Marowski. Detroit: Gale Research, 1985.
Compilation of materials on Thomas' fiction including a biographical head-note and excerpts from reviews of *Marked by Fire* and *Bright Shadow*.

Selected Title

Marked by Fire
Childress, Alice. "*Marked by Fire*." *The New York Times Book Review* 87 (April 18, 1982): 38.
Generally favorable review praising the admirable simplicity of Thomas' style and her ability to find a "marvelous fairy tale quality in everyday happenings." Praises the novel's unforgettable characters but questions the believability of some plot events. Focusing on a child's recovery after she is raped by a respected church member, Thomas expresses the best and worst times of a small black community.

ALICE WALKER

Biography

Christian, Barbara. "Alice Walker." In *Afro-American Fiction Writers After 1955*, edited by Thadious M. Davis and Trudier Harris. Vol. 33 of *Dictionary of Literary Biography*. Detroit: Bruccoli Clark, 1984.
Substantial reference entry including biographical sketch and analysis of Walker's writing through the mid-1980's. Emphasizes her concern with exploring the relationship between the degree of freedom experienced by black women within and beyond the black community, and the ability of that community as a whole to survive. As a southerner, Walker views the land as a potential resource for survival and creativity. Biographical section notes the importance of Walker's childhood in a sharecropping family; her developing sense of commitment to the freedom of the black community; the difficulties she encountered when she became pregnant as one of the few black students at a wealthy white college; the wide range of her literary influences; and the central importance of her mother to her writing.

Davis, Thadious M. "Alice Walker." In *American Novelists Since World War II*, edited by James E. Kibler, Jr. Vol. 6 of *Dictionary of Literary Biography*. Detroit: Bruccoli Clark, 1980.
Lengthy reference entry including sketch of Walker's biography and analysis of *The Third Life of Grange Copeland* and *Meridian*. Emphasizes the importance of Walker's Southern background to her vision of the unity of social, moral, and aesthetic sensibilities. Biographical section describes the importance of Walker's Southern family background; her education and marriage, which took place primarily in the North; and her eventual return to the South. She draws Southern blacks, particularly women, without stereotyping or romanticizing them. She looks to the past as a source of values capable of contributing to individual and communal transcendence over suffering.

Howard, Lillie P. "Alice Walker." In *American Women Writers*, vol. 4, edited by Lina Mainiero. New York: Frederick Ungar, 1982.
Biographical entry including brief commentary on *The Third Life of Grange Copeland* and *Meridian*. Notes that Walker is dedicated to the continuation of black American traditions.

Kirschner, Susan. "Alice Walker's Nonfictional Prose: A Checklist, 1966-1984." *Black American Literature Forum* 18 (Winter, 1984): 162-163.
Useful checklist of Walker's essays, published lectures, reviews, interviews, and published letters.

McDowell, Margaret B. "Alice (Malsenoir) Walker." In *Contemporary Novelists*, 4th ed., edited by D. L. Kirkpatrick. New York: St. Martin's Press, 1986.
Reference entry including biographical outline, list of publications, and analysis of Walker's first three novels. Observes that while the metaphysical complexities of *Meridian* precluded popular success, its balancing of the need for revolution against the sustaining of traditional black values may make it the most significant of Walker's novels. *The Color Purple* is a "lively fable suggesting an alternative vision of possibilities for the Black individual."

O'Brien, John, ed. *Interviews with Black Writers*. New York: Liveright, 1973.
Interview covering topics such as the early influences on Walker's writing; her writing process; the lack of recognition given black women writers; and the role of feminism in her work. Walker comments on the theme of change in *The Third Life of Grange Copeland*, which O'Brien's headnote identifies as her most important achievement.

Steinem, Gloria. "Do You Know This Woman? She Knows You: A Profile of Alice Walker." *Ms.* 10 (June, 1982): 35, 37, 89-94.
Lengthy biographical essay emphasizing Walker's importance as a populist writer whose reputation developed not in the literary world but among "ordinary readers." Published prior to the publication of *The Color Purple*, the essay predicts that it will be a "popular and literary event that transforms an intense reputation into a national one." Walker describes the influence of her early reading on her fiction; her feelings about the violence in her work; her marriage; and her plans for teaching courses on African women writers.

Tate, Claudia C. *Black Women Writers at Work*. New York: Continuum, 1983.
Includes an interview with Walker in which she comments on the nonlinear narrative form of *Meridian*; the impact of the media on interactions between black male and black female writers; the place of black women writers in literary politics; the importance of folk heros in her work; and her mother's influence on her writing.

Walker, Alice. "*One* Child of One's Own: A Meaningful Digression within the Work(s)." In *The Writer on Her Work*, edited by Janet Sternburg. New York: W. W. Norton, 1980.
Essay beginning with Walker's statement that a woman writer should have one child, because a larger number would limit her freedom of movement. Discusses the relationship between biological motherhood and artistic creation; and the implicit and explicit racism of the white women's movement. Concludes with a lyrical evocation of "Our Mother" as the collective spiritual voice of black women.

_____ . "Writing *The Color Purple*." In *Black Women Writers, 1950-1980: A Critical Evaluation*, edited by Mari Evans. Garden City, N.Y.: Anchor Press, 1984.
Describes the origins and development of *The Color Purple*. Comments on her characters' refusal to "visit" her as long as she was living in New York City and the financial difficulties she encountered once she left.

Commentary

Adams, Timothy Dow. "Alice Walker." In *Critical Survey of Long Fiction*, vol. 7, edited by Frank N. Magill. Englewood Cliffs, N.J.: Salem Press, 1983.
Lengthy reference entry including biographical sketch and analysis of Walker's first three novels. Analysis focuses on Walker's belief that radical change is possible even under the least promising conditions. Her work focuses on the survival mechanisms of Southern black women. Her prose style is characterized by a distinctive combination of lyricism and unflinching realism. Combining feminism with a broad concern for minorities everywhere, Walker's work has been shaped by a broad range of influences, including Jean Toomer, Hurston, Flannery O'Connor, and Albert Camus.

"Alice Walker." In *Contemporary Literary Criticism*, vol. 5 (1976) and vol. 6 (1976), edited by Carolyn Riley and Phyllis Carmel Mendelson; vol. 9 (1978), edited by Dedria Bryfonski; vol. 19 (1981), edited by Sharon R. Gunton; vol. 27 (1984), edited by Jean C. Stine; and vol. 46 (1988), edited by Daniel G. Marowski and Roger Matuz. Detroit: Gale Research.
Compilations of materials relating to Walker's writing. Entry in vol. 46 includes biographical headnote. Various entries reprint commentary by Gloria Steinem, Trudier Harris, Bettye J. Parker-Smith, Klaus Ensslen, Peter Erickson, and Mary Helen Washington. Vols. 27 and 46 includes several reviews reflecting the debate over *The Color Purple*. Other volumes focus primarily on reviews of Walker's earlier work, including *The Third Life of Grange Copeland* (vol. 5) and *Meridian* (vol. 9).

Bell, Bernard W. "The Contemporary Afro-American Novel, 1: Neorealism." In *The Afro-American Novel and Its Tradition*. Amherst: University of Massachusetts Press, 1987.
Walker's novels tailor the tradition of critical realism to fit into the form of the folk romance in order to reinforce the theme of black feminism. The class and racial struggles in Walker's fiction are primarily sexual. The higher consciousness she seeks is based on an insider's view of black working-class history and the socialized ambivalence of black women, in addition to her outsider's view of the conflict of white women with capitalism.

Bradley, David. "Novelist Alice Walker: Telling the Black Woman's Story." *The New York Times Magazine* (January 8, 1984): 25-37.
Lengthy essay, including biographical sketch, by a black male novelist. Frequently cited as evidence of the tension between black male and black women novelists. Describing his personal meetings with Walker and his ambivalent response to her early fiction, Bradley credits her with helping to shape his commitment to writing. Highly critical of Walker's stylistic weaknesses, Bradley expresses his anger over her popularity and her "high level of enmity toward black men." Bradley concludes that while he "does not like her as much as I once did," there is no one "possessed of more wisdom."

Buncombe, Marie H. "Androgyny as Metaphor in Alice Walker's Novels." *CLA Journal* 30 (June, 1987): 419-427.
Argues that Walker employs androgyny as a metaphor for the wholeness of the black experience. She calls for redefinition of terms such as "masculine," "feminine," and "lesbian" whose conventional usage has led to a polarization of black men and black women and therefore to a falsification of black history. Focuses analysis on Grange Copeland and Shug Avery from *The Color Purple*.

Byerman, Keith E. "Women's Blues: The Fiction of Toni Cade Bambara and Alice Walker." In *Fingering the Jagged Grain: Tradition and Form in Recent Black Fiction*. Athens: University of Georgia Press, 1985.
Argues that Walker uses the folk sensibility as part of her attempt to transcend the history of suffering, but that this transcendence paradoxically negates the folk worldview according to which history must be lived through rather than transcended. The utopian form of *The Color Purple* moves Walker outside the tradition that generates the sewing, the blues singing, and Celie's own voice. Byerman's analysis of *The Third Life of Grange Copeland* and *Meridian* center on Walker's generation of rituals that enable her protagonists to realize the healed, growing self that the folk world makes possible.

Callahan, John F. "Reconsideration: The Higher Ground of Alice Walker." *The New Republic* 171 (September 14, 1974): 21-22.
Observes that "reading Alice Walker is like hearing John Coltrane's *Alabama*." Although each work seems almost unbearable in its recognition of violence and oppression, Walker's writing manages to transmit the theme of open-ended wholeness. She suggests that the first step beyond oppression is accepting responsibility for one's own actions. Her power, like that she associates with Jean Toomer, is derived from her ability to be simultaneously "masculine" and "feminine" in her perceptions.

Christian, Barbara. "Alice Walker: The Black Woman Artist as Wayward." In *Black Women Writers, 1950-1980: A Critical Evaluation*, edited by Mari Evans. Garden City, N.Y.: Anchor Press, 1984.

Like many other contemporary black women novelists, Walker focuses on the struggle of black people, particularly black women, to claim their own lives through a deepening of self-knowledge and love. What is distinctive in Walker is her willingness to focus on the "forbidden" as a possible path to truth, a willingness reflected in her criticism of the abstract rhetoric of liberation current at the beginning of her career. Organically spare rather than elaborate, her concentrated distillation of language paradoxically enables her to expand rather than restrict her vision. Includes lengthy analysis of each of Walker's novels.

_____ . "Novels for Everyday Use: The Novels of Alice Walker." In *Black Women Novelists: The Development of a Tradition, 1892-1976*. Westport, Conn.: Greenwood Press, 1980.
Walker's is the most significant treatment of the Southern black sensibility as a resource for addressing the conflict between the human spirit and social patterns. Like quilters, black women must salvage bits and pieces of their past and re-create them in their own image. The unheralded creativity of black women provides the foundation of Walker's vision. Includes lengthy discussions of *The Third Life of Grange Copeland* and *Meridian*.

Davis, Thadious M. "Alice Walker's Celebration of Self in Southern Generations." *Southern Quarterly* 21, no. 4 (1983): 39-54. Reprinted in *Women Writers of the Contemporary South*, edited by Peggy Prenshaw. Jackson: University Press of Mississippi, 1984.
Discussion of Walker's treatment of the relationship between individual identity and communal context across the generations in the black south. Emphasizes Walker's consciousness of the role of the artist in clarifying issues of identity. Discusses the impact of the family on individual identity; Walker's treatment of violence; and the theme of reparation. She is particularly sympathetic to the older women who carry the legacy of survival.

Dixon, Melvin. "Keep Me from Sinking Down: Zora Neale Hurston, Alice Walker, and Gayl Jones." In *Ride Out the Wilderness: Geography and Identity in Afro-American Literature*. Urbana: University of Illinois Press, 1987.
The return to self and landscape is a constant theme in each of Walker's novels. Like Hurston, Walker uses the South as an image of the cultural underpinnings that must accompany political movements if they are to have lasting effect. Discusses the importance of the garden image; Walker's problematic response to Richard Wright; and the importance of black music in her work.

Erickson, Peter. " 'Cast Out Alone/ To Heal/ And Re-Create/ Ourselves': Family-Based Identity in the Work of Alice Walker." *CLA Journal* 23 (September, 1979): 71-94.

Identifies the concern with intrafamily relationships as the crucial theme of Walker's writing. She uses the family as an imaginative structure capable of organizing experience. Following *The Third Life of Grange Copeland* her approach to the theme undergoes a significant change as her focus shifts from the relationship between grandfather and father to that between mother and daughter. Meridian's rediscovery of the church marks an implicit reconciliation with her mother.

Freeman, Alma S. "Zora Neale Hurston and Alice Walker: A Spiritual Kinship." *Sage* 2 (Spring, 1985): 37-41.
Compares three of Walker's characters, including the title character of *Meridian*, with Janie Crawford in *Their Eyes Were Watching God* to demonstrate the spiritual kinship between Walker and Hurston. All four women begin their lives imprisoned by conventional sexual roles that conflict with their own history and self-images. Fighting against racism and sexual oppression, they choose between lives of continued subservience or opt to take control of their own experience.

Harris, Trudier. "Folklore in the Fiction of Alice Walker: A Perpetuation of Historical and Literary Traditions." *Black American Literature Forum* 11 (Spring, 1977): 3-8.
Examines Walker's use of folklore to comment on racial problems and, frequently, to chastise black characters for their attitudes about themselves. Walker's use of folk materials, particularly the image of the conjure woman, recalls that of Hurston and Charles W. Chesnutt. Includes a discussion of the significance of storytelling in the relationship between Ruth and Grange in *The Third Life of Grange Copeland*.

Johnson, Charles. "The Women." In *Being and Race: Black Writing Since 1970*. Bloomington: Indiana University Press, 1988.
Brief comment by a black male novelist, focusing primarily on *The Color Purple*, which is no longer a book, but a cultural event. Although not as strong an artistic achievement as Walker's first two novels, *The Color Purple* is the literary expression of a social revolution of the highest importance. Criticizes Walker's portrayal of black men, described as "thinly rendered strawmen" who serve as "foils for the unfailingly wise, heroic women." The novel is marred by a failure to capture the "spirit of place" and a thinness of characterization.

Marcus, Laura. "Feminism into Fiction: The Women's Press." *Times Literary Supplement* (September 27, 1985): 1070.
Reviews reprint editions of *The Color Purple* and *The Third Life of Grange Copeland*. *The Color Purple* uses a vivid and idiosyncratic vernacular prose to

conceal its polemical statement. Walker's language keeps the plausibility of Celie's awakening and the fairy-tale quality of the ending from becoming major problems. *The Third Life of Grange Copeland* embarks on themes to which Walker returns in later works: individual responsibility; the movement from repetition to progress; and the redemptive power of love.

Mickelson, Anne Z. "Winging Upward: Black Women: Sarah E. Wright, Toni Morrison, Alice Walker." In *Reaching Out: Sensitivity and Order in Recent American Fiction by Women*. Metuchen, N.J.: Scarecrow Press, 1979.
Discusses *Meridian* along with Walker's early short stories to demonstrate her commitment to the spiritual health of black people. The central movement in Meridian's life is toward her decision that her place is with poor Southern blacks. Her mysticism and sense of mission identify Meridian as a type of saint without detracting from Walker's treatment of the details of her relationship with her mother, her marriage, and her commitment to social justice.

Parker-Smith, Bettye J. "Alice Walker's Women: In Search of Some Peace of Mind." In *Black Women Writers, 1950-1980: A Critical Evaluation*, edited by Mari Evans. Garden City, N.Y.: Anchor Press, 1984.
Emphasizes Walker's use of the South as a spiritual balance and an ideological base from which to construct her characters. Discusses the affinity between this position and the land-base theory of Booker T. Washington. Suggests that, while Walker has always been an "apologist" in the sense that she has acknowledged the actual conditions of black women, only with *The Color Purple* does she commit herself to their elevation and defense. Although Walker's characters would resist many of her formulations, their distinguishing attribute is the "tremendous quality with which they carry their suffering."

Royster, Philip M. "In Search of Our Father's Arms: Alice Walker's Persona of the Alienated Darling." *Black American Literature Forum* 20 (Winter, 1986): 347-370.
Argues that much of the hostile response to Walker's portrayal of black men results from the fact that in her fiction autobiographical fantasies of sexuality and aggression masquerade as realistic characterizations. Despite her self-image as "alienated rescuer," she has little real awareness of her relationship with her audience, thereby subverting her intentions. Contrasts Walker's defeatism with the more positive vision of Toni Morrison's *Tar Baby*.

Sadoff, Dianne F. "Black Matrilineage: The Case of Alice Walker and Zora Neale Hurston." *Signs* 11 (Autumn, 1985): 4-26.
Applies Harold Bloom's theory of the "anxiety of influence" and Sandra Gilbert and Susan Gubar's revision focusing on the "anxiety of authorship" to

Walker's celebration of Hurston. Sadoff argues that Walker misreads Hurston as a celebrator of liberated heterosexual love, repressing issues such as her concern with punishing dominant males such as Tea Cake. Concludes that the double bind of race and gender skews literary influence toward creative affirmation.

Spillers, Hortense J. " 'The Permanent Obliquity of an In[pha]llibly Straight': In the Time of the Daughters and Fathers." In *Daughters and Fathers*, edited by Lynda E. Boose and Betty S. Flowers. Baltimore: Johns Hopkins University Press, 1989.
Theoretically grounded discussion of Walker's short story "The Child Who Favored Daughter" and *The Color Purple* in relation to the treatment of incest in Afro-American fiction. Examining the ways in which the historical disruption of black families alters patterns of repression and disclosure in European and Euro-American writing, Spillers revoices Freudian/Lacanian understandings of incest and concludes that the "romance" of black fiction is "a tale of origins that brings together once again children lost, stolen, or strayed from their mothers."

Wade-Gayles, Gloria. *No Crystal Stair: Visions of Race and Sex in Black Women's Fiction*. New York: Pilgrim Press, 1984.
Discusses the treatment of relationships between black men and black women, and those between mothers and daughters in *The Third Life of Grange Copeland* and *Meridian*. Walker shows how tragically the lives of black women can be shaped by racial violence, sexual abuse, and class oppression. In *The Third Life of Grange Copeland*, Josie's anger stands out against a background of oppression and loneliness. Devotion and sacrifice are the central themes of *Meridian*.

Walker, Robbie. "Coping Strategies of the Women in Alice Walker's Novels: Implications for Survival." *CLA Journal* 30 (June, 1987): 401-418.
Employs a social psychology model based on "risk appraisal" and "locus of control"—the extent to which individuals perceive problem resolutions to be in their control—to analyze the coping strategies of Mem and Margaret in *The Third Life of Grange Copeland* and Celie in *The Color Purple*. Although Alice Walker's characters are frequently lumped together as victims of deprivation and brutality, each responds in a unique way. The belief in self-determination differentiates Walker's characters who merely survive from those who survive whole.

Washington, J. Charles. "Positive Black Male Images in Alice Walker's Fiction." *Obsidian II* 3 (Spring, 1988): 23-48.

Defends Walker against Trudier Harris' and David Bradley's claims that she is unrelentingly hostile in her portrayal of black men. Argues that Walker's fiction contains numerous positive images and that the tension between black men and black women is grounded in a realistic assessment of the nexus of political and economic forces in the black community. She gives praise when appropriate, but does not shrink from necessary criticism.

Washington, Mary Helen. "An Essay on Alice Walker." In *Sturdy Black Bridges: Visions of Black Women in Literature*, edited by Roseann P. Bell, Bettye J. Parker, and Beverly Guy-Sheftall. Garden City, N.Y.: Anchor Press, 1979.
Identifies Walker's distinguishing characteristic as her evolutionary treatment of black women, who move from total victimization to a developing consciousness that gives them some control over their lives. In both *The Third Life of Grange Copeland* and *Meridian*, Walker portrays the pattern of movement from numbness through political awakening to creative expansion accompanied by an attempt to reintegrate themselves into their culture in order to discover its value.

Willis, Susan. "Alice Walker's Women." In *Specifying: Black Women Writing the American Experience*. Madison: University of Wisconsin Press, 1987.
Throughout Walker's novels, the journey over geographic space is a metaphor for personal growth and historical transformation. In *The Third Life of Grange Copeland*, Walker suggests that black community must be based on the experience and transcendence of enslavement to both the plantation and to wage labor. In her later novels, black remains the symbol of underclass status. Includes an extended discussion of two relatively minor characters, Wile Chile and Louvinie, from *Meridian*.

Selected Titles

The Color Purple
Awkward, Michael. "*The Color Purple* and the Achievement of (Comm)unity." In *Inspiriting Influences: Tradition, Revision, and Afro-American Women's Novels*. New York: Columbia University Press, 1989.
Explores the ways in which Walker revoices aspects of *Their Eyes Were Watching God* to create a vision of the possible resolution of separation which includes formal, individual, and tribal dimensions. Walker's notion of the generational transmission of the artistic spirit through underappreciated folk forms plays a crucial role in *The Color Purple*. In an environment characterized by patriarchal domination, Celie's letters serve as the major outlet for her muzzled creative spirit.

Blount, Marcellus. "A Woman Speaks." *Callaloo* 18 (Spring/Summer, 1983): 118-122.
Favorable review emphasizing the way in which the novel draws together the conventions of black women's fiction, including the identity and sexuality which bind Celie and Shug in an ideal sisterhood. Walker expresses a profound spirit of reconciliation positing a faith in unqualified redemption unusual in Afro-American fiction. Relates Walker's narrative form to the tradition of women's epistolary novels.

Bovoso, Carole. "Books." *Essence* 13 (October, 1982): 20.
Favorable review of *The Color Purple* as one of the rare books in which the extraordinary courage of black women "comes shining through." Walker reveals truths about men and women, blacks and whites, God and love. Concludes with the statement that the novel is "one of the great books of our time."

Chambers, Kimberly. "Right on Time: History and Religion in Alice Walker's *The Color Purple*." *CLA Journal* 31 (September, 1987): 44-62.
Examines Walker's innovative understanding of time as a source of redemptive vision in *The Color Purple*. Walker's sense of time is rooted in folklore, which provides enduring patterns for understanding human behavior. An awareness of God coincides with the major steps in the lives of all of Walker's characters. Ultimately a new sense of timelessness as promise rather than endurance emerges to assert the possibility of recovering what had been lost.

Fifer, Elizabeth. "The Dialect and Letters of *The Color Purple*." In *Contemporary American Women Writers: Narrative Strategies*, edited by Catherine Rainwater and William J. Scheick. Lexington: University Press of Kentucky, 1985.
Discusses Walker's use of the epistolary form as the key to understanding her central theme that "how we tell the stories of our lives determines the significance and outcome of the narratives that are our lives." Noting that both Celie and Nettie gradually develop feminist consciousness, Fifer emphasizes Walker's use of the letters to reinvent and juxtapose events in a manner that resists the potentially programmatic quality of her archetypal characters.

Gates, Henry Louis, Jr. "Color Me Zora: Alice Walker's (Re)Writing of the Speakerly Text." In *The Signifying Monkey: A Theory of Afro-American Literary Criticism*. New York: Oxford University Press, 1988.
Emphasizes the "act of ancestral bonding"—which contrasts sharply with the anxiety and conflict characteristic of the relationship between black male writers and their literary predecessors, who are most frequently white males—represented in Walker's rewriting of the narrative strategy of *Their Eyes Were Watching God* in *The Color Purple*. Where Hurston represents Janie's self-

discovery as the narrative "enunciation of her own doubled self," Walker represents Celie's growth of self-consciousness as an "act of writing" which brings that self into being. Placing *The Color Purple* at the end of the chain of "repetition and difference" at the center of the Afro-American narrative tradition, Gates also emphasizes the similarity of Walker's spiritual vision to that of the nineteenth century black religious visionary Rebecca Cox Jackson.

Guy, David. "A Correspondence of Hearts." *The Washington Post Book World* 12 (July 25, 1982): 1, 8.
Favorable review. Argues that where Walker's previous novels have sometimes been too ideological, *The Color Purple* marks a perfect synthesis of material and vision. Attributes the negative images of whites and black males not to Walker, but to Celie's perspective. Walker's fable of the modern world implies that only by removing themselves from the relationship of oppressor and oppressed can people hope to make themselves free.

Hamilton, Cynthia. "Alice Walker's Politics or the Politics of *The Color Purple*." *Journal of Black Studies* 18 (March, 1988): 379-391.
Harsh criticism of Walker's novel as an expression of the narcissistic spirit of American culture. Her portrayal of black families passing on cultural pathology reinforces the Republican belief that the problem of the black poor is not their problem. Like Mary Wollstonecraft, Walker believes that the way out of oppression is "to assume bourgeois values and style." Argues that *The Color Purple* ultimately articulates an "ideology of submission."

Harris, Trudier. "*The Color Purple*: Stereotypes and Silence." *Black American Literature Forum* 18 (Winter, 1984): 155-161.
Strongly worded statement from a black woman critic condemning the failure of critics to address the serious weaknesses in *The Color Purple*. Harris observes that for many readers the novel reinforces stereotypes and contrasts the responses of black and white feminists. Among the problems Harris identifies are the fabulist/fairy-tale narrative which contradicts the novel's message, and the superficial political rhetoric, which makes the novel read "like a political shopping list of the IOUs Walker felt that it was time to repay."

Henderson, Mae G. "*The Color Purple*: Revisions and Redefinitions." *Sage* 2 (Spring, 1985): 14-18.
By subverting the conventions of the traditionally Eurocentric male form of the epistolary novel, Walker asserts her right to authorship and, by extension, gives voice to the black women who have been silenced in life as well as in literature. Argues that Walker's art is liberating inasmuch as it reconstructs and reclaims the past of women and community. The novel moves from male-female coupling to a new variation of the eternal triangle in which women complement each other rather than compete.

Hernton, Calvin C. "Who's Afraid of Alice Walker? *The Color Purple* as Slave Narrative." In *The Sexual Mountain and Black Women Writers: Adventures in Sex, Literature, and Real Life*. Garden City, N.Y.: Anchor Press, 1987.

Lengthy essay discussing the response to both the book and film versions of *The Color Purple*. Provides an overview of hostile commentary before defending both treatments. *The Color Purple* is best viewed as a slave narrative tracing Celie's rise from brutalization to liberation, which is imaged in her ability to participate in the womanist energy associated with the porch.

Kelly, Ernece B. Review of *The Color Purple*. *CLA Journal* 27 (September, 1983): 91-96.

Favorable review of *The Color Purple* as a "moral fable" on the theme that men are victims of any culture that encourages them to indulge in spiritually fatal domination over women, but that they can learn to move beyond their victimization. Argues that Walker's treatment of the lesbian theme is interesting in part because neither Shug nor Celie draws her support and strength from women "exclusively or even preponderantly." Walker's use of the epistolary tradition, which has historically embraced absurdist qualities, demonstrates that black English is by no means a limited mode of expression.

Miller, Jane. "Women's Men." In *Women Writing About Men*. New York: Pantheon, 1986.

The Color Purple is a story of women's rebellion, a "regenerative and affirmative turning of the tables on men, whose brutality towards women may be understood but must also be resisted." Walker, who has previously created comic, loving, sad, and angry portraits of men, offers the men in *The Color Purple* a "miraculous redemption" as a by-product of women's creativity.

Mootry-Ikerionwu, Maria K. Review of *The Color Purple*. *CLA Journal* 27 (March, 1984): 345-348.

Generally unfavorable review emphasizing the shortcomings of Walker's characterization of Celie, who seems a bit stupid and elemental. Although the transformation of the male characters makes a statement on androgyny, it is not a strong conclusion. While Walker's ideas are interesting, her craft is not sufficiently polished.

Pinckney, Darryl. "Black Victims, Black Villains." *The New York Review of Books* 34 (January 29, 1987): 17-20.

Generally unfavorable review of both the book and film versions of *The Color Purple*. Although Walker makes a claim to historical truth, she participates fully in the present trend of novels which treat the struggles of black people in an insular manner, failing to address the socioeconomic and political sources of their suffering. Spielberg's movie reveals the melodrama beneath the novel's feminist rhetoric. Criticizes Walker's presentation of black males as raging tyrants incapable of reflection. Walker transforms Hurston's folk wisdom into feminist clichés and a vague transcendentalism.

Prescott, Peter S. "A Long Road to Liberation." *Newsweek* 99 (June 21, 1982): 67-68.
Identifies *The Color Purple* as a "novel of permanent importance," commenting on Walker's ability to create difficulties and then transcend them. Praising Walker's skillful use of black English, Prescott identifies the redemptive power of love as the central theme and emphasizes that such love in *The Color Purple* is based on female bonding.

Ross, Daniel W. "Celie in the Looking Glass: The Desire for Selfhood in *The Color Purple*." *Modern Fiction Studies* 34 (Spring, 1988): 69-84.
Argues that the mirror scene initiates the process through which Celie begins to come to terms with her body, which is the necessary precondition for finding her voice. By accepting her feelings of desire, Celie reappropriates the body that was taken from her by male brutality. Only after she has made this transition can she connect with self, others, community, and Creation.

Shelton, Frank. "Alienation and Integration in Alice Walker's *The Color Purple*." *CLA Journal* 28 (June, 1984): 382-392.
Discusses the treatment of the motif of alienation from God and nature to explore Walker's vision of the ways in which change can occur in the lives of her characters. Both her women and men work through problems of racism, sexism, and violence to achieve a wholeness attained virtually without political action.

Smith, Barbara. "Sexual Oppression Unmasked." *Callaloo* 22 (Fall, 1984): 170-176.
Highly favorable review heralding Walker as the first writer to create an extended literary work whose subject is the sexual politics of black life as experienced by ordinary black people. The novel also provides the first positively and fully depicted lesbian relationship between two black women set in a traditional black community. Comments that many favorable reviews avoid addressing its actual themes.

Smith, Dinitia. "Celie, You a Tree." *The Nation* 235 (September 4, 1982): 181-183.
Favorable review emphasizing the central importance of relationships between women to the successful resolution of the struggle between redemption and revenge. No writer has made the pain of racism, especially in the frequently ignored world of rural black women, more palpable than Walker. Despite the occasional didacticism of Walker's prose, *The Color Purple* is a major advance in her work. At its best, it bears comparison with Faulkner.

Stade, George. "Womanist Fiction and Male Characters." *Partisan Review* 52 (1985): 264-270.

Discusses the controversy over *The Color Purple*, which Stade does not view as feminist because "it does not argue the equality of the sexes; it dramatizes, rather, the virtues of women and the vices of men." Relates this unexplained awfulness of men to other recent novels by women, who portray heroines leaving stifling relationships to find happiness in an artistic career or relationships with other women. Comments that such "womanist fiction" is justified if it helps women live more effectively and notes that most Western literature is filled with equivalently "mannist" characters.

Tavormina, M. Teresa. "Dressing the Spirit: Clothworking and Language in *The Color Purple*." *Journal of Narrative Technique* 16 (Fall, 1986): 220-230.

Examines Walker's use of the familiar analogy between spinning words and spinning yarns, between "text and textile." Walker emphasizes that both language and clothing are means of self-expression, although they can also be turned into forms of repression. Examines images of clothing, sewing, and quilting in relation to personalized forms of language such as dialect and letter-writing. Walker's theme is that it is necessary to lovingly "dress" the spirits of self and others.

Towers, Robert. "Good Men Are Hard to Find." *The New York Review of Books* 29 (August 12, 1982): 35-36.

Mixed review concluding that no other novelist has so successfully tapped the poetic resources of subliterate black idiom, but criticizing Walker for structural failings in "what is clearly intended to be a realistic novel." The account of Africa fails because Walker does not endow Nettie with an individual voice. Emphasizes the importance of the theme of women's bonding and Walker's defense of Southern black religion.

Tucker, Lindsey. "Alice Walker's *The Color Purple*: Emergent Woman, Emergent Text." *Black American Literature Forum* 22 (Spring, 1988): 81-95.

The Color Purple is a truly modernist text that evinces a high awareness of the role of language in the shaping of vision. Drawing on traditions of quilting, song, and needlework, Walker demonstrates what the nature of an independent black women's discourse might be. Her use of the epistolary form is particularly effective since it is a convention used primarily by women that focuses attention on the disruption between speaker and listener.

Wall, Wendy. "Lettered Bodies and Corporeal Texts in *The Color Purple*." *Studies in American Fiction* 16 (Spring, 1988): 83-97.

Views Walker as a postmodernist who uses the epistolary genre as a form of revisionary history that emphasizes the plurality of possible meanings. Discusses Celie as a figure whose body has been made to submit to patriarchal authority. Celie learns to reshape these forces through her letters, which provide a "second body" mediating her relationship with power.

Wallace, Michele. "Blues for Mr. Spielberg." *The Village Voice* (March 18, 1986): 21-26.

Lengthy discussion of the transformation of *The Color Purple* from novel into film, emphasizing Walker's position in the movement of black women writers attempting to reconstruct "black female experience as a positive ground." Argues that Walker's revolutionary impulses in the first half of the novel are undermined by the second half, which offers abrupt and premature solutions. Responding to the call of Walker's utopian vision, Spielberg "juggles film cliches and racial stereotypes fast and loose, until all signs of a black feminist agenda are banished, or ridiculed beyond repair."

Walsh, Margaret. "The Enchanted World of *The Color Purple*." *Southern Quarterly* 25 (Winter, 1987): 89-107.

Argues that reading *The Color Purple* in the context of fairy tale patterns helps explain the function of the unpleasantness and exaggeration that has generated some negative response to the novel. Basing her discussion on the work of Bruno Bettelheim, Walsh identifies the "enchanted heart" in Walker's theme of the victory of a simple young girl over her degraded circumstances and the transformation of a beastly young man into a princely sage of wisdom and grace.

Watkins, Mel. "Some Letters Went to God." *The New York Times Book Review* 87 (July 25, 1982): 7.

Identifies *The Color Purple* as Walker's most impressive novel, bringing into sharper focus the themes of her previous work, including her central concern with the estrangement and violence that mark the relationship between her black men and women. Her narrative style, convincing because of its folk voice, is not intrusive, but forces intimate identification with Celie. Identifies the "somewhat pallid portraits of the males" and the weakness of Nettie's letters from Africa as flaws in "a striking and consummately well-written novel."

Wesley, Richard. "*The Color Purple* Debate: Reading Between the Lines." *Ms.* 15 (September, 1986): 62, 90-92.

Defense of *The Color Purple* by a black male critic who criticizes the tendency of some commentators to establish themselves as "guardians of the black image." Noting that the wildly divergent reactions to the novel testify to the power of Walker's probing into the soul of the nation, Wesley argues that the negative responses of black men have been generated primarily by those who maintain a belief in the sacrosanct quality of the Black Power ideology of the

1960's. Wesley finds "little that was offensive as far as the images of black men portrayed in either the novel or in the movie."

Meridian

Barthold, Bonnie J. "Women: Chaos and Redemption." In *Black Time: Fiction of Africa, the Caribbean, and the United States*. New Haven, Conn.: Yale University Press, 1981.

Focuses on the theme of the ambiguities of motherhood. Although she lives in a world where motherhood is linked with death, Meridian generates a mythic vision of motherhood in which the death of one child represents a threat to all children. Walker rebels against temporal chaos by insisting on the archetypal identity of "Woman" and "Mother" and refusing to embody "what is extrinsic to the mythic truth of a traditional past."

Callahan, John F. "The Hoop of Language: Politics and the Restoration of Voice in *Meridian*." In *In the African-American Grain: The Pursuit of Voice in Twentieth-Century Black Fiction*. Urbana: University of Illinois Press, 1988.

Discusses *Meridian* as a response to the desperation of the early 1970's. Attempting to envision an authentic personal and public voice, Walker's technique fuses discontinuous, apparently irreconcilable voices and perspectives. While those around Meridian demand *correct* political responses, Walker's protagonist struggles to find the *right* response. Silence and solitude, in Meridian's process, provide an essential prologue to speech and social action.

Cooke, Michael G. "Intimacy: The Interpenetration of the One and the All in Robert Hayden and Alice Walker." In *Afro-American Literature in the Twentieth Century: The Achievement of Intimacy*. New Haven, Conn.: Yale University Press, 1984.

Identifies Walker as one of the writers who has done most to realize the meaning of intimacy, which Cooke views as the keynote of modern Afro-American literature. *Meridian* illuminates the inner struggle and public cost of genuine intimacy and reveals the varieties of false intimacy. Walker's choice of an eccentric heroine is a key to a successful strategy of inviting the reader to participate in the construction of reality.

DuPlessis, Rachel Blau. "Beyond the Hard Visible Horizon." In *Writing Beyond the Ending: Narrative Strategies of Twentieth-Century Women Writers*. Bloomington: Indiana University Press, 1985.

Views *Meridian* as a "collective biography of a multiple individual, who articulates social and spiritual questions." Walker challenges the Afro-American cultural strategy of "mainstreaming" by telling the stories of many women, thereby locating Meridian's individual story in a narrative multiplicity that acknowledges conflict and the centrality of women's experience. Among the major themes are the triumph over many forms of violation and the transformation of the conventional meaning of death in the novel's resolution.

Harris, Norman. "*Meridian*: Answers in the Black Church." In *Connecting Times: The Sixties in Afro-American Fiction*. Jackson: University Press of Mississippi, 1988.
Views *Meridian* as an examination of the impact of the civil rights movement on Afro-American life with detailed attention to three areas: the process of parental and institutional socialization that alienates blacks from their heritage; problems between black men and black women; and the ascendancy of nationalist thought in the movement. Harris focuses on the ways in which characters are able to use the black church as a basic resource in their quest for freedom and literacy. Those who are alienated from the church fail to actualize their potential.

Karl, Frederick R. "The Female Experience." In *American Fictions, 1940-1980*. New York: Harper & Row, 1983.
Discusses *Meridian* in the context of a broad survey of contemporary fiction by women. Identifies a crucial focus in Walker's complex novel in her concern with thoughts which have no outlet, psychological states which have no resolution. The Wild Child provides an emblem of Meridian's possible fate and reinspires her commitment to social change.

McDowell, Deborah E. "The Self in Bloom: Alice Walker's *Meridian*." *CLA Journal* 24 (March, 1981): 262-275.
Walker's most artistically mature writing, *Meridian* expands her concern with black women to embrace universal concerns about autonomy, self-reliance, and self-realization. Although Meridian confronts an extremely hostile environment, she flourishes by fashioning an identity on the artifacts of her own heritage rather than from the Western tradition. Emphasizing the cyclic imagery of death and rebirth, McDowell views the novel as a variation on the traditional *Bildungsroman*.

McGowan, Martha J. "Atonement and Release in Alice Walker's *Meridian*." *Critique* 23, no. 1 (1981): 25-36.
Examines Walker's attempt in *Meridian* to move beyond the image of black women as victims to an exploration of their roots and possibilities. The recurring image of The Sojourner makes it clear that Meridian's spiritual renewal must come from the strength of her bond with black womanhood. Walker replaces Meridian's impossible goal of sainthood with what may ultimately be only a new revised version.

Marcus, Greil. "Limits." *The New Yorker* 52 (June 7, 1976): 133-136.
Thoughtful review discussing *Meridian* as a revoicing of the theme of existential heroism from Albert Camus' *The Rebel*. Walker confronts the problem of the "ethic of rebellion," particularly the paradox that the very murder necessary to the defense of the "right" cannot be "permitted to survive itself." Argues that Meridian's dilemma stems from the fact that the connections that Meridian's parents have made are beyond her grasp. Questions Walker's decision to make Meridian into a saintly figure, because "If only saints can bear such questions, we can forget them."

Nadel, Alan. "Reading the Body: Alice Walker's *Meridian* and the Archaeology of Self." *Modern Fiction Studies* 34 (Spring, 1988): 55-68.
Meridian is an attempt to mend the disruptions in black life and reconstruct an alternative black tradition. Treating narrative as archaeology, Walker focuses her analysis on the ways in which Meridian's body and name incorporate a range of larger social tensions. Nadel discusses the difficulty of reconstructing the past either through activism or artifacts, since both are infiltrated by the oppressive context. Includes a provocative discussion of Meridian's use of Anne-Marion's letters as a way of bridging the gap between artifact and activism.

Piercy, Marge. Review of *Meridian*. *The New York Times Book Review* (May 23, 1976): 5.
Favorable review emphasizing the power of Walker's protagonist, who attempts to make real the notions of holiness and commitment. Although Piercy does not find the ending successful, she praises Walker's ability to bring a saintly character to life. *Meridian* is a "tight, fascinating novel" that accomplishes "a remarkable amount."

Rumens, Carol. "Heirs to the Dream." *Times Literary Supplement* (June 18, 1982): 676.
Favorable review observing that although the question of racial equality is central to Walker's concern, it is sometimes diminished by the more urgently personal quest for sexual justice. Walker's deepest concern is with the impact of political and moral issues on individual relationships. In Meridian, Walker creates a convincing secular saint whose collapse and survival symbolize a kind of spiritual journey.

Stein, Karen F. "*Meridian*: Alice Walker's Critique of Revolution." *Black American Literature Forum* 20 (Spring/Summer, 1986): 129-141.
Responding to the failure of the civil rights movement to acknowledge black women's selfhood, Walker shifts her attention in *Meridian* from the concept of revolution to the more powerful idea of transformation. Walker's protagonist resists rigid definitions of herself, including those embedded in conceptions of martyrdom and false revolutionary consciousness, in order to survive.

Weston, Ruth D. "Inversion of Patriarchal Mantle Images in Alice Walker's *Meridian*." *Southern Quarterly* 25 (Winter, 1987): 102-107.
Argues that Walker inverts the religious symbolism of the patriarchal mantle in order to assert the potential power of the female imagination. Associates Meridian with ecstatic prophets such as Elijah, and Truman, as her successor, with Elisha.

The Third Life of Grange Copeland

Butler, Robert James. "Making a Way Out of No Way: The Journey in Alice Walker's *The Third Life of Grange Copeland*." *Black American Literature Forum* 22 (Spring, 1988): 65-79.
Discusses Walker's adaptation of the journey motif which links the American and Afro-American traditions. Rather than directing their journeys to a specific place, both traditions exult in nonteleological movement through indefinite space. Central to *The Third Life of Grange Copeland* is the thematic tension between the characters' desire for a stable life centering on a "home" and their desire for radical change brought about through open-ended journeying. In a world of severely limited options, Walker endorses movement and open space over stasis and restriction.

Coles, Robert. "To Try Men's Souls." *The New Yorker* (February 27, 1971): 104-106.
Favorable review contrasting Walker's emphasis on the human dimension of racial experience with approaches that reduce human tragedy to a "history of exploitation and oppression." Comments on Walker's ability to tell us about the inner lives of the black people who become the "social dynamite" of the urban ghettos. Rather than writing a social novel or a protest novel, Walker engraves the centuries of black life in America on the reader's consciousness with her lyrical prose.

Ensslen, Klaus. "Collective Experience and Individual Responsibility: Alice Walker's *The Third Life of Grange Copeland*." In *The Afro-American Novel Since 1960*, edited by Peter Bruck and Wolfgang Karrer. Amsterdam: B. R. Gruner, 1982.
Focuses on the unresolved tension between Walker's individualistic emphasis on moral regeneration and her commitment to addressing the political problems of the black community. Structuring her novel around the central opposition of moral decay (Brownfield) and moral self-discovery (Grange), Walker develops the theme of self-expression around the women characters. Stressing the need for an end to the self-destruction of black men and women, she provides no insight as to how the renewed family can be reintegrated into the black community.

Gaston, Karen C. "Women in the Lives of Grange Copeland." *CLA Journal* 24 (March, 1981): 276-286.

Observing that most reviewers have failed to recognize the importance of Margaret, Mem, Fat Josie, and Ruth in *The Third Life of Grange Copeland*, Gaston identifies the strength, tenacity, and love of black women as Walker's central concern. Countering stereotypical images of black women, these four characters often subvert their strength through love. More than simply foils to Grange and Brownfield, Walker's women characters play a central thematic role because they inspire Grange to direct Ruth toward racial and sexual liberation.

Harris, Trudier. "Fear of Castration: A Literary History." In *Exorcising Blackness: Historical and Literary Lynching and Burning Rituals*. Bloomington: Indiana University Press, 1984.

Discusses the theme of "symbolic castration" in relation to Grange and Brownfield in *The Third Life of Grange Copeland*. Both men fit into the category of black men who have been emasculated by the sharecropping system. Although Grange allows himself to be reduced to bestiality when he attempts to run away from his responsibility, he is ultimately able to rise above his degradation. In contrast, Brownfield surrenders his humanity by uncritically adopting the white image of him as a "bad nigger."

_____ . "Three Black Women Writers and Humanism: A Folk Perspective." In *Black American Literature and Humanism*, edited by R. Baxter Miller. Lexington: University Press of Kentucky, 1981.

Focuses on the process through which Grange accepts himself and learns to interact with other human beings. Following an abortive series of attempts to evade responsibility or attain freedom through geographical movement, Grange ultimately refuses to recognize any values other than those defined by his own humanity.

Hellenbrand, Harold. "Speech, After Silence: Alice Walker's *The Third Life of Grange Copeland*." *Black American Literature Forum* 20 (Spring/Summer, 1986): 113-128.

Examines the theme of silence in *The Third Life of Grange Copeland* in relation to Walker's combination of two major strains in black fiction: the chronicle of a black family, and the tale of racial confrontation. In its focus on Grange, which Hellenbrand compares at length with Richard Wright's portrait of Bigger Thomas, the novel dramatizes the convergence of racial antagonism and family history. The aspects of the novel focusing on Ruth, however, point toward the reconstitution of female identity and family life that become Walker's preoccupations in her later novels.

Hendin, Josephine. Review of *The Third Life of Grange Copeland*. *Saturday Review* 53 (August 22, 1970): 55-56.

Generally favorable review emphasizing Walker's insightful exploration of the problems of respectable blacks. Her primary theme is the depletion of love and the erosion of the sources of affection. While her presentation of the problem has depth, she "disappoints" by explaining Grange's conversion in political cliches that ignore the depth of the suffering she describes.

Hogue, W. Lawrence. "History, the Feminist Discourse and *The Third Life of Grange Copeland.*" In *Discourse and the Other: The Production of the Afro-American Text*. Durham, N.C.: Duke University Press, 1986.

Illustrating the historical oppression of black women and undermining stereotypical images, *The Third Life of Grange Copeland* produces a feminist representation of history. A careful examination of Grange demonstrates Walker's use of individual characters to espouse ideological forms. Employs a theoretical framework emphasizing the ways in which black writers create a variety of responses to a shared literary, political, and historical context.

MARGARET WALKER (ALEXANDER)

Biography

Baytop, Adrianne. "Margaret Walker." In *American Women Writers*, vol. 4, edited by Lina Mainiero. New York: Frederick Ungar, 1982.
Biographical entry including brief commentary on *Jubilee*. Bibliography lists entries in other reference works.

Egejuru, Phanuel, and Robert Elliot Fox. "An Interview with Margaret Walker." *Callaloo* 6 (May, 1979): 29-35.
Includes Walker's comments on the role of politics and religion in *Jubilee*. Walker comments that she was attempting to present different points of view, rather than make a political statement. She views black religion as an expression of the doubleness of black culture. Also contains Walker's comments on the failure of literary critics to recognize the achievements of black women, including Fauset and West, during the Harlem Renaissance.

Emanuel, James A. "Margaret (Abigail) Walker." In *Contemporary Novelists*, 4th ed., edited by D. L. Kirkpatrick. New York: St. Martin's Press, 1986.
Reference entry including biographical outline, list of publications, and analysis of *Jubilee*. Emanuel emphasizes the historical richness of the novel, which is an enlargement of the experiences of Walker's great-grandmother. Quotes Walker's speech to the 1968 Urban League Conference in which she celebrates the Afro-American spirit as an articulation of "primacy of human personality and the spiritual destiny of all mankind."

Freibert, Lucy M. "Southern Song: An Interview with Margaret Walker." *Frontiers* 9, no. 3 (1987): 51-56.
Interview included in special issue on women in the South. Among the topics discussed are the unifying principle of Walker's various roles; the influence of her parents and teachers; the significance of Langston Hughes, W.E.B. DuBois, and Richard Wright for her development; several of her works-in-progress, including a planned sequel to *Jubilee*; her treatment of the relationship between black and white women in *Jubilee*; her feelings about relationships between black and white women in the contemporary South; her response to Hurston, Larsen, and Brooks; her sense of connection with Flannery O'Connor and Carson McCullers; her criticism of *The Color Purple*; and her admiration for *Maud Martha*.

Pettis, Joyce. "Margaret Walker." In *Afro-American Writers 1940-1955*, edited by Trudier Harris. Vol. 76 of *Dictionary of Literary Biography*. Detroit: Bruccoli Clark, 1988.

Reference essay including a substantial biographical sketch, analysis of Walker's poetry, and a brief discussion of *Jubilee* as a realistic treatment of the daily life and folklore of the slave community. Biographical section describes Walker's Southern upbringing; her early immersion in a wide range of literature; her education at Northwestern and Iowa University; her involvement with the Works Progress Administration; her relationship with Richard Wright; and her teaching career.

Rowell, Charles. "Poetry, History, and Humanism: An Interview with Margaret Walker." *Black World* 25, no. 2 (1975): 4-17.
Interview focusing on Walker's humanistic vision. She comments on the uses of history in her novel; the general topic of novelists as historians; her admiration for younger writers such as Ishmael Reed and Sam Greenlee; and her ambivalent feelings concerning the Black Arts movement.

Tate, Claudia C. *Black Women Writers at Work*. New York: Continuum, 1983.
Includes an interview with Walker, incorporating an excerpt from Walker's unpublished autobiography and an unpublished manuscript concerning the role of black women in American literature, which includes brief comments on Hurston and Harper. In addition, Walker comments at length on the major points of her biography of Richard Wright; and on a symposium on black women writers she organized.

Walker, Margaret. "How I Wrote *Jubilee*." Chicago: Third World Press, 1972.
Monograph in which Walker describes the origins and writing of *Jubilee*. She emphasizes the importance of the oral tradition, particularly as it came down through her own family, to the content of the novel. The most important source of contextual information concerning *Jubilee*.

_____ . "Interview." In *Mississippi Writers Talking, II*, edited by John Griffin Jones. Jackson: University Press of Mississippi, 1983.
Interview in which Walker discusses her family background; the importance of education in her upbringing; her relationship with Richard Wright; the process of writing her poetry and *Jubilee*; contemporary racial relations; the civil rights movement; and the significance of various aspects of southern culture.

_____ . "On Being Female, Black, and Free." In *The Writer on Her Work*, edited by Janet Sternburg. New York: W. W. Norton, 1980.
Autobiographical essay centering on Walker's belief that a philosophical state of mind provides her with a sense of solidity. Walker discusses her early determination to become a writer; her education and apprenticeship; her feelings concerning racism; and the situation of the black woman writer throughout the world.

Walker, Margaret, and Nikki Giovanni. *A Poetic Equation: Conversations Between Margaret Walker and Nikki Giovanni*. Washington, D.C.: Howard University Press, 1974.

Series of discussions between Walker and a young black woman poet concerning their shared concerns, both aesthetic and political. Walker comments on a wide range of issues, including her sense of the past and future directions of the civil rights movement and changes in the cultural position of the Afro-American writer.

Selected Title

Jubilee

Bell, Bernard W. "The Contemporary Afro-American Novel, 2: Modernism and Postmodernism." In *The Afro-American Novel and Its Tradition*. Amherst: University of Massachusetts Press, 1987.

A neoslave narrative based on folk material and Vyry's quest for freedom, *Jubilee* creates fiction from the oral history of Walker's family and the recorded history of the United States. In Vyry, Walker creates one of the most memorable women characters in contemporary Afro-American fiction, in part because of her challenge to stereotypical images of nineteenth century black womanhood. There is little ironic distance at any point in the novel

Carby, Hazel. "Ideologies of Black Folk: The Historical Novel of Slavery." In *Slavery and the Literary Imagination*, edited by Deborah E. McDowell and Arnold Rampersad. Baltimore: Johns Hopkins University Press, 1987.

Though the sources of *Jubilee* are in memories and oral culture, Walker transforms the material through the structure of the social realist novel. Carefully avoiding romantic invocation of an undifferentiated rural folk, Walker rewrites folk ideology to address the social transformations of the 1960's. Contains a detailed comparison of *Jubilee* with *Gone with the Wind*.

Chapman, Abraham. "Negro Folksong." *Saturday Review* 49 (September 24, 1966): 43-44.

Favorable review praising *Jubilee* as an innovative response to the hackneyed genre of Civil War writing. Evoking the folk experience and attitudes of Southern blacks, Walker reverses the image of blacks who exist only on the margins of the plantations. No previous novel has provided such an accurate picture of the everyday life of the slaves. At times Walker's historical project results in a loss of literary form, but generally she writes with the "indirection and compact suggestiveness of the poet."

Christian, Barbara. "Ordinary Women: The Tone of the Commonplace." In *Black Women Novelists: The Development of a Tradition, 1892-1976*. Westport, Conn.: Greenwood Press, 1980.

A massive historical novel, *Jubilee* retells the Civil War romance from the perspective of the slave. Using folklore as a major structural element, Walker makes her story representative of the experience of an entire culture. Rather than dramatizing the humiliation of slavery or the extraordinary heroism of individual slaves, Walker emphasizes the practical slave culture that allowed black people to survive as a race. The novel is occasionally marred by an unresolved tension between the personal drama of Vyry's life and Walker's desire to incorporate a wider historical context.

Daniel, Walter C. "Margaret Walker's Brother Ezekiel: Priest-Prophet of the 'Invisible Church.'" In *Images of the Preacher in Afro-American Literature*. Washington, D.C.: University Press of America, 1981.
Brother Ezekiel embodies the essential tension in Afro-American culture. Ezekiel is simultaneously the official spokesman for the religion of the masters and a central figure in the formation of the institutional support system for the slave community. Ezekiel's ability to survive among the whites while serving as a conductor on the underground railroad highlights the dual function of the "invisible church" in the slave community.

Dykeman, Wilma. "A Talent for Survival." *The New York Times Book Review* 71 (September 25, 1966): 52.
Mixed review praising *Jubilee* as an ambitious and uneven novel. Vyry is one of the most memorable women in contemporary fiction, and Walker presents a compelling image of the triumph of the human spirit over many kinds of bondage. At times, however, she succumbs to the problems of fiction as sociology and creates stereotypes in the interest of presenting an accurate image of the daily life of the slaves.

Gwin, Minrose C. "*Jubilee*: The Black Woman's Celebration of Human Community." In *Conjuring: Black Women, Fiction, and Literary Tradition*, edited by Marjorie Pryse and Hortense J. Spillers. Bloomington: Indiana University Press, 1985.
Investigates the "organic connection between humanism and religion" portrayed in Walker's novel. Expressing a vision of humanity as flawed but capable of moral insight and spiritual change, *Jubilee* concerns the freedom of self through the acknowledgement of a self-imposed bondage to the human duty of nurturing others. Vyry's willingness to forgive, as imagined by a black woman writer in the context of the 1960's, is a significant black acknowledgement of cross-racial female bonds of suffering.

Klotman, Phyllis Rauch. "'Oh Freedom'—Women and History in Margaret Walker's *Jubilee*." *Black American Literature Forum* 11 (Winter, 1977): 139-145.

Rejecting comparisons with romances such as *Gone With the Wind*, Klotman identifies *Jubilee* as a part of the Afro-American recovery of history based on the oral tradition. Emerging from the tradition of the slave narrative, *Jubilee* shares the tripartite structure of bondage, escape, and freedom. Walker emphasizes the role of women in preserving the heritage.

Powell, Bertie J. "The Black Experience in Margaret Walker's *Jubilee* and Lorraine Hansberry's *The Drinking Gourd.*" *CLA Journal* 21 (December, 1977): 304-311.

Discusses Walker's presentation of the slave experience. The slave owner John Dutton, plantation mistress Big Missy, and overseer Ed Grimes demonstrate the exploitation of blacks. Walker also shows how the slaves used religion, romance, and family life as ways of finding a meaningful life.

Schraufnagel, Noel. "Accommodationism in the Sixties." In *From Apology to Protest: The Black American Novel.* Deland, Fla.: Everett/Edwards, 1973.

In the apologetic tradition of black fiction, Walker emphasizes the ability of blacks to survive great tribulations. Walker's protagonist is an enduring black matriarch who maintains her Christian humility and respect for the decadent white aristocrats. Walker presents numerous stereotypes, including a Faulknerian portrait of a decaying Southern family. *Jubilee* is nonetheless a relatively competent historical study.

Times Literary Supplement. Review of *Jubilee.* (June 29, 1967): 583.

Identifies the novel as a source of "heartbreaking" historical background relevant to civil unrest in the American ghettoes. Although there are too many sections of undigested history and much of the characterization is stereotypical, Walker nonetheless brings new vitality to an old story. Among the novel's strengths are Walker's effective use of Negro spiritual phraseology to comment on Vyry's indignities, and her precise sense of the importance of objects and everyday household ritual.

DOROTHY WEST

Biography

Ferguson, SallyAnn H. "Dorothy West." In *Afro-American Writers 1940-1955*, edited by Trudier Harris. Vol. 76 of *Dictionary of Literary Biography*. Detroit: Bruccoli Clark, 1988.
Substantial reference entry including biographical sketch and analysis of *The Living Is Easy* as one of the first explorations of the ironic possibilities of the black urban life style. Biographical discussion emphasizes West's editorial support of black writing during the 1930's; her family background; her formal education; her early short stories; her friendships with numerous Harlem Renaissance figures; her travels in Russia; and her recent work on a second novel. Discussion of *The Living Is Easy* focuses on the theme of "values gone awry."

McDowell, Deborah. "Conversations with Dorothy West." In *The Harlem Renaissance Re-examined*, edited by Victor A. Kramer. New York: AMS Press, 1987.
Interview covering topics such as the beginnings of West's writing career; her involvement in the Harlem Renaissance; her work with *Challenge* magazine; the writing and reception of *The Living Is Easy*; and her recent life. West observes that Cleo's negative traits are related to her desire to make conditions better for future generations.

Roses, Lorraine Elena. "Dorothy West at Oak Bluffs, Massachusetts, July 1984." *Sage* 2 (Spring, 1985): 47-49.
Interview with West including her comments on the origins of her style; Claude McKay as her literary mentor; the relationship between her character Simeon Binney and Monroe Trotter; the influence of her mother; and the outline of her second unpublished novel, *The Wedding*, which she says has been accepted by Harper and Row.

Weyan, N. Jill. "Dorothy West." In *American Women Writers*, vol. 4, edited by Lina Mainiero. New York: Frederick Ungar, 1982.
Biographical entry including brief commentary on *The Living Is Easy*. Concludes that while West's novel was promising, it is a disappointment that she failed to follow it up with other novels.

Selected Title

The Living Is Easy
Berzon, Judith R. *Neither White Nor Black: The Mulatto Character in American Fiction*. New York: New York University Press, 1978.

The most satisfying artistic study of the black bourgeoisie, *The Living Is Easy* offers a brilliantly ironic scrutiny of the middle-class preoccupation with color, background, and conspicuous consumption. Cleo feels compelled to mutilate her "Rabelaisian soul, her creativity" in order to gain acceptance into the bourgeoisie. Her tragic flaw—her inability to respect the integrity of individual human beings—ultimately brings a plague down upon her house.

Bone, Robert. "The Contemporary Negro Novel." In *The Negro Novel in America.* New Haven, Conn.: Yale University Press, 1965.
A bitingly ironic novel, *The Living Is Easy* deals with the ruthless success-drive in the black middle class, which exacts a staggering toll in ruined personalities. West never subordinates psychological interest to social criticism. She is particularly masterful in her presentation of minor characters.

Cromwell, Adelaide M. Afterword to *The Living Is Easy.* Old Westbury, N.Y.: Feminist Press, 1982.
The Living Is Easy furnishes a glimpse of an aspect of Afro-American history overshadowed by the emphasis on slavery and racism. The small group of blacks West describes has all but disappeared in fiction and in fact. Contains extensive biographical sketch including information on West's family background; her involvement with *Challenge* magazine and the younger group of Harlem Renaissance writers; her attitude toward the Communist Party; and her life on Martha's Vineyard in the 1970's.

Harris, Trudier. "A Different Image of the Black Woman." *Callaloo* 16 (October, 1982): 146-151.
Review of reprint edition emphasizing West's presentation of a type of black woman not frequently portrayed in literature. An accomplished liar who subordinates human relationships to social climbing, Cleo defies easy categorization. One of the novel's weaknesses is West's failure to explain adequately why other characters make such self-destructive commitments to the protagonist. Although West's style is pedestrian, this weakness is outweighed by the originality of her material.

Perry, Margaret. "The Short Story." In *Silence to the Drums: A Survey of the Literature of the Harlem Renaissance.* Westport, Conn.: Greenwood Press, 1976.
One of the few sources to consider West's Harlem Renaissance-era short fiction. Notes the influence of Dostoevskian approaches to the theme of moral, psychological, physical, and emotional confinement. Argues that the psychological soundness of West's characterizations is not supported by an adequate style.

Schraufnagel, Noel. "The Revolt against Wright." In *From Apology to Protest: The Black American Novel*. Deland, Fla.: Everett/Edwards, 1973.
Classifies *The Living Is Easy* as an "accommodationist" novel whose primary purpose is to satirize the emptiness of the middle class, which is more interested in social status than its own humanity. Although West fails to maintain her objectivity towards Cleo, the novel is interesting for its presentation of an antithesis to the stereotype of the black woman as enduring and sympathetic matriarch. Cleo fulfills the opposite role through her selfishness and perverted sense of values.

Wade-Gayles, Gloria. "Journeying from Can't to Can." In *No Crystal Stair: Visions of Race and Sex in Black Women's Fiction*. New York: Pilgrim Press, 1984.
Emphasizes Cleo's struggle to control her life in the same way men are able to control theirs. Unable to do so, she grows resentful of male power and female passivity. Although she functions in the role of wife, she attempts to use the role to chart her own destiny. Gives detailed attention to Cleo's refusal to engage in sex with her husband.

Washington, Mary Helen. "I Sign My Mother's Name: Maternal Power in Dorothy West's *The Living Is Easy*." In *Invented Lives: Narratives of Black Women, 1860-1960*. Garden City, N.Y.: Anchor Press, 1987.
Focuses on West's attempt to come to terms with the complex influence of her mother. Quotes from an interview in which West credits her discovery of her own creative voice to the memory of her mother's power. Washington observes, however, that the maternal influence is also the source of the class- and color-consciousness that provides a central tension in *The Living Is Easy*. West sounds an array of feminist themes—the need for female community, anger over the limitations of women's lives—but an ambivalent narrative perspective frequently undercuts Cleo's strengths.

SHERLEY ANNE WILLIAMS

Biography

Greene, Cheryll Y. "A Conversation with Sherley Anne Williams." *Essence* 16 (March, 1986): 33.
Interview including Williams' comments on her purpose in writing *Dessa Rose*; the issue of empowerment; the male-female and black-white relationships in the novel; the difficulty of balancing academic and creative pursuits; and her plans for a trilogy set in working-class California.

Howard, Lillie P. "Sherley Anne Williams." In *Afro-American Poets Since 1955*, edited by Trudier Harris and Thadious M. Davis. Vol. 41 of *Dictionary of Literary Biography*. Detroit: Bruccoli Clark, 1985.
Discussion of Williams' poetry and critical prose accompanied by a substantial biographical sketch. Examines Williams education, family life, and the relationship of her critical insights to her creative work. A member of what she calls the "Neo-Black" movement, Williams shares the belief in a black aesthetic growing from shared racial memory and a common future. Like Hurston, Williams moves comfortably between written and oral traditions.

Tate, Claudia C. *Black Women Writers at Work*. New York: Continuum, 1983.
Includes an interview with Williams in which she discusses the importance of the black female perspective in her work; her use of the blues; the difference in perspective of black male and black female writers; and her sense of the relationship between her criticism, creative work, and teaching duties.

Selected Title

Dessa Rose
Bucknell, Katherine. "Slaves to the Slaves." *Times Literary Supplement* (July 17, 1987): 765.
Mixed review emphasizing the theme that individual personalities rather than social roles were the determining factor in human relations under slavery. Williams' belief that the a determined and clever slave could win freedom through violence or trickery is provocative, but hard to believe. Although *Dessa Rose* creates a more subtle and differentiated image of human relations under slavery, it perpetuates the cliché that blacks have deeper emotions than whites.

Davenport, Doris. Review of *Dessa Rose*. *Black American Literature Forum* 20 (Fall, 1986): 335-340.

Favorable review-essay identifying *Dessa Rose* as "literary revenge" for the betrayal of black history by some white writers. The novel's structure, content, and style emphasize both revenge and reclamation/celebration. Williams subtly redefines several Afro-American literary traditions, including that of the slave narrative. Identifies the confrontation between Dessa and Rufel over "mammy" as a turning point that emphasizes how little whites actually know of black experience.

Gillespie, Marcia. "The Seraglio, the Plantation—Intrigue and Survival." *Ms.* 15 (September, 1986): 20-21.
Favorable review praising Williams' ability to construct a convincing novel from historical fragments. Dessa Rose is a woman in process, whose essential spirit has survived despite her brutal experience. Although the white and black women in the novel cannot become friends, each serves as a catalyst for the other's struggle for freedom.

Kelly, Ernece B. Review of *Dessa Rose*. *CLA Journal* 30 (June, 1987): 515-518.
Favorable review emphasizing Williams' intricate picture of the ways in which blacks and whites influence one another's psyches, despite the mutual mistrust that keeps them from believing one another's stories. A historical novel with issues of racial and sexual repression at its heart, *Dessa Rose* uses irony and humor to create a richly textured picture of a South quite different from that of *Gone with the Wind*.

McDowell, Deborah E. "Negotiating Between Tenses: Witnessing Slavery After Freedom—*Dessa Rose*." In *Slavery and the Literary Imagination*, edited by Deborah E. McDowell and Arnold Rampersad. Baltimore: Johns Hopkins University Press, 1989.
Although the presence of multiple, contradictory versions of the story testifies to Williams' grasp of postmodernist technique, *Dessa Rose* resists "the postmodern orthodoxy of undecidability and relativism." Williams participates in the critiques of the nature of the subject and of binary oppositions, but she grounds her critique in a network of specific material circumstances. Like the female slave narrators who shift emphasis from victimization to creative resistance, Dessa Rose ultimately assumes authority over her own story.

Schultz, Elizabeth. "And the Children May Know Their Names." *Callaloo* 35 (Spring, 1988): 371-377.
Favorable review linking *Dessa Rose* with the tradition of the slave narrative. Like the slave narrators, Dessa liberates herself through the articulation of her own experience and attempts to liberate her descendants through the creation of a narrative in which she represents their history. Williams makes personal and communal knowledge of history fundamental, emphasizing the need for conscious and imaginative rewriting of history.

Wallace, Michele. "Slaves of History." *The Women's Review of Books* 4 (October, 1986): 1, 3-4.
Favorable review emphasizing Williams' successful solution of the problems involved with writing an historical novel expressing the slave woman's point of view. Williams turns the problem of point of view to her advantage by decentering patriarchal authority and focusing on the rhetorical play of relativistic perspectives. This illumines the ephemeral quality of the antebellum records. Wallace discusses the treatment of women in *Dessa Rose*, concluding with an endorsement of its vision of friendship as "the collective struggle that ultimately transcends the stumbling blocks of race and class.

Werner, Craig. "Black Dreams of Faulkner's Dreams of Blacks." In *Faulkner and Race*, edited by Doreen Fowler and Ann J. Abadie. Jackson: University Press of Mississippi, 1987.
Discusses *Dessa Rose* as a repudiation of William Styron's *The Confessions of Nat Turner*. Williams echoes several motifs introduced in the work of William Faulkner, most importantly the destructive impact of the failure to engage in real dialogue with members of other races and genders. Williams contrasts the self-destructive quality of Nehemiah's approach to history with the tense, but real, cooperation between the white woman Ruth and the black protagonist.

HARRIET WILSON

Biography

Gates, Henry Louis, Jr. "Harriet E. Adams Wilson." In *Afro-American Writers Before the Harlem Renaissance*, edited by Trudier Harris. Vol. 50 of *Dictionary of Literary Biography*. Detroit: Bruccoli Clark, 1986.

Biographical essay relating the limited information available concerning Wilson's life and the history of her book, which received no commentary between 1859 and 1983. Presents *Our Nig* as a major example of genre fusion between the predominantly black masculine slave narrative and the predominantly white women's sentimental novel. The resulting synthesis is peculiarly black and female, assuring the novel's continuing importance in Afro-American and American literature.

──────────── . "Parallel Discursive Universes: Fictions of the Self in Harriet E. Wilson's *Our Nig*." In *Figures in Black: Words, Signs, and the "Racial" Self*. New York: Oxford University Press, 1987.

Recounts Gates's rediscovery of *Our Nig* and presents the findings of his research into Wilson's life. Emphasizes the originality of Wilson's indictment of both irresponsible black abolitionists and racist Northern white women. The book is unique in American fiction because it uses the interracial marriage as a source of plot development rather than as social commentary. Includes a chart detailing the correspondences between the plot of *Our Nig* and the events of Wilson's life.

Shockley, Ann Allen. "Harriet E. Adams Wilson." In *Afro-American Women Writers, 1746-1933*. Boston: G. K. Hall, 1988.

Biographical headnote to excerpt from *Our Nig* presenting the known events of Wilson's life and discussing her "fictionalized memoir of a free—yet unfree —black northern woman."

Commentary

Bell, Bernard W. "The Early Afro-American Novel: Historical Romance, Social Realism and Beyond." In *The Afro-American Novel and Its Tradition*. Amherst: University of Massachusetts Press, 1987.

Biographical sketch with discussion of *Our Nig* identifying Wilson's major autobiographical theme as Northern white racism and hypocrisy. Reflecting Wilson's double consciousness, the quotations introducing each chapter suggest the unusually wide scope of her reading. Formally, Wilson synthesizes the sentimental novel and the slave narrative, romance and autobiography. Inverting the structure of the white woman's novel to create a black woman's novel, *Our Nig* is notable for its open-ended conclusion, which places the burden of closure on her readers.

Dearborn, Mary V. "Strategies of Authorship in American Ethnic Women's Fiction: Midwiving and Mediation." In *Pocahontas's Daughters: Gender and Ethnicity in American Culture*. New York: Oxford University Press, 1986.
Examines the reasons why *Our Nig* remained unread for more than a hundred years. The history of the text highlights the ways in which the ethnic female text is a tradition of mediation. The presence of authenticating documents—prefaces, appendices, explanations—in the text itself testifies to this dynamic. Frado's experience within the novel parallels that of the author in the real world.

Fox-Genovese, Elizabeth. "To Write My Self: The Autobiographies of Afro-American Women." In *Feminist Issues in Literary Scholarship*, edited by Shari Benstock. Bloomington: Indiana University Press, 1987.
Brief discussion of *Our Nig* in relation to the tradition of autobiographical writing by black women. Like Harriet Jacobs in *Incidents in the Life of a Slave Girl*, Wilson constructs her fictionalized autobiography around the metaphor of the journey. Unlike most of her contemporaries, Wilson's text presents the white woman, rather than a man, as the primary enemy.

Selected Title

Our Nig
Brown, Beth. Review of *Our Nig*. *CLA Journal* 29 (March, 1986): 378-386.
Descriptive review ranking the historical importance of *Our Nig* with that of *Uncle Tom's Cabin*. Wilson's style is comparable to those of other nineteenth century black writers such as William Wells Brown, Frank Webb, and Sutton Griggs. Summarizes the similarities between Wilson's novel and the typology of nineteenth century women's fiction described by Nina Baym.

Carby, Harriet. " 'Hear My Voice, Ye Careless Daughters': Narratives of Slave and Free Women before Emancipation." In *Reconstructing Womanhood: The Emergence of the Afro-American Woman Novelist*. New York: Oxford University Press, 1987.
Brief discussion arguing that *Our Nig* should be viewed as an allegory of a slave narrative, a "slave" narrative set in the "free" North. A comparison of Wilson's book with the autobiography of Nancy Prince highlights Wilson's decision to seek patronage not from Northern whites but from the black

community. Her direct appeal to the black community marginalizes the white readership. Wilson recasts the conventions of the sentimental novel via slave narratives to produce a unique allegorical form.

Kinney, James. "Abolition and Civil War, 1850-1865." In *Amalgamation! Race, Sex, and Rhetoric in the Nineteenth-Century American Novel*. Westport, Conn.: Greenwood Press, 1985.
Places *Our Nig* in the context of literary treatments of miscegenation during the antebellum era. Like Frank Webb's *The Garies and Their Friends*, *Our Nig* attempts to free the issue from the limiting context of slavery and abolition. Wilson makes it clear that Frado, who shows no concern for the problem of slavery, experiences an alienation derived from her feeling of not belonging. The exceptional realism of the book in the age of the sentimental novel suggests an autobiographical basis.

O'Meally, Robert. "Slavery's Shadow." *Callaloo* 20 (Winter, 1984): 157-158.
Review commenting on Wilson's relation to Afro-American literary history and to the nineteenth century "sentimental reform novel." Despite its wooden prose, *Our Nig* is an intriguing book, in part because of the significance Wilson attaches to blackness. As in *Huckleberry Finn* and *Benito Cereno*, blackness in *Our Nig* signifies the American hunger for freedom.

SARAH WRIGHT

Biography

Guilford, Virginia B. "Sarah Wright." In *Afro-American Fiction Writers After 1955*, edited by Thadious M. Davis and Trudier Harris. Vol. 33 of *Dictionary of Literary Biography*. Detroit: Bruccoli Clark, 1984.
    Substantial reference entry including biographical sketch with detailed analysis of *This Child's Gonna Live*. Sees Wright's importance in her function as a writer who explores the full range of experience to extract what is most significant even if the resulting shattering of façades is painful. She embraces her roots without rejecting values from other cultures. Biographical section notes the importance of her parents' philosophy of life to Wright's work; her education at Howard University; her involvement with the Harlem Writers' Guild; and the difficulties she has experienced as an uncompromising writer attempting to make a living in New York City.

Wright, Sarah E. "The Negro Woman in Literature." *Freedomways* (First Quarter, 1966): 8-13.
    Transcript of remarks presented at a symposium held at the New School for Social Research. Wright comments that the demand for black manhood frequently takes the form of attacks on black women. Criticizes the sexual exploitiveness of the publishing industry and the relegation of black women to the lowest rungs of the social ladder.

Selected Title

This Child's Gonna Live
Amini, Johari. "This Child's Gonna Live." *Negro Digest* 18 (August, 1969): 51-52.
    Favorable review praising Wright's ability to use her technical capabilities to bring her characters to life. Wright's insights into the conflicts of black marriage and family life remain relevant. Not simply a woman's novel, it is a book for black people.

Harris, Trudier. "Three Black Women Writers and Humanism: A Folk Perspective." In *Black American Literature and Humanism*, edited by R. Baxter Miller. Lexington: University Press of Kentucky, 1981.
    Focuses on the tension between Christianity and the humanistic values of African-American folklore in the experience of Mariah Upshur. Mariah's struggle is to maintain her humanity in a world of petty jealousies and hypo-

critical Christians. Forced to develop a code of behavior capable of protecting her emotional life and directing her interaction with others, she embraces her folk ancestors' belief in the fundamental necessity of freedom.

Howe, Irving. "New Black Writers." *Harper's* 239 (December, 1969): 130-146.
Unfavorable review criticizing the novel as a black militant version of *Green Pastures*. The novel has some interest as local color, but the patches of authentic detail clash with basic narrative failures. Wright's lack of sophistication and the failures of her language are reflected in the "incongruous" alternation of folk-like dialogue and her angry political outbursts.

Killens, John Oliver. "An Appreciation." In *This Child's Gonna Live*. Old Westbury, N.Y.: Feminist Press, 1986.
Praises Wright's novel as "an overwhelming metaphor of the Black experience" in America. Triply oppressed as a black working-class woman, Mariah is a figure of "unparalleled heroism." Combining love and tenderness with the reality of oppression, *This Child's Gonna Live* presents a complex image of the black psyche. Mariah's main struggle is for her own self respect.

Mickelson, Anne Z. "Winging Upward: Black Women: Sarah E. Wright, Toni Morrison, Alice Walker." In *Reaching Out: Sensitivity and Order in Recent American Fiction by Women*. Metuchen, N.J.: Scarecrow Press, 1979.
The most important element of Wright's novel is the intensity of her effort to register in its own terms the reality of black suffering during the 1930's. Many of the problems Wright identifies are rooted directly in moral/social codes derived from patriarchal Old Testament religion. Her treatment of older women demonstrates the ways in which the oppressed can become the oppressors. Although none is entirely successful, each of the women in *This Child's Gonna Live* is reaching for some sense of self-definition.

Schraufnagel, Noel. "Apologetic Protest in the Sixties." In *From Apology to Protest: The Black American Novel*. Deland, Fla.: Everett/Edwards, 1973.
An impressive novel from a stylistic viewpoint, *This Child's Gonna Live* presents a valuable examination of the use of violence; the sexual aspects of racism; and the psychological effects of white racism. The stream-of-consciousness narrative reflects the feverish turmoil of the characters' lives.

Wade-Gayles, Gloria. "Journeying from Can't to Can." In *No Crystal Stair: Visions of Race and Sex in Black Women's Fiction*. New York: Pilgrim Press, 1984.
Wright's treatment of sexism and religious narrow-mindedness is inseparable from her treatment of racism, which is the dominant theme of the novel. *This Child's Gonna Live* is constructed around two contrasting worlds within the black community: man's world and woman's place. Mariah recognizes that

each of these worlds is extremely limited in relation to white power. Emphasizes the role of the church in placing limitations on black women's experience.

Whitlow, Roger. "1960 to the Present: Satire, the Past—and Themes of Armageddon." In *Black American Literature: A Critical History*. Chicago: Littlefield, Adams, 1974.
Brief analysis of *This Child's Gonna Live* accompanied by a biographical sketch of Wright. Praises Wright's precise rendering of dialect and her treatment of folk humor, both of which compare favorably with Hurston's. Wright's portrayal of human misery, like Petry's in *The Street*, is particularly powerful because there is nothing Mariah can do to reduce the suffering of herself and her children.

BLACK AMERICAN
WOMEN
NOVELISTS

INDEX

INDEX

INDEX

INDEX

016.8130 Werner, Craig
09   Hansen.   19,178
Wer
          Black American women
          novelists.

016.8130 Werner, Craig
09   Hansen.   19,178
Wer
          Black American
          women
          novelists.

DATE	BORROWER'S NAME